Regrounding
Maqāṣid al-Sharīʿah

*The Qur'anic Semantics and Foundation
of Human Common Good*

Dedication

To People Who Think ...

Regrounding Maqāṣid al-Sharīʿah

The Qurʾanic Semantics and Foundation of Human Common Good

MOHAMED EL-TAHIR EL-MESAWI

with

WALEED FEKRY FARIS

DAWOOD A. YAHYA AL-HIDABI

International Institute for Muslim Unity | Islamic Book Trust
Kuala Lumpur
2022

Published by
International Institute for
Muslim Unity (IIMU)
Jalan Gombak
53100 Kuala Lumpur, Malaysia
www.iium.edu.my

In collaboration with
Islamic Book Trust
607 Mutiara Majestic, Jalan Othman
46000 Petaling Jaya, Selangor,
Malaysia
www.ibtbooks.com

Islamic Book Trust is affiliated with The Other Press.

Perpustakaan Negara Malaysia   Cataloguing-in-Publication Data

Mohamed El-Tahir El-Mesawi
   Regrounding Maqāṣid al-Sharīʿah: The Quranic Semantics of Human and
   Foundation of Human Common Good / Mohamed El-Tahir El-Mesawi,
   Waleed Fekry Faris & Dawood A. Yahya al-Hidabi.
   ISBN 978-967-0526-97-3
   1. Maqāṣid (Islamic law).
   2. Humanity.
   I. Waleed Fekry Faris.
   II. Dawood A. Yahya al-Hidabi.
   III. Title.
   340.5911

Cover design by Hoda and Amirah El-Mesawi.

Printed by
SS Graphic Printers (M) Sdn. Bhd.
Lot 7 & 8, Jalan TIB 3
Taman Industri Bolton
68100 Batu Caves, Selangor

Contents

Foreword   vii

Introduction   xi

1. *Ḥifẓ al-Dīn and Ḥifẓ a-Nasl:* Enhancing Human Spiritual Morality and Safeguarding Mankind   1

Introduction   1

Ḥifẓ al-Dīn: meaning and scope   2

     1. *Dīn*: From semantical analysis to conceptual formulation   2

     2. *Dīn*: Content and magisterium   15

     3. *Ḥifẓ al-dīn*: Ways and means   34

Ḥifẓ al-nasl: meaning and purpose   37

     1. A Qur'anic semiotics of nasl   37

     2. *Ḥifẓ al-nasl*: means and ways   45

Dīn and a *nasl*: The eternal essential nexus   49

2. *Ḥifẓ al-Nafs:* Sanctifying Human Life and Protecting Personal Selves   75

Introduction   75

Nafs: Semantics and conceptualization   76

Anchoring *ḥifẓ al-nafs*: Human dignity   79

The Sharī'ah Approach to *ḥifẓ al-nafs*   92

1. The positive proactive aspect of *ḥifẓ al-nafs*   94

2. The preventive 'reactive' aspect of *ḥifẓ al-nafs*   96

Conclusion   103

3. *Ḥifẓ al-'Aql* and *Ḥifẓ a-Māl*: Building Human Rationality and Realizing Economic Well-being   117

Introduction   117

Ḥifẓ al-'Aql: Meaning and Significance   118

1. The semantics of *'aql*   118

2. Protecting the mind and enhancing human rationality   122

Ḥifẓ a-Māl: Meaning and Purpose   128

1. The Qur'anic semantics of *māl* and the ontology of economic wealth   128

2. *Māl* and wealth in the value scheme of Islamic jurisprudence   137

3. Justice and need fulfilment: Pearls of wisdom from Ibn Khaldūn and al-Ghazālī   142

4. *Infāq*: Towards a humane economy   158

Conclusion   169

Epilogue   191

Select Bibliography   197

Notes on the Authors   209

Index   211

Foreword

Although intensively drawing on classical original Arabic sources, the work presented here to the English-speaking world is not a translation of, nor an appendage to, the already overworked field of *maqāṣid al-Sharīʿah*. Rather, it is an original attempt to open up and widen the foundational textual sources of the idea of *maqāṣid* by bringing in related and relevant Qur'anic terms that the scholars of the *maqāṣid* have presumably overlooked. Once these Qur'anic terms are adequately identified and analyzed, they would become the base on which the *maqāṣid* could be regrounded. As a result of such a process, the field of the *maqāṣid* would receive further gains to those already developed by al-Shāṭibī and his predecessors and successors. To this end, the authors have employed a semantic-conceptual analysis approach, which is unavoidably linguistic and theoretical or abstract. Their unmistakable goal, however, is to develop a new and deeper perspective that leads to a better understanding of religion and reality.

Far from claiming absolute novelty, the authors navigate their way confidently through a rich intellectual tradition out of which this work evolved. They analyze and incorporate the insights of the pioneer scholars who exerted enormous effort on the analysis and classification of the Qur'anic terms—from Muqātil al-Balkhī, al-Ḥakīm al-Tirmidhī and al-Rāghib al-Iṣfahānī to al-Ghazālī and others in the past. However, the fountain of semantic and conceptual analysis of the Qur'anic terms did not dry up with the works of the scholars of the classical and post-classical era. A new generation emerged in our age. Here the authors focus on the works of contemporary Muslim intellectuals like, for instance, Ibn Ashur, Mawdūdī, al-Turabi, al-Attas, and al-Fārūqī; the five scholars who carried, each on his own way, the method of conceptual analysis far afield.

It is worth pointing out that one of the authors of this work is not a dispassionate scientific student of Islam and Islamic thought, as some scholars and experts might project themselves. He is strongly concerned with social and political reform and hence this work is an attempt to come to grips with the question of how to, methodologically speaking, rejuvenate the Muslim mind in such a way as would enable it to come to terms with the challenges of a totally new world. Much of his earlier published works present a persistent and continuous effort to explicate and augment the *maqāṣid* approach by redefining the meanings and broader significance of its basic terms; that is, *dīn, nafs, nasl, 'aql* and *māl*. His and his colleagues' aim is to make the *maqāṣid* approach accessible for those who are genuinely intent on overcoming the intellectual stagnation and improving Muslims' miserable social, cultural, economic and political conditions.

The linguistic analysis of the Qur'anic terminology to uncover the enduring values and eternal principles of Revelation is, in the main, reliable. However, it necessitates a profound look into issues concerning being as such. This is because the theory of *maqāṣid* and its three categories (*ḍarūriyyāt, ḥājiyyāt* and *taḥsīniyyāt*), being essentially of ethical nature, are predicated on an articulation of being. Exhibiting clear awareness of this dimension, the authors have succeeded to balance the Qur'anic semantic fields of the category of the five necessities (i.e., *dīn, nafs, nasl, 'aql* and *māl*) with an adequate Qur'anic understanding of the concept of being. No doubt, any ethical discourse that confines itself to language alone will certainly be a futile exercise. Such pitfall did not escape the intellectual awareness of the authors who therefore made sure to demonstrate and emphasize the interconnectedness among being, language and universal values.

The book thus paves the way for a new sensibility and a wider intellectual methodological horizon in both Qur'anic and *maqāṣid* studies. The authors made it clear right from the outset that their effort aims at a reinstatement or reformulation of *maqāṣid al-Sharīʿah* by regrounding them on the Qur'anic core values and worldview. The three main chapters focus on "Enhancing human spiritual morality, and safeguarding mankind", "Sanctifying human life and protecting personal selves" and "Building human rationality and realizing economic well-being". The reorganization of the five categories in this manner makes life and the human self the bridge between the other four values. Most important of all, it develops a distinct concept of Islamic humanism that encompasses both the hierarchy of values and their shared nexus. While doing so, the authors show keen awareness of the danger of making values relative to the human agent. Therefore, they rather opted for a position that makes them relational both in their interconnectedness and with regard to the human beings.

Needless to say, the *maqāṣid*-oriented approach as developed by Muslim jurisprudents has its origins in the Qur'an. This may suggest that the authors of the present book are overdoing things by emphasizing (if not overemphasizing) the semantic approach in comprehending the five universal necessities constituting the first category of the Sharīʿah goals, namely the *ḍarūriyyāt*. Such impression, however, does not hold. Coupled with serious reflections on being and values, the semantic-conceptual analysis conducted by the authors has actually led to an innovative and inspiring discourse on *maqāṣid al-Sharīʿah*, opening up hitherto rarely systematically explored dimensions in this crucial area of Islamic scholarship which has far-reaching implications for matters of real and day-to-day life. Though their effort cannot be claimed to have come up with definitive solutions to all issues raised by this book, nonetheless it provides us with a set of principles and informative postulates needed for any further meaningful study on *maqāṣid*.

Eltigani Abdulqadir Hamid, Qatar University, Doha

Ibrahim Mohamed Zein, Hamad University, Doha

Introduction

The present book has been in the making for more than two years since it started as a rough idea. That idea initially came up as a suggestion by one agency at the International Islamic University Malaysia, IIUM to produce a small booklet that could serve as a general introduction and accessible manual for the general administrative staff and clerks of the university educating them on the basic notions and general categories of the Sharīʿah objectives (*maqāṣid al-Sharīʿah*). This suggestion came about in response to the move by the top management of the university, especially its rector, to engage intellectually and practically with the Seventeen Sustainable Development Goals (SDGs) adopted by the United Nations in its 2015 summit and embodying its 2030 Agenda for Sustainable Development; these goals came into force in January 2016 as a sequel or substitute to the 2000 Millenium Development Goals (MDGs). The theory of *maqāṣid al-Sharīʿah* has been taken as the guiding Islamic framework and prism for that engagement,[1] and it was in this context that the need arose to enlighten IIUM community on its basics by producing such a simplified work.

The three of us, Waleed F. Faris, Dawood A. Y. al-Hidabi and I, were tasked with the abovementioned project. After a few discussion sessions on the overall plan of the booklet and its general outlines, we agreed to divide it into three chapters that should cover the five necessary universals (*al-kulliyyāt al-ḍarūriyyah al-khamsah*) whose realization constitutes the highest goals of the Sharī'ah according to the established taxonomy of Muslim legal theorists and jurists. The first chapter, assigned to El-Mesawi, had to deal with the two goals pertaining to religion and progeny, namely *ḥifẓ al-dīn* and *ḥifẓ al-nasl*. The second chapter, assigned to Faris, had to focus on the goal relating to life, that is, *ḥifẓ al-nafs*. Finally, the third chapter, taken up by al-Hidabi, had to take care of the two goals relating to the intellect as well as property and wealth, notably *ḥifẓ al-'aql* and *ḥifẓ al-māl*.

As can be seen, the way the focus and subject matter of each chapter were determined does not follow strictly the generally agreed upon classification of the five necessary universals usually ordered as follows: *ḥifẓ al-dīn, ḥifẓ al-nafs, ḥifẓ al-'aql, ḥifẓ al-nasl* and *ḥifẓ al-māl*. This, in fact, did not come up in our discussions as an issue to be addressed one way or another, and therefore we did not then think about the matter nor did we contemplate any idea of developing a new classification of these *ḍarūriyyāt*. Yet, it seems as if we were intuitively guided to a new way of considering their order, as I will show later. For the time being, a note is in order to shed some light on the direction our effort was destined to take in such a manner that has totally departed from the initial idea: to come up with a general or introductory manual suitable to an ordinary audience mostly with very little or no academic background in the subject. As each of us embarked, somewhere in October or November 2019, on his respective task with a time frame to submit the first draft within three to four months, I personally, and most probably my colleagues too, came to realize that a good number of simplified and introductory small-sized works on *maqāṣid al-Sharī'ah* were already available in a good quality both in content and form. These booklets were either originally written for such purpose, or a brief and simplified summary of some well-known extensive works on the subject.[2]

Realizing this made me think that there was no point in continuing with the original idea of writing a manual-like text, as doing so will amount to no more than mere replication at least in terms of content, albeit not necessarily in language and style of presentation. Accordingly, I decided to rather invest my effort in testing and exploring an idea that has been lingering in my mind and pressing itself on me for quite a number of years alongside with my teaching and research experience and as a result of reasonably learned acquaintance with the fast growing body of literature on the subject of *maqāṣid* (especially in Arabic and English), dealing with different aspects thereof: historical, methodological and epistemological as well as practical and pragmatic. That idea is that the study of the Sharīʿah goals needs a serious revision of its methodological and epistemological tenets in such a way as would liberate it from its dominating essentially legalistic paradigm and both widen and deepen its theoretical and methodological framework, as will be explained shortly.

Somewhere in early May 2020 during the complete lockdown imposed in Malaysia due to the worldwide Covid-19 pandemic, each of us had completed a first draft of the part assigned to him. After an exchange of those drafts in order for the contributors to comment on one another's piece, the whole material was entrusted to me for streamlining and final editing. Owing to the difference of academic background and training of each one of us, and due also to the impact of the initial idea behind the booklet project targeting a specific audience, our contributions revealed themselves to be quite divergent from one another in both content and style of presentation, notwithstanding the wealth of insights each of us had come up with. So, a round of conversations mostly through email and Whatsapp was needed to resolve this issue, following which an agreement was reached whereby I was delegated to undertake the task of reworking the whole stuff in order to refine its conceptual and methodological unity, and substantiate and sharpen its arguments, with emphasis on making the semantic approach bear on all parts of the work. This, indeed, put me in front of a big and challenging task. Undertaking this task required a great deal of further research in quest of Qur'anic, linguistic and exegetical materials needed to ground and consolidate that approach in a coherent, if not unified, manner throughout the constituent parts of the book. And so it was; the result has been a completely different output from what had been envisaged more than two years ago in orientation, method and substance.

Having said that, the book now in the reader's hand needs to be put in a proper intellectual and historical perspective.[3] One could easily notice in the literature on *maqāṣid* produced over the last three to four decades that some of the abovementioned aspects, especially the historical, have been treated quite fairly. Many works have been produced which systematically analyze the contributions of earlier Muslim scholars, especially in the context *uṣūl al-fiqh,* and present their views in a language and style easily accessible to a wider audience that is mostly unequipped to navigate safely in the ocean of classical sources. In similar vein, serious efforts have been made to recast, contextualize, relevantize and actualize the theory of *maqāṣid* and carry it to novel theoretical and practical levels and concerns. Special attention has been given to emerging and ever-increasing and changing social, cultural, economic and political issues that go beyond the particular interests and preoccupations of individuals and small groups, so as to embrace the overall condition and general interest of society and the common good of all, not only with regard to Muslims but also at a wider human and global level. The central motto inspiring a great deal of the intellectual effort invested in the study of *maqāṣid al-Sharīʿah,* particularly by Muslim authors, is that this theory provides an appropriate and much-needed frame for the reinvigoration of *ijtihād* and revitalization of Islamic thought required so as to come to terms with the challenges of the modern world. Hence, terms such as *ijtihād maqāṣidī* and *tafkīr maqāṣidī* have become part of the widely circulated jargon in the intellectual and academic arena manifested in university dissertations, monographs, journal articles and conference papers.[4]

A justified realization underlying all this, one could safely say, is that the idea of *maqāṣid* as articulated by many outstanding scholars in the past and in modern times conceptually and holistically reflects and embodies the Islamic worldview, system of values and legal injunctions in a way that clearly brings to the forefront the centrality of human essential and common good in the teachings of Islam. However, with countable exceptions, the abundant literature that has been accumulating in the name of *maqāṣid* remains to a great extent imprisoned in the juridical-legalistic paradigm that was developed over the centuries by such great jurisprudents and theological philosophers as Abū al-Maʿālī al-Juwaynī, Abū Ḥāmid al-Ghazālī, Fakhr al-Dīn al-Rāzī, Sayf al-Dīn al-Āmidī, etc.

A common feature of the treatment of the subject of *maqāṣid al-Sharīʿah* by most legal theorists and jurists prior to Abū Ishāq al-Shāṭibī (d. 790/1388) was their focus on a limited body of Qur'anic verses and Prophetic traditions which are considered to have a legal import by virtue of their grammatical forms and syntactical structure carrying varying degrees of prescriptive and proscriptive nature. Hence, they came to be known as *āyāt* and *aḥādīth al-aḥkām*, dangerously implying that the bulk of the Qur'anic revelation and Prophetic guidance has, if at all, only little and indirect bearing on the legislation for the social, cultural, economic and political matters of human life. In addition to that, there is another element that had a negative effect on the jurisprudential treatment of the subject of *maqāṣid*. It is a recurrent fact in *uṣūl al-fiqh* works that one essential evidence usually adduced to prove the indispensability and enduring nature of the five necessary universals (*al-kulliyyāt al-ḍarūriyyah*) is the existence in the Sharīʿah of specific penalties (*ʿuqūbāt*) for their violation, such as just retribution (*qiṣāṣ*) for homicide and theft punishment (*ḥadd al-sariqah*), a situation at which Ibn Ashur is the first, and perhaps the only one in modern times, to express uneasiness and reservation.[5]

Considering this great methodological and epistemological shortcoming in the legal discourse on *maqāṣid* which literally marginalized most of the Qur'anic guidance on human affairs, it was al-Shāṭibī in the eighth/fourteenth century who actually rose to systematically reset things on a proper track. To this end, he adopted a holistic approach to the Qur'an based on an inductive method of thematic inference (*istiqrā'*) in dealing with its verses seen from the perspective of their chronological sequence in order to arrive at the universals (*kulliyyāt*) and general principles underlying all juridical details and particulars of the Sharīʿah. His purpose was to effect a total reconstruction and re-structuring of the discipline of *uṣūl al-fiqh* in which *maqāṣid al-Sharīʿah* are not only the most important subject or theme or only occupy a prominent place therein, but also function as the unifying axis of all the topics and sub-topics of that discipline as expounded in his masterpiece *al-Muwāfaqāt*. The foremost premise underlying al-Shāṭibī's whole endeavour is twofold. First is the fact that "the primary intention of the Lawgiver (*qaṣd al-Shāriʿ ibtidāʾan*) in laying down the Sharīʿah" is to secure "the interests and well-being (*maṣāliḥ*) of human beings (*ʿibād*) in both this life (*ʿājil*) and the Hereafter (*ājil*)."[6] All other purposes that may be deduced from the Qurʾan and which al-Shāṭibī himself discussed extensively are in fact offshoots and ramifications of this fundamental goal and serve it in different ways.[7] The second fact is that the Qurʾan is "the comprehensive ultimate source (*kulliyyat*) of the Sharīʿah, the mainstay of Religion, the wellspring of wisdom, and the paradigm of the [Divine] message."[8] Likewise, the Sharīʿah universals are expressed and laid out throughout the Makkan and Madīnan Qurʾanic revelations in different forms and contexts and through multiple particulars and details in such an interrelated manner that a thematic continuity runs through the Qurʾan and links up its sūrahs and verses as an integral whole projecting those universals as being the fundamentals and foundation of the Sharīʿah.[9] These two premises constitute an integral part of al-Shāṭibī's epistemic foundation for the study of the Sharīʿah and of *maqāṣid* as its core.

However, the great lesson and purpose of al-Shāṭibī's effort aimed at effecting an epistemological and methodological reformulation of *uṣūl al-fiqh* and a reorientation of the study of *maqāṣid al-Sharīʿah* seems to have, regrettably, escaped the intellectual attention of many, indeed most, of those engaged in the discourse on the Sharīʿah objectives, despite the verbally high acclaim usually attached to his book in many Muslim academic and intellectual circles. One might even encounter people claiming to specialize in the study of *maqāṣid* and aspiring to practise *ijtihād maqāṣidī* without having read at least once the central part of *al-Muwāfaqāt* where al-Shāṭibī explicates in an unprecedented way and detail the structure and categories of *maqāṣid*, let alone the other four parts in which he elaborates his epistemology and methodology. It is not rare to detect that talks about al-Shāṭibī and references to his views and ideas to support a certain opinion or position simply draw on secondary sources, with the result of those ideas and views being distorted and put out place, as those using them do not have any sense of their original context and of the kind of reasoning informing them. In many cases, what is learnt from the great work of the Andalusian theorist is limited to the notion of *maṣlaḥah* and its classification into *ḍarūrī, ḥājī* and *taḥsīnī*, taken in a general and vague manner, thus failing to realize and make sense of the richness of hermeneutical and methodological discussions and epistemological outlook that guided al-Shāṭibī's project of intellectual renewal. As al-Najjar justly lamentated, just as al-Shāṭibī's breakthrough in theorizing about *maqāṣid al-Sharīʿah* was unique or unprecedented (*yatīmah*) compared to what had preceded it, so it remained in relation to what followed it. Subsequent works on *uṣūl al-fiqh* went on just reproducing what had already been said time and again by pre-al-Shāṭibī legal theorists.[10] Exceptions of course there are, but just to confirm the rule.

Be that as it may, it would not be an exaggeration to speak of a *maqāṣid* turn in the study of the Sharīʿah, which is of course a welcome intellectual and methodological development in contemporary Islamic juristic discourse. In fact, one may also speak of some kind of cultural fashion that has attracted various categories of learned and unlearned writers and speakers who are thrust onto the stage by different motives and for varied purposes. One general and common trait characterizing the discourse of many of such riders is a clear lack of sound knowledge of the theoretical roots, methodological parameters and historical development of the notion of *maqāṣid*, let aside its connections with the wider spectrum of disciplines in the Islamic intellectual and scholarly tradition. Many a writer is in relation to it like someone who picks up a piece of fruit of which he/she has no idea about its nature and characteristics, the type of tree producing it, and the way of consuming or making use of it. Knowingly or unknowingly, in good or bad faith, this may give rise to different forms of misuse and abuse of such a great idea to serve as a justificatory means or cover-up for ideas and/or practices that deeply and squarely run counter to the teachings of Islam in form or substance or in both at the same time.

To just give a few examples of such aberrant trends, one can point to the view claiming that *maqāṣid al-Sharī'ah* can be employed as a tool of abrogation to repeal the legal import and rules enacted in some of the Qur'anic verses which are allegedly not suitable to the values, mentality, attitudes and tastes of the modern world! It is not far-fetched to say that such a move simply undermines the very sources from which the idea of *maqāṣid* has been inferred. Another approach to *maqāṣid al-Sharī'ah* that might run the risk of sliding into even more dangerous consequences is what one can describe as ethical naturalism and intellectual historicism which may end up playing down or even suspending a good deal of the revealed rules and norms of personal and collective conduct in the name of general or vague amorphic notions of human natural or universal moral values. Concepts such as *fiṭrah* and *maqāṣid* are used to serve as a gate for the way out of the bounds of the Sharī'ah, even though the latter are enunciated explicitly in clear-cut and unequivocal terms.[11]

Opposite to such modernist and modernizing trends is the literalist traditionalist camp which has been enjoying weighty presence and exercising wide influence in many Muslim academic institutions, thus shaping in varying degrees the study of the Islamic scriptural sources and intellectual traditions. Generally speaking, the members of this camp do not see any horizon or possibility for the understanding of the Qur'anic discourse and Prophetic traditions except what the forefathers have bequeathed, let alone to open up to and benefit from the new methodologies and conceptual frameworks which the humanities and social sciences may often provide for the study of human cultural and social life. Indeed, there are among this camp ultra-traditionalist and ultra-literalist tendencies that restrict the correct and acceptable interpretation and understanding of the teachings of Islam to only a school or even certain individual scholars to the exclusion of all others, especially those with remarkable levels of rational intellectualism, no matter how steeped in the knowledge of scriptural sources they might be. Though the influence of such tendencies has been receding over the last few decades due to various reasons, their spectre cannot be said to have disappeared. In fact, they can regain authority as a result of psychological and cultural reactions in which political manipulation can easily come into play, just as it did in their ascendancy.

Between these two extremes lies the larger and mainstream body of contemporary Islamic scholarship and intellectualism which, despite its nuances and differences, strives for a balanced, learned, enlightened, original and viable interpretation and understanding of Islam in its textual sources and intellectual and cultural legacies. Its main and ultimate goal is to enable Muslims to live in the modern world and act positively as constructive partners with the rest of mankind in facing the multiple problems and crises besetting and threatening the human population of the globe. This mainstream and middlemost position shuns the modernist and post-modernist intellectual fashions inclined to confuse, dilute and obliterate the teachings of Islam as well as the literalist traditionalism that adamantly fixates and freezes the understanding and application of those teachings at a specific historical moment or geographical area of the past. Unlike both camps, it seeks to strike a just and creative balance between the *Text* and *Context*, between idealism and realism, between the individual and community, between localism and globalism, between particularism and universalism, so that Muslims today and in the future are not uprooted and deracinated from the spiritual and historical sources of their individual and collective self, nor alienated and estranged from the realities and concerns of the world in which they live.[12]

With the above-described considerations in mind, the present book germinated and took final shape both in terms of methodology and content, form and substance. Taking the Qur'an as the major source for the purpose of exploring the deep roots, interconnections and dimensions of the five necessary universals (*al-kulliyyāt al-ḍarūriyyah: dīn, nafs, ʿaql, nasl* and *māl*) on which there is an almost universal consensus among Muslim scholars of the past and present as being the ultimate and cardinal goals of the Sharīʿah. Semantic-conceptual analysis has been the main method employed in dealing with the relevant key terms, though not in an exhaustive manner covering all possibly related vocabulary. While embracing the spirit that animated al-Shāṭibī's efforts, the present work departs from him in terms of method and style.

This undertaking does not lay ground to any claim of novelty for such an approach in dealing with the Qur'anic text.[13] Nevertheless, it can confidently be affirmed that its application is new as far as discoursing on *maqāṣid al-Sharī‘ah* is concerned. So far, as we have already pointed out, most of the discourse on this important theory has been confined to the hermeneutical parameters and technical language of Islamic jurisprudence, both as legal theory and methodology (*uṣūl al-fiqh*) and as applied positive law (*fiqh*), not denying the fact that, historically and methodologically speaking, the very notion of *maqāṣid al-Sharī‘ah* is an essential product and legitimate baby of this area of Islamic learning and scholarship, but certainly not disconnected from the other constituent disciplines of what the Moroccan philosopher Taha Abderrahmane calls the Arabic-Islamic semiotic field (*al-majāl al-dilālī al-islāmī al-‘arabī*),[14] notably the study of the Qur'an as being the foundational text of Islamic life and culture.[15]

Yet, to continue dealing with it within the confines of jurisprudence alone will only perpetuate its unjustified severance from its most profound Qur'anic underpinnings, thus missing the richness of meaning, the width of intellectual horizon and practical implications it can gain by linking it to a wider semantic and conceptual field in the Qur'an that sheds more light on its relationship with certain essential components of the Islamic worldview, notably with respect to questions of values and being, or axiology and ontology. Hence, there is a legitimate and urgent need for what may be described as semantic and conceptual regrounding of *maqāṣid al-Sharī‘ah* in the Qur'an, a task that is humbly attempted in the present monograph. This regrounding can enable us to uncover and bring into stronger relief the interconnectedness and multidimensionality of human common good sustaining and grounding the Islamic way of life as enjoined in the Qur'an and exemplified in the Prophetic model.[16] The idea that *maqāṣid al-Sharī‘ah* revolve around human good has actually been at the centre of all intellectual theorization on it since it made its appearance in *uṣūl al-fiqh* literature, indeed before that at the hands of the eminent philosopher al-‘Āmirī (d. 381H).[17] As rightly argued by Taha Abderrahmane, "the science of goodness, *ʿilm al-ṣalāḥ*, is what *maqāṣid al-Sharīʿah* is all about, thus addressing one fundamental question: how to be a good human being, and how to do good things."[18]

As it evolved along the lines of the initial division of tasks among the contributing authors, a reordering of the five necessary universals has emerged that clearly departs from the historically established classification in which life usually comes as number two next to religion, while offspring ranks as number four after intellect and prior to wealth. By occupying the third and middle position in relation to the other four necessary universals, life appears to be the one essential value which serves as the bridge linking the other four. An important and deep meaning that can be discerned behind this 'intuitive' reordering is that life is in actual fact the object on which the other things are predicated, and in the absence of which they can never hold. The notion of life here is not confined to human life, but it also includes all manifestations of life, starting from the Life of the Eternal and Absolute, *al-Ḥayy al-Qayyūm*, Who is the source of all life and bestows being on all else in the seen and unseen realms of existence.

As it stands, our work may be deemed to offer a food for serious thought to an increasing number of researchers and thinkers who are intent on looking more critically into the existing body of social science disciplines and theories many of which are wrought with varying degrees of methodological reductionism and materialistic conceptualism. A burgeoning new discourse is taking shape in some academic institutions in the Muslim world in search of alternative approaches in the study of human social affairs that would embrace the human condition and reality in all its aspects and dimensions. Some would consider *maqāṣid al-Sharīʿah* as providing an appropriate conceptual framework to bridging the gap between Islamic studies and the social sciences and humanities in Muslim educational institutions. Others would find in this Islamic theory epistemological and methodological tools for the reorientation and indigenization of Western-grown sciences of man and society.[19]

Having said that, it is a matter of both duty and honour for me to express my deep gratitude to a number of people who have contributed in different ways to the production of this work. First of course, I should at the same time thank and congratulate my two co-authors, Dawood al-Hidabi and Waleed Fares, for their cooperative, fruitful and creative effort without which the book would not have got its present shape. Bringing together the intelligence and acumen of a mechanical and aerospace engineer, an educationist and an Islamic studies student, this work may inspire further and more focused efforts of cross-border and interdisciplinary research. Second, Eltigani A. Hamid and Ibrahim M. Zein were very generous to carefully read a semi-final draft of the work and grace it with an enlightening joint foreword. Their encouraging and constructive remarks were significant in drawing my attention to certain methodological and intellectual flaws that needed rectification. I am very grateful to both of them, indeed. Third, my daughters Hoda and Amirah have always been ready for assistance even at the expense of their immediate preoccupations and urgent tasks. While Hoda provided a number of sample designs for the book cover, Amirah worked on improving the selected one. Both deserve my infinite love and deep thankfulness. Fourth, I should highly value the decision by the International Institute for Muslim Unity, IIMU to include this book in its list of publications and co-publish it with such a leading and professional publisher as Islamic Book Trust, IBT. Last but not least, IBT team, especially publication officer Mohd. Yusoff Sultan and Mohamad Mohideen, have been very cooperative, accommodative, and efficient throughtout the different stages of the book production, even when last minute corrections and amendments need to be made. My great appreciation goes to all and each of them and to their boss and old time friend Hj. Koya Kutty.

And God knows best.

Mohamed El-Tahir El-Mesawi
Kuala Lumpur/Gombak
Jumādā al-Awwal 1443/December 2021

Notes

[1] See in this respect, Abdul Rashid Moten (ed.), *Spirituality and Sustainability: Experiences of the International Islamic University Malaysia* (Kuala Lumpur: IIUM Pess, IIUM, 1st print, 2021); also his *Humanising Education: Maqāṣid al-Sharīʿah and Sustainable Development* (Kuala Lumpur: IIUM Pess, IIUM, 1st print, 2021).

[2] Most of the works referred to are published by the International Institute of Islamic Thought under the series name *IIIT Books in Brief*. They include, among others, the following titles: Jasser Auda, *Maqāṣid al-Sharīʿah: A Beginner's Guide* (London-Washington: The International Institute of Islamic Thought, 1429AH/2008CE); Mohammad Hashim Kamali, *Maqāṣid al-Sharīʿah Made Simple* (London-Washington: The International Institute of Islamic Thought, 1429AH/2008CE), also his *Actualization (Tafʿīl) of the Higher Purposes of Sharīʿah* (London-Washington: The International Institute of Islamic Thought & Kuala Lumpur: International Institute of Advanced Islamic Studies Malaysia, 1441AH/2020CE); Muhammad al-Tahir Ibn Ashur, *Treatise on Maqāṣid al-Sharīʿah* (London-Washington: The International Institute of Islamic Thought, 2013); Musfir bin Ali al-Qahtani, *Understanding Maqāṣid al-Sharīʿah: A Contemporary Perspective* (London-Washington: The International Institute of Islamic Thought, 2015).

[3] In order to keep this introduction within reasonable limits, it is not of its purpose to embark on producing historical details on how the independent study of *maqāṣid al-sharīʿah* has evolved throughout the twentieth century well into the twenty-first up to the present. It would therefore suffice to point out what can be considered as landmarks. The year 1946 can be seen as the real and vigorous start of this intellectual and academic movement by the publication in Tunisia of Muhammad al-Tahir Ibn Ashur's *Maqāṣid al-Sharīʿah al-Islāmiyyah* in which he called for the establishment of a new and independent discipline by the name *ʿIlm Maqāṣid al-Sharīʿah*. Almost eighteen years later, this work was followed by the Moroccan Allal al-Fasi's *Maqāṣid al-Sharīʿah al-Islāmiyyah wa-Makārimuhā* published in 1963. These two books did not, however, instigate any immediate and serious intellectual response in the study of Islamic jurisprudence and legal theory in Muslim academic institutions. So we had to wait until the 1990s when a take-off took place and *maqāṣid* started to become an increasingly attractive subject of academic and intellectual interest in Muslim circles and beyond. As a result, some sort of rediscovery and reintroduction of *maqāṣid al-sharīʿah* has become a highly visible trend in Islamic studies. See my remarks in this respect in, Muhammad al-Tahir Ibn Ashur, *Maqāṣid al-Sharīʿah al-Islāmiyyah*, edited and subjoined with a lengthy study by Mohamed El-Tahir El-Mesawi (Amman: Dār al-Nafaes, 4th edn., 1440/2019 [2001]), pp. 66-70 & 114-115; Mohamed El-Tahir El-Mesawi (ed.), *Maqāṣid al-Sharīʿah: Explorations and Implications* (Petaling Jaya, Malaysia: Islamic Book Trust, 2018), pp. ix-xii.

[4] Among many others reference can be made here to the works of scholars such as Abdelmajid al-Najjar, Abderrahmane b. Moammar al-Sanussi, Ahmad al-Raysuni, Farid al-Ansari, al-Hassan Shaheed, Gamal al-Din Atya, Hamadi al-Ubaydi, Ibrahim al-Kaylani, Ibrahim Bayyoumi Ghanem, Ihsan Mir Ali, Ismail al-Hassani, Jasser Auda, Musfir al-Qahtani, Hassan Jabir, Muhammad Hashim Kamali, Muhammad Khalid Masud, Naamane Djeghim, Noureddine al-Khadmi, Mohamed Hendou, Taha Jabir al-Alwani, Yusuf al-Qaradawi, Yusuf Hamid al-Alim.

[5] Commenting on the view upheld by some scholars that the preservation of honour (ʿirḍ) is indispensable and hence belongs to the category of ḍarūriyyāt by reason of the severity of the ḥadd punishment prescribed by the Sharīʿah for slander, Ibn Ashur says, "We do not, however, see any necessary correlation between what is indispensable and that whose violation incurs the ḥadd penalty." Muhammad al-Tahir Ibn Ashur, Treatise on Maqāṣid al-Sharīʿah, translated from the Arabic and annotated by Mohamed El-Tahir El-Mesawi (London-Washington: The International Institute of Islamic Thought, 1427/2006), p. 123. See also his remarks concerning just retribution and its role in the protection of human life (p. 120). A few decades after Ibn Ashur, the eminent Lebanese scholar Muhammad Mahdi Shmasuddin expressed his reservation and criticism regarding the jurists' view on the number of the so-called juridical Qur'anic verses. In his opinion, this view is due to a narrow and atomistic methodological and epistemological approach to the Qur'an as well as to the affairs of human society. Muhammad Mahdi Shmasuddin, al-Ijtihād wa'l-Tajdīd fi'l-Fiqh al-Islāmī (Beirut: al-Muʾassasah al-Dwliyyah, 1st edn., 1419/1999), pp. 82-84

[6] Abū Isḥāq Ibrāhīm b. Mūsā al-Shaṭibī, al-Muwāfaqāt fī Uṣūl al-Sharīʿah, ed. Abdullah Draz (Beirut: Dār al-Kutub al-ʿIlmiyyah, 1422/2001), vol. 1/2, pp. 3-4; also its English version, The Reconciliation of the Fundamentals of Islamic Law, trans. Imran Ahsan Khan Nyazee (London: Garnet Publishers, 2014), vol. 2, p. 3.

[7] Al-Shāṭibī, al-Muwāfaqāt fī Uṣūl al-Sharīʿah, vol. 1/2, pp. 7-313; The Reconciliation of the Fundamentals of Islamic Law, vol. 2, pp. 9-242.

[8] Al-Shāṭibī, al-Muwāfaqāt, vol. 2/3, p. 250.

[9] Al-Shāṭibī, al-Muwāfaqāt, vol. 2/3, pp. 3-18. See also, Wael B. Hallaq, "The Primacy of the Qur'an in al-Shāṭibī's Legal Theory," in Wael B. Hallaq & Donald P. Little (eds.), Islamic Studies Presented to Charles J. Adamas (Leiden-New York-Kobenhavn-Koln: E.J. Brill, 1st edn., 1991), pp. 69-90; pp. 24-29; also his "On Inductive Corroboration, Probability and Certainty in Sunni Legal Thought", in Nicholas Heer (ed.), Islamic Law and Jurisprudence (Seattle and London: University of Washington Press, 1990), pp. 24-29; Mohamed El-Tahir El-Mesawi, "From al-Shāṭibī's legal hermeneutics to thematic exegesis of the Qur'an," Intellectual Discourse, vol. 20, No. 2 (2012), pp. 194-207. See also, Hamadi al-Ubaydi, al-Shāṭibī wa-Maqāṣid al-Sharīʿah (Damascus: Dār Qutaybah, 1st edn., 1412/1992), pp.165-178 & 189-195; Ahmad al-Raysuni, Imām al-Shāṭibī's Theory of the Objectives and Intents of Islamic Law, translated from the Arabic by Nancy Roberts (London-Washignton: The International Institute of

Islamic Thought, 1426/2005), pp. 136-168; Farid al-Ansari, *al-Muṣṭalaḥ al-Uṣūlī ʿinda al-Shāṭibī* (Cairo: Dār al-Salām, 1ˢᵗ edn., 1431/2010), pp. 283-294.

[10] Abdelmajid al-Najjar, *Fuṣūl fi'l-Fikr al-Islāmī bi'l-Maghrib* (Beirut: Dār al-Gharb al-Islāmī, 1ˢᵗ edn., 1992), p. 143.

[11] This only shows how profoundly secularist and historicist epistemological and methodological doctrines have infiltrated and impacted the minds so that attempts are being made to play down and undermine, consciously or unconsciously, the authority of the Qur'an in Muslim personal and collective life, since history has proven the impossibility of removing it altogether, despite the systematic and concerted onslaught on the Qur'an that has been going on for one hundred years at least. So, explaining away the revealed text and distorting and confusing its messages seem to be a better strategy than direct attack. See in this connection, Abdelmajid al-Najjar, *al-Qirā'ah al-Jadīdah li'l-Naṣṣ al-Dīnī* (Damascus: Markaz al-Rāyah li'l-Tanmiyah al-Fikriyyah, 2006); Ahmad Idris Al-Taʿan, *al-ʿAlmāniyyūn wa'l-Qur'ān al-Karīm: Tārīkhiyyat al-Naṣṣ* (Riyadh: Dār Ibn Ḥazm, 1428/2007); Kotb al-Raissouni, *al-Naṣṣ al-Qur'ānī min Tahāfut al-Qirā'ah ilā Ufuq al-Tadabbur: Madkhal ilā Naqd al-Qirā'āt wa-Ta'ṣīl ʿIlm al-Tadabbur al-Qur'ānī* (Rabat: Ministry of Endowments and Islamic Affairs, 1ˢᵗ edn., 1431/2010); Mohammad Salim al-Naimi, *al-Qirā'ah al-Ḥadāthiyyah li'l-Naṣṣ al-Qur'ānī wa-Atharuhā fī Qaḍāyā al-ʿAqīdah* (Cairo: Dār Miṣr al-ʿArabiyyah, 2016); Harald Motzki, "Alternative accounts of the Qur'an Formation," in Jane Dammen McAuliffe (ed.), *The Cambridge Companion to the Qur'an* (Cambridge: Cambridge University Press, 2006), pp. 59-75; Walid A. Saleh, "The Etymological Fallacy and Qur'anic Studies: Muhammad, Paradise, and Late Antiquity", in Angelika Neuwirth *et al.* (eds.), *The Qur'ān in Context: Historical and Literary Investigations into the Qur'ānic Milieu* (Leiden-Boston: Brill, 2010), pp. 649-698.

[12] See in this respect, Ahmad al-Raysuni (ed.), *Iʿmāl al-Maqāṣid bayna al-Tahayyub wal'-Tasayyub* (London: Al-Furqan Islamic Heritage Foundation, 1ˢᵗ edn., 1435/ 2014).

[13] The systematic semantic analysis of Qur'anic terms aimed at understanding specific topics in the Islamic Scripture in modern times can rightfully be attributed to the late Japanese scholar Izutsu whose contributions in this regard date as far back as the late 1950s. See, Toshihiko Izutsu, *Ethico-Religious Terms in the Qur'an* (Montreal-Kingston-London-Ithaca: Queen's University Press, 2002 [1959]); *God and Man in the Qur'an: Semantics of the Qur'anic Weltanschauung* (Kuala Lumpur: Islamic Book Trust, 2002 [1964]). But it should be noted that prior to these works Izutsu had already laid down, though partly, the philosophical foundation of his semantic-conceptual methodology in his *Language and Magic: Studies in the Magical Function of Speech* (Kuala Lumpur: Islamic Book Trust, 2012 [1956]). In the Arab-Islamic academic and intellectual milieus reference can be made especially to Chahid Bouchikhi, Eltigani Abdelgadir Hamid and Abderrahman Helali who have contributed a good number of articles and papers employing the semantic-conceptual method in dealing with a variety of subjects.

[14] Taha Abderrahmane, *Tajdīd al-Manhaj fī Taqwīm al-Turāth* (Beirut-Casablanca: al-Markaz al-Thaqāfī al-ʿArabī, 3rd edn., 2007), pp. 237-420.

[15] For a comprehensive account of the intellectual roots and historical development of the *maqāṣid* theory, see Mohamed El-Tahir El-Mesawi, "*Maqāṣid al-Sharīʿah*: Meaning, Scope and Ramifications", *Al-Shajarah* (ISTAC Journal of Islamic Thought and Civilization), vol. 25, No. 2 (2020), pp. 263-286.

[16] It is worth pointing out, in this connection, that al-Najjar's work on *maqāṣid* can still be seen as a pioneering effort in this direction. See, especially, Abdlemajid al-Najjar, *Maqāṣid al-Sharīʿah bi-Abʿād Jadīdah* (Beirut: Dār al-Gharb al-Islāmī, 1st edn., 2006); also his *Qaḍāyā al-Bīʾah min Manẓūr Islāmī* (Doha: Ministry of Endowment and Islamic Affairs, 1429/1999).

[17] Abū al-Ḥasan al-ʿĀmirī, *Kitāb al-Iʿlām bi-Manāqib al-Islām,* ed. Ahmed Abdelhamid Ghorab (Riyadh: Muʾassasat al-Aṣālah, 1408/1988), pp. 95-150; also *Arbaʿ Rasāʾil Falsafiyyah,* ed. Saeed al-Ghanimi (Tunis-Beirut: Dār al-Tanwīr, 2015), pp. 182-213. Most probably, al-ʿĀmirī was inspired and influenced by his teacher in Islamic jurisprudence Abū Bakr al-Qaffāl al-Shāshī (d. 365H) who devoted his book *Maḥāsin al-Sharīʿah* to explaining how the teachings of Islam revolve around what is good and beneficial to human beings.

[18] Taha Abderrahmane, *Suʾāl al-Manhaj: Fī Ufuq al-Taʾsīs li-Unmūdhaj Fikrī Jadīd* (Beirut: al-Muʾassasah al-ʿArabiyyah liʾl-Fikr waʾl-Ibdāʿ, 1st edn., 2015), p. 74.

[19] See for example, Abdullah Mohamed El-Amin El-Naim (ed.), *Maqāṣid al-Sharīʿah: Naḥwa Iṭār liʾl-Baḥth fiʾl-ʿUlūm al-Ijtimāʿiyyah waʾl-Insāniyyah* (Damascus: Dār al-Fikr, 1st edn., 1430/2009); Mazin Muwaffaq Hashim, *Maqāṣid al-Sharīʿah al-Islāmiyyah: Madkhal ʿUmrāni* (Hernden, Virginia: The International Institute of Islamic Thought, 1st edn., 1435/2014); Sari Hanafi, *ʿUlūm al-Sharʿ waʾl-ʿUlūm al-Ijtimāʿiyyah: Naḥwa Tajāwuz al-Qaṭīʿah* (Beirut: Markaz Nuhḥū, 1st edn., 2021), esp. pp. 695-715; Ibrahim al-Bayyoumi Ghanem, *Tajdīd al-Fuṣūl fī Fiqh Maqāṣid al-Sharīʿah* (Cairo: Mufakkirūn, 1440/2019).

CHAPTER ONE

Ḥifẓ al-Dīn and *Ḥifẓ al-Nasl*: Enhancing Human Spiritual Morality and Safeguarding Mankind

Introduction

Together with other things *ḥifẓ al-dīn* and *ḥifẓ al-nasl* (lit. preservation of religion and preservation of progeny) stand on top of the pyramid and hierarchy of the goals that the Sharīʿah seeks to realize by means of its rules and commands in the different arenas of human life. God, the Almighty Creator and all-Merciful Sustainer, has enunciated the Sharīʿah in the Qurʾan and Prophetic Sunnah for the sake of bringing about human beings' benefit and well-being (*maṣlaḥah*) in this world and in the Hereafter, while at the same time averting and/or removing any harm (*mafsadah*) that might affect them. Likewise, *ḥifẓ al-dīn* and *ḥifẓ al-nasl* consist of protecting and enhancing religion and progeny which, alongside with *ḥifẓ al-nafs*, *ḥifẓ al-ʿaql*, and *ḥifẓ al-māl*, make up the category of the universal necessities or necessary universals known in Islamic jurisprudence as *al-kulliyyāt al-ḍarūriyyah*, or shortly as *al-ḍarūriyyāt*. Though *ḥifẓ al-nasl* is usually ranked as number four by almost all Muslim legal theorists and jurists preceding only *ḥifẓ al-māl*, we have deemed it appropriate to link them together in this chapter for reasons that will become clear throughout the following discussion.

In the ethico-legal system of the Sharīʿah these *ḍarūriyyāt* are complemented, consolidated and realized through a wide range of purposes, rules, and mechanisms subsumed in Islamic jurisprudence under the next two categories of *ḥājiyyāt* (needs) and *taḥsīniyyāt* (improvements or embellishments). Likewise, they constitute the foundation and pillars of human life and existence in the absence of which society and civilization collapse, if they ever come into being in the first place. Their realization, protection and promotion are therefore a matter of utmost priority in the theory of *maqāṣid al-Sharī'ah* (or the Sharī'ah objectives). This is because these universal necessities are the cornerstone, and stand at the root, of all kinds of benefit and good that human beings seek in order to fulfil different types of their needs, material and immaterial, so that their life functions properly and smoothly in a way that brings about well-being, gratification and happiness.

Ḥifẓ al-Dīn: meaning and scope

1. Dīn: From semantical analysis to conceptual formulation

In both the Arabic language and Qur'anic usage, the term *dīn* has a wide range of meanings that may not be easily captured and encapsulated by the English word 'religion' and its synonyms in other Western languages, nor would it be accurately interpreted and understood through the prism of Western history and intellectual traditions, especially within the orbit of Enlightenment rationalism and modernity's secular humanism over the last few centuries.[1] Neither in the Qur'anic usage, nor in the Arabic language, does this term refer simply to faith and belief in God as Creator and Sustainer of the world and obedience to Him by performing ritual acts of worship, such as prayer and pilgrimage. Nor is the meaning of *dīn* restricted to the rules of personal conduct and private life or even to family matters, such as marriage, divorce, inheritance, etc. Indeed, as will be made clear below, this term signifies all such things and much more.

The Arabic lexicographical tradition is of great help in enabling us to realize the variety and richness of meaning of the term *dīn* in the Arabic language itself prior to the technical or special usage of revelation; it offers us a starting point to grasp its much wider Qur'anic import depending on the contexts of its occurrence. The term in question is derived from the root *d.y.n.* From this same root are derived many other words (in the form of nouns, verbs and adjectives) connoting different meanings the variation of some of which goes as far as contrariness, thus falling under what is known in Arabic lexicology and linguistics as *aḍdād* (i.e., a kind of homonyms in which a word has two contrary meanings).[2]

This linguistic phenomenon of contrariness in signification is also reflected in the term *dīn* itself.[3] According to al-Attas, to whom we shall return later for deeper insights, whatever the many primary significations of this term, they can be reduced to four basic meanings, namely "(1) *indebtedness*, (2) *submissiveness* [and obedience], (3) *judicial power*, (4) *natural inclination or tendency*."[4] Further examination of the available lexicographical sources, however, reveals other meanings that are no less basic than these four. We shall limit ourselves to only three of such meanings which, together with what al-Attas has identified, will help us construct the total picture of the concept of *dīn* as can be grasped from the Qur'an. The first item in our addendum is requital and reckoning denoted by the words *ḥisāb* and *jazā'*. As will become clearer in the following exposition, despite the undeniable overlapping of meaning between judicial power (number 3 in al-Attas' list) and reckoning, the latter meaning brings immediately to attention one central Qur'anic concept that the former does not, or at least not as much clearly. The second meaning of *dīn* to be supplemented to al-Attas's list is that of faith or creed denoted by the word *millah*. Lastly, we have the sense of tradition and custom conveyed by the words *ʿādah* and *da'b*.[5]

As we shall see below, these essential meanings around which revolve the various significations of the term *dīn* and its derivatives are expressed in many Qur'anic contexts whether by the use of this term itself or by other terms belonging to the same semantic field in the Qur'anic discourse. Since very early in Muslim history the Qur'an has been the focus of intellectual reflection on many accounts and for different, yet not unrelated, purposes. Its language, style and message are the pivot of all that. In this context, the Qur'anic vocabulary and its significance and import have preoccupied the minds of many scholars throughout Muslim intellectual history, notably what has come to be known as *wujūh* and *naẓā'ir* whereby special focus is put on terms denoting more than one meaning.

Based on the oldest extant literature, Muqātil al-Balkhī (d. 150 AH/767 AD) can be seen as the first to have devoted a reasonably focused, though not exhaustive, effort to trace the different meanings connoted by a list of one hundred eighty-six terms depending on the Qur'anic contexts in which they are used. In his book on polysemy and homonymy in the Qur'an, opening with the term *hudā* and closing with that of *fisq*, we are presented with five meanings of the term *dīn* that are recurrent throughout its text and occur, as it appears from the verses cited by al-Balkhī as evidence, in Makkan as well as Madīnan sūrahs. These meanings consist of the following.

1. Belief in the oneness of God (*tawḥīd*), as evidenced by a number of verses such as (al-Zumar, 39:2), "it is We who have bestowed this revelation upon thee from on high, setting forth the truth: so worship Him, sincere in thy faith in Him alone!"

2. Judgement and requital (*ḥisāb*) as expressed in sūrah al-Fātiḥah (1:4) by the phrase describing God as "Lord of the Day of Judgement!"

3. Law and command (*ḥukm*), as conveyed in the verse of sūrah al-Nūr (24:2) prescribing the punishment for adultery: "As for the adulteress and the adulterer—flog each of them with a hundred stripes, and let not compassion with them keep you from [carrying out] this law of God."

4. The total body of teachings revealed by God enjoining human beings to serve and worship Him (*alladhī yadīnu Allāhu bihi al-ʿibād*), as denoted by the statement (al-Fatḥ, 48:28) that "He [God] it is who has sent forth His Apostle with the [task of spreading] guidance and the religion of truth, to the end that He make it prevail over every [false] religion."

5. The last Qur'anic meaning of *dīn* as identified by al-Balkhī is

> that of creed and faith as conveyed in verses such as (al-Naḥl,
> 16:123): "And lastly, We have inspired thee, [O Muḥammad ,
> with this message:] 'Follow the creed of Abraham (*millata
> Ibrāhīm*), who turned away from all that is false, and was not of
> those who ascribe divinity to aught beside God'."[6]

Following in al-Balkhī's footsteps, a number of works on the same topic were produced over the centuries up to the present, varying mainly in detail and scope, but not in approach and orientation. Regardless of whether or not the authors of such works (including Muqātil himself) adopted a specific order of any kind in arranging their entries of the Qur'anic vocabularies they examined, there is a common feature that is characteristic of most of them. They do not seem to have reflected upon and analyzed the relationships (conceptual or otherwise) among the different (contextual) meanings they identify in respect of each vocabulary, exception being made of al-Ḥakīm al-Tirmidhī and, to a lesser extent, al-Rāghib al-Iṣfahānī. Likewise, in their entries on the term *dīn* most of them would start with reproducing almost verbatim and in similar sequence the significations listed by al-Balkhī without adding to it anything substantial, thus perhaps implying that these five significations are the essential meanings of the term *dīn* in the semantic world of the Qur'an.[7]

The importance of al-Tirmidhī's work, at least on the theoretical level, lies in the fact that, as he clearly indicates, whatever different connotations a word might have in the Qur'an, such variations are only contextual and circumstantial, for they are in fact expressions of one and the same essential meaning and truth.[8] The idea al-Tirmidhī seems to embrace is that the variety of significations of Qur'anic key terms is a manifestation of different aspects of one axis or core meaning underpinning and uniting all those significations and pointing to an essential truth and reality beyond them. According to El-Awa, this view opened the door for a big change in the way people had been thinking about the Qur'anic vocabulary, which developed into a trend or school among linguists of the Arabic language.[9]

Guided by this proposition or thesis, al-Tirmidhī proceeds to examine a list of eighty-one terms beginning with *hudā* (guidance) and ending with *sabīl* (path, way). Thus, for him, submission and awe (*khuḍūʿ* and *khushūʿ*) constitute the essential meaning underlying and connecting together the five sub-meanings of the term *dīn* in the Qur'an, namely the profession of the oneness of God (*tawḥīd*), judgement and requital (*ḥisāb*), law and command (*ḥukm*), sincerity of faith, and obedience to the teachings of Islam (*ikhlāṣ, īmān* and *islām*). In his view, the sense of "*khuḍūʿ* and *al-khushūʿ* starts at the heart and spreads out to the different organs (of the human body, *arkān*), thus manifesting itself through those organs' obedience to [God's] commands, abstinance from His prohibitions, acceptance of His laws, and total self-submission to Him."[10]

In quite similar vein, al-Iṣfahānī mentions that, in addition to indebtedness, tradition, judgement and requital, *dīn,* being synonymous with *sharīʿah*, most importantly denotes in the Qur'an submission (*ṭāʿah*) out of sincerity (*ikhlāṣ*) that is free from coercion (*ikrāh*), as taught in many verses such as (al-Baqarah, 2:256): "There shall be no coercion in matters of religion (*lā ikrāha fī'l-dīn*)." Sincere and true submission to the divine will and commands as conveyed in the Sharīʿah, al-Iṣfahānī ascertains, cannot obtain under coercion (*al-ikhlāṣ fīhi lā yata'attā fīhi al-ikrāh*).[11] It is worthy of mention here that almost all the Qur'anic significations of *dīn* identified by al-Iṣfahānī and those preceding him have been incorporated by al-Zabīdī in his massive Arabic lexicon,[12] which clearly indicates the close relationship and mutual fertilization between the study of the Qur'an and Arabic lexicography.

The insights offered by such earlier scholars on the semantic and conceptual meaning of the term *dīn* as briefly surveyed above, especially al-Tirmidhī and al-Iṣfahānī, will reverberate in the works of a number of modern Muslim thinkers, though not necessarily through straightforward appropriation, but most probably by way of influence and inspiration. Three thinkers come immediately into prominence here, namely the Pakistani Abul Aʿla Mawdūdī (1903-1979), the Sudanese Hassan al-Turabi (1932-2016) and the Malaysian Syed Muhammad Naquib al-Attas (1931-), although they were not the first to have devoted considerable effort to the study of religion in the Islamic context both as concept and system of belief and conduct. Before or contemporaneously with them, other eminent scholars had made significant contributions that still remain landmarks in contemporary Islamic thought. Six names at least come to mind whose works are worthy of special attention in their own right, namely the Turkish Ahmed Izzet Pasha (known as Ahmet İzzet Furgaç, 1864-1937), the Egyptians Mohammed Farid Wajdi (1878-1954), Mustafa Abdel Raziq (1885-1947), Muhammad A. Draz (1894-1958) and Ali Sami al-Nashshar (1917-1980), and the Indian Wahiduddin Khan (1925-2021).[13]

All these scholars were in quest of systematic and original response to the socio-historical and intellectual challenges facing Islam and Muslims in an increasingly secularized and globalized world generated mainly by the forces of European enlightenment and modernity. Not contenting themselves with merely emulating the inherited methodologies established by the past generations of Muslim scholarship, they were passionately engaged in profound reflection on how to rejuvenate Islamic thought and ground their thinking in the fundamental and foundational textual sources of Islam by developing a new hermeneutics and methodology.

However, the views of the six scholars just mentioned will be excluded from the following discussion and our focus will rather be on the previous three. This exclusion is mainly due to methodological reasons, as the thrust of the approach adopted in the present work is semantic-conceptual analysis, in which respect Mawdūdī, al-Turabi and al-Attas stand as good, if not exemplary, representatives.[14] Within the context of this methodological and hermeneutical orientation, these three thinkers offered both analytic and constructive conceptualizations of the term *dīn* in the Qur'an bringing forth hitherto not sufficiently and systematically theorized dimensions and implications thereof. Thus, they have paved the way for a new theorizing about religion and exhibit undisputed intellectual originality, regardless of their indebtedness to earlier scholars. Furthermore, they did not take modern Western conceptions, and approaches to the study of religion as their springboard in their intellectual inquiry on the meaning and implications of the concept of *dīn,* though such theories and approaches most probably were not absent from their minds, at least in their broad propositions and general conclusions. Instead, they took the semantic and conceptual analysis of the Qur'anic vocabulary as the bedrock of their reflections and reasoning.

Following a chronological order as we have done with earlier (classical and post-classical) scholars, we shall start with Mawdūdī. On the linguistic plane, the latter reduces the primary significations of the term *dīn* to four basic meanings. These meanings include sovereignty and supreme authority; obedience and submission to such authority; a system of laws and rules of action to be observed and followed; and lastly judgement and requital in consideration of loyalty and obedience to, or rebellion and transgression against, those laws and rules. In the Qur'an, Mawdūdī then observes, the term *dīn* is used on many occasions in one or the other of these four meanings, but in other cases it conveys all of them at the same time in the sense of a whole system (*niẓām kāmil*), as indicated by many verses which he cites to this effect.[15]

In Mawdūdī's view, the Qur'anic use of the term *dīn* in the four meanings mentioned above is more or less the same as it used to be understood by the Arabs before the Qur'anic revelation. However, a much more important fact which is characteristic of the Qur'an is that this term has been used in a rather comprehensive sense as an all-inclusive concept (*muṣṭalaḥ jāmi' shāmil*) denoting a complete way of life (*niẓām ḥayāt kāmil*) encompassing man's thinking, beliefs, morality, and behaviour in all walks of life. This way of life is one "in which a person gives submission and obedience to someone whom he regards as having the ultimate authority, shapes his conduct according to the bounds and laws prescribed by that being, looks to him for recognition and honour as well as reward for loyal service, and fears the disgrace or punishment that could result from any failure on his part."[16] For Mawdūdī, the Qur'anic concept of *religion* in the comprehensive sense just explained lays the foundation for a specific mode of thought and action, not only in one particular sector of human life nor for a specific community, but for all mankind and in all spheres of life and sectors of society, contrary to modern Western conceptions of religion. In this sense, it applies most perfectly to Islam as described by the Qur'an itself.[17]

Taking into account that most of Mawdūdī's works predate those of al-Turabi and al-Attas, it is improbable that they were unaware of his views. Nonetheless, what is of interest to us here is that both of them have opened a new angle in analyzing the conceptual structure of the term *dīn* in the Qur'an, thus putting into sharp relief its internal relationships and fundamental unity, which makes their contributions both interesting and inspiring.[18]

According to al-Turabi, religion as expressed by the term *dīn* consists, on the human side, of a relationship of obedience (*khaḍā'ah*) and humbleness (*ḍarā'ah*) by virtue of which one submits oneself freely to a sublime being, God, and on the basis of which one would establish and arrange one's relations with the different realms of existence. This is because the religious significance (*al-ma'nā al-dīnī*) of the world does not lie in that world as such, but in its being both the theatre and object of the human being's action and pursuit (*kasb*), for religion is in essence a firm conviction (*mawqif i'tiqād*) entailing a vision of the world, whereby one recognizes the absolute truth of God's divinity and oneness as the Creator and Sustainer as well as the createdness of all beings except Him, and believes in the veracity of the knowledge and information brought by Revelation on matters of the Unseen and in the justice of its legal order and commands (*aḥkām al-shar'*). Likewise, religion pertains to man's attitude of total submission to the will of God in harmony with the rest of the creation.[19]

Seen from the upper side of that relationship, religion refers to the body of divine teachings on the realities of the physical and metaphysical realms of existence, to the system of commands and obligations constituting the way of worshipping God (*minhāj al-'ibādah*), as well as to the divine call to humans to act in accordance with such commands and obligations. On this level, the term *dīn* is an expression of religion in its ideal and complete form as revealed by God, as indicated in the Qur'an (Āl 'Imrān, 3:19, 83; al-Ḥajj, 22:78; al-Ṣaff, 61:9).[20]

On a third level, the term *dīn* has to do with the human being's experience of striving to live in accordance with the imperatives of religion and to realize its values and norms in the face of the transient circumstances of life in different socio-historical contexts. It thus consists of a person's actual religiosity (*tadayyun*) and the degree of success or failure to bring one's acquired religion (*kasb dīnī*) as closer as possible to the sublime values and ideal norms of religion, in a continuous effort and struggle to subject one's life to the requirements of those values and norms by changing one's conditions and removing or overcoming the challenges one faces on the way. Likewise, religion in this sense pertains to what al-Turabi describes as *ibtilā'* or trial through which one would worship God in all domains of life by wrestling with its changing circumstances and upholding one's religion. This sense of religiosity and religious experience as trial and acquisition applies to both the individual and community, in the intellectual as well as practical domains by virtue of the fact that religion pertains to all these. In this respect, the term *dīn* is found in the Qur'an either attributed to the agent of religious accomplishment (*ṣāḥib al-kasb al-basharī*) or used in an indefinite form whose signification can be easily determined in light of the context and other circumstantial evidence, as can be realized from a number of verses (Āl 'Imrān, 3:85; al-Nisā', 4:146; al-An'ām, 6:70; Yūsuf, 12:76; al-Ḥujurāt, 49:16).[21] Moreover, and closely connected with the meaning of religion just discussed, there is the sense of *dīn* as God's judgement and reward or otherwise in the Hereafter of a person for what he/she has acquired and achieved in worshipping Him measured by the criteria of ideal religion, as can be clearly understood from other Qur'anic verses (al-Fātiḥah, 1:3; al-Ṣāffāt, 37:53).[22]

Furthermore, there is in al-Turabi's scheme one fifth mode of Qur'anic usage of the term *dīn* whereby it denotes all the previous meanings at the same time, thus confirming and affirming the idea of religion as unity and wholeness. Using this term to express all such meanings at the same time suggests to the mind that one should make utmost effort to unite one's actual 'acquired religion' with the high ideals and sublime norms of religion, thus striving to live up to, and establish, absolute truth, though one never attains complete unity with that truth due to the very limitations of human nature itself. Were the

Qur'an to use different words to express these different meanings and aspects of religion, al-Turabi argues, there would be serious risk of believing in the existence of certain stagnant level or status (*maqām*) and petrified specific forms (*ashkāl*) of religiosity, both as consciousness and experience or thought and action, to which one should stick rather than to strive through various forms for higher levels towards the perfect model of religion. While warning against such perception, al-Turabi does not deny or overlook the fact that there is in religion in general and in Islam in particular an immutable core which does not change over time. In other words, man's continuous quest and struggle in religion is geared towards filling up, or at least reducing, the gap between the actual and the ideal, the *what-is* and the *ought-to-be*.

Likewise, the Qur'an does not only underline the unity and wholeness of religion by shunning all kinds of reductionism, partiality and bifurcation in the understanding and practice thereof. It also, more importantly, underlines the unity of human life itself through bringing all its spheres and aspects within the purview of religious teachings and norms as enshrined in the Qur'an and the Prophet's example and traditions. Thus understood, religion exemplifies the very spirit of *Tawḥīd* and aligns human life individually and collectively with the cosmic unity of the universe which runs according to God's will.[23]

On quite similar methodological lines, al-Attas undertakes a semantic and conceptual analysis of the term *dīn* adding deeper philosophical and sociological elements to the reflections of Mawdūdī and al-Turabi. In what follows an account of his insights will be provided without reproducing those points and details on which he concurs with the other two scholars. According to al-Attas, although the many primary significations of the term *dīn* in the Qur'an and the Arabic language are apparently contrary to each other, they are "all conceptually interconnected, so that the ultimate meaning derived from them all presents itself as a clarified unity of the whole," this whole being what is "described as the Religion of Islam, which contains within itself all the relevant possibilities of meaning inherent in the concept of *dīn*."[24] What is clearly implied here is that the various divine teachings enshrined in the Qur'an and the Prophetic traditions are a translation and manifestation of the unified essential meanings couched in the concept *dīn*.

In line with this fundamental view al-Attas proceeds to offer quite unprecedented reflections on, and profound analysis of, the meaning of *indebtedness* showing the essential relationship between religion and human social life seen as deeply and ontologically rooted in the metaphysical realm of existence. Being co-derivative of *dīn* the verb *dāna* "conveys the meaning of being indebted, including various other meanings connected with *debts*." From this emerges the state of finding oneself in debt or *dāʾin* (also *madīn*) in which respect one has to subject oneself "to the law and ordinances governing debts and also, in a way, to the creditor, who is likewise designated as a *dāʾin*." For to al-Attas, this situation underscores the fact that one is under *obligation,* which naturally involves judgement (*daynūnah*) and conviction (*idānah*), as the case may be.[25]

Together with their contraries inherent in the verb *dāna,* al-Attas expounds, such significations "are practicable possibilities only in organized societies involved in commercial life in *towns* and *cities,* denoted by *mudun* and *madāʾin*." As he unambiguously says, by its very nature a city, town, or *madīnah,* requires "a *judge, ruler* or *governor*—a *dayyān*," thus giving rise before the mind's eye to "a picture of civilized living; of societal life of law and order and justice and authority."[26] This, moreover, presupposes "the existence of a *mode* or *manner of acting* consistent with what is reflected" in law, order, authority, and socio-cultural refinement, hence embodying a *state of being* "that is *customary* or *habitual*." This brings to our attention "the logic behind the derivation of the other primary significations of the concept *dīn* as *custom, habit, disposition* or *natural tendency*," thus underscoring the fact that "the concept *dīn* in its most basic form indeed reflects in true testimony the natural tendency of man to form societies and obey laws and seek just government."[27] To al-Attas, the idea of *kingdom* or *cosmopolis,* which emerges from these significations as something inherent in the concept of *dīn,* is of utmost importance "in helping us attain a more profound understanding" of this concept in relation to "the religious and spiritual aspects of man's existential experience."[28]

Being mutually connected and conceptually unified within the concept *dīn*, the above primary significations quintessentially express "human 'secular' relations."[29] When it comes to "the relationship between man and God and what God approves of man's relations with his fellow-men," al-Attas further explains, such significations "undergo profound synthesis and intensification at once true to the experience of the Religion of Islam as the objective faith, beliefs and practices and teachings experienced and lived by each and every member of the Muslim Community as well as by the Community as a whole."[30] Likewise, the idea of *being indebted* in the religious context can be explained by answering the following twofold question: "what is the nature of debt?, and to whom the debt is owed?" The simple and straightforward answer is that "man is indebted to God, his Creator and Provider, for bringing him into existence and maintaining him in his existence," for man "was once nothing and did not exist, and now he is," as clearly stated in the Qur'an (Al-Mu'minūm 23:12-14). This same truth "applies to all ages of man from the beginnings of his existence in time."[31]

That being so, one's sense of being indebted for one's creation and existence can in no real way be attributed to one's parents, for one knows very well that they "too are subject to the same process by the same Creator and Provider."[32] This means that man "owns absolutely nothing to 'repay' his debt;" the only thing he owns is "*his own consciousness* of the fact *that he is himself the very substance* of the debt."[33] Thus, al-Attas infers, the only way for human beings to 'repay' their existential debt is through giving themselves up to their Lord and Master who has brought them into existence, by sincerely and consciously enslaving themselves "for the sake of God in order to fulfil His Commands and Prohibitions, and thus to live out the dictates of His Law."[34] Hence, religion is in actual fact a conscious return to God in respect of which Islam provides a social order encompassing all aspects of human physical, material, and spiritual existence "in a way which, here and now, does justice to the individual as well as the society; and to the individual as a physical being as well as the individual as spirit, so that a Muslim is at once himself and his community, and his community is also he, since every other single member strives, like him, to realize the same purpose in life and to achieve the same goal."[35]

As a matter of fact, the notion of indebtedness, especially of human beings to God, has been expressed in different ways in the Qur'an. The following verse will suffice to highlight this most fundamental fact in human existence.

> *O mankind! It is you, who stand in need (fuqarā') of God, whereas He alone is self-sufficient (al-ghaniyy), the One to whom all praise is due.* (Fāṭir, 35:15)

Faqr or poverty, al-Ghazālī explains, "is to lack what one needs. Lacking what is not needed cannot be called poverty. When what is needed exists (*mawjūd*) and is attainable, the person in need is not poor (*faqīr*)." In light of this semantic clarification, al-Ghazālī goes on to expound the ontological and existential meaning of poverty. As he puts it, "everything existing besides God Exalted is poor, because it is dependent on the perpetuity of existence, in the second sense; and the perpetuation of its own existence is acquired through God's favour and grace. Were there in existence a being whose existence is not dependent on another, then it would be the 'absolutely self-sufficient' (*al-ghaniyy al-muṭlaq*)," and there is none other than God with such a quality as clearly stated in the verse.[36] Of course, poverty and indebtedness as existential features of the human condition logically entail the sense of human beings' ontological dependence on God who "is the Creator of all things" and to whom "belong the keys of the heavens and the earth" (al-Zumar, 39:62-63).[37]

The foregoing exposition makes it clear that the plurality and diversity of significations which the term *dīn* encompasses has engaged the attention of Muslim scholars since very early times, both as a linguistic and Qur'anic phenomenon. It has thus incited profound reflections on the meaning, nature, essence, characteristics and scope of religion. Commenting on this phenomenon, al-Kafawī observes that those diverse significations "are unified in essence, but different in consideration (*muttaḥidah bi'l-dhāt wa-mutaghāyirh bi'l-iʿtibār*)."[38] To express the same point in different terms, while the basic meaning of the term *dīn* concerns the essence of the phenomenon of religion as an integrated total reality, its apparently different sub-meanings reflect the different dimensions and diverse historical manifestations of that phenomenon in the real world of human life.

Our survey of those reflections in their chronological order has enabled us to see the historical development of the understanding of the central term *dīn* from mainly linguistic consideration to conceptual articulation and intellectual theorization through a gradual and cumulative process. Arguably, that development reflects one way or another some of the concerns pressed on the minds by the general socio-cultural and political environments in which the respective authors lived and points to a steady methodological refinement and intellectual and theoretical maturity, thus opening new vistas of thought and inquiry.

2. Dīn: *Content and magisterium*

The foregoing semantic and conceptual analysis of the term *dīn* has brought us to a vantage point wherefrom we can advance to investigate with more focus the content, substance, ramifications and implications of this all-encompassing concept as can be realized from different Qur'anic statements and contexts. In other words, we are now in a position to explore the magisterium of religion in the Qur'anic perspective and as exemplified by the teachings of Islam. Therefore, our next investigation concerns the domain or domains covered and managed by religion as taught in the Islamic scripture.

As described in the Qur'an, Islam is the true religion in the sight of God through which He has perfected for Muslim believers in particular and mankind in general the religious laws embodying the way for self-surrender to Him. (Āl 'Imrān, 3:19; al-Māi'dah, 5:3) In light of the above explanation of the concept of *dīn*, this means that its teachings as enshrined in the Qur'an and elaborated by the Prophet (peace be upon him) do not concern only matters of right belief and good personal behaviour or the affairs of family life, no matter how important they are. Rather, those teachings cover all aspects of human life and existence both at the individual and collective levels and throughout the different stages of the human journey in this world. Accordingly, setting up the norms and criteria of good and evil and truth and falsehood, and laying down rules and laws to regulate human social, economic and political interactions and relations within and among societies and nations, all those are part and parcel of Islamic teachings. This feature of Islamic teachings clearly underscores the social and communal nature of Islam as a way of life caring for both the individual and the community.

The wide and holistic significance of the concept of *dīn* as elucidated above can easily be grasped more clearly by reflecting on certain Qur'anic verses in which this term occurs either directly or by implicit reference to it. Citing only a few of such verses will suffice here. Thus we read in sūrah al-Baqarah (2:256):

> *There is no compulsion in religion (dīn): true guidance has become distinct from error, so whoever rejects false gods and believes in God has grasped the firmest hand-hold, one that will never break.*

In this verse as well as many others, the word *dīn* in the Qur'anic usage clearly "denotes both the contents of and the compliance with a morally binding law; consequently it signifies 'religion' in the widest sense of this term, extending over all that pertains to its doctrinal contents and their practical implications, as well as to man's attitude towards the object of his worship [i.e. God]."[39] This means that in the Qur'an the term *dīn* simultaneously connotes what may be described as theory and practice. In other words, it includes what we should think and believe about God and other articles of faith as well as how we should behave and act in our worldly life. The all-encompassing meaning of the term *dīn* can be made much clearer by looking into some of God's instructions to Prophet Muḥammad on what he shall call people for, as we can see in the following verses of sūrah al-An‘ām (6:151-153):

> [151] *Say, 'Come! I will tell you what your Lord has really forbidden you. Do not ascribe anything as a partner to Him; be good to your parents; do not kill your children in fear of poverty'—We will provide for you and for them—'stay well away from committing obscenities, whether openly or in secret; do not take the life God has made sacred,*

except by right. This is what He commands you to do: perhaps you will use your reason. [152] Stay well away from the property of orphans, except with the best [intentions], until they come of age; give full measure and weight, according to justice'—We do not burden any soul with more than it can bear—'when you speak, be just, even if it concerns a relative; keep any promises you make in God's name. This is what He commands you to do, so that you may take heed'— [153] this is My path, leading straight, so follow it, and do not follow other ways: they will lead you away from it.

These verses summarize the essentials of the religious message which the last of God's messengers was assigned to convey to mankind. This message consists of the following things: 1. establishing sound faith and belief in the Oneness of God, 2. inculcating kindness to parents, 3. caring for children rather than getting rid of them for fear of poverty, 4. safeguarding people's immune lives, 5. keeping away from obscene acts and immoral conduct, 6. avoiding violation and usurpation of orphans' property, 7. observing justice and fairness in all kinds of dealings, 8. speaking the truth, 9. fulfilling promises, and 10. following God's straight path and shunning all other ways. Thus, the expression "what your Lord has really forbidden you" at the beginning of the verses means what God actually has forbidden humans to do and what He has enjoined them to do,[40] as is clear from the list.

It is reported that Prophet Muḥammad's cousin and companion 'Abd Allāh b. 'Abbās upheld the view that these verses (and those of sūrah al-Isrā', 17:22-38) are of the kind of determined or unequivocal verses (*āyāt muḥkamāt*) mentioned in sūrah Āl 'Imrān (3:7) as they pertain to matters agreed upon in all divine laws revealed to mankind (*sharā'i' al-khalq*), likewise not subject to abrogation.[41] Being "clear in and by themselves" in contradistinction to the allegorical or equivocal verses (*mutashābihāt*), the *muḥkamāt* are described in the verse referred to by Ibn 'Abbās as "the essence of the divine writ (*umm al-kitāb*) because they comprise the fundamental principles underlying its message and, in particular, its ethical and social teachings: and it is only on the basis of these clearly enunciated principles that the allegorical passages [of the Qur'an] can be correctly interpreted."[42] To state the matter in somewhat different (anthropological) terms, if the *muḥkamāt* verses constitute the unalterable core of revelation over the centuries, their content constitutes "the spiritual, moral and legislative (*tashrīʿī*) foundation on which the whole social structure stands"[43] throughout history.

Enunciated in clear and unequivocal terms, these 'Ten Commandments' (*al-waṣāyā al-ʿashr*) reflect in a comprehensive manner all the dimensions of human life and existence: spiritual and moral, emotional and intellectual, material and physical, personal and societal, private and collective, economic and political. They thus constitute all-inclusive principles (*uṣūl kulliyyah jāmiʿah*) covering all matters of right belief, good morality and virtuous conduct and action, and shunning all kinds of falsehood, vice and evil deeds.[44] In other words, they revolve around a set of fundamental values that are necessary for the human social edifice and survival. These core values are mentioned and emphasized in different ways throughout the Qur'an either wholly or partly, in detail or in general terms, in such a way that the reader of the Qur'an is time and again reminded of their importance and of the necessity to observe them.[45]

As an instance of the first manner of bringing them to human consciousness mention can be made of sūrahs al-Isrā', al-Mu'minūm and al-Furqān. In al-Isrā' (17:22-38) they are described as part of the knowledge of right and wrong or *ḥikmah* (wisdom) which God revealed to Prophet Muḥammad for the purpose of conveying it to all mankind, thus reflecting the nature of his universal message as one of grace and mercy to all the worlds (al-Anbiyā', 21:107). In al-Mu'minūn and al-Furqān (23:1-6, 57-60 & 25:63-74) we are rather presented with some of the main qualities of people observing such commandments. Interestingly, the ten things mentioned specifically in al-Anʿām and al-Isrā' constitute the core values which Muslim capable agents (*mukallafūn*) are enjoined to attain in their life struggle individually and collectively, and around which revolves the intellectual discourse on *maqāṣid al-Sharīʿah*.[46]

Since the message of the Qur'an and Prophet Muḥammad's mission are a continuation, rectification, consolidation and elaboration of the eternal truths contained in earlier divine messages to mankind,[47] it is of much significance that the Qur'anic verses listing the ten commandments mentioned above are immediately succeeded by a reference to what had been earlier vouchsafed to Prophet Moses,[48] as if to remind us that the commandments revealed to him are in essence the same as what Prophet Muḥammad was enjoined to teach mankind.[49] Likewise, they stand at the heart of the universal values constituting the necessary framework and essential ground for human common good and well-being throughout the ages till the end of the world; hence not being subject to alteration or abrogation in all divinely revealed books.[50]

According to Ibn Ashur, these commandments as stated in the Qur'an can be classified in three categories. The first one, starting with "Do not ascribe anything as a partner to Him", concerns what brings reform (*iṣlāḥ*) in the overall condition of society. The second, beginning by "Stay well away from the property of orphans", pertains to what regulates people's dealings (*taʿāmul*) with each other. The third category, starting from "this is My path, leading straight, so follow it", provides the general principle of all divine guidance (*jamiʿ al-hudā*) and what may cause deviation from it.[51] Hence, the message of the Qur'an and the religion of Islam are of the same eternal essence of divine guidance conveyed to mankind by successive prophets before Muḥammad b. ʿAbd Allāh (peace be upon him), God's last messenger, as clearly indicated in sūrah al-Shūrā (42:13):[52]

> *In matters of religion (dīn), He has ordained to you that which He had enjoined upon Noah—and into which We gave thee [O Muḥammad] insight through revelation as well as that which We had enjoined upon Abraham, and Moses, and Jesus: Steadfastly uphold the [true] faith, and do not break up your unity therein.*

There is no denying the fact that the successive dispensations of divine revelation referred to in the verse differed with regard to the specific details and particular laws and rules conveyed in each one of them. The reason behind this is that such details and particular rules were intended to suit the circumstances of the specific socio-cultural and historical context within which each prophet had to carry out his mission as well as and the conditions of the people to whom they were conveyed. Muslim Qur'an exegetes are almost one that the sameness or similarity of the messages of those prophets lies principally in the unchanging universal "spiritual and ethical principles underlying all revealed religions."[53] As al-Iṣfahānī clearly states, the above verse "refers to the fundamentals (*uṣūl*) that are equally the same among [different] religious communities (*milal*), such as the knowledge of God the Exalted, hence not subject to abrogation."[54]

In al-Qurṭubī's view, the above-cited verse clearly informs Prophet Muḥammad's community that what has been brought to them by the last messenger is the same as what had been revealed before to Noah and other prophets after him. It is one and the same religion consisting of "the fundamentals (*uṣūl*) in respect of which the law (*sharī'ah*) does not change, thus including the oneness of God (*tawḥīd*), prayer, almsgiving, fast, pilgrimage, getting closer and nearer to God by good deeds and through total submission to Him inwardly and outwardly (*bil'qalbi wa'l-jāriḥah*), truthfulness and keeping of promises (*al-wafā' bi'l-'ahd*), delivering trusts (to those entitled thereto), fostering kinship ties (*ṣilat al-raḥim*), renunciation of disbelief, prohibition of homicide, of fornication and of harming people in any way, as well as aggression against animals (for no reason), keeping away from ignoble practices (*danā'āt*) and all that blemishes good character." All such things, the Andalusian scholar ascertains, constitute "one single religion and one unified tradition confirmed by all prophets."[55]

Recapitulating and synthesizing what previous scholars had to say on the verse, Ibn Ashur states that *the one common* message of all God's prophets consists of "common fundamentals of faith (*uṣūl al-dīn*) concerning God's necessary attributes as well as of the principles of the law and universals of legislation (*kulliyyāt al-tashrī'i*). Foremost of these is the Oneness of God succeeded by the five necessary universals (*al-kulliyyāt al-khams al-ḍarūriyyah*) and the general needs (*ḥājiyyāt*) in the absence of which the human social order does not function properly."[56] Moreover, not only has the last and final revelation (the Qur'an) of *islām* (in the sense of submission and self-surrender to God) contained all such universal religious and ethical truths and essential moral values supplemented with new details, but it has also presented them in a new mould endowing them with dynamic and adaptable principles of intellectuality and rationality and clearly establishing their strong connection with human nature.[57]

In addition to the term *dīn* discussed above, there are in the Qur'an other terms that express almost the same meaning, or at least some essential aspects thereof. One of those terms comes immediately to the mind and is frequently and widely mentioned in written and oral discourses among both Muslims and non-Muslims, namely the term *sharīʿah* (and its co-derivative *shirʿah*, which is less popularly used). Being derived from the root *sh.r.ʿ*, the primary significations connoted by these and other derivatives can be subsumed under the following basic meanings, namely, 1. fountainhead and source; 2. way and path; 3. sameness and equality; 4. custom and tradition; 5. institution or promulgation, and 5. manifestnes, clarity and elevation.[58] These meanings seem to revolve around the essential idea of a prescribed law or an established religion as being a clear and right way of belief and practice leading to well-being and salvation.[59] This will come into more prominence by examining the Qur'anic usage of the verb *sharaʿa* and its two nouns *sharīʿah* and *shirʿah* derived from the same root.

The verb *sharaʿa* occurs twice in sūrah al-Shūrā, verses 13 and 21, while the nouns *sharīʿah* and *shirʿah* occur once each in sūrah al-Jāthiyah (45:18) and sūrah al-Māʾidah (5:48), respectively. It will be enlightening to consider them according to the chronological order of their revelation. Describing the nature of what Prophet Muḥammad was taught through Revelation, God Almighty addressed His messenger in the following terms in sūrah al-Jāthiyah (45:18):

> *Now [O Muḥammad] We have set you on a path (sharīʿah) by which the purpose (of life) may be fulfilled. So follow it, and do not follow the desires of those who lack true] knowledge.*

The path referred to in the verse is none else than what God has revealed to Prophet Muḥammad concerning both belief and action. Accordingly, we may define *sharīʿah* in a technical sense as being the total body of Qur'anic and Prophetic teachings laying down the norms and rules which people have to follow in order to live their lives in both belief and action in accordance with God's will by obeying His commands, thus doing what is permissible and abstaining from what is prohibited. Hence, *sharīʿah* is the path leading us to attain well-being and happiness in this life and blessing and salvation in the next. In light of what has been said on the meaning, content and scope of *dīn* and its interconnectedness with that of *sharīʿah* in the Qur'an we can easily understand why *ḥifẓ al-dīn* (or preservation of religion) has been placed by Muslim scholars in the category of the universal and necessary objectives of the ethical system and legal code of Islam, known as *maqāṣid al-Sharīʿah*.

First and foremost, in the Islamic outlook, it is religion and religious faith that establish and maintain the essential vertical bond between human beings and God, their Creator and ultimate Lord, Sustainer and Provider (*Rabb* & *Razzāq*). Without His creative will and power, human beings and all creatures in the world and the universe will not have come into existence nor would they be self-sustained and self-sufficient. In other words, and as a matter of fact, we are indebted to God for our very being and existence, for it is He who has given us life and provided for us the means of sustenance and survival on earth which He made subservient to us. Thus, human beings' indebtedness to God and dependence on Him are total and absolute, unlike all kinds of dependence and indebtedness that might bind us with other beings in the world.[60] It would therefore be sheer ingratitude and ungratefulness to forget God and turn away from Him. By remembering and worshipping God the way He has taught us to do (in the Qur'an and through the example of His messenger), we actually express our gratitude and thankfulness to Him and strive to get as closer to Him as our human capacities allow us. This relationship with God is at the origin of all human spirituality and morality and has far-reaching implications for human life and existence in the world.

Second, just as religion establishes and enhances our vertical relationship with the Creator who is the absolute and most exalted being, it promulgates the values, norms and rules aimed at guiding and governing our behaviour and actions and regulating our horizontal relationships and interactions with fellow human beings and the natural world with all that exists therein. As such, both types of human beings' relation to God and His creation have a definitively spiritual and ethical character no matter how strong or weak human spirituality and ethicality might be. This fact brings them up to be in consonance with the order of the world, inasmuch as they strive to live out the values and ideals they are taught by religion. As the Qur'an makes it clear (al-Baqarah, 2:30; al-Aḥzāb, 33:72), God Almighty chose mankind from among all heavenly and terrestrial creatures and appointed her as His vicegerent and trustee on earth (*khilāfah* and *amānah*).

To assume this high position and noble status, human beings have been provided with a moral and legal code which they should follow in their personal conduct and social intercourses both as individuals and groups, and also in their dealing with the different kinds of creatures sharing with them the immediate world of nature and the wider universe in multiple seen and unseen ways. The essentials of this code have been taught to mankind through successive prophets, such as Noah, Abraham, Moses, and Jesus, and it is Prophet Muḥammad , God's last messenger, who was given the final and complete version through the Qur'an. (al-Shūrā, 42:13; al-Mā'idah, 5:3)

In other words, the great significance of *ḥifẓ al-dīn* stems from the fact that religion in the Islamic context is the source of moral values and legal norms pertaining to the meaning and criteria of what is good and evil, lawful and unlawful. God is not only a creator giving life to human beings and providing material sustenance for them, He also teaches them wisdom and ordains for them the proper laws that shall govern the life affairs of both individuals and society. God is therefore the ultimate Lawgiver and Legislator (*ḥākim* and *shāri'*). This is what the Qur'an (al-A'rāf, 7:54) has expressed in clear-cut terms as an all-inclusive maxim: "verily, His is all creation and all command. Hallowed is God, the Sustainer of all the worlds."

What has been said so far about the wide-ranging meaning of the term *dīn* in the Qur'an can further be clarified and emphasized by reflecting on a verse that is frequently quoted to the effect of the comprehensive nature of the teachings of Islam. The verse in question is the first one in the following passage from sūrah al-Dhāriyāt (51:56-58):

[56]I created jinn and mankind only to worship Me (ya'budūn): [57]I want no provision from them, nor do I want them to feed Me— [58]God is the Provider, the Lord of Power, the Ever Mighty.

The expression *ya'budūn* has been understood by many Muslim scholars not simply in the narrow sense of worship taking specific forms of ritual devotion on specific times or days such Fridays and Sundays and in specific places such as mosques, churches, synagogues or temples. Not excluding this meaning and aspect of worship or underestimating its importance, the above expression more importantly signifies knowing God and having conscious willingness to conform to His will and plan inasmuch as humans are capable to understand such will and plan. For Muslims at least, God has explicitly made His will and plan known to mankind through the Qur'an and the Prophetic example. This means that obeying God's prescriptions and abstaining from His prohibitions in all domains of human life (not only in matters of ritual devotion) is an equally important aspect of worship or *'ibādah*. Hence, the meaning of worship in Islam extends far beyond ritual devotions to include all kinds of endeavour and activity the Muslim undertakes with the sincere intention and commitment to submit himself to the divine will, while at the same time seeking to fulfil his needs and attain his well-being and welfare in this world.[61] As succinctly articulated by Asad, "the innermost purpose of all rational beings is their cognition (*ma'rifah*) of the existence of God and, hence, their conscious willingness to conform their own existence to whatever they may perceive of His will and plan: and it is this twofold concept of cognition and willingness that gives the deepest meaning of what the Qur'an describes as 'worship' ('*ibādah*)."[62] As such, *'ibādah* provides human life and existence with meaning and purpose putting mankind in synchrony with the whole universe.[63]

The preceding explication of the meaning and scope of religion in the Qur'an is in fact grounded in a more fundamental Islamic view on the relation of religion with human nature. Humans are by nature religious beings or *homo religiosus*. This means that they are endowed with a natural innate disposition to religious belief and practice, in the sense that human nature consists of an "inborn, intuitive ability to discern between right and wrong, true and false, and, thus, to sense God's existence and oneness."[64] Likewise, the human inclination to religion and religiousness is not, as many theorists on human affairs would have us believe, a result of merely and ultimately external influences of natural factors and socio-historical circumstances, nor simply conditional upon early "primitive" socio-cultural stages of their existence on earth; hence its reality amounting to a bygone fact in the historical development of mankind and therefore susceptible to substitution by other things.[65] On the contrary, religion emanates from, and is rooted in, an innate disposition or God-given nature of the human species. Religiosity is thus inscribed in the very constitution of human beings thanks to an existential primordial pact (*mīthāq*) with their Creator as mentioned in sūrah al-A'rāf (7:172):

> *And whenever thy Sustainer brings forth their offspring from the loins of the children of Adam, He [thus] calls upon them to bear witness about themselves: 'Am I not your Sustainer?'—to which they answer: 'Yes, indeed we bear witness thereof!'*

As upheld by a number of eminent Muslim Qur'an exegetes, it is question in this verse of a metaphoric representation (*tamthīl, takhyīl*) of divine power and command bringing forth the continuous recurrence of God's creation of human beings in such a way as would always reflect their ontological relationship and existential indebtedness to Him as their Lord and Sustainer.[66] It is on account of this pact[67] that "the ability to perceive the existence of the Supreme Power is inborn in human nature", notwithstanding the fact that this instinctive cognition "may or may not be subsequently blurred by self-indulgence or adverse environmental [i.e. socio-cultural] influences."[68] The latter fact has been clearly depicted in a famous Prophetic tradition stating, in one of its versions, that

> *Every child is born in the natural disposition (fiṭrah); his parents then turn him into a Jew (yuhawwidānih), a Christian (yunaṣṣirānih), or a Magian (yumajjisānih). Just like an animal delivers a child with limbs intact, do you detect any flaw therein?*[69]

Irrespective of its various recensions, this tradition can be seen as an explanation of the above verse as well as of the verse of sūrah al-Rūm (30:30) which ordains the Prophet thus:

And so, set thy face steadfastly towards the [one ever-true] religion, turning away from all that is false, in accordance with the natural disposition (fiṭrah) with God has instilled into mankind (nās): [for,] not to allow any change to corrupt what God has thus created—this is the [purpose of the one] ever-true faith; but most people know it not.

Singling out the "three religious formulations" of Judaism, Christianity and Magianism which were "best known to the contemporaries of the Prophet," the abovementioned ḥadīth clearly contrasts them with *fiṭrah* or the natural disposition consisting, as stated earlier, "in man's instinctive cognition of God and self-surrender (*islām*) to Him." Thereupon the Prophet draws our attention to what causes human beings to deviate from that original disposition or inborn nature. Though the parents are specifically mentioned as responsible for such deviation, they in fact have "the much wider meaning of 'social influences' or 'environment'."[70]

No matter what mishaps and adversities might befall human beings and cause them to go astray and get alienated from their original nature or *fiṭrah*, they will however continue carrying within themselves its deep-seated seeds thanks to that primordial covenant. This means, as Seyyed H. Nasr puts it, that "[m]en and women still bear the echo of [the] 'yes' deep down within their souls, and the call of Islam is precisely to this primordial nature, which uttered the 'yes' even before the creation of the heavens and earth."[71] Likewise, the essential purpose of the long chain of divine messages in history, in which the Qur'an stands as continuation and culmination, has been to reform human primordial nature by reviving, consolidating and nurturing that which is ontologically rooted in each and every human self and by channeling and synthesizing its potentials and different and sometimes, if not often, conflicting instinctive drives in a constructive manner in accordance with higher values and sublime ideals.[72] As such, the message of the Qur'an "concerns, above all, the remembrance of a knowledge deeply embedded in our being, the confirmation of a knowledge that saves, hence the stereological function of knowledge in Islam."[73]

As the Andalusian mystic philosopher Ibn Barrajān (d. 536/1141) stated, humanity has been endowed with divine guidance through two types of pact or covenant. The first one is *mīthāq al-rubūbiyyah* mentioned in the verse quoted above, and the other is *mīthāq al-nubuwwah* mentioned in sūrah Āl 'Imrān (3: 81) according to which,

> *God accepted, through the prophets, this solemn pledge [from the followers of earlier revelation]: 'If, after all the revelation and the wisdom which I have vouchsafed unto you, there comes to you an apostle confirming the truth already in your possession, you must believe in him and succour him. Do you'—said He—'acknowledge and accept My bond on this condition?' They answered: 'We do acknowledge it.' Said He: 'Then bear witness [thereto], and I shall be your witness'.*

In Ibn Barrajān's opinion, whatever has been taught in the Qur'an and earlier revelations is actually a reminder, reviver and elaboration of the first *mīthāq*, that is the existential pact.[74] What Ibn Barrajān calls *mīthāq al-rubūbiyyah* has been described by some scholars as the primordial (*awwal*) and general or universal (*ʿāmmi*) covenant.[75] It pertains, as already indicated, to human beings' relationship with God as their Creator and Lord, just as He is the Creator and Lord of all existents in the world, and falls under what Ibn Taymiyyah describes as God's cosmic command (*amr kawnī*) or creative will (*irādah takwīniyyahi*). As for *mīthāq al-nubuwwah*, it pertains to God's relation with humans as Legislator and Lawgiver who commands them on how they ought to behave, and falls under Ibn Taymiyyah's concept of God's legislative cammand (*amr sharʿi*) or religious moral will (*irādah dīniyyah amriyyah*) whose channel is revelation and prophethood.[76] Considering *mīthāq al-rubūbiyyah* as a primordial reality, we can furthermore speak of it as an "unmediated and universal" covenant between God and all humanity which constitutes "the basis of all later and specific covenants mediated by the prophets."[77]

As argued by Jaffer, the idea of covenant "is central to the the Qur'anic worldview."[78] Looking at the concept of covenant from the perspective of the Qur'anic modes of argumentation and their logical structure, Gwynne has rightly inferred that "the Covenant [in the Qur'an] may be called the cosmic rule, the unshakable basis for the moral reasoning that God requires from human beings. It validates divine commandments, defines the human condition, provides premises in categorical syllogisms, affirms or denies antecedents to yield known consequents, and supplies the criteria that distinguish better from worse and good from evil."[79] It is indeed of great significance that this covenant has been described in the Qur'an as God's bond (*'ahd Allāh*) which has been established in human beings' nature and which people break, thus cutting "asunder what God has bidden to be joined" and spreading "corruption on earth" (al-Baqarah, 2:27). This bond or covenant, in Asad's opinion, "apparently refers to man's moral obligation to use his inborn gifts – intellectual as well as physical – in the way intended for them by God." As he further elaborates, the establishment of "this bond arises from the faculty of reason which, if properly used, must lead man to a realization of his own weakness and dependence on causative power and, thus, to a gradual cognition of God's will with reference to his own behaviour."[80]

As can be realized from the foregoing exposition, the Qur'anic concept of *fiṭrah* as signifying the human primordial nature that entails innate cognition of God and its relationship to the notion of *mīthāq* as a recurrent event in human existence (inherited and born anew in each and every individual) are inextricably interrelated. Both of them revolve around the same essential universal truth about human nature and existence and their ontological rootedness.[81] Accordingly, we are presented with a conception of human nature according to which people are not born *tabula rasa* or a blank slate with regard to religion and morality. Understood in like manner, the concepts of *fiṭrah* and *mīthāq* enable us, following Bennabi, to see religion "as a cosmic phenomenon, governing man's thought and civilization, just as gravitation governs matter and conditions it evolution." It thus "appears to be inscribed in the order of the universe as a law characteristic of the human spirit that gravitates in diverse orbits, from the Unitarian Islam to the most primitive fetishism, around one and the same center, always dazzling and forever mysterious."[82] As expressed by the French philosopher Bergson, the "truth is that religion, being co-extensive with our species" as human beings, "must pertain to our structure."[83] Likewise, there existed in the past, and could exist to-day, "human societies with neither science nor art nor philosophy. But there has never been a society without religion."[84]

Likewise, humanity is in a continuous covenant with God existentially and ontologically by virtue of creation and ethically and historically through revelation.[85] It is in view of the inalienable relationship between human nature and the primordial and, at the same time, recurring covenant that Muslim scholars in general uphold the idea that the sense of good (*khayr*) and evil (*sharr*), goodness (*ḥusn*) and ugliness (*qubḥ*), and truth (*ḥaqq*) and falsehood (*bāṭil*), and the capacity to distinguish between them are moored in the innate human nature by a divine stamp. According to *al-qāḍī* ʿAbd al-Jabbār, "all that the agent (*mukallaf*) has to do or abstain from God has inscribed its sumtotal or essentials (*jumaluhu*) in the minds," with its details and particulars not necessarily within the power of reason to circumscribe; hence the conformity of the obligations (*takālīf*) to reason, be that in rational theology (*ʿaqliyyāt*) and jurisprudence (*sharʿiyyāt*), or in human dealings (*muʿāmalāt*), including the distinction between harm (*ḍarar*) and benefit (*nafʿ*).[86] Commenting on verse 30 of sūrah al-Rūm according to which God created man in an unchangeable original nature (*fiṭrah*), Shah Wali Allah states that this original nature "is nothing other than the essentials of piety and sin and their general axioms (*uṣūl al-birr wa'l-ithm wa kulliyyātuhumā*), not their ramifications and extremities," hence consisting of the universal "religion (*dīn*) which does not differ according to the differing of eras and that all of the prophets agree on it."[87] Clearly realizing the significance of history and experience in the cumulative development of human cognition and discernment, Ibn Ashur attempted to reformulate what most of earlier scholars had expressed in different fashions. Thus, for him,

> [T]he fundamentals of *fiṭrah* (*uṣūl fiṭriyyah*) consist of what God has instilled in human beings, whom He has created for the purpose of inhabiting the world. They are therefore suited to the orderly functioning of the world in the most appropriate manner. Hence, they correspond to the teachings of Islam that

God has willed for putting the world to rights and removing disorder from it. The Qur'anic description of Islam as *fiṭrat Allāh* likewise means that its fundamentals (*uṣūl*) originate in man's natural disposition. To those fundamentals are subjoined principles and sub-principles belonging to the widespread and universally accepted virtues that Islam came to confirm and enhance, for they constitute part of the good manners deeply rooted in human life and emanating from good purposes free from harmful effects. When left on its own, *fiṭrah* may not attest to such manners or to their opposites. However, when they happened, they proved agreeable to it and it therefore accepted them in such a way that they became firmly established in it. Likewise, they are attributable to the fundamentals of *fiṭrah*.[88]

Considering Islam as *dīn al-fiṭrah* or the religion of human nature, therefore, means that its teachings on both belief and practice are consonant with, and suitable to, the internal and external mould and order of the human creation.[89] Put differently, "Islam thus presupposes a *religio naturalis* with which all humans are equally endowed."[90]

Yet, while proposing the notion of religious naturalism one has to be careful not to fall into the trap of the so-called "natural religion" theories. In the wake of European Enlightenment thought, many of such theories advocated the idea of 'natural religion' not only as antithetical and substitute to divinely revealed religion (as generally understood in the monotheistic religious traditions of Judaism, Christianity and Islam) and what is often described as scriptural and institutional or positive religion, but also as straightforward rejection of the existence of a supernatural realm and metaphysical world. Like many other phenomena, religion has been mostly reduced to the physical world and, at best, to a kind of psychologism determined by physical and biological factors and shaped by socio-cultural circumstances and historical happenings. In like manner, naturalistic theories of religion have mostly ended up with God-less new religion(s), 'chemicalized and despritualized spirituality', thus heralding the kind of New Age 'spiritism' and 'alternative spirituality' axed around consumerism and hedonism and steeped in an unmistakable sense of paganism! Consequently, instead of being properly explained and made sense of, religion is rather despised, explained away and altogether dismissed.[91]

These reservations in respect of the so-called natural religion seem to have been at the back of the mind of the Dominican student of Islam Jacques Jomier (1914-2008) in his important work on the Qur'an. Summarizing his reflections on the three major verses on *mīthāq, amānah* and *fiṭrah* (Qur., 7:172, 33:72 & 30:30), he thus put the matter: "Moreover, this natural theology [of the Qur'an] is embodied in a positive religion to which the third verse refers, with its laws, obligations and exclusions; in short, [it is embodied] in a whole system of sacralised life (*vie sacralisée*) that is specific to Islam and depends on particular choices affirmed to have been revealed."[92]

From our analysis of the term *dīn* and other related terms (i.e. *'ibādah, sharī'ah, mīthāq,* and *fiṭrah*) a very crucial idea emerges consisting of the fact that religion in the Qur'anic semantic and conceptual world has a fundamentally integrative function in human life and thought, whereby all dimensions and aspects of human existence and spheres of the lifeworld are or should be operating in unison and symbiosis with the cosmic order of the universe. Other than its semantic and conceptual roots as demonstrated in that analysis, this crucial idea of religion as an integrative or unifying force of the individuals and society has been explicitly expressed and underlined on different occasions in the Qur'an. In one case (Āl 'Imrān, 3:103), the early Muslim community and, for that matter, all Muslims over the ages are enjoined "to hold fast, all together, unto the bond with God (*ḥabl Allāh*)," not to "draw apart from one another" and to "remember the blessings which God has bestowed" on them by bringing "their hearts together," making them brethren after having been enemies, and saving them from "the brink of a fiery abyss". In another case (al-Anfāl, 8:62-63), the Prophet Muḥammad himself is reminded of God's favour on him as He strengthened him "with His succour" by giving him "followers whose hearts He has brought together," for if the Prophet himself had "expended all that is on earth", he "could not have brought their hearts together, but God did bring them together."

To express it in Iqbal's philosophical language, the integrative function of religion in the Qur'anic perspective in actual fact "follows from the unity of the all-inclusive Ego [God] who creates and sustains all egos" wherefrom also "follows the essential unity of all mankind." Likewise, prayer, one of Islam's most prominent and regular acts of devotional and ritual worship, exemplifies the unifying purpose of religion in Islam. As Iqbal puts it, the "Islamic form of association in prayer, therefore, besides its cognitive value, is further indicative of the aspiration to realize this essential unity of mankind as a fact of life by demolishing all barriers which stand between man and man." Hence, the "division of mankind into races, nations, and tribes, according to the Qur'an, is for purposes of identification only," as stated in the Qur'an (al-Ḥujurāt, 49:13).[93]

The idea of the integrative function of religion in the Islamic perspective played an important role in shaping, for example, Ibn Khaldūn's theory of social cohesion and solidarity (ʿaṣabiyyah). Though apparently overshadowed by political considerations pertaining specifically to the question of the rise, expansion and decline of states,[94] this theory was an attempt to resolve one "central problem: what is it that keeps men together in society? What is it that leads them to identify with a social group, to accept and observe its norms, to subordinate their own individual interests to it, in some measure to accept the authority of its leaders, to think its thoughts and to internalize its aims?"[95]

To this effect, Ibn Khaldūn ascertains that "[d]ynasties of wide power and large royal authority have their origin in religion." His explanation of this phenomenon is that since "royal authority results from superiority (taghallub), and superiority results from cohesion and the coming together of individual desires in agreement to press their claims," it is only by God's help "that hearts come together and become united" in which respect God, most exalted He be, says (al-Anfāl, 8:63): "If you had expended all the treasures on earth, you would have achieved no unity among them." As the author of the *Muqaddimah* further expounds, the profound reason (*sirr*) behind this "is that when the hearts succumb to false desires and are inclined toward the world (*dunyā*), mutual jealousy and widespread differences arise. [But] when they are turned toward the truth and reject the world and whatever is false, and advance toward God, they become one in their outlook. Likewise, jealousy disappears, differences diminish, and mutual cooperation and support flourish. As a result, the extent of the state widens, and the dynasty grows."[96]

Not very much satisfied with, though undoubtedly appreciative of, Ibn Khaldūn's view on the role of religion because of its being, at least apparently, limited to the formation and consolidation of the state, Bennabi attempted to look at the integrative function of religion from a broader psycho-sociological and historical perspective embracing human social existence in its civilizational manifestations and at its most fundamental level. Religion, he concurs with German philosopher Hermann von Keyserling, provides human beings with the *principe du sens,* that is, the principle of meaning, and functions as the catalyst factor (*catalyseur*) of the essential constituents and dimensions of human society and civilization.[97]

Taking human natural needs and instinctual drives and impluses as its object and *matériel* constituting what Bennabi describes as the vital energy of mankind, religion transforms the human soul, shapes the individuals' conduct, and conditions and channels their instincts toward a higher purpose and for a greater mission. It moralizes the hearts in society by setting up for them such a higher end (*finalité*), and uplifting human consciousness to an objective that endows life with meaning and purpose; thus, it establishes the essential bond that brings people together and gives them a clear sense of direction and orientation through a multilayered network of relations and intercourses that enable them to act constructively and harmoniously as an integrated whole. This, according to Bennabi, is the purport of the Qur'anic verse (al-Anfāl, 8:63) quoted above. By so doing, religion enhances human agency in history and liberates the individual as well as the society from all sorts of materialistic determinism, be they natural or social and historical.[98]

3. Ḥifẓ al-dīn: Ways and means

Now that we have clarified the concept of *dīn* and shown its essential and inalienable relationship with human nature in the Qur'an, a fact that serious scientific and historical research cannot forego or overlook, the question that calls for answer is the following: how is *ḥifẓ al-dīn* to be attained by Muslims in their daily lives at the personal and social levels as members of their particular societies, the Muslim *ummah* and humanity at large?

Like the other universal necessities constituting the higher goals of the Sharīʿah, *ḥifẓ al-dīn* concerns the individual and society concurrently. This is only natural since, as we have already seen, the teachings of the Qur'an and the Prophet have both a personal and social character. Likewise, the preservation of religion is to be achieved in two different, yet interrelated and complementary, ways. The first way is positive or proactive and consists of establishing the foundations of religion and strengthening its presence in real life. The second is reactive or preventive and consists of removing and averting whatever confusion and/or distortion affecting it.

This twofold approach to the preservation of religion concerns both its theoretical and practical aspects, that is to say, our knowledge of its teachings and the way we should implement them in the different arenas of life. Thus, at the individual level *ḥifẓ al-dīn* means to salvage and strengthen the faith of every individual Muslim from being affected by anything that might undermine and distort his/her beliefs and derail or corrupt his/her behaviour based on them. As for the community as a whole, it means to prevent anything that might violate and destroy its fundamentals, which includes defending Muslim land and sovereignty and preserving the means of Islamic learning and education among the present and future generations of the Muslim community.

In other words, in order for *ḥifẓ al-dīn* to be properly realized, Muslims need to have adequate knowledge of what Islam is about, especially in matters of faith and belief right from the Oneness of God and His attributes to the authenticity and integrality of the Qur'an and prophethood of Muhammad [99] as the last messenger to whom God's final message to mankind was revealed. Next, they need to have sound knowledge of the values and norms as well as practical duties and obligations and rules of conduct which they are supposed to carry out and abide by individually and collectively in submission to the will of God and as a manifestation of their sincere worship to Him. Such knowledge has to be based on clear rational understanding leading to unshakable conviction and sincere commitment. This, of course, requires the existence of a proper and vibrant and multidimensional system of education whose aim is not solely to provide individuals and groups with the necessary knowledge enabling them to be aware and cognizant of their duties and obligations as well as and rights and entitlements within the context of their own society and the world at large; it should also educate them on how to pursue and attain the latter and fulfil and discharge the former.

Education here should not be understood in a narrow sense restricting it to formal education at the primary, secondary and tertiary levels with bestowal of official certificates, and ending at a certain stage of one's life, notwithstanding the importance and decisive impact of such education. More importantly, it should be understood as a continuous process of learning, cognitive and intellectual development and skill acquisition advancing and intensifying in tandem with one's physical and mental growth as well as the expansion of one's roles and responsibilities in society throughout the different stages of life. Likewise, it must include all kinds of non-formal educational and training activities through all available and efficient means: at mosques and seminaries, and through all possible channels of communication including the virtual world of the internet and its offshoots. All such media and channels need to be wisely and efficiently used to disseminate sound and correct knowledge and information that would not only equip the people with mechanical skill and practical efficiency and expediency, but would also inculcate in them the sense of wisdom, goodness, dignity, virtue, sincerity, justice, responsibility, accountability, respect, care, togetherness, compassion, clemency, benevolence, etc.[100]

Combining both streams of formal and informal education integrated through a unity of vision and purpose, education thus understood should not be geared to only nurture and bring about good and nice individuals whose goodness and uprightness is reflected and realized only within the narrow confines of their belonging to a specific community or socio-political entity and state through subjecting themselves to its order and laws. It should rather strive to produce persons embodying the spirit, values and qualities of goodness and justice of truly universal human beings behaving in accordance with such values and qualities wherever they might be and with whomever they might interact, within or without the context of their citizenship or faith-community.[101]

Understandably, knowledge of the religious teachings of Islam is not pursued for the sake of knowledge as such, nor is, for that matter, any other type of knowledge in the Islamic worldview, be it in the natural physical sciences, in human and social science disciplines or in technology and practical skills. All knowledge that enriches the mind, nurtures rational thinking, uplifts the spirit and soul and develops and refines the person's abilities has to be pursued not for the sake of just being preserved in any form of storage from one's memory to one's gadgets. Its primary goal is that it should be internalized and acted upon. That is to say, it should be sought for the sake of applying it to its relevant objects and situations on the path to human development, well-being and accomplishment in a balanced manner, imbibed and illuminated with value, meaning and purpose. For, as a maxim goes, knowing is the principle of doing, and doing is the end of knowing. To state this wisdom differently, knowledge without action is means without end and purpose, just like a fruitless and useless tree. Pursuit and acquisition of knowledge thus perceived should therefore be a means to wisdom, virtue and excellence both in the theoretical and practical sense. It should thus shine over and reverberate in people's activities, interactions and relations as an integrated collective body and not simply as isolated, floating and uprooted individuals, thus shaping their personality and behaviour and strengthening their ties and unity of purpose.[102]

Ḥifẓ al-nasl: meaning and purpose

1. A Qur'anic semiotics of nasl

Generally speaking, the phrase *ḥifẓ al-nasl* refers to the protection of human offspring and progeny. But what does the term *nasl* exactly mean so we may understand its protection properly?

The term *nasl* has occurred only twice in the Qur'an. Its first occurrence, according to the established order of the sūrahs, is in al-Baqarah (2:205), while the second is in al-Sajdah (32:8). Hence, we read the following passages in both sūrahs in the order just mentioned:

1. *²⁰⁴Now there is a kind of man whose views on the life of this world may please thee greatly, and [the more so as] he cites God as witness to what is in his heart and is, moreover, exceedingly skilful in argument ²⁰⁵But whenever he prevails (tawallā), he goes about the earth spreading corruption and destroying [man's] tilth and progeny [ḥarth & nasl]: and God does not love corruption. ²⁰⁶When he is told, 'Beware of God,' his arrogance leads him to sin. Hell is enough for him: a dreadful resting place.*

2. *⁴It is God who has created the heavens and the earth and all that is between them in six days, and is established on throne of His almightiness. You have none to protect you from God, and none to intercede for you [on Judgement Day]: will not, then, bethink yourselves? ⁵He governs all that exists, from the celestial space to the earth; and in the end all shall ascend unto Him [for judgement] on a Day the length whereof will be [like] a thousand years of your reckoning. ⁶Such is He who knows all that is unseen as well as what is seen, the Almighty, the Merciful, ⁷who makes most excellent everything He creates. He first created man from clay, ⁸then He made his descendants (naslahu) out of the essence of a humble fluid,⁹ and then He forms him in accordance with what he is meant to be, and He breathes into him of His spirit: and [thus, O men,] He endows you with hearing, and sight, and feelings as well as minds: [yet] how seldom are you grateful.*

Let us start with the second passage which was revealed before the first one, as it belongs to a Makkan sūrah, while the first one was revealed later in the early Madīnan period. As we can clearly see, the first four verses (4-6) of the passage provide a description of God's all-inclusive creative power and absolute knowledge as Master of the universe, who controls everything in it both seen and unseen. Then, verses 7-8 move on to inform us about the origin of the human being (*insān*) and the way his procreation takes place. Following a brief prelude concerning perfection and excellence in God's creation, two important facts about man are brought to our attention: that he has been originally created "from clay" (*ṭīn*), and that his offspring (*naslahu*) is made out of the extract of "a humble fluid" (*mā' ma-hīn*).[103] This last expression refers to the combination in the womb of the male's sperm and the female's egg, ultimately resulting in the formation of the human embryo through different stages till its delivery in the form of a male or female baby, a process that is fully described elsewhere in the Qur'an.[104]

One point that is of special interest for us here is that from the physical and chemical point of view man comes from lower or base materials both in terms of original constitution and initial process of formation, thus apparently showing not much difference from other kinds of animals in so far as the common process from which they ensue is concerned. Nevertheless, this lower material or base physical status is soon raised up and ennobled by the divine spirit breathed into the human being at a certain stage of his/her embryonic development, following which he/she is endowed "with hearing, sight, feelings and mind".[105] Likewise, human beings are put on a much higher level and raised to a special status as a distinct species among the various kinds of creatures inhabiting the world of nature.

Going back now to the passage from sūrah al-Baqarah, the following points can be made. Regardless of the historical circumstance or special occasion of their revelation,[106] these verses have rather a general or universal import. They describe a specific category of people (call them hypocrites, malicious, or anything else) who would appeal to others and please them with all kinds of good words and nice external appearance, thus giving the impression of being good persons, and affirming their goodness even by swearing by God and invoking Him as witness unto themselves. However, they turn into totally different people as soon as they leave you or become equipped with power and authority (both meanings are simultaneously expressed by the verb *tawallā*). This unexpected or sudden change in character is manifested in their going around "the earth spreading corruption and destroying [man's] tilth and progeny (*ḥarth & nasl*)." An immediate and apparent meaning of the terms *ḥarth* and *nasl* pertains to people's agricultural and animal produce as being the source and basis of their livelihood.

Nonetheless, these two terms have a much deeper and wider sense which pertains to the family and human procreation and reproduction; hence, the "destruction of tilth and progeny" stands synonymous with upsetting family life and, consequently, the entire social fabric. [107] This latter meaning is corroborated by other Qur'anic verses (al-Baqarah, 2:187 & 222-223) depicting the intimacy between the spouses as making each of them a garment (*libās*) for the other and their sexual relationship as tilth or *ḥarth*. [108] It is from this psycho-physical reality that ensues the human offspring or progeny, in which respect "the spiritual relationship between man and woman" is stipulated as their "indispensable basis."[109] This is because, before being born and coming to the light of the sun, each individual has a pre-embryonic and pre-natal potential existence in the separate bodies of his/her parents in the form of "seminal fluid issuing from the loins" of the father "and the pelvic arch" of the mother, as clearly indicated in the Qur'an (al-Ṭāriq, 86:5-7).

From the foregoing discussion, it becomes clear how much significant the term *nasl* is despite its extremely limited use in the Qur'an. Another important and closely related term has been used in the Qur'an in different forms and contexts thirty times at least, namely the term *dhurriyyah* which unequivocally denotes progeny, offspring and children. [110] Yet, it has been part of the great wisdom of Muslim scholarship to choose the infrequently used term *nasl* to express one of the fundamental goals of the Sharīʿah denoted by the expression *ḥifẓ al-nasl*. The wisdom behind this seems to be that this term refers to the very origin and foundation as well as cosmic nature of human life taking the form of a universal law governing the process of human procreation and coming into being, and reflecting both God's plan and purpose in the creation.

Accordingly, we can confidently say that the preservation and safeguarding of offspring starts in the pre-natal stage of existence and does not wait until human beings are born, as we shall see below. We cannot, however, embark on the next discussion before bringing to the fore another term that is directly connected to that of *nasl* as explained above, namely the term *nasab* which has also been used in the Qur'an and is frequently mentioned by Muslim scholars in conjunction with *ḥifẓ al-nasl* under the phrase *ḥifẓ al-nasab*.[111] It is very telling that the two terms *nasl* and *nasab* occur together in one and the same verse in a manner that clearly indicates their strong connection. Hence, we read in the Qur'an (al-Furqān, 25:54):

> *And He [God] it is who has created human beings (bashar) from water, and has made them into kindred by blood (nasab) and kindred by marriage (ṣihr); for your Lord is all powerful!*

Before looking into the specific meaning of the term *nasab* and its correlate *ṣihr*, it is important to relate it to another crucial term and concept in the Qur'anic discourse on nature and the creation, i.e. water, and which constitutes the immediate background to the term under consideration. In the above-cited verse attention is drawn to a natural phenomenon in the sea whereby two bodies or kinds of water, one sweet and the other salty, meet together without anyone transgressing the other, as God has set up a barrier between them (al-Furqān, 25:53; also al-Raḥmān, 55:19-20).[112] Then a shift is made in the present verse to talk about man's creation from water. This brings to the mind a cosmic fact mentioned in the Qur'an as part of the manifestation of God's creative power and majesty over all existing beings, namely that He has "made of water every living thing," (al-Anbiyā', 21:30), and that He "has created all animals (*kulla dābbah*) out of water" (al-Nūr, 24:45).[113]

As such, the creation of human beings from water belongs to a cosmic phenomenon and falls under a universal law of nature governing organic life in the world, whether in the general sense pertaining to water as a *sine qua none* condition for vegetative and animal life (as mentioned in the Qur'an not less than fifty times), or in the specific sense of begetting and procreation. In the latter sense, it is question of an already mentioned specific kind of water consisting of "a seminal fluid issuing from the loins [of man] or *ṣulb* and the pelvic arch [of woman] or *tarā'ib*" (al-Ṭāriq, 86:6-7). The combination and merging of these two kinds of water in the woman's womb results in the successive stages of a new human being's embryonic development described in astonishing details by the Qur'an (al-Ḥajj, 22:5 & al-Mu'minūn, 23:12-14). Hence, the Qur'anic assertion that God has created all people (*nās*) "out of a male and a female" and made them "into nations and tribes," so that they should "recognize one another." (al-Ḥujurāt, 49:13)

Two essential facts emerge from the last paragraph which help us realize the significance of the concepts of *nasab* and *ṣihr* mentioned in the verse quoted above. First, human procreation and reproduction emanate from a natural God-ordained process of the combination of special extracts in the human body. Second, these extracts and their combination and merging cannot obtain without the involvement of the male-female pair, or man and woman, through natural sexual intercourse befitting their biological constitution and physical structure, like any other animal species in the world, let aside the psycho-emotional dimension animating and shaping that relationship. This most fundamental aspect of human life and existence stems from another important fact about mankind in the Qur'an according to which God has created man and woman from one and the same original human reality or entity (*nafs wāḥidah*) and instilled in them a natural inclination towards each other that is the source of love, compassion, tenderness, tranquility, companionship and intimacy, expressed by such Qur'anic terms as *raḥim, mawaddah, raḥmah* and *sakīnah*. (al-Nisā', 4:1; al-An'ām, 6: 98; al-A'rāf, 7:189; al-Naḥl, 16:72; al-Rūm, 30:21; al-Zumar, 39:6)[114] As Eaton put it, "[n]ot for nothing has God created the two sexes and inspired in them a passion to unite, and this is a cause for wonder rather than for reproach."[115]

In Islam as in most (if not all) religious and non-religious ethical-legal traditions in human history until the present, the necessary and suitable context of this phenomenon is marriage, a fact and act that have been over millennia sanctioned both morally and socially as the only acceptable framework for sexual relationship between man and woman that provides the basis of legitimacy of offspring, thus establishing the notions of filiation (*bunuwwah*), motherhood (*umūmah*) and fatherhood (*ubuwwah*) on natural cosmic laws and time-honoured moral values and social norms. These three types of feelings and ties are actually an expression of what can be described as the fourfold emotional, spiritual, intellectual and social nature or character of the family, not merely as an institution for human reproduction, but for both procreation and education.

That the male-female human pair has been created from one single entity is an important theme portrayed in the Qur'an as one of the greatest signs (*āyāt*) of God's creative power and profound cosmic wisdom, constituting one of His unlimited blessings to mankind, thus being the source from which arises human communal life in the form of parents, children, grand-children and so on. All three aspects are at once encapsulated in the verse of al-Naḥl (16:72) referred to previously, thus addressing human beings,

> *God has given you mates of your own kinds and has given you, through your mates, children and children's children (banīna wa-ḥafadah), and has provided for your sustenance out of the good things of life. Will men, then, [continue to] believe in things false and vain, and thus blaspheme against God's blessings?*

This verse succeeds an enumeration of different natural and social phenomena which are linked in varying degrees of strength and immediacy to human existence in both positive and negative ways (65-71). Underlining the four aspects indicated earlier as one of the greatest manifestations of the divine wisdom and power that makes the human species unique and essentially different from all kinds of animals, not least of which the mutual love and care amongst its individuals, the verse ends with making the point that all this constitutes compelling evidence that none other than the one true God deserves to be worshipped, if not for anything but in recognition of, and gratefulness for, the many bounties He has bestowed on the humankind.[116] Likewise, "Parents, their children and grand-children and the love and compassion between them constitute an immutable pattern of God in creation."[117] This clearly lays the ground in Islam for the notion of the family in both its nuclear and extended forms as "an intrinsic order of nature," thus constituting the basic institution in human society.[118]

It is from this sanctioned and institutionalized natural relationship that arises what the Qur'an has described as *nasab* and *ṣihr*. *Nasab* embodies the essential natural bond or blood relationship between parents and children, whereby the latter are properly attributed to the former. It thus gives rise to the primary layer or immediate constituents of the family system, which includes the spouses and their descendants, and may also include their ascendants. From it emanates also the sense of descent, origin, belonging and identity in the hearts and minds of the children and that of owning and prolongation at the level of the parents. *Ṣihr* (or *muṣāharah*), on the other hand, refers to the second-level or supplementary relationships that emerge as a result of marriage, thus bringing together within a wider web of relations people who are not connected by blood. This phenomenon is usually designated by the term in-laws.

These two kinds of human ties are at the origin, indeed *the* origin, of all kinds of human social relationships. Both of them entail mutual expectations on the part of the parties involved. Such expectations may vary depending on the ethical-legal systems prevailing in different societies and civilizations, but they are quite well-defined in the Sharī'ah in terms of the obligations and rights of each party. Family rights and obligations in the Islamic context are not mere private family matters that do not concern the rest of society, though their administration falls on the family members to handle privately. In so far as that administration runs properly in a spirit of equity and harmony, no interference of any external party of whatever kind is warranted. But the moment it starts cracking and becomes dysfunctional, the need arises for such interference. This is because any ills befalling the family are very consequential for the whole society.[119]

To these bonds, mankind owes her most spontaneous and natural human feelings and noble values of love, tenderness, compassion, kindness, forbearance and sacrifice, as well as the sense of worth, belonging and unity of origin. Likewise, marriage and the constitution of the family are a response to, and fulfilment of, the instinctive natural inclination God has ingrained in the male-female pair, and are the right means not only to emotional and sexual gratification, but also to social integration. While they satisfy a wide range of essential needs (biological, emotional, social, etc.) for the individuals at each stages of their lives, not least of them the sexual need, they most importantly serve the greater purpose of the survival, preservation and continuation of the human species on earth in accordance with God's will and plan, whence the idea that marriage in Islam is an act of spiritual piety besides its moral worth and social significance.[120] All of this has been beautifully and suggestively described as one of the manifestations of God's wonders in the creation (al-Rūm, 30:21):

> *And among His wonders is this: He creates for you out of your own kind (min anfusikum), so that you might incline towards them, and He engenders love and tenderness between you: in this, behold, there are messages indeed for people who think!*

This is most probably the reason why Muslim jurists wavered on whether marriage is a contract like other types of contracts or something sacramental, notwithstanding the fact that it cannot be conceived and fulfilled without satisfying certain conditions in the absence of which the validity of marriage will be at stake. Indeed, there can be no wonder as to the juristis' hesitation regarding the nature of the marriage contract, since the Qur'an has described marriage as "a most solemn pledge (*mīthāqan ghalīẓā*)." (al-Nisā', 4:21)[121] The institution of marriage and the family in the Qur'an is thus presented as "a source of protection in which children can be nurtured."[122] Let us remember a very important fact in the Qur'anic account of human genesis, namely the fact that Adam was not put alone in the Garden nor alone when sent to dwell and labour in earth, but with his pair or mate (*zawj*), as communal or social life can only be possible with both of them together as the two necessary and complementary apsects or sides of the human reality.[123]

2. Ḥifẓ al-nasl: means and ways

What has been said is only a little light on the fathomless wisdom underlying God's creation of the humankind with such a distinctive nature setting it apart from and above all kinds of the animal genus, whatever physical and non-physical features it might have in common with them. Human difference is indeed a matter of kind and essence, not merely of degree.[124] This little light, however, is sufficient to help us perceive and appreciate the high importance attached to marriage and the family in the teachings of Islam and the Muslim ethos and tradition. This importance is reflected in the large space and big amount of details given them in the ethical norms and legal rules of the Sharīʿah in clearly incomparable degree with other areas of Islamic legislation, thus covering all possible and imaginable aspects from the pre-marital stage to the post-separation stage whether by death or dissolution and divorce. This special status is due to the fact that marriage and the family constitute the fundamental social institution providing the necessary natural and proper ecology for the physical, psychological, moral, spiritual and intellectual development of the human being at very crucial stages of his/her life, thus shaping his/her personality in a considerable if not decisive manner.

In light of what has been said, we can understand why *ḥifẓ al-nasl* and its correlate *ḥifẓ al-nasab* partake in the high ranks of the goals of the Sharīʿah, regardless of whether both of them belong to the category of *ḍarūriyyāt* or only the first, with the second falling within that of the *ḥājiyyāt*. But there is no doubt as to their strong interconnectedness as has been shown above. For one, *ḥifẓ al-nasl* consists of ensuring human procreation and reproduction and safeguarding it from cessation. This is because, since individuals as such are by nature subject to death no matter how long their lifespan might be, procreation is necessary for their replacement. If it decreases or ceases, this will result in the diminution or extinction of the human species itself. It is in this light that we can see the great significance of Islam's uncompromising condemnation and rejection of all kinds of abnormal sexual behaviour and all types of homosexuality, let aside what latter-day perverse and corrupted minds popularize as same-sex marriage, no matter what justifications their 'genius' might invent.

The reason behind this is plain and straightforward. Irrespective of any religious and moral considerations, such abnormal homosexual behaviour and relationship are first and foremost a transgression against, and violation of, the biological laws governing the very physical constitution and structure of the human being as well as a total aberration from the universal norms of nature governing animal behaviour. It goes without saying that no sensible person with the weakest mind and slightest commonsense would in any fanciful manner expect any sort of procreation and begetting out of such practices. It is actually a level of physical deterioration, moral debauchery and intellectual degeneration that no creature in the animal world would in any way fall into, thanks to their being normally and genuinely guided by their natural instincts and inborn drives.

There should be no wonder then that the Qur'an has considered, through prophet Lot's voice, sodomy and, for that matter, all homosexual conduct and relations as a "cutting of the way of nature" (al-'Ankabūt, 29:29), as their ultimate and necessary consequence is the breakdown of the essential and only natural means to human existence and survival. It is a representation of what the Qur'an describes as man's reduction "to the lowest of the low (*asfal sāfilīn*)", hence falling from "the best conformation (*aḥsan taqwīm*)" in which God has created man (al-Tīn, 95:4-5) and betraying and violating his "original, positive disposition",[125] that is his *fiṭrah* or normative human nature. Rather than being a distortion or alteration in the physical structure of the human being, this reduction or degeneration consists of moral and intellectual decline as well as corrupt behaviour and ignoble deeds. According to Ibn Ashur, the way this moral, intellectual and behavioural degeneration takes place is explained by the above-cited famous *fiṭrah* tradition, which begins with mentioning the parents by virtue of being the closest to the child and the first external factors to influence him/her with whatever good or bad ideas they teach him/her.[126]

Furthermore, since the Sharī'ah as a divinely instituted system looks beyond the mere biological survival and physical continuation of mankind, it is equally concerned about lineal association and identity of offspring through the regulation of marriage and institution of the family. Hence, the importance of *ḥifẓ al-nasab* which contemplates a very critical purpose in human social life and existence, as already explained. It aims at cultivating and fostering the inborn natural feelings of love of both parents and children. Uncertainty or doubt about the offspring's lineal belonging to their parents weakens and even destroys the latter's natural innate inclination to protect their children, take care of them and ensure their well-being and balanced physical growth and mental development by upbringing, education, and maintenance until they reach the age of maturity and self-reliance. Similarly, the dubiousness of lineal attribution removes from the children the feeling of gratitude, gratefulness and filial devotion towards their parents; and it is this very feeling that actually makes the children take care of them when they reach old age. It thus becomes abundantly clear how crucial *ḥifẓ al-nasab* is for a morally and materially sustainable family and social life of both children and parents.[127]

Accordingly, it can be ascertained that *ḥifẓ al-nasab* is both an expression and fortification of the spiritual, moral and social dimensions of *ḥifẓ al-nasl*. That is why the Sharīʿah has instituted severe penalties for both adultery (*zinā*) and slander (*qadhf*). While the punishment on adultery aims to prevent all unlawful non-marital sexual relationships and to ensure purity and certainty of lineage identity of offspring, the penalty on slander combats gratuitous accusations and harmful tarnishing of people's character and undermining of their social status and personal dignity. Hence, both kinds of punishment are geared toward the protection of the biological and moral condition of the human person as well as the social fabric at a very essential level.[128] "It is precisely because Islam goes so far as accepting the natural instincts, and sanctifying them, that it is obliged to 'draw the line' so firmly and to punish with such severity departures from the norm and excursions beyond the limits established by the religious Law [Sharīʿah]. The requirements of social and psychological equilibrium, the need to protect women and the security of children are the motives that determine this Law, and, since the whole social structure is anchored in the family, its infringements threaten society as a whole and are punished accordingly."[129]

It will now have become crystal clear how the realization of this fundamental goal of the Sharīʿah can be achieved both in positive-proactive and defensive preventive terms, which may not require further elaboration, at least as far as the conceptual framework and overall picture are concerned. People, that is Muslims, mostly know, or at least are supposed to know, a good deal of the Sharīʿah moral values and legal norms and rules pertaining to family life and affairs, be they prescriptive, prohibitive or exhortative. Yet, one very important thing is seldom given the attention it deserves. It is question here of the art of living good family life and providing proper parenting so that the family becomes a truly blissful haven for the healthy physical and mental growth of the children and the positive and balanced development of their personality, by virtue of its educational vocation and not only its procreational function, as stated earlier.

Whatever the power of the naturalness and instinctive sense of parenthood in the psyche of human beings both males and females, parenting is something that should not be taken for granted as a fact of nature. Like many other aspects of human life and society, it is, generally speaking, neither an inborn natural skill nor can it be acquired by mere intuition or through *ad hoc* learning. This is more so in our age when the idea of parenthood, and motherhood in particular, is the target of continuous attacks by different kinds of both intended and unintended socio-cultural influences. Parenting is rather an art, something to be learnt and acquired through processes of proper education and training. Such learning and acquisition presuppose and require an adequate and efficient educational system and a conducive socio-cultural atmosphere that inculcate in people's minds and souls a positive sense of parenthood (both as fatherhood and motherhood) and its corollary of parenting as one of the most cherished human vocations, indeed the most cherished one, especially at a time when systematic efforts are being made on a large scale to devalue and undermine the notion of marriage and severe all family bonds, thus eroding all types of emotions, values and ties supporting, and emanating from, them.[130]

The argument underlying the preceding reflections may not be in serious need for further elaboration. Only the unlearned and deniers of the truth will fail to realize the deep-seated and far-reaching crisis besetting most societies at their very heart, manifesting itself in utter erosion of the notion of marriage and the shattering apart of the family institution, in a way never experienced before in the history of mankind. It is a crisis in the wake of which the natural has been considered unnatural, the normal abnormal, insanity wisdom, and beast-like behaviour, or even worse, the norm of humanity, civility and progress. It is a crisis where the fanciful and illusionary is represented as the real, and falsehood as the truth.

As eminent sociologist Sorokin warned long time ago, the crumbling of the principal socio-cultural value of the sanctity and inviolability of marriage and the family is one of the most flagrant aspects of the global and multifaceted crisis of our age into the abyss of which "sensate culture" has pushed mankind, leading to different kinds of psycho-social and cultural ills of egotism, hedonism, ennui, disillusionment, criminality, suicide, etc.[131] It is indeed much more alarming and threatening that the devaluation of marriage and disintegration and collapse of the family are not the work and result of mere historical events and social dynamics. They are rather intended goals of destructive agents and the agenda of dominating forces that systematically target the family and family values both directly and indirectly in multiple ways and by different means from forthright objectification and self-objectification of women to commercialization of sex and conceptual vilification and ideological destruction.[132]

Dīn and a *nasl*: The eternal essential nexus

The previous discussion and elaboration of the meaning, scope and significance of the terms of *dīn* and *nasl* and their place and function in human life and existence would have hopefully made clear their inextricable relationship. With this essential connection between them they form the two most solid rocks on which human society and civilization stand, biologically, physically and socially as well as spiritually, morally and mentally, thus giving human life the core of its fullest, if not its fullest.[133] This fundamental connection has been put in strong relief by the Qur'an on a number of occasions. Pointing out two such instances will suffice to make this point. Thus, at the beginning of sūrah al-Nisā' (4:1), human being s are enjoined by God as follows:

> *O Mankind! Be conscious of your Sustainer, who has created you out of one living entity, and out of it created its mate, and out of the two spread abroad a multitude of men and women. And remain conscious of God, in whose name you demand [your rights] from one another, and of these ties of kinship. Verily, God is ever watchful over you.*

As a call to all human beings irrespective of their gender, race, or belief, this verse reminds them of their essential unity of origin as fashioned by God, their Creator, Provider and Sustainer, who alone deserves to be venerated and worshipped. Thus, the unity of the human race (*waḥdat al-nawʿ*) and the unity of belief (*waḥdat al-iʿtiqād*) are mentioned together to bring into focus the crucial interconnectedness of faith in God and submission to His commands on the one hand, and the consideration of the rights of fellow humans, especially offspring, next of kin and orphans, on the other.[134] It is very much revealing that this command to be God-conscious and observant of the rights of the next of kin (*arḥām*) comes at the very opening of the sūrah which contains the largest part of the essential rules and commandments concerning marriage, the family and related social and financial matters of dowry, maintenance, inheritance, etc.[135]

The second instance occurs in sūrah al-Isrā' (17:22-23) which reads:

> [22]*Do Not set up any other deity side by side with God, lest thou find thyself disgraced and forsaken, for thy Sustainer has ordained that you shall worship none but Him.* [23]*nd do good unto [thy] parents. Should one of them, or both, attain to old age in thy care, never say 'uff' to them or scold them, but [always] speak unto them with reverent speech.*

It follows from this that "[w]hereas God is the real, ultimate cause of man's coming to life, his parents are its outward, immediate cause."

For this reason, the call to man not to take any deity besides God "is followed by the injunction to honour and cherish one's parents." Likewise, these and the subsequent verses up to verse 39 are meant "to show that kindness and just dealings" between human beings "are an integral part of the striving for the good of the life to come."[136] In other words, the preservation of faith and protection of offspring go hand in hand in such a way that they cannot part ways only at the expense of a balanced, realistic and meaningful human life and existence at the level of both the individual and society, provided their implications are fully realized and pursued. This leaves no doubt as to the great wisdom of considering *ḥifẓ al-dīn* and *ḥifẓ al-nasl* as part of the universal essential goals of the Sharīʿah.[137]

While religion provides meaning and purpose for human life by answering ultimate existential questions and instituting the enduring values and ideals for the human endeavour,[138] the establishment and proper functioning of the family "constitute the foundation of human civilization and the integrating factor" of the human social order.[139] We may further formulate this as follows. It is through marriage and the family that the human being comes to life and existence as a manifestation of the species, whereas it is through religion that their life and existence are endowed with meaning and purpose as God's dignified and accountable creature.[140] It would thus be mere fooling of oneself to imagine human life and existence with only one of its two sources of provenance and sustenance or manipulate such sources in a demoniac fashion in the name of distorted conceptions of reason or science or both; hence God's all-encompassing and conclusive decree: "Verily, His is all creation and command. Hallowed is God, the Sustainer of all the worlds." (al-Aʿrāf, 7:54)

It will not be out of context to argue in light of our discussion on *fiṭrah* and *mīthāq* that, stemming from the original human nature understood in a holistic manner, the marriage relationship between man and woman is the first historical covenant in human culture and civilization preceding all other covenants, thus being at the very root, indeed *the* root, of human society and making the family its first unit and basic institution. Following al-Fārūqī, it will not be far from the truth to argue that marriage and the family constitute the greatest manifestation on earth of human responsibility and obligation, *taklīf*, which is "the basis of man's humanity, its meaning and content," thus putting mankind "on a higher level than the rest of creation, indeed than the angels." This is a definitive characteristic of Islamic humanism and constitutes "the cosmic significance"[141] of the human species, hence making its true difference.

Notes

[1] Syed Muhammad Naquib al-Attas, *Islam and Secularism* (Kuala Lumpur: International Institute and Civilization, 1993), p. 51. On the different, often conflicting, approaches to the study of religion: its meaning, nature, origin and functions, see for example, F. Max Muller, *Lectures on the Science of Religion* (New York: Scribner, Armstrong, and Co., 1874), *esp.* pp. 3-127; also his *Origine et Développement de la Religion étudiés á la Lumière des Religions de l'Inde*, translated from English by J. Darmesteter (Paris: C. Reinwald et Co., 1879); Mustafa Abdel Raziq, *al-Dīn wa'l-Waḥy wa'l-Islām* (Cairo: Hindawi Foundation for Education and Culture, 2014 [1945]), pp. 13-20; Ali Sami al-Nashshar, *Nash'at al-Dīn: al-Naẓariyyāt al-Taṭawwuriyyah wa'l-Mi'allihah* (Cairo: Dār al-Salām, 1430/2016 [1948]); Mohammed Abd Allah Draz, *al-Dīn: Buḥūth Mumahhidah li-Dirāsat Tārīkh al-Adyān* (Cairo: Hindawi Foundation for Education and Culture, 2016 [1952]); Mircea Eliade, *The Scared and the Profane: The Nature of Religion,* translated from the French by Williard R. Trask (New York: Harcourt, Brace & World, Inc., 1959); also his, *The Quest: History and Meaning in Religion* (Chicago & London: The History of Chicago University Press, 1969); Wilfred Cantwell Smith, *The Meaning and End of Religion* (Minneapolis: Fortress Press, 1991 [1962]), pp. 15-50; W.S.F. Pickering, *Durkheim's Sociology of Religion: Themes and Theories* (Cambridge, UK: James Clarke Co. Ltd, 1984); Thomas A. Idnopulos & Brian G. Wilson (eds.), *What is Religion? Origins, Definitions, and Explanations* (Leiden-Boston-Koln: Brill, 1998); James Thrower, *Religion: The Classical Theories* (Edinburgh: Edinburgh University Press, Year: 1999); Aaron W. Hughes (ed.), *Theory and Method in the Study of Religion* (Leiden-Boston: Brill, 2013); Brent Nongbri, *Before Religion: A History of a Modern Concept* (New Haven and London: Yale University Press, 2013); Daniel L. Pals., *Nine Theories of Religion* (New York: Oxford University Press, 2015). It is to be noted, however, that steady positive developments can be noticed in the study of religion and evaluation of its place in human life in Western scholarship, thus driving away from the reductionalist positivist and materialist (often denigrating and dismissive) stances. Yet, James's treatment of the subject still remains one of the most inspiring and constructive works. William James, *Varieties of Religious Experience: A Study in Human Nature*, centenary edition with a foreword by Micky James & new introduction by Eugene Taylor and Jeremy Carrette (London & New York: Routledge, 2002); Thomas J. Green, *Religion for a Secular Age: Max Müller, Swami Vivekananda and Vedanta* (London and New York: Routledge, 2016).

[2] For a good account on the phenomenon, scope and functions of *aḍdād* in the Arabic language see, Mohammed Hossein Al Yasin, *al-Aḍdād fi'l-Lughah* (Baghdad: Maṭba'at al-Ma'ārif, 1st edn., 1394/1974); Hussain Nassar, *Madkhal Ta'rīf al-Aḍdād* (Cairo: Maktabat al-Thaqāfah al-Dīniyyah, 1st edn., 1423/2003). As for works devoted to the collection of words embodying this phenomenon see for example, Abū 'Alī Muḥammad b. al-Mustanīr Quṭrub (d. 206H), *Kitāb al-Aḍdād*, ed. Hanna Haddad (Riyadh: Dār al-'Ulūm, 1st edn., 1405/1984); Muḥammad b. al-Qāsim al-Anbārī (d. 327H), *Kitāb Aḍdād*, ed. Muhammad

Abu al-Fadl Ibrahim (Sidon-Beirut: al-Maktabah al-ʿAṣriyyah, 1407/1987); Abū al-Ṭayyib ʿAbd al-Wāḥid b. ʿAlī al-Lughawī al-Ḥalabī (d. 351H), *Kitāb al-Aḍdād fī Kalām al-ʿArab* (2 vols.), ed. Izzat Hassan (Damascus: al-Majmaʿ al-ʿIlmī al-ʿArabī, 1963).

[3] Al-Khalīl b. Aḥmad al-Farāhīdī, *Kitāʿb al-ʿAyn,* edited and rearranged alphabetically by Abdul Hameed Hendaoui (Beirut: Dār al-Kutub al-ʿIlmiyyah, 1st edn., 1424/2003), vol. 2, pp. 61-62; Abū al-Faḍl Jamāl al-Dīn Muḥammad b. Makram Ibn Manẓūr, *Lisān al-ʿArab* (Beirut: Dār Sader Publishers, n. d.), vol. 13, pp. 166-171; al-Sayyid Muḥammad Murtaḍā al-Ḥusaynī al-Zabīdī, *Tāj al-ʿArūs min Jawāhir al-Qāmūs* (Kuwait: al-Majlis al-Waṭanī liʾl-Thaqāfah waʾl-Funūn waʾl-Ādāb, 1419/1998), vol. 35 (ed. Mustafa Hegazy), pp. 49-61. See also, Edward William Lane, *An Arabic-English Lexicon* (Beirut: Librairie du Liban, 1968), vol. 3, pp. 942-945. It should be pointed out that the meanings we have added to the list of al-Attas will be taken up by him in his detailed analysis of the concept *dīn*, as we will see later.

[4] Al-Attas, *Islam and Secularism,* p. 52 (italics in the original). See also (pp. 52-84) his insightful and profound analysis of the derivatives of the root *d.y.n.* together with other terms belonging to the same semantic field, thus supporting these four basic meanings and showing their functional interconnectness in making up the comprehensive concept of religion in Islam.

[5] See on all the seven meanings mentioned here, al-Farāhīdī, *Kitāb al-ʿAyn,* vol. 2, pp. 61-62; Abū Bakr b. Durayd, *Kitāb Jamharat al-Lughah,* ed. Ramzi Baalbakki (Beirut: Dār al-ʿIlm liʾl-Malāyīn, 1st edn., 1987), pp. 699; Abū al-Ḥusayn Aḥmad b. Fāris b. Zakariyā al-Lughawī, *Mujmal al-Lughah,* ed. Zuhair Abdul Muhsin Sultan (Beirut: Muʾassasat al-Risālah, 2nd edn., 1407/1986), vol. 2, p. 342; Kāfī al-Kufāt al-Ṣāḥib Ismāʿīl b. ʿAbbād, *al-Muḥīṭ fiʾl-Lughah,* ed. Muhammad Hassan Al Yasin (Beirut: ʿĀlam al-Kutub, 1st edn. 1414/1994), vol. 9, pp.359-361; Abū al-Ḥassan ʿAlī b. Ismāʿīl al-Mursī Ibn Sīdeh, *al-Muḥkam waʾl-Muḥīṭ al-Aʿẓam,* ed. Abdul Hameed Hendaoui (Beirut: Dār al-Kutub al-ʿIlmiyyah, 1st edn., 1421/2000), vol. 9, pp. 398-401; Ibn Manẓūr, *Lisān al-ʿArab,* vol. 13, pp. 169-171; al-Zabīdī, *Tāj al-ʿArūs,* vol. 35, pp. 52-53; al-Idārah al-ʿĀmmah liʾl-Muʿjamāt wa-Iḥyāʾ al-Turāth, *al-Muʿjam al-Kabīr* (Cairo: The Academy of the Arabic Language, so far 8 volumes each with a different publication date), vol. 7 (1425/2004), pp. 723-731; Lane, *An Arabic-English Lexicon,* vol. 3, pp. 943-945.

[6] Muqātil b. Sulaymān al-Balkhī, *al-Wujūh waʾl-Naẓāʾir fiʾl-Qurʾān al-Karīm,* ed. Ahmad Farid al-Muzayyidi (Beirut: Dār al-Kutub al-ʿIlmiyyah, 1st edn., 1429/2008), pp. 38-39.

[7] Hārūn b. Mūsā al-Qāriʾ (d. 170 AH), *al-Wujūh waʾl-Naẓāʾir fiʾl-Qurʾān al-Karīm,* ed. Hatim Salih al-Damin (Baghdad: Dāʾirat al-Āthār waʾl-Turāth, Ministry of Culure & Information, 1409/1988), pp. 120-121; Abū Ḥātim al-Rāzī, *Kitāb al-Zīnah,* ed. Said al-Ghanimi (Beirut/Freiburg: Al-Kamel Verlag, 2015), vol. 1, pp. 404-409; Abū Hilāl al-ʿAskarī (d. 400 AH), *Taṣḥīḥ al-Wujūh waʾl-Naẓāʾir,* ed. Mohamed Othman (Cairo: Maktabat al-Thaqāfah al-Dīniyyah, 1st edn., 1428/2007),

pp. 217-218; al-Ḥussain b. Muḥammad al-Dāmaghānī (d. 478 AH), *Qāmūs al-Qur'ān: Iṣlāḥ al-Wujūh wa'l-Naẓā'ir fi'l-Qur'ān al-Karīm,* ed. Abdulaziz Sayyid al-Ahl (Beirut: Dār al-ʿIlm li'l-Malāyīn, 4th edn., 1983), pp. 178-179; Jamāl al-Dīn Abū al-Faraj ʿAbd al-Raḥmān Ibn al-Jawzī, *Nuzhat al-Aʿyūn al-Nawāẓir fī ʿIlm al-Wujūh wa'l-Naẓā'ir,* ed. Mohamed Abdulkarim Kadim al-Radi (Beirut: Mu'assasat al-Risālah, 1st edn., 1404/1984),pp. 297-299; Majd al-Dīn Muḥammad b. Yaʿqūb al-Fayrūzābādī, *Baṣā'ir dhawī al-Tamyīz fī Laṭā'if al-Kitāb al-ʿAzīz,* ed. Abdul Alim al-Tahawi (Cairo: al-Majlis al-Aʿlā li'l-Shu'ūn al-Islāmiyyah, 1393/1973), vol. 2, pp. 615-617; Aḥmad b. Yūsuf b. ʿAbd al-Dā'im al-Samīn al-Ḥalabī, *ʿUmdat al-Ḥuffāẓ fī Tafsīr Ashraf al-Alfāẓ,* ed. Mohamed Bassel Uyun al-Soud (Beirut: Dār al-Kutub al-ʿIlmiyyah, 1st edn., 1417/1996), vol. 2, pp. 34-36; Ahmed bin Muhammad al-Buraydi & Fahd b. Ibrahim al-Ḍāliʿ, *Mawsūʿat al-Wujūh wa'l-Naẓā'ir fi'l-Qur'ān al-Karīm* (Riyadh: Dār al-Tadmuriyyah, 1436/2014), pp. 480-483. For both a moderate and radical critical evaluation of this genre of the study of the Qur'an see, respectively, Salwa Mohamed El-Awa, *al-Wujūh wa'l-Naẓā'ir fi'l-Qur'ān al-Karīm* (Cairo-Beirut: Dār al-Shurūq, 1st edn., 1419/1998); Abdul Jabbar Fathi Zaydan al-Hamadani, *Lā Wujūh walā Naẓā'ir fī Kutub al-Wujūh wa'l-Naẓā'ir* (Mosul: n.p., 2nd edn., 1438/2018).

[8] Al-Ḥakīm al-Tirmidhī, *Taḥṣīl Naẓā'ir al-Qur'ān,* ed. Hosni Nasri Zaydan (Cairo: Matbaat al-Saadah, 1st edn., 1389/1969), p. 19.

[9] El-Awa, *al-Wujūh wa'l-Naẓā'ir fi'l-Qur'ān al-Karīm,* p. 23.

[10] Al-Ḥakīm al-Tirmidhī, *Taḥṣīl Naẓā'ir al-Qur'ān,* pp. 119-120.

[11] Al-Rāghib al-Iṣfahānī, *Mufradāt Alfāẓ al-Qur'ān,* ed. Safwan Adnan Dawoodi (Damascus: Dār al-Qalam & Beirut: al-Dār al-Shāmiyyah, 4th edn., 1430/2009), p. 323 & 450. Commenting on this verse, Muhammad Asad has the following to say: "On the strength of the above categorical prohibition of coercion (*ik-rah*) in anything that pertains to faith or religion, all Islamic jurists (*fuqahā'*), without any exception, hold that forcible conversion is under all circumstances null and void, and that any attempt at coercing a non-believer to accept the faith of Islam is a grievous sin: a verdict which disposes of the widespread fallacy that Islam places before the unbelievers the alternative of 'conversion or the sword'." *The Message of the Qur'an,* p. 69, note 249.

[12] Al-Zabīdī, *Tāj al-ʿArūs,* vol. 35, pp. 54-56.

[13] The specific works of these scholars which we have in mind are, respectively, *al-Dīn wa'l-ʿIlm* or *Religion and Science* (1948), *Dā'irat Mʿārif al-Qrn al-ʿIshrīn* (1910, vol. 4, pp. 109-112), *al-Dīn wa'l-Waḥy wa'l-Islām* or *Religion, Revelation and Islam* (1945), *Nash'at al-Dīn* or *The Birth of Religion* (1949), *al-Dīn: Buḥūth Mumahhidah li-Dirāsat Tārīkh al-Adyān:* (1952), and *al-Dīn fī Muwājahat al-ʿIlm: Religion versus Science* (1971).

[14] The concern of these scholars about the question of approach and methodology has been expressed in different ways and on different occasions in their works, which lies beyond our purpose to explore. It would suffice here to point out some references for the benefit of whoever is interested in this aspect of

their intellectual legacy. See in this respect, Sayyid Abul Aʻla Mawdūdī, *Towards Understanding The Qurʾān*, abridged version of *Tafhīm al-Qurʾān*, translated and edited by Zafar Ishaq Ansari (Leicester: The Islamic Foundation, 1988/1408), vol. 1, pp. 1-31; *al-Muṣṭalaḥāt al-Arbaʻah fiʾl-Qurʾān*, translated from Urdu by Muhammad Kazim Sabbaq (Kuwait: Dār al-Qalam, 5th edn., 1391/1971), pp. 7-12; *Mūjaz Tārīkh Tajdīd al-Dīn wa-Ihyāʾihi & Wāqiʿ al-Muslimīn wa-Sabīl al-Nuhūḍi bihim* (Beirut: Dār al-Fikr al-Hadith, 2nd edn., 1386/1967), pp. 49-138; *al-Mabādiʾ al-Asāsiyyah li-Fahm al-Qurʾān*, trans. from Urdu by Khalil Ahmad Hamidi (Kuwait: al-Dār al-Kuwaitiyyah, 1st edn., 1388/1968); Hasan al-Turabi, *Qaḍāyā al-Tajdīd: Naḥwa Manhaj Uṣūlī* (Beirut: Dār al-Hādī, 1421/2000); al-Attas, *Islam and Secularism*, esp. pp. 97-167 and *Prolegomena to the Metaphysics of Islam* (Kuala Lumpur: International Institute and Civilization, ISTAC, 2001), pp. 1-39 (Introduction).

[15] Mawdūdī, *al-Muṣṭalaḥāt al-Arbaʻah fiʾl-Qurʾān*, pp. 119-129.

[16] Ibid., p. 126 & 129.

[17] Abul Aʻla al-Mawdūdī, *al-Dīn al-Qayyim* (Beirut: Muʾassasat al-Risālah, 1404/1984), p. 10.

[18] This should not imply denying that other scholars, whose works have not come to our attention, might have contributed something on close or similar methodological lines.

[19] Al-Turabi, *Qaḍāyā al-Tajdīd*, p. 32.

[20] Ibid., pp. 32-33.

[21] Ibid., pp. 33, 99-102, 105-107. For a succinct account of al-Turabi's ideas on religiosity and *ibtilāʾ* and their theoretical and practical implications for his understanding of *ijtihād* and *tajdīd*, see Abdullahi Ali Ibrahim, *Manichaean Delirium: Decolonizaing the Judiciary and Islamic Renewal in Sudan, 1898-1985* (Leiden-Boston: 2008), pp. 332-345. The theme of religiosity and "acquired religion" in the sense articulated by al-Turabi has been taken up and developed by the Tunisian scholar Abdelamjid al-Najjar in a more elaborate manner in different works of his, notably in his book *Fī Fiqh al-Tadayyun Fahman wa-Tanzīlan*, 2 vols. (Doha: Ministry of Endowments [Awqaf] and Islamic Affairs, Ummah Book Series, 1989).

[22] Al-Turabi, *Qaḍāyā al-Tajdīd*, p. 34.

[23] Ibid., pp. 34-44, 192& 196-222.

[24] Al-Attas, *Islam and Secularism*, pp. 51-52. (all italics used in our citations from al-Attas are in the original)

[25] Ibid., p. 52. Note the feature of contrariness of significations in the term *dīn* as clearly manifested in the two meanings of the word *dāʾin*, ie. creditor and debtor.

[26] Ibid., pp. 52-53.

[27] Ibid., p. 54.

[28] Ibid.

[29] Ibid.

[30] Ibid., pp. 54-55.

[31] Ibid., p. 55.

[32] Ibid., p. 56.

[33] Ibid., p. 57.

[34] Ibid.

[35] Ibid., p. 66.

[36] Abū Ḥāmid Muḥammad b. Muḥammad b. Muḥammad b. Aḥmad al-Ghazālī, *Iḥyā' 'Ulūm al-Dīn* (Jeddah: Dār al-Minhāj, 1432/2011), vol. 8, pp. 11-12; Anthony F. Shaker (trans.), *al-Ghazālī on Poverty & Abstinence* (Cambridge: Islamic Texts Society, 2019), pp. 7-8.

[37] Numerous are the verses of the Qur'an which underline human indebtedness to and dependence on God by indicating their signs and manifestations in human beings themselves and in the world around them. This is one of the central themes of the Qur'an that deserves independent study.

[38] Abū al-Baqā' Ayyūb b. Mūsā al-Kafawī, *al-Kulliyyāt: Mu'jam fi'l-Muṣṭalaḥāl wa'l-Furūq al-lugha wiyyah*, ed. Adnan Darwish and Mohamed Almasri (Beirut: Mu'assasat al-Risālah, 1419/1998, p. 444.

[39] Muhammad Asad, *The Message of the Qur'an* (Kuala Lumpur: Islamic Book Trust, 2001), p. 69, note 249.

[40] Abd al-Rahman Hassan Habannakah al-Maydani, *Ma'ārij al-Tafakkur wa-Daqa'iq al-Tadabbur* (Damascus: Dār al-Qalam, 1st edn., 1423/2002), vol. 11, p. 470.

[41] Abū Ja'far Muḥammad b. Jarīr al-Ṭabarī, *Tafsīr al-Ṭabarī: Jāmi' al-Bayān 'an Ta'wīli Āyi al-Qur'ān*, ed. Abdullah bin Abdul Muhsin al-Turki *et al.* (Cairo: Hajar li'l-Ṭibā'ah wa'l-Nashr wa'l-Tawzī' wa'l-I'lān, 1422/2001), vol. 5, p. 193; Abū Isḥāq Aḥmad b. Muḥammad b. Ibrāhīm al-Tha'labī, *al-Kashf wa'l-Bayān 'an Tafsīr al-Qur'ān*, ed. Salah Ba-Uthman *et al.* (Jeddah: Dār al-Tafsīr, 2015/1436), vol. 9, p. 28 & 33; Athīr al-Dīn Muḥammad b. Yūsuf b. 'Alī b. Yūsuf Ibn Ḥayyān known as Abū Ḥayyān al-Andalusī al-Gharnāṭī, *Tafsīr al-Baḥr al-Muḥīṭ*, ed. Abdul Razzaq al-Mahdi (Beirut: Dār Iḥyā' al-Turāth al-'Arabī 1423/2002), vol. 4, p. 322.

[42] Asad, *The Message of the Qur'an*, p. 81, note 5. It is to be noted that both categories of *muḥkamāt* and *mutashābihāt* Qur'anic verses have been the subject of a continuous debate among scholars as to their meaning, scope and the relationship between them. The *mutashābihāt*, especially, have raised many issues of linguistic, exegetical, juristic and theological nature, and the debate thereupon resulted in different, if not contradictory, views. For reasonable accounts addressing the various issues and presenting the different views in this respect, see for example:

Al-Ṭabarī, *Jāmi' al-Bayān*, vol. 5, pp. 188-233; Abū Manṣūr Muḥammad b. Muḥammad b. Maḥmūd al-Māturīdī, *Ta'wīlāt Ahl al-Sunnah*, ed. Majdi Basalum (Beirut: Dār al-Kutub al-'Ilmiyyah, 1st edn., 1426/2005), vol. 2, pp. 303-313; al-Sayyid al-Sharīf al-Raḍiyy, *Ḥaqā'iq al-Ta'wīl fī Mutashābih al-Tanzīl*, ed. Muhammad al-Rida Al Kashif al-Ghita (Beirut: Dār al-Aḍwā', 1406/1986), pp.

1-14; Abū Saʿd al-Muḥsin b. Muḥammad b. Karāmah al-Bayhaqī, al-Ḥākim al-Jashmī, *al-Tahdhīb fī al-Tafsīr*, ed. Abdul Rahman b. Sulayman al-Salimi (Cairo: Dār al-Kitāb al-Miṣrī & Beirut: Dār al-Kitāb al-Lubnānī, 1440/2019), vol. 2, pp. 1097-1102; Fakhr al-Dīn Muḥammad b. Ḍiyāʾ al-Dīn ʿUmar al-Rāzī, *Tafsīr al-Fakhr al-Rāzī,* known as *al-Tafsīr al-Kabīr,* known as *Mafātīḥ al-Ghayb* (Beirut: Dār al-Fikr, 1401/1981), vol. 7, pp. 189-192; Abū ʿAbd-Allah Aḥmad b. Abī Bakr al-Qurṭubī, *al-Jāmiʿ li-Aḥkām al-Qurʾān waʾl-Mubayyin limā Taḍammanahu minaʾl-Sunnati wa-Āyi al-Furqān,* ed. Abdullah bin Abdul Muhsin al-Turki *et al.* (Beirut: Muʾassasat al-Risālah, 1427/2006), vol. 5, pp. 16-29; Taqī al-Dīn Aḥmad Ibn Taymiyyah, *al-Iklīl fīʾl-Mutashābih waʾl-Taʾwīl,* ed. Mohammad al-Shaymi Shehata (Alexandria, Egypt: Dār al-Īmān, n. d.), pp. 6-52; Badr al-Dīn Muhammad b. ʿAbd Allāh al-Zarkashī, *al-Burhān fī ʿUlūm al-Qurʾān,* ed. Mohammad Abdul Fadl Ibrahim (Cairo: Maktabat Dār al-Turāth, 3rd edn., 1404/1984), vol. 2, pp. 68-89; Muḥammad Jamāl al-Dīn al-Qāsimī, *Maḥāsin al-Taʾwīl,* ed. Mohammed Fuad Abd al-Baqi (Cairo: Dār Iḥyāʾ al-Kutub al-ʿArabiyyah, 1376/1957), vol. 4, pp. 751-796; Sayyid Qutb, *Fī Ẓilāl al-Qurʾān* (Cairo-Beirut: Dār al-Shurūq, 32nd edn., 1423/2003), vol. 3, p. 1229; Muhammad al-Tahir Ibn Ashur, *Tafsīr al-Taḥrīr waʾl-Tanwīr* (Tunis: al-Dār al-Tūnusiyyah liʾl-Nashr, 1984), vol. 3/3, pp. 153-169; Mohammad Hossein al-Tabatabaʾi, *al-Mīzān fī Tafsīr al-Qurʾān* (Beirut: Muʾassasat al-Aʿlamī liʾl-Maṭbūʿāt, 1417/1997), vol. 3, pp. 66-78 & his *al-Jawāhir al-Nūrāniyyah fīʾl-ʿUlūm waʾl-Maʿārif al-Insāniyyah* (Beirut: Dār al-Maḥajjah al-Bayḍāʾ, 1426/2005), pp. 68-98.

In Appendix I to his *Message of the Qurʾan* (pp. 1179-1183) titled "Symbolism and Allegory in the Qurʾan", Asad has provided a condense and useful synthesis of the issues and views pertaining to the matter at hand.

[43] Eltigani Abdelgadir Hamid, *al-Naṣṣ al-Qurʾānī wa-Uṣūl al-Ijtimāʿ al-Siyāsī: Madākhil Taʾsīsiyyah* (Doha: Muntadā al-ʿAlāqāt al-ʿArabiyyah al-Dawliyyh, 2020), p. 51.

[44] Muhammad Abdu and Muhammad Rashid Rida, *Tafsīr al-Qurʾān al-Ḥakīm* known *Tafsīr al-Manār* (Cairo: Maṭbaʿat al-Manār, 1st edn., 1338H), vol. 8, p. 183 & 285.

[45] The description of these commandments as *al-waṣāyā al-ʿashr* goes back to very early times in Muslim history and is said to have originated during the generation of the Prophet's Companions. The choice of this nomenclature has been inspired by the statement following these commandments: "This is what He commands you to do, so that you may take heed" (*dhālikum waṣṣākum bihi laʿallakum tadhdhakkarūn*). For a detailed analysis of the significance and implications of these commandments, see, al-Rāzī, *al-Tafsīr al-Kabīr*, vol. 13, pp. 243-248; Mahmud Shaltut, *Tafsīr al-Qurʾān al-Karīm* (Cairo: Dār al-Shurūq, 18th edn., 1424/2004), pp. 307-346; also his *al-Waṣāyā al-ʿAshr* (Cairo: Dār al-Shurūq, 5th edn., 1404/1984); Ibn Ashur, *Tafsīr al-Taḥrīr waʾl-Tanwīr*, vol. 5/8, pp. 155-175; al-Tabatabaʾi, *al-Mīzān fī Tafsīr al-Qurʾān*, vol. 7, pp. 385-394.

[46] See for example, Abū Isḥāq Ibrāhīm b. Mūsā al-Shāṭibī, *al-Muwāfaqāt fī Uṣūl al-Sharīʿah*, ed. Abdullah Draz (Beirut: Dār al-Kutub al-ʿIlmiyyah, 1422/2001), vol. 1/2, pp. 3-313; also its English version *The Reconciliation of the Fundamentals of Islamic Law*, trans. Imran Ahsan Khan Nyazee (London: Garnet Publishers, 2014), vol. 2, pp. 3-321; Ibn Ashur, *Treatise on Maqāṣid al-Sharīʿah*, pp. 91-133 & 238-340; Yusuf Hamid al-ʿAlim, *al-Maqāṣid al-ʿĀmmah li'l-Sharīʿah al-Islāmiyyah* (London-Washington: The International Institute of Islamic Thought, 1413/1993), pp. 203-568.

[47] This is clearly expressed by the concept of confirmation (*taṣdīq*) and determining authority (*haymanah*) in sūrah al-Māʾidah (5:48), thus depicting the relationship between the Qurʾan and previous scriptures: "And unto thee [O Prophet] have We vouchsafed this divine writ, setting forth the truth, confirming (*muṣaddiqan*) the truth of whatever there still remains of earlier revelations and determining what is true therein (*muhayminan ʿalayh*)." The participle *muhaymin*, which is derived from the quadriliteral verb *haymana*, denotes the meaning of prevalence and control, "and is used here to describe the Qurʾan as the determinant factor in deciding what is genuine and what is false in the earlier scriptures." Asad, *The Message of the Qurʾan*, p. 184, note 64. According to Ibn Ashur, the verse refers to two aspects of the Qurʾan's relationship with earlier revealed scriptures. On the one hand, it has confirmed in the previous revealed laws (*sharāʾiʿ*) pertaining to *maṣlaḥah* whatever is universal and does not change according to nations and times, hence it is *muṣaddiq* in the sense that it verifies and ascertains their truth (*muhaqqiq wa muqarrir*). On the other hand, the Qurʾan has annulled certain teachings in those scriptures and abrogated many rules in them which were related to temporary and particular benefits (*maṣāliḥ*) in which respect specific conditions of peoples had been taken into consideration. Ibn Ashur, *Tafsīr al-Taḥrīr wa'l-Tanwīr*, vol., 4/6, p. 221. For more of Ibn Ashur's insights on this and other related issues, see *Treatise on Maqasid al-Sharīʿah*, pp. 134-145.

It should be pointed out, however, that the import and implications of this verse have been a subject of theological debate and at the root of differences in juristic opinion among Muslim scholars from very early times until the modern era. See in this regard, al-Māturīdī, *Taʾwīlāt Ahl al-Sunnah*, vol. 3, pp. 532-533; al-Ṭabarī, *Jāmiʿ al-Bayān*, vol. 8, pp. 485-491; Abū Jaʿfar Muḥammad b. al-Ḥasan al-Ṭūsī, *al-Tibyān fī Tafsīr al-Qurʾān*, ed. Ahmed Habib Kasir al-ʿAmili (Beirut: Dār Iḥhyāʾ al-Turāth al-ʿArabī, n. d.), vol. 3, pp. 543-544; Muhammad ʿIzzat Darwazeh, *al-Tafsīr al-Ḥadīth* (Beirut: Dār al-Gharb al-Islāmī, 2ⁿᵈ edn., 1421/2000), vol. 9, pp. 147-152; Tabatabaʾi, *al-Mīzān fī Tafsīr al-Qurʾān*, vol. 5, pp. 356-357. See also fresh looks at this issue of the Qurʾan and earlier scriptures in, Holger M. Zellentin (ed.), *The Qurʾan's Reformation of Judaism and Christianity: Return to the Origins* (London and New York: Routledge, 2019).

[48] Thus we read in al-Anʿām (6:154): "*And once again: We vouchsafed the divine writ unto Moses in fulfilment [of Our favour] upon those who persevered in doing good, clearly spelling out everything, and [thus providing] guidance and grace, so that they might have faith in the [final] meeting with their Sustainer.*" In an even much clearer way, the Qurʾan more

specficilly refers to Moses' tablets in which he received the Ten Commandmants. Likewise, we read in sūrah *al-Aʿrāf* (7:145): "*And We ordained for him in the tablets [of the Law] all manner of admonition, clearly spelling out everything. And [We said:] 'Hold fast unto them with [all thy] strength, and bid thy people to hold fast to their most goodly rules'.*"

[49] Muqātil b. Sulaymān, *Tafsīr Muqātil Ibn Sulaymān,* ed. Abdallah Mahmoud Shehatah (Beirut: Dār Iḥyāʾ al-Turāth al-ʿArabī, 1st edn., 1423/2002), vol. 1, p. 597; al-Rāzī, *al-Tafsīr al-Kabīr,* vol. 14, pp. 4-5; Ahmad b. Yūsuf al-Samīn al-Ḥalabī, *al-Durr al-Maṣūn fī ʿUlūm al-Kitāb al-Maknūn,* ed. Ahmed Mohamed al-Kharrat (Damascus: Dār al-Qalam, n.d.), vol. 5, p. 226; Abdu & Rida, *Tafsīr al-Qurʾān al-Ḥakīm,* vol. 8, pp. 200-203; al-Tabatabaʾi, *al-Mīzān fī Tafsīr al-Qurʾān,* vol. 7, pp. 394-396; Hassan al-Turabi, *al-Tafsīr al-Tawḥīdī* (Beirut/London: Dār al-Sāqī, 1st edn., 2004), vol. 1, p. 664 & 671.

[50] For a comprehensive comparison between The Qurʾanic version of the Ten Commandments and those of the Bible (New and Old Testaments), see M.A. Draz, *Introduction to the Qurʾan,* trans. Ayeshah Abdel-Haleem (London/New York: I.B. Tauris, 2000), pp. 66-88; Rashad Abdullah al-Shami, *al-Waṣāyā al-ʿAshr fiʾl-Yahūdiyyah: Dirāsah Muqārinah fiʾl-Masīḥiyyah waʾl-Islām* (Dār al-Zahrāʾ liʾl-Nashr, 1414/1993); Sebastian Guenther, "The Ten Commandments and the Qurʾan," *Journal of Qurʾanic Studies,* vol. 9, No. 2 (2007), pp. 22-58. As for the Ten Commandments as received by Moses see, *The Scofield Study Bible III* (Oxford-New York: Oxford University Press, 2002 [1909], Deuteronomy 5: 6-21, pp. 261-262. For an insightful contemporary reading of Moses' com-mandments, see Leon R. Kass, *Founding God's Nation: Reading Exodus* (New Haven & London: Yale University Press, 2021).

[51] Ibn Ashur, *Tafsīr al-Taḥrīr waʾl-Tanwīr,* vol. 5/8, p. 156; *cf.* al-Turabi, *al-Tafsīr al-Tawḥīdī,* vol. 1, pp. 670-671.

[52] We shall come later again to this verse in our discussion of the term *sharīʿah* which is in the Qurʾan closely connected with the concept *dīn.*

[53] Asad, *The Message of the Qurʾan,* p. 885, note 12. See also, al-Māturīdī, *Taʾwīlāt Ahl al-Sunnah,* vol. 9, p. 111; Abū al-Qāsim Jār Allāh Maḥmūd b. ʿUmar al-Zamakhsharī al-Khuwārizmī, *Tafsīr al-Kashshāf,* ed. Khalil Maʾmoun Sheha (Beirut: Dār al-Maʿrifah, 1430/2009), p. 975; Abū Muḥammad ʿAbd al-Ḥaqq b. Ghālib Ibn ʿAṭiyah al-Andalusī, *al-Muḥarrar al-Wajīz fī Tafsīr al-Kitāb al-ʿAzīz,* ed. Abdul Salam Abdul Shafi Mohammad (Beirut: Dār al-Kutub al-ʿIlmiyyah, 2nd edn., 1422/2001),vol. 5, p. 29; al-Ṭūsī, *al-Tibyān fī Tafsīr al-Qurʾān,* vol. 9, p. 150; al-Ḥākim al-Jashmī, *al-Tahdhīb fī al-Tafsīr,* vol. 9, pp. 6226-6227; al-Rāzī, *al-Tafsīr al-Kabīr,* vol. 27, p. 157; Nāṣir al-Dīn Abū al-Khayr ʿAbd Allāh b. ʿUmar b. Muḥammad al-Shīrāzī al-Shāfiʿī al-Bayḍāwī, *Anwār al-Tanzīl wa-Asrār al-Taʾwīl,* ed. Mohammed Abdur-Rahman (Beirut: Dār Iḥyāʾ al-Turāth al-ʿArabī, n. d.), vol. 5, p. 78; Abū Ḥayyān al-Andalusī, *Tafsīr al-Baḥr al-Muḥīṭ,* vol. 7, pp. 677-678; al-Qāsimī, *Maḥāsin al-Taʾwīl,* vol. 14, pp. 5231-5232; Muhammad al-Tahir Ibn Ashur, *Uṣūl al-Niẓām al-Ijtimāʿī fiʾl-Islām,* ed. Mohamed El-Tahir El-Mesawi (Amman: Dār al-Nafaes, 1st edn., 1421/2001), pp. 25-28; al-Tabatabaʾi, *al-Mīzān fī Tafsīr al-Qurʾān,* vol. vol. 8, pp. 312-323; vol. 18, pp. 28-30.

[54] Al-Iṣfahānī, *Mufradāt Alfāẓ al-Qur'ān*, p. 450.

[55] Al-Qurṭubī, *al-Jāmiʿ li-Aḥkām al-Qur'ān*, vol. 18, pp. 452-453.

[56] Ibn Ashur, *Tafsīr al-Taḥrīr wa'l-Tanwīr*, vol. 12 /25, p. 50; *Treatise on Maqāṣid al-Sharīʿah*, pp. 78-90. See also, A. Ezzati, *Islam and Natural Law* (London: Islamic College for Advanced Studies Press, 2002); Seyyed Hossein Nasr, *The Heart of Islam: Enduring Values for Humanity* (London & New York: Harper-Collins, 2002), pp. 113-306.

[57] Ibid. In this respect, Ibn Ashur refers the reader to his book devoted to the subject of *maqāṣid al-sharīʿah* as containing an elaboration of the general ideas expounded here. See also, Mohamed al-Kattani, *Manẓūmat al-Qiyam al-Marjiʿiyyah fi'l-Islām* (Rabat: Markaz al-Dirāsāt wa'l-Abḥāth fi'l-Qiyam, Rabita Mohamadia des Oulémas, 2nd edn., 1433/2011), pp. 67-84.

[58] See for example, al-Farāhīdī, *Kitāb al-ʿAyn*, vol. 2, pp. 323-324; Abū Manṣūr Muḥammad b. Aḥmad al-Azharī (d. 370H), *Tahdhīb al-Lughah*, ed. Abdel Salam Haroun (Cairo: al-Dār al-Miṣriyyah li'l-Ta'līf wa'l-Tarjamah, 1st edn. 1384-1387/1964-1967), vol. 1, pp. 424-428; Ibn Sīdeh, *al-Muḥkam wa'l-Muḥīṭ al-Aʿẓam*, vol. 1, pp. 369-371; Majd al-Dīn Muḥammad b. Yaʿqūb al-Fayrūzābādī, *al-Qāmūs al-Muḥīṭ*, ed. Anas Mohamed al-Shami and Zakaria Jabir Ahmad (Cairo: Dār al-Ḥadīth, 1429/2008), p. 854; Ibn Manẓūr, *Lisān al-ʿarab*, vol. 8, pp. 175-178; al-Zabīdī, *Tāj al-ʿArūs*, vol. 21, pp. 259-269; Lane, *Arabic-English Lexicon*, vol. 4, pp. 1534-135.

[59] Ibn Manẓūr, *Lisān al-ʿArab*, vol. 8, p. 176; Lane, *Arabic-English Lexicon*, vol. 4, p. 1535.

[60] Gai Eaton, *Remembering God: Reflections on Islam* (Cambridge: Islamic Texts Society, 2000), pp. 10-11.

[61] For the interpretation of the meaning of *ʿibādah* as we have summarily explained it, see for example, al-Māturīdī, *Ta'wīlāt Ahl al-Sunnah*, vol. 9, pp. 594-596; al-Thaʿlabī, *al-Kashf wa'l-Bayān*, vol. 24, pp. 565-568; Ibn ʿAṭiyyah, *al-Muḥarrar al-Wajīz*, vol. 5, pp. 181-182; al-Rāzī, *al-Tafsīr al-Kabīr*, vol. 29, pp. 233-235; al-Qurtubī, *al-Jāmiʿ li-Aḥkām al-Qur'ān*, vol. 19, pp. 506-508; Shaykh al-Islām Taqī al-Dīn Aḥmad b. ʿAbd al-Ḥalīm Ibn Taymiyyah, *al-ʿUbūdiyyah*, ed. Ali Hassan Abdulhamid (al-Ismāʿīliyyah: Dār al-Aṣalah, 3rd edn., 1419/1999), pp. 136-140; Abu'l-Fidā' Ismāʿīl b. ʿUmar Ibn Kathīr al-Qurashī al-Dimashqī, *Tafsīr al-Qur'ān al-ʿAẓīm*, ed. Sami bin Mohammed Salamah (Riyadh: Dār Ṭaybah, 1420/1999), vol. 7, p. 425; Qutb, *Fī Ẓilāl al-Qur'ān*, vol. 6, pp. 3387-3388; Ibn Ashur, *Tafsīr al-Taḥrīr wa'l-Tanwīr*, vol. 13 /27, pp. 25-28; al-Tabataba'i, *al-Mīzān fī Tafsīr al-Qur'ān*, vol. 18, pp. 392-394; Yusuf al-Qaradwi, *al-ʿIbādah fi'l-Islām* (Cairo: Maktabat Wahbah, 24th edn., 1416/1995); Hassan al-Turabi, *al-Īmān: Atharuhu fī Ḥayāt al-Insān* (Jeddah: Manshūrāt al-ʿAṣr al-Ḥadīth, 1404/1984 [1394/1974]), pp. 31-66; Sayyid Abul Aʿlā Mawdūdī, *Worhsip in Islam: An Indepth Study bof ʿIbādah, Ṣalāh and Ṣawm*, translated and edited by Ahmad Imam Shafaq Hshemi (Lesicestershire: The Islamic Foundation, 2014 CE/1435 AH).

[62] Asad, *The Message of the Qurʾan*, p. 965, note 38; al-Attas, *Islam and Secularism*, pp. 68-72.

[63] Qutb, *Fī Ẓilāl al-Qurʾān*, vol. 6, p. 3387.

[64] Asad, *The Message of the Qurʾan*, p. 741, note 27.

[65] In an ideologically and hastily proclaimed secular age, many philosophic and social-scientific theories across different disciplines have since the middle of the nineteenth century gained ascendancy and prevalence, with a clear aim not only to downplay the importance of religion but also to explain it away and prognosticate its disappearance and end altogether. It was the French sociologist Durkheim, among others, who provided the theoretical and methodological ground for this thesis. Recognizing religion's importance in social regulation and its admirable "integrative function" over the centuries thanks to its moral norms and commands, he however insisted that "we need only substitute an empirically observable reality—society—for God, and the nature and authority of moral rules is entirely demystified." Robert Alun Jones, *The Development of Durkheim's Social Realism* (Cambridge, UK & New York: Cambridge University Press, 2004), p. 96. And it was most probably in line with this historicizing theorization about religion that Durkheim developed his views on professional ethics and civic morals as independent of, and substitute to, religious ethics, so as to suit a post-Christian society, as articulated in his posthumously published work ethics and morals. (Bryan S. Turner in his Introduction to Emile Durkheim, *Professional Ethics and Civil Morals,* trans. Cornelia Brookfield [London and New York: Routledge, 1992], p. xxxi).

Neverthelss, and contrary to nineteenth-century theories of religion "which treated religion as primarily a cognitive activity which was false from a scientific point view" as a result of human beings' "understanding of natural reality" (Turner, ibid., p. xxi), the last five to six decades have witnessed a lot of accumulated historical, empirical and theoretical research across the different social-science disciplines that have revisited the propositions and conclusions of those theories and debunked many of them, which is beyond our purpose here to deal with. Yet, it should be pointed out that cognitive and phenomenological approaches seem to play an important role in this development. See for example, Peter L. Berger, *A Rumor of Angels: Modern Society and the Rediscovery of the Supernatural* (New York: Anchor Books, 1970); also his *The Social Reality of Religion* (Middlesex, England: Penguin Books, 1973); first published in 1967 as *The Sacred Canopy*); also (ed.), *The Desecularization of the World: Resurgent Religion and World Politics* (Washington, DC: Ethics and Public Policy Center, 1999); Pascal Boyer, *The Naturalness of Religious Ideas: A Cognitive Theory of Religion* (California: University of California Press, 1994); Roy A. Pappaport, *Ritual and Religion in the Making of Humanity,* (Cambridge, UK : Cambridge University Press, 1999); Jensine Andersen (ed.), *Religion in the Mind: Cognitive Perspectives on Religious Belief, Ritual, and Experience* (Cambridge, UK: Cambridge University Press, 2001); Huston Smith, *Why Religion Matters* (New York: HarperSanFransico, 2001); Basia Spalek & Alia Imtoual (eds.), *Religion, Spirituality and the Social Sciences: Challenging Marginalisation* (Bristol: The Policy Press, University of B ristol, 2008); Jefferey Schloss & Michael Murray (eds.), *The Believing Pramate: Scientific, Philosophical, and Theological Reflections on the Origin of Religion* (Oxford-New York: Oxford University Press, 2009); William Grassie, *The New Sciences of Religion: Exploring Spirituality from the Outside In and Bottom Up* (New York: Palgrave MacMillan, 2010); Roger Trigg, *Religion in Public Life: Must Faith Be Privatized?* (Oxford, UK & New York: Ixford University Press, 2007); also his *Beyond Matter: Why Science Needs Metaphysics* (West Conshohocken, Pennsylvania: Templeton Press, 2015).

[66] See for example, al-Māturīdī, *Ta'wīlāt Ahl al-Sunnah*, vol. 5, pp. 83-85; al-Zamakhsharī, *Tafsīr al-Kashshāf*, p. 395; Abū ʿAlī al-Faḍl b. al-Ḥasan al-Ṭabarsī, *Majmaʿ al-Bayān fī Tafsīr al-Qur'ān*, ed. Hashim al-Rasuli al-Mahallati & Fadlullah al-Tabatabe (Beirut: Dar El-Marefah, 1408/1988), vol. 3-4, pp. 765-767; al-Ḥākim al-Jashmī, *al-Tahdhīb fī'l-Tafsīr*, vol. 4, pp. 2773-2774; al-Rāzī, *al-Tafsīr al-Kabīr*, vol. 15, pp. 53-57; al-Qurṭubī, *al-Jāmiʿ li-Aḥkām al-Qur'ān*, vol. 9, p. 375; al-Bayḍāwī, *Anwār al-Tanzīl wa-Asrār al-Ta'wīl*, vol. 3, p. 41; Abū al-Faḍl Shihāb al-Dīn al-Sayyid Maḥmūd al-Alūsī al-Baghdādī, *Rūḥ al-Maʿānī fī Tafsīr al-Qur'ān al-ʿAẓīm wa'l-Sabʿ al-Mathānī* (Cairo: Idārat al-Ṭibāʿah al-Munīriyyah, n.d.), vol. 9, pp. 102-106; al-Qāsimī, *Maḥāsin al-Ta'wīl*, vol. 7, pp. 2897-2899; Darwazeh, *al-Tafsīr al-Ḥadīth*, vol. 2, pp. 531-533; Qutb, *Fī Ẓilāl al-Qur'ān*, vol. 3, pp. 1391-1396; Ibn Ashur, *Tafsīr al-Taḥrīr wa'l-Tanwīr*, vol. 5/9, pp. 165-171; al-Tabataba'i, *al-Mīzān fī Tafsīr al-Qur'ān*, vol. 8, pp. 312-316.

[67] It is not out of context to point out here that one of the great Muslim scholars of our time, Mawdūdī, has rejected the allegorical interpretation of covenant which, in his view, explains away its being an actual event that did take place. His argument, worthy of consideration, goes as follows: "If someone considers calling all human beings together in one assembly impossible, that shows, more than anything else, the woeful paucity of his imagination. For if someone accepts that God has the power to create countles human beings in succession, there is no reason to suppose that He did not have the power to create them all at some given moment prior to the creation of the universe, or that He will be unable to resurrect them all at some given moment in the future." *Towards Understanding the Qur'an*, vol. 3, p. 98.

[68] Asad, *The Message of the Qur'an*, p. 276, note 139. See also Ibn Ashur, *Tafsīr al-Taḥrīr wa'l-Tanwīr*, vol. 15/30, pp. 423-428; Qutb, *Fī Ẓilāl al-Qur'ān*, vol. 6, p. 3933; Darwazeh, *al-Tafsīr al-Ḥadīth*, vol. 2, p. 165; al-Maydani, *Maʿārij al-Tafakkur wa-Daqā'iq al-Tadabbur*, vol. 2, pp. 397-399.

[69] Abū ʿAbd Allāh Muḥammad b. Ismāʿīl al-Bukhārī, *Ṣaḥīḥ al-Bukhārī* (Damscus-Beirut: Dār Ibn Kathīr, 1st edn., 1423/2002), 'Kitāb al-Janā'iz', ḥadiths 1358, 1359 & 1385, pp. 327-328 & 334; Abū al-Ḥussain Muslim b. al-Ḥajjāj al-Qushayrī al-Naysābūrī, *Ṣaḥīḥ Muslim*, ed. Mohammed Fuad Abd al-Baqi (Cairo: Dār Iḥyā' al-Kutub al-ʿArabiyyah, 1st edn., 1412/1991), 'Kitāb al-Qadar', ḥadīth 2658, vol. 4, pp. 2047-2049; Mālik b. Anas, *al-Muwaṭṭa'*, ed. Mohammed Fuad Abd al-Baqi (Beirut: Dār Iḥyā' al-Turāth al-ʿArabī, 1406/1985), 'Kitāb al-Janā'iz', ḥadīth 52, vol. 1, p. 241.

[70] Asad, *The Message of the Qur'an*, p. 741, note 27.

[71] Nasr, *The Heart of Islam*, pp. 6-7. *Cf.* Ismail Raji al-Faruqi, *Islam and Other Faiths*, edited by Ataullah Siqqiqui (Leicester: The Islamic Foundation & Nerendon, Virginia: The International Institute of Islamic Thought, 1419/1998), pp. 44-50.

[72] Qutb, *Fī Ẓilāl al-Qur'ān*, vol. 3, pp. 1391-1396 & vol. 5, pp. 2766-2767; Muhammad Qutb, *Dirāsāt fi'l-Nafs al-Insāniyyah* (Cairo/Beirut: Dār al-Shurūq, 10th edn., 1414/1993), pp. 211-270; also his *Manhaj al-Tarbiyyah al-Islāmiyyah* (Cairo/Beirut: Dār al-Shurūq, 14th edn., 1414/1993), pp. 18-215; Fathi al-Durayni, *Khaṣā'iṣ al-Tashrīʿ al-Islāmī fi'l-Siyāsah wa'l-Ḥukm* (Beirut: Resalah Publishers, 2nd edn., 1429/2008), pp. 84-85; al-Turabi, *al-Tafsīr al-Tawḥīdī*, vol. 1, pp. 765 & 781. Based on a profound discussion of the meaning, origin and function of religion and its relationship with, and difference from myth, the renowned philosopher Ernst Cassirer had the following statement to make in respect of its relationship with human natural instincts: "Religion had not the power, nor could it ever tend, *to suppress or eradicate these deepest instincts of mankind. It had to fulfil a different task—to use them and lead them into new channels.* The belief in the 'sympathy of the Whole' is one of the firmest foundations of religion itself." *An Essay on Man* (New Haven and London: Yale University Press, 1992 [1944]), p. 95. Itallics added.

[73] Nasr, *The Heart of Islam*, p. 7.

[74] ʿAbd al-Salām b. ʿAbd al-Raḥmān b. Muḥammad Ibn Barrajān, *Tanbīh al-Afhām ilā Tdabbur al-Kitāb al-Ḥakīm wa-Taʿarruf al-Āyāt wa'l-Naba' al-ʿAẓīm*, ed. Ahmed Fareed al-Muzayyidi (Beirut: Dār al-Kutub al-ʿIlmiyyah, 1st edn., 1434/2013), vol. 1, pp. 565-567 & vol. 2, p. 390-391; see also, Gerhard Böwering and Yousef Casewit (eds.), *A Qur'ān Commentary by Ibn Barrajān of Seville: Īḍāḥ al-ḥikma bi-aḥkām al-ʿibra* (Leidon-Boston: Brill, 2014), p. 83.

[75] Al-Ṭabarī, *Jāmiʿ al-Bayān*, vol. 10, p. 551; al-Bayḍāwī, *Anwār al-Tanzīl wa-Asrār al-Ta'wīl*, vol. 3, p. 42; al-Alūsī al-Baghdādī, *Rūḥ al-Maʿānī*, vol. 9, p. 99.

[76] Ibn Taymiyyah also uses other terms, such as *irādah kawniyyah qadariyyah* and *irādah sharʿiyyah dīniyyah*, to express the same basic ideas. See, Taqī al-Dīn Ibn Taymiyyah, *Majmūʿat al-Rasā'il wa'l-Masā'il* (Beirut: Dār al-Kutub al-ʿIlmiyyah, 2nd edn., 1412/1992), vol. 2, pp. 159-160 & 325-333; *Majmūʿ Fatāwaā Shaykh al-Islām Aḥmad Ibn Taymiyyah*, complied by Abd al-Rahman b. Muhammad b. Qasim & his son Muhammad (al-Madinah: King Fahd Complex for the Printing of the Holy Qur'an, 1425/2004), vol. 2, pp. 411-413; vol. 8, pp. 187-190 & 197-200 & vol. 11, pp. 265-271. For informative analysis of the cognitive, moral and theological and scio-political dimensions and implications of Ibn Taymiyyah's conceptualization of *fiṭrah* and *mīthāq*, see, M. Sait Dzervarli, "Divine Wisdom, Human Agency and *fiṭra* in Ibn Taymiyya's Thought," in Birgit Krawietz and Georges Tamer (eds.), *Islamic Theology, Philosophy and Law: Debating Ibn Taymiyya and Ibn Qayyim al-Jawziyyah* (Berlin/Boson: De Gruyter, 2013), pp. 38-60; Livnat Holtzman, "Human Choice, Divine Guidance and the *Fiṭra* Tradition: The Use of Hadith in Theological Treatises by Ibn Taymiyya and Ibn Qayyim al-Jawziyya," in Yossef Rapoport & Shahab Ahmed (eds.), *Ibn Taymiyya and his Times* (Karachi: Oxford University Press, 2010), pp. 166-178; Ovamir Anjum, *Politics, Law and Community: The Ibn Taymiyyah Moment*

(Cambridge/New York: Cambridge University Press, 2012), chap. 6, pp. 128-265; Abdullah bin Nafie al-Da'jani, *Manhaj Ibn Taymiyyah al-Ma'rifī* (al Khobar/London: Takween Studies and Research, 2ⁿᵈ edn., 1436/2015), pp. 3383-426 & 668-681; Sophia Vasalou, *Ibn Taymiyya's Theological Ethics* (New York: Oxforn University Press, 2016), pp. 56-104. The distinction and relationship between the notions of divine creative and legislative will and command is also clearly upheld by al-Shāṭibī. See *al-Muwāfaqāt*, vol. 1/2, p. 23; vol. 2/3, pp. 90-92 & vol. 2/4, p. 91.

[77] Seyyed Hossein Nasr *et al.*, *The Study Quran* (New York: Harper Collins Publishers, 2015), p. 467.

[78] Tariq Jaffer, "Is There Covenant Theology in Islam", in Majid Daneshgar & Walid A. Saleh (eds.), *Islamic Studies Today: Studies in Honor of Andrew Rippin* (Leiden-Boston: Brill, 2017), pp. 98-121, at 99.

[79] Rosalind Ward Gwynne, *Logic, Rhetoric and Legal Reasoning in the Qur'an: God's Arguments* (Abingdon, Oxfordshire, UK & New York: RoutledgeCurzon, 2004), p. 24. The covenant theme in the Qur'an has attracted increasing scholarly interest over the last few decades, not least for its theological and ethical significance. See for example, Bernard Weiss, "Covenant and Law in Islam," in Edwin B. Firmage *et al.* (eds.), *Religion and Law: Biblical-Judaic and Islamic Perspectives* (Winona Lake: Eisenbrauns, 1990), pp. 49-83; Wadad Kadi [al-Qadi], "The Primordial Covenant and Human History in the Qur'an," in *Proceedings of the American Philosophical Society*, vol. 147, No. 4 (December 2003) pp. Nora S. Eggen, "The *Mīthāq*: A Study in Trust Relationships in the Qur'an," in Håkan Rydving (ed.), *Micro-Level Analyses of the Qur'ān* (Uppsala: Uppsala Universitet, 2014), pp. 47-75; Joseph E. B. Lumbard, "Covenant and Covenants in the Qur'an," *Journal of Qur'anic Studies*, vol. 17, No. 2 (2015), pp. 1-23; Andrew J. O'Connor, "Qur'anic Covenants Reconsidered: *mīthāq* and *'ahd* in Polemical Context," *Islam and Christian-Muslim Relations*, vol. 30, No. 1 (2019), pp. 1-22.

[80] Asad, *The Message of the Qur'an*, p. 9, noe 19.

[81] See for instance, al-Māturīdī, *Ta'wīlāt Ahl al-Sunnah*, vol. 8, pp. 271-272 & vol. 5, p. 83; al-Sharīf al-Murtaḍā 'Alī b. al-Ḥusayn al-Mūsawī al-'Alawī, *Ghurar al-Fawā'id wa-Durar al-Qalā'id*, known as *Amālī al-Murtaḍā*, ed. Muhammad Abul Fadl Ibrahim (Beirut: al-Maktabah al-'Aṣriyyah, 1426/2005), vol. 1, pp. 54-56 & vol. 2, pp. 73-76; Abū Muḥammad al-Ḥusain b. Mas'ūd al-Baghawī, *Tafsīr al-Baghawī: Ma'ālim al-Tanzīl*, ed. Mohammed Abdullah al-Nimr *et al.* (Riyadh: Dar Taibah, 1412 H), vol. 6, p. 270; al-Zamakhsharī, *Tafsīr al-Kashshāf*, p. 395 & 830; Ibn Barrajān, *Tanbīh al-Afhām*, vol. 2, pp. 390-391; vol. 4, pp. 337-339; Ibn 'Aṭiyah, *al-Muharrar al-Wajīz*, vol. 4, p. 336-337; al-Ḥakim al-Jashmī, *al-Tahdhīb fī'l-Tafsīr*, vol. 4, pp. 2773-2778 & vol. 8, pp. 5618-5620; al-Rāzī, *al-Tafsīr al-Kabīr*, vol. 13, p. 53 & 56 & vol. 25, pp. 120-121; al-Qurṭubī, *al-Jāmi' li-Ahkām al-Qur'ān*, vol. 16, pp. 425-426; Abū Ḥayyān, *Tafsīr al-Baḥr al-Muḥīṭ*, vol. 4, pp. 532-533 & vol. 7, pp. 223-224; Ibn Kamal Pasha, *Tafsīr Ibn Kamal Pasha*, vol. 8, p. 137 & vol. 4, pp. 186-187; Ibn Ashur, *Tafsīr al-Taḥrīr wa'l-Tanwīr*, vol. 5/9, pp. 165-171 & vol. 10/21, pp. 89-94; al-Tabataba'i, *al-Mīzān fī Tafsīr al-Qur'ān*, vol. 8, pp. 312-316 & vol. 16, pp. 183-187; al-Turabi, *al-*

Tafsīr al-Tawḥīdī, vol. 1, p. 765; Morteza al-Motahhari, *al-Fiṭrah*, translated from the Persian by Jaafar Sadiq al-Khalili (Beirut: Muassasat al-Biʿthah, 2ⁿᵈ edn., 1412/1992), pp. 195-208; Ali bin Abdullah bin Ali al-Qarni, *al-Fiṭrah: Ḥaqīqatuhā wa-Madhāhib al-Nāsfihā* (Riaydh: Dār al-Muslim, 1424H), pp. 469-581; Nasr *et al.*, *The Study Quran*, pp. 466-469 & 991; Ayatullah Jawad al-Amuli, *al-ʿAqīdah min khilāl al-Fiṭrah fiʾl-Qurʾān* (Beirut: Dār al-Ṣafwah, 1429/2009).

[82] Bennabi, *The Qurʾanic Phenomenon*, p. 262.

[83] Henri Bergson, *The Two Sources of Morality and Religion*, translated by R. Ashley Audra and Cloudesley Brerton (Westport, Connecticut: Greenwood Press, 1974 [1935]), p. 166. Notwithstanding the importance of Bergson's statement, his view of religion as having gradually evolved "towards gods of increasingly marked personality" until it reached the concept of "a single deity" (p. 168 and *passim*) is certainly open to debate and criticism from the perspective of mono-theistic, especially Qurʾanic, thought which sees the matter in a rather opposite direction. Instead, paganism and plurality of deities are considered as the result of strayness and deviation from the original norm consisting of unitarian belief in God as the one creator and sustainer of the world, the sense of whose existence is engrained in human nature. For a recent and more comprehensive compara-tive study on the originality and inborn nature of religious monotheistic belief, see Umar al-Faruq Abd-Allah, *al-Īmān Fiṭrah: Dirāsah liʾl-Īmān al-Fiṭrī fiʾl-Qurʾān waʾl-Sunnah wa-Kathīr minaʾl-Milal waʾl-Niḥal* (Abu Dhabi: Dār al-Faqīh, 1ˢᵗ edn., 1435/2014).

[84] Ibid., p. 92.

[85] See in this respect, Joseph E. B. Lumbard, "Humanity in Covenant with God", in George Archer, Maria M. Dakae, and Daniel A. Madigan (eds.), *The Routledge Companion to the Qurʾan* (London and New York: Routledge, 2022), pp. 58-68.

[86] Al-Qāḍī ʿAbd al-Jabbār, *Kitāb al-Majmūʿ fiʾl-Muḥīṭ biʾl-Taklīf*, 3 vols., ed. J. J. Houben *et al.* (Beirut: Dar El-Machreq Editeurs, n.d.), vol. 1, p. 22. This view has been held in one form or another, explicitly or implicitly, by many Muslim schol-ars of different theological and juristic schools, even though one's school might be a staunch opponent of the Muʿtazilites of whom al-Qāḍī was a prominent au-thority. The latter school was, among other things, much criticized for its doctrine on reason's power to judge things based on their inherent qualities of goodness and evilness, famously known as *taḥsīn* and *taqbīḥ* *ʿaqliyyan*. See for example, ʿIzz al-Dīn ʿAbd al-ʿAzīz b. ʿAbd al-Salām, *al-Qawāʿid al-Kubrā* known as *Qawāʿid al-Aḥkām fī Iṣlāḥ al-Anām*, ed. Nazih Kamal Hammad and Othman Jomaa Dhamiraiyyah (Damasucs: Dār al-Qalam, 1ˢᵗ edn., 1421/2000), vol. 1, pp. 6-26; Abū al-ʿAbbās Taqī al-Dīn Aḥmad b. ʿAbd al-Ḥalīm Ibn Taymiyyah, *Darʾ Taʿāruḍ al-ʿAql waʾl-Naql*, ed. Muhammad Rashad Salim (Riyadh: Imam Mohamed Ibn Saud Islamic University, 2ⁿᵈ edn., 1411/1991), vol. 8, pp. 444-469; also his, *Majmūʿ Fatāwā Shaikh al-Islām Aḥmad Ibn Tyamiayh*, vol. 11, p. 335-354; Abū ʿAbd Allāh Muḥammad b. Abī Bakr b. Ayyūb Ibn Qayyim al-Jawziyyah, *Miftāḥ Dār al-*

Saʿādah wa-Manshūr Wilāyat al-ʿIlm wa'l-Irādah, ed. Abdul Rahman bin Hassan bin Qa'id (Makkah al-Mukarramah: Dār ʿĀlam al-Fawā'id, 1ˢᵗ edn., 1432H), vol. 2, pp. 965-135; Ibn Ashur, *Tafsīr al-Taḥrīr wa'l-Tanwīr,* vol. 5/8, pp. 63-64, 82-84 & vol. 5/9, pp. 134-136.

[87] Shāh Walī Allāh, *Ḥujjat Allāh al-Bālighah,* ed. Mohamed Sharif Sakr (Beirut: Dār Iḥyā' al-Turāth, 1413/1992), vol. 1, p. 85 & pp. 174-175; also, Shāh Walī Allāh, *The Conclusive Argument from God,* trans. Marcia K. Hermansen (Leiden-New York-Koln: EJ. Brill, 1996), p. 72 & pp. 148-150. *Cf.* Jacques Jomier, *Dieu et l'homme dans le Coran: l'aspect religieux de la nature humaine joint à l'obéissance au prophète de l'Islam* (Paris, Les Editions du CERF, 1996), pp. 31-52.

[88] Ibn Ashur, *Treatise on Maqāṣid al-Sharīʿah,* pp. 83-84.

[89] Ibn Ashur, *Treatise on Maqāṣid al-Sharīʿah,* pp. 82-86; *Tafsīr al-Taḥrīr wa'l-Tanwīr,* vol. 15/30, pp. 422-429 & vol. 10/21, pp. 89-94; *Uṣūl al-Niẓām al-Ijtimāʿī fi'l-Islām,* pp. 32-45; Qutb, *Fī Ẓilāl al-Qur'ān,* vol. 5, p. 2767; al-Attas, *Islam and Secularism,* pp. 61-76. For a systematic and elaborate discussion in this respect see, Yasien Mohamed, *Human Nature in Islam* (Kuala Lumpur: A.S. Noordeen, 1419/1998), pp. 15-17; Mohamed El-Tahir El-Mesawi, "Human nature and the universality of the Sharīʿah: Fiṭrah and Maqāṣid al-Sharīʿah in the works of Shāh Walā Allāh and Ibn ʿĀshūr," *Al-Shajarah,* vol. 14, No. 2 (2009), pp. 167-205.

[90] Maḥmūd ʿAwān, "The Faith community and World Order in the perspective of Islam," in Ismāʿīl Rājī al Fārūqī (ed.), *Trialogue of Abrahamic Faiths* (Herndon, Virginia: International Institute of Islamic Thought, 1411/1991), p. 85.

[91] See for example, David Hume, *Dialogues Concerning Natural Religion and Other Writings,* edited by Dorothy Coleman (Cambridge, UK • New York: Cambridge University Press, 2007); Ali Sami al-Nashshar, *Nash'at al-Dīn,* pp. 38-93; Daniel C. Dennet, *Breaking the Spell: Religion as a Natural Phenomenon* (New York: Viking Penguin, 2006); Charles Taylor, *Secular Age* (Cambridge, Massachusetts & London: The Belknap Press of Harvard University Press, 2007), pp. 505-535 & *passim;* George Makari, *Soul Machine: The Invention of the Modern Mind* (New York: W. W. Norton & Company, 2016); Peter Gay, *The Enlightenment: An Interpretation,* vol. 1: *The Rise of Modern Paganism* (New York • London: W.W. Norton & Company, 1966); Paul Heelas, *The New Age Movement: The Celebration of the Self and the Sacralization of Modernity* (Oxford, UK and Malden, Massachusetts: Blackwell Publishers, 1996); Steven Sutcliffe and Marion Bowman (eds.), *Beyond New Age: Exploring Alternative Spirituality* (Edinburgh: Edinburgh University Press, 2000); Hugh B. Urban, *New Age, Neopagan, and New Religious Movements: Alternative Spirituality in Contemporary America* (Oakland, CA: University of California Press, 2015); April D. DeConick, *The Gnostic New Age: How a Countercultural Spirituality Revolutionized from Antiquity to Today* (New York: Columbia University, 2016); Murphy Pizza, James R. Lewis (eds.), *Handbook of Contemporary Paganism* (Leiden-Boston: Brill, 2009); Eric Steinhart, *Believing in Dawkins: The New Spiritual Atheism* (Gewerbestrasse, Switzerland: Palgrave Macmillan, 2020).

[92] Jomier, *Dieu et l'homme dans le Coran*, p. 39. See his discussion on the three verses on pp. 31-38.

[93] Muhammad Iqbal, *The Reconstruction of Religious Thought in Islam*, edited and annotated by M. Saeed Sheikh (Stanford, California: Stanford University Press, 2012), p. 75. *Cf.* Hassan al-Turabi, *al-Ṣalāt ʿImād al-Dīn* (Al Safa, Kuwait: Dār al-Qalam, 5th edn., 1414/1994), pp. 124-147; also, *al-Īmān: Atharuhu fī Ḥayāt al-Insān*, pp. 115-141.

[94] ʿAbd al-Raḥmān b. Muḥammad Ibn Khaldūn, *Muqaddimat Ibn Khaldūn*, ed. Darwish al-Juwaydi (Sidon-Beirut: al-Maktabah al-ʿAṣriyyah, 2nd edn., 1416 /1996), pp. 143-150; also its English translation by Franz Rosenthal: *The Muqaddimah: An Introduction to History* (London: Routledge and Kegan Paul, 1958), vol. 1, pp. 311-327.

[95] Ernest Gellner, *Muslim Society* (Cambridge, UK-New York: Cambridge University Press, 1984[1981]), p. 86.

[96] Ibn Khaldūn, *Muqaddimat Ibn Khaldūn*, p. 146. Except for slight modifications, the translation of Ibn Khaldun's words is by Rosenthal, *The Muqaddimah*, vol. 1, pp. 319-320.

[97] Malek [Malik] Bennabi, *Les Conditions de la Renaissance* (Algiers: Editions ANEP, 2005), p. 63.

[98] Ibid., pp. 55-89; also Malik Bennabi, *The Question of Culture*, translated by Abdel Wahid Lu'lu'a, and revised by Mohamed El-Tahir El-Mesawi (Kuala Lumpur: Islamic Book Trust – London: The International Institute of Islamic Thought, 1423/2003), pp. 41-52. For further details on Bennabi's sociological and cultural theorizing on the place and role of religion in human life and civilaztion see, Mohamed El-Tahir El-Mesawi, "Religion, Society, and Culture in Malik Bennabi's Thought," in Ibrahim M. Abu-Rabiʿ (ed.), *The Blackwell Companion to Contemporary Islamic Thought* (Malden, USA-Oxford, UK-Carlton, Australia: Blackwell Publishing Ltd, 2006), pp. 216-256.

[99] Following the many unsuccessful efforts undertaken mainly in European Christian and Orientalist circles for centuries to undermine the truthfulness and authenticity of Prophet Muḥammad's prophethood, the Qur'an has come under systematic attack since the early 20th century, especially in the wake of the so-called reviosionist turn in Qura'nic studies in many Western academic and intellectual circles, radically questioning the textual integrity and veracity of the historical transmission of the Qur'an. The main purpose of such a campaign is to undermine the authority of the Islamic scripture in Muslim life and culture.

[100] For more details on the different aspects and forms of Islam's twofold strategy for the protection of religion see, al-Shāṭibī, *al-Muwāfaqāt*, vol. 1/2, pp. 7-8; Ibn Ashur, *Treatise on Maqāṣid al-Sharīʿah*, p. 120; al-ʿAlim, *al-Maqāṣid al-ʿĀmmah*, pp. 203-270; al-Najjar, *Maqāṣid al-Sharīʿah bi-Abʿād Jadīdah*, pp. 59-83; Ihsan Mir Ali, *al-Maqāṣid al-ʿĀmmah li'l-Sharīʿah al-Islāmiyyah bayna al-Aṣālah wa'l-Muʿāṣarah* (Damascus: Dār al-Thaqāfah li'l-jamīʿ, 1st edn., 1430/2009), vol. 1, pp. 211-399; Muhammad Qutb, *Manhaj al-Tarbiyyah al-Islāmiyyah* (Cairo-Beirut: Dār al-Shurūq, 14th edn. 1414/1993); Syed Muhammad Naquib al-Attas (ed.), *Aims and Objectives of Islamic*

Education (London: Hodder & Stoughton / Jeddah: King Abdulaziz University, 1979); also his *Islam and Secularism*, pp. 149-167; Majid Irsan al-Kilani, *Falsafat al-Tarbiyyah al-Islāmiyyah* (Makkah al-Mukarramah: Maktabat al-Manārah-Jeddah: Dār al-Manārah, 1ˢᵗ edn., 1407/1987); also *Ahdāf al-Tarbiyyah al-Islāmiyyah* (al-Madīnah al-Munawwarah: Maktabat al-Turath, 2ⁿᵈ edn., 1408/1988); Syed Ali Ashraf & Paul H. Hirst (eds.), *Religion and Education: Islamic and Christian Approaches* (Cambrodge: The Islamic Academy, 1994); J. Mark Halstead, "An Islamic Concept of Education", *Comparative Education*, vol. 40, No. 4 (2004); Hassan Abdullah Hassan, *al-Jāmiʿah al-Ḥaḍāriyyah: Mafhūmuhā wa-Waẓā'ifuhā wa-Mutaṭallabātuhā* (Herndon-Amman: The International Institute of Isllamic Though, IIIT, 1ˢᵗ edn., 1442/2021).

¹⁰¹ Al-Attas, *Islam and Secularism*, p. 148.

¹⁰² For more details see, al-Ghazālī, *Iḥyā'*, vol. 1, pp. 20-80, 141-154 & 181-216, also his *Mīzān al-ʿAmal* (Jeddah: Dār al-Minhāj, 2ⁿᵈ edn., 1441/2020), pp. 64-81 & 107-229; Muhammad al-Tahir Ibn Ashur, *Alaysa al-Ṣubḥu bi-Qarīb*, ed. Mohamed El-Tahir El-Mesawi (Amman: Dār al-Nafaes, 1441/2020), pp. 23-30 & 189-268; Ahmed Fuad al-Ahwani, *al-Tarbiyyah fi'l-Islām* (Cairo: Dār al-Maʿārif, 1968); al-Attas, *Islam and Secularism*, pp. 143-167; also his "Preliminary Thoughts on the Nature of Knowledge and Definition and Aims of Education," in al-Attas (ed.), *op. cit.*, pp. 19-47; Abul Hasan Ali al-Hasani al-Nadwi, *Abḥāth ḥawla al-Taʿlīm wa'l-Tarbiyyah al-Islāmiyyah,* compiled ny Syed Abdul Majid al-Ghouri (Damascus-Beirut: Dār Ibn Kathīr, 1ˢᵗ edn., 1423/2002); Mohamed Mounir Morsi, *al-Tarbiyyah al-Islāmiyyah: Uṣūluhā wa-Taṭawwurahā fi'l-Bilād al-ʿArabiyyah* (Cairo: Dār al-Maʿārif, 1987), pp. 40-129; Abdul Karim Bakkar, *Ḥawla al-Tarbiyyah wa'l-Taʿlīm* (Damasucus: Dār al-Qalam, 3ʳᵈ edn., 1432/2011); Jamilah Alam al-Huda, *al-Naẓariyyah al-Islāmiyyah fi'l-Tarbiyyah wa'l-Taʿlīm* (2 vols.), translated from Persian by Abbas Safi (Beirut: Center of Civilization for the Development of Islamic Thought, 1ˢᵗ edn., 2011); Fathi Hasan Malkawi, *al-Fikr al-Tarbawī al-Islāmī al-Muʿāṣir* (Herndon-Amman: International Institute of Isllamic Though, IIIT, 1ˢᵗ edn., 1442/2021); Sebastian Günther, "'Only Knowledge That Distances You from Sins Today Saves You from Hellfire Tomorrow': Boundaries and Horizons of Education in al-Ghazālī and Ibn Rushd," in Sebastian Günther (ed.), *Knowledge and Education in Classical Islam: Religious Learning between Continuity and Change* (Leiden-Boston: Brill, 2020), vol. 1, pp. 260-297; Luca Patrizi "The Metaphor of the Divine Banquet and the Origin of the Notion of *Adab*," in Günther, *op. cit.*, vol.1, pp. 517-538.

¹⁰³ In this connection other terms are used in the Qur'an denoting the same basic idea seen in different lights or highlighting different aspects and stages, such as *ṭīn, sulālah, nuṭfah, maniy, mā' dāfiq, ʿalaq/ʿalaqah, amshāj*, etc. For a comprehensive study of these and other related matters in light of modern medical science, see Muhammad Ali al-Bar, *Khalq al-Insān bayna al-Ṭibb wa'l-Qur'ān* (Jeddah: al-Dār al-Suʿūdiyyah, 4ᵗʰ edn. 1403/1983), pp. 109-231; see also Nabih Abdul Rahman Othman, *Muʿjizat Khalq al-Insān bayna al-Ṭibb wa'l-Qur'ān* (Makkah al-Mukarraman: Muslim World League, n.d.), pp. 33-73.

¹⁰⁴ See for example, al-Anbyā', 23:12-14; al-Ḥajj, 22:5; Ghāfir, 40:67; al-Ṭāriq, 86:5-7.

[105] See also al-Naḥl, 16: 78; al-Muʾminūn, 23: 78; al-Aḥqāf, 46: 26; al-Mulk, 67: 23.

[106] On the specific occasion(s) of revelation (*sabab al-nuzūl*) of these verses see for example, al-Ṭabarī, *Jāmiʿ al-Bayān*, vol. 3, pp. 571-577; al-Māturīdī, *Taʾwīlāt Ahl al-Sunnah*, vol. 3, p. 101; al-Rāzī, *al-Tafsīr al-Kabīr*, vol. 5, p. 266; al-Qurṭubī, *al-Jāmiʿ li-Aḥkām al-Qurʾān*, vol. 3, pp. 381-382; Ibn Ashur, *Tafsīr al-Taḥrīr wa'l-Tanwīr*, vol. 2, p. 266.

[107] Asad, *The Message of the Qurʾan*, pp. 53-54, notes 188 & 198. See also, al-Ṭabarī, *Jāmiʿ al-Bayān*, vol. 3, pp. 580-589; al-Māturidī, *Taʾwīlāt Ahl al-Sunnah*, vol. 2, p. 101; al-Zamkhsharī, *al-Kashshāf*, p. 123; al-Ṭabarsī, *Majmaʿ al-Bayān*, vol. 1, p. 534; al-Rāzī, *al-Tafsīr al-Kabīr*, vol. 5, pp. 216-220; Ibn Kemal Pasha, *Tafsīr Ibn Kemal Pasha*, vol. 2, p. 77; Abū al-Ṭayyib Ṣiddīq bin Hassan bin ʿAli al-Hussain al-Qinnūjī al-Bukhārī, *Fatḥ al-Bayān fī Maqāṣid al-Qurʾān*, ed. Abdullah bin Ibrahim al-Ansari (Sidon-Beirut: al-Maktabah al-ʿAṣriyyah, 1412/1992), vol. 1, pp. 416-417; Ibn Ashur, *Tafsīr al-Taḥrīr wa'l-Tanwīr*, vol. 2, pp. 269-270; al-Tabatabaʿi, *al-Mīzān fī Tafsīr al-Qurʾān*, vol. 2, pp. 97-98; al-Turabi, *al-Tafsīr al-Tawḥīdī*, vol. 1, pp. 158-159 & 168.

[108] Al-Māturīdī, *Taʾwīlāt Ahl al-Sunnah*, vol. 3, p. 101.

[109] Asad, *The Message of the Qurʾan*, p. 59, note 211.

[110] See for example, al-Baqarah, 2:134, 138 & 266; Āl ʿImrān, 3: 34 & 38; al-Nisāʾ, 4:9; al-Anʿām, 6:84, 87 & 133; al-Aʿrāf, 7:172; Yūnus, 10:83; al-Raʿd, 13:38; Ibrāhīm, 14:37; al-Isrāʾ, 17:2; Maryam, 19: 38; al-Furqān, 25:74; Ya Sīn, 36:41; 58; al-Ṭūr, 52:21.

[111] See, Shihāb al-Dīn Aḥmad b. Idrīs al-Qarāfī, *Sharḥ Tanqīḥ al-Fuṣūl fī Ikhtiṣār al-Maḥṣūl*, ed. Ahmed Farid al-Muzayyidi (Beirut: Dār al-Kutub al-ʿIlmiyyah, 1428/2007), p. 377; Najm al-Dīn Abū al-Rabīʿ Sulaymān b. ʿAbd al-Qawīy b. ʿAbd al-Karīm b. Saʿīd al-Ṭūfī, *Sharḥ Mukhtaṣar al-Rawḍah*, ed. Abdullah bin Abdul Muhsin al-Turki (Beirut: Muʾassasat al-Risālah, 2nd edn., 1419/1998), vol. 3, p. 209; Kamāl al-Dīn Muḥammad b. Abd al-Waḥid b. ʿAbd al-Ḥamīd b. Masʿūd Ibn al-Humām, *al-Taḥrīr fī Uṣūl al-Fiqh al-Jāmiʿ bayna Iṣṭilāḥay al-Ḥanafiyyah wa'l-Shāfiʿiyyah* (Cairo: Maṭbaʿat Musṭafā al-Bābī al-Halabī wa-Awlādih, 1351 H), p. 433; Tāj al-Dīn ʿAbd al-Wahhāb b. ʿAli al-Subkī, *Jamʿ al-Jawāmiʿ fī Uṣūl al-Fiqh*, ed. Abdul Munʿim Khalil Ibrahim (Beirut: Dār al-Kutub al-ʿIlmiyyah, 1424/2003), p. 92; Shams al-Dīn Muḥammad b. Ḥamzah b. Muḥammad al-Fanārī al-Rūmī, *Fuṣūl al-Badāʾiʿ fī Uṣūl al-Sharāʾiʿ*, ed. Mohmamed Hassan Mohammed Hassan Ismail (Beirut: Dār al-Kutub al-ʿIlmiyyah, 1st edn., 1427/2006), vol. 2, p. 346; Ibn Ashur, *Treatise on Maqāṣid al-Sharīʿah*, pp. 12-123.

[112] Modern science of oceanography has discovered that in places where two different seas meet, there is a barrier between them. Such a barrier divides the two seas so that each one of them has its own temperature, salinity, and density. For example, Mediterranean seawater is warm, saline, and less dense, compared to Atlantic seawater.

[113] For an interesting and illuminating comparative study of the importance and significance of water in the Bible, the Qurʾan, and the monotheistic tradi-

tions see, Denise Masson, *L'Eau, le Feu, la Lumière d'après la Bible, le Coran et les traditions monothéistes* (Paris: Desclée de Bouwer, 1985), pp. 11-98.

[114] For an anthropologically and sociologically informed analysis of these and other related Qur'anic terms aimed at constructing an alternative paradigm in the study of human association and society, see Hamid, *al-Naṣṣ al-Qur'ānī wa-Uṣūl al-Ijtimāʿ al-Siyāsī*, pp. 37-106; see also, Mohamed El-Tahir El-Mesawi, *Gender Issues in Islam: Recovering the Measure and Restoring the Balance,* with comments by Serene Jones and edited by Fethi B. Jomaa Ahmed (Doha: Research Center for Islamic Legislation and Ethics, 2019), pp. 38-43.

[115] Gai Eaton, *Islam and the Destiny of Man* (Kuala Lumpur: Islamic Book Trust, 2001 [1985]), p. 65.

[116] Ibn Ashur, *Tafsīr al-Taḥrīr wa'l-Tanwīr*, vol. 6/14, pp. 217-219.

[117] Ismāʿīl Rājī al Fārūqī, "The nation-state and social order in the perspective of Islam," in al Fārūqī (ed.), *op. cit.*, p. 49.

[118] Ibid.

[119] For a more detailed treatment of the matters briefly described here, see Ḥammūdah ʿAbd Al-ʿĀṭī, *The Family Structure in Islam* (Petaling Jaya, Malaysia: The Other Press, 2008), pp. 50-97; Ibn Ashur, *Treatise on Maqāṣid al-Sharīʿah,* pp. 247-266; al Fārūqī, *Al Tawḥīd*, pp. 130-133; Mohamed al-Kaddi al-Umrani, *Fiqh al-Usrah al-Muslimah fi'l-Mahājar* (Beirut: Dār al-Kutub al-ʿIlmiyyah, 1st edn., 1422/2001), vol. 1, pp. 163-204; Zainab Abdul Salam Abul Fadl, *al-ʿArḍ al-Qur'ānī li-Qaḍāyā al-Nikāḥ wa'l-Furqah* (Cairo: Dār al-Ḥadīth, 1427/2006); Zainab Taha al-Alwani, *al-Usrah fī Maqāṣid al-Sharīʿah* (Herndon: International Institute of Isllamic Though, IIIT, 1ST edn., 1434/2013); Ramon Harvey, *The Qur'an and the Just Society* (Edinburgh: Edinburgh University Press, 2019), 142-158; Ysusf al-Qaradawi, *Fiqh al-Usrah wa-Qaḍāyā al-Mar'ah* (Turkey: al-Dār al-Shāmiyyah, 1st edn., 1438/2017), pp. 359-458.

[120] Al-Ghazālī, *Iḥyā'*, vol. 3, pp. 93-184 & *passim* (*Kitāb Ādāb al-Nikāḥ*); al-Ḥākim al-Jashmī, *al-Tahdhīb fi'l-Tafsīr*, vol. 8, pp. 5613-5614; Burhān al-Dīn Abū al-Ḥassan b. ʿUmar al-Biqāʿī, *Naẓm al-Durar fī Tanāsub al-Āyāt wa'l-Suwar* (Cairo: Dār al-Kitāb al-ʿArabī, n.d.), vol. 15, pp. 67-69; Abdu and Rida, *Tafsīr al-Qur'ān al-Ḥakīm*, vol. 4, pp. 352; Ibn Ashur, *Tafsīr al-Taḥrīr wa'l-Tanwīr*, vol. 10/21, pp. 70-72; Tabataba'i, *al-Mīzān fī Tafsīr al-Qur'ān*, vol. 16, pp. 171-172; El-Mesawi, *Gender Issues in Islam.*

[121] Accordingly, Muslim jurists of different schools maintain that "marriage contracts are based on virtue and quality (*mukāramah*), while sales are based on measure and quantity (*mukāyasah*)." See for example, Abū al-Walīd Ibn Rushd (the Grandson), *The Distinguished Jurist's Primer* (*Bidāyat al-Mujtahid wa Nihāyat al-Muqtaṣṣid*), translated from the Arabic by Imran Ahsan Khan Nyazee (Reading, Berks, UK: Garnet Publishing, 2003), vol. 2, p. 8; Yaḥyā ibn Sharaf al-Nawawī, *Sharḥ Ṣaḥīḥ Muslim* (Beirut: Dār Iḥyā' al-Turāth al-ʿArabīṭ, n. d.), vol. 9, p. 202; Abū ʿAbd Allāh Muḥammad al-Anṣārī al-Raṣṣāʿ, *Sharḥ Ḥudūd Ibn ʿArafah*, ed. Muhammad Abu al-Ajfan & al-Tahir al-Maamouri (Beirut: Dār al-Gharb al-Islāmī, 1993), vol.1, p. 326.

[122] Harvey, *The Qur'an and the Just Society*, p. 143.

[123] See, al-Baqarah, 2:35-36; al-Aʿrāf, 7:24-25. Of course, together with the human pair that was descended from the Garden to the Earth was a third companion, Iblīs or Satan. But from the very beginning, Adam and his mate were clearly informed of, and warned against, this companion as their first and ultimate and most dangerous foe.

[124] For a profound philosophical discussion in this regard, see Mortimer J. Adler, *The Difference of Man and the Difference it Makes* (New York: Fordham University Press, 2005 [1967]) & *Intellect: Mind Over Matter* (New YorkCollier Books, 1990). See also, Mary Midgley, *Beast and Man: The Roots of Human Nature* (London and New York: Routledge, 2002 [1979]); Roy F. Naumeister, *The Cultural Animal: Human Nature, Meaning and Social Life* (Oxford and New York: Oxford University Press, 2005).

[125] Asad, *The Message of the Qur'an*, p. 1149, note 3.

[126] Ibn Ashur, *Tafsīr al-Taḥrīr wa'l-Tanwīr*, vol. 15/30, pp. 422-429; *Treatise on Maqāsid al-Sharīʿah*, pp. 83-84; see also, al-Tabataba'i, *al-Mīzān fī Tafsīr al-Qur'ān*, vol. 20, pp. 365-367.

[127] Ibn Ashur, *Treatise on Maqāsid al-Sharīʿah*, pp. 122-123; Harvey, *The Qur'an and the Just Society*, p. 143.

[128] Harvey, *The Qur'an and the Just Society*, pp. 185-195.

[129] Eaton, *Islam and the Destiny of Man*, p. 65. For a fairly detailed and profound maqasid-informed discussion of the notions of *ḥifẓ al-nasl* and *ḥifẓ al-nasab* and their sociological and ethical dimensions, see, Ibn Ashur, *Treatise on Maqāṣid al-Sharīʿah*, pp. 247-269.

[130] For comprehensive *maqāṣid*-informed juristic discussions on the topic of *ḥifẓ al-nasl* and related issues that have been been raised here, see, Al-ʿAlim, *al-Maqāṣid al-ʿĀmmah*, pp. 393-465; al-Najjar, *Maqāṣid al-Sharīʿah bi-Abʿād Jadīdah*, pp. 145-180; Farida Sadiq Zouzou, *al-Nasl: Dirāsah Maqāṣidiyyah fī Wasā'il Hifẓihi fī Ḍaw' al-Taḥaddiyyāt al-Muʿāṣirah* (Riyadh: Maktabat al-Rushd, 1427/2006). *Cf.* Harvey, *The Qur'an and the Just Society*, pp. 185-195. See also, Kamal Ibrahim Morsi, *al-ʿAlāqah al-Zawjiyyah wa'l-Ṣiḥḥan al-Nafsiyyah fī'l-Islam wa-ʿIlm al-Nafs* (Kuwait: Dār al-Qalam, 2nd edn., 1415/1995), also his *al-Zawāj wa-Binā' al-Usrah* (Kuwait: Dār al-Qalam, 1st edn., 1425/2004); Raed Jamil Okasha & Monzer Arafat Zaytoun (eds.), *al-Usrah al-Muslimah fī Ẓill al-Taghayyurāt al-Muʿāṣirah* (Herndon: International Institute of Islamic Thought & Amman: Dār al-Fath, 1st edn., 1436/2015), pp. 23-312; Abdullah Nasih ʿUlwan, *Tarbiyyat al-Awlād fī'l-Islām*, 2 vols.(Cairo: Dār al-Salām, 21st edn. 1412/1992).

[131] Ptirim Sorokin, *The Crisis of Our Age* (Oxford, England: Oneworld Publications, 1992 [1941]), pp. 168-173.

[132] Since the second half of the nineteenth century at least, the family, both as concept and institution, has been in the West the target of an almost endless onslaught by different kinds of theories and ideologies across the board of the

social sciences and humanities. This onslaught has taken more alarming dimensions going beyond academic and intellectual circless and assuming legal and institutional forms as part of concerted socio-political agendas adopted and pushed by different types of bodies, including international organizations such as the UN and its satellite institutions, especially in the wake of their infiltration by radical feminism tinted with Marxian-Freudianism and its latter-day product genderism. The amount of literature in this regard is indeed so huge that it cannot be circumscribed in a note or even a chapter. Therefore, only a very limited sample of such literature shall be mentioned here. See for example, Friedrich Engels, *The Origin of the Family, Private Property and the State* (Newtown, Australia: Resistance Books, 2004 [1884]); David Cooper, *The Death of the Family* (Middleessex, England: Pelican Books, 1972); Teresa Brennane (ed.), *Between Feminism and Psychoanalysis* (New York and London: Routledge, 1st edn., 1989); Judith Buttler, *Gender Trouble: Feminism and the Subversion of Identity* (New York an d London: Routledge, 1st edn., 1990); Linda L. Layne, *Motherhood Lost: A Feminist Account of Pregnancy Loss in America* (New York and London: Routledge, 2003); Muthanna Amin al-Kurdustani & Kamelia Helmy Mohammed, *al-Jandar: al-Mansha', al-Madlūl, al-Athar* (Amman: Jamʿiyyat al-ʿAfāf al-Khayriyyah, 1st edn., 1425/2004); Ann Taylor Allen, *Feminism and Motherhood in Western Europe, 1890-1970* (New York: Palgrave MacMillan, 2005); Muthanna Amin al-Kurdustani, *Ḥarakāt Taḥrīr al-Mar'ah mina'l-Musāwāt ila'l-Jandar* (Cairo: Dār al-Qalam, 1st edn., 1425/2004); Rachel M. Calogero *et al.* (eds.), *Self-Objectification in Women: Causes, Consequences, and Counteractions* (Washington, DC: American Psychological Association, 2011); Narges Rodker, *Fiminizme (al-Ḥarakah al-Niswiyyah): Mafhūmuhā, Uṣūluhā al-Naẓariyyah wa-Tayyārātuhā al-Ijtimāʿiyyah*, translated from the Persian by Hiba Dhafir (Beirut: al-Markaz al-Islāmī li'l-Dirāsāt al-Istrātījiyyah, 1440/2019); Kamelia Helmy Mohammed, *al-Mawāthīq al-Dawliyyah wa-Atharuhā fī Hadm al-Usrah: Bidāyatan min Ta'sīs Munaẓẓamāt al-Umam al-Muttaḥidah fī 1945 ḥattā Awā'il 2019* (Self-publishing, 1st edn., 1441/2020); Okasha & Zaytoun, *op. cit.,* pp. 315-654; Isabel Crowhurst et al. (eds.), *Third Sector in Sex Work and Prostitution* (London and New York: Routledge, 2021).

[133] The parabolic use of rock and the expression of "the fullest of life" here are borrowed from the renowned paleontologist Stephen Gould (d. 2002) who strongly argued for the necessity of religion and science each of which "covering a central facet of human existence," in accordance with his "principle of respectful noninterference". Stephen Jay Gould, *Rocks of Ages: Science and Religion in the Fullest of Life* (New York: The Ballantine Publishing Group, 1999), p. 5.

[134] Ibn Ashur, *Tafsīr al-Taḥrīr wa'l-Tanwīr*, vol. 3/4, pp.214-215. See also, Abū Ḥayyān, *Tafsīr al-Baḥr al-Muḥīṭ*, vol. 3, pp. 217-225.

[135] Ibn Ashur, *Tafsīr al-Taḥrīr wa'l-Tanwīr*, vol. 3/4, p. 213; Raymond Farrin, "Sūrat al-Nisā' and the Centrality of Justice," *Al-Bayān: Journal of Qur'ānic and Hadīth Studies,* No. 14 (1015), pp. 1-17 (at 3-6).

[136] Asad, *The Message of the Qur'an*, p. 504, note 26.

[137] Al Fārūqī, *Al Tawḥīd*, p.131.

[138] See in this respect, Abbas Mahmoud al-Aqqad, *al-Falsafah al-Qur'āniyyah*, in *Mawsūʿat Aʿmāl ʿAbbās Maḥmūd al-ʿAkkād: The Complete Works of al-Akkad* (Beirut: Dar al-Kitab al-Lubnani. Cairo: Dar al-Kitab al-Masri, 3rd edn., 1438/2017), vol. 7, pp. 23-40, 104-164 & 177-184; also his *al-Insān fi'l-Qur'ān*, in *CWA*, vol. 8, pp. 367-416; Sayyid Qutb, *Muqawwimāt al-Taṣawwur al-Islāmī* (Cairo-Beirut: Dār al-Shurūq, 5th edn., 1418/1997). Making the case for the necessity of both religion and science for human existence, Stephen Gould had the following to say: "Science tries to documnent the factual character of the natural world, and to develop theories that coordinate and explain these facts. Religion, on the other hand, operates in the equally important, but utterly different, realm of human purposes, meanings and values—subjects that the factual domain of science might illuminate, but can never resolve." Gould, *Rocks of the Ages*, p. 4.

[139] Ibn Ashur, *Treatise on Maqāṣid al-Sharīʿah*, p. 247.

[140] al-Akkad, *al-Falsafah al-Qur'āniyyah*, pp. 11-12 & *al-Insān fi'l-Qur'ān*, pp. 367-404.

[141] Ibid., pp. 62-63 & 67-76. *Cf.* al-Turabi, *al-Īmān*, pp. 54-62.

CHAPTER TWO

Ḥifẓ al-Nafs: Sanctifying Human Life and Protecting Personal Selves

Introduction

Ḥifẓ al-nafs is usually mentioned by Muslim legal theorists and jurists after *ḥifẓ al-dīn*, thus being second in their taxonomy of the necessary universal goals of the Sharīʿah (*al-kulliyyāt al-ḍarūriyyah*, or simply *al-ḍarūriyyāt*) adopted by most of those scholars. This phrase refers to the protection of the human life and self from all sorts of harm and aggression without any valid and established reason, such as committing homicide and causing harm to other people in any form. Putting *ḥifẓ al-nafs* in such a high rank reflects the crucial importance of the sanctity and inviolability of the personal life and existence of human beings who are the main constituents of human society and agents of history and civilization, and in whose absence society itself remains mere, if not beyond, imagination.

The protection and promotion of the human self and life in Islam is not confined to the material and physical aspects of human existence. Rather, it has a comprehensive meaning that includes, besides what has been mentioned, other equally, if not more, important dimensions of the human person: spiritual, intellectual, moral, psychological and social. Put differently, the Islamic view of human life and existence is holistic and integrative, not partial, reductionist and disintegrative. In what follows a general and brief exposition of the

Sharīʿah approach to safeguarding human life is provided.

Nafs: Semantics and conceptualization

In order to pave the ground for our discussion of the meaning, significance and means of *ḥifẓ al-nafs* as envisaged in the teachings of Islam, there is need for a general view of the semantics of the term *nafs* itself. Starting with lexicography, we are told by al-Farāhīdī that *nafs*, pl. *nufūs* [also *anfus*], has different meanings. It is "the soul, *rūḥ*, on which the life of the body depends (*bihi ḥayāt al-jasad*); each human being is a *nafs,* male and female alike, including Adam may peace be with him." It is also said of "everything as such (or in itself: *kullu shay'in bi-ʿaynih*)."[1] Abū ʿUbayd (d. 401AH), Ibn Sīdeh (d. 458AH), Ibn Manẓūr (d. 711AH) and al-Zabīdī (d. 1125 AH) report in slightly different wordings that a certain Abū Isḥāq, most probably al-Zajjāj (d. 311 AH), stated that *nafs* in Arabic speech (*kalām al-ʿArab*) is used in two ways: the first one is to signify the soul or spirit (*rūḥ*), such as saying that someone's *nafs* went off (*kharajat nafsuh*); the second is to refer to something in "its totality and essence (*jumlatu al-shay' wa-ḥaqīqatih*)," such as stating that "so and so killed himself (*qatala nafsahu*), meaning that he caused destruction to himself."[2] Ibn Sīdeh, however, was quick to point out, just before citing Abū Isḥāq's words, that there was a difference between *nafs* and *rūḥ*, a matter that was not of the purpose of his book, as he said.

If it is the case that the terms *nafs* and *rūḥ* are not synonyms, thus referring to two different things, the question as to what sort of relationship there might be between their referents and the human body, etc. has been the subject of a rich and complex debate involving scholars of different intellectual backgrounds. Linguists, exegetes, jurists, theologians, philosophers and mystics all have offered various explanations and interpretations of such terms, thus attempting to fathom the nature and manifestations of the reality to which they refer in human existence and consciousness, for which purpose they made use of whatever scientific sources and methods of knowledge at their disposal. Nonetheless, it is not the aim of this chapter to summarize the different views and positions which informed and shaped that debate, let alone to analyze their underlying respective arguments, notwithstanding the illuminating lights they shed on the different aspects of the problem.[3]

One of the many significations of the term *nafs* seems to be paramount or at least most re-current in that debate, namely that it refers to the totality and essence of a thing. Therefore, we shall take this sense as our springboard for reasons that will become clear in the rest of this section. Accordingly, as prominent lexicographers since al-Khalīl b. Aḥamd have indicated in slightly different terms, *nafs* is said of "man in his totality" (*al-nafsu yuʿabbaru bihā ʿan al-insān jamīʿih*), of man's "whole self and essence", of "man" (*insān*) or of "man as a whole: his soul and body" (*al-insān jamīʿuhu, rūḥuhu wa-jasaduh*), both as "male and female".[4]

Thus denoting the sense of integral entity or self (*dhāt*), comprising all the constituents and dimensions of the human being both inwardly and outwardly as embodied and concretized in the human body, the term *nafs* has been used in different Qur'anic contexts to convey the same meaning, notably in the singular form. The word *nafs* occurs in the Qur'an two hundred ninety-five times in the singular (140) and plural (155) forms, both in Makkan and Madīnan sūrahs, long, medium and short. Furthermore, it is used alone as subject, object or attributed to possessive singular and plural pronouns of the first, second, and third person.[5] Far from laying claim to any detailed analysis of this general statistical data, we shall rather confine ourselves to highlighting certain facts and providing some examples. That shall bring to the mind the main argument of the present discussion.

Regardless of its grammatical functions in the various contexts of its 140 occurrences in the Qur'an in the singular form, in roughly 99 (71%) of those instances the term *nafs* clearly refers to the human being, person or self in a generic sense. Thus, *nafs* is equivalent in meaning to the term *insān*, itself occurring 65 times in mainly, if not exclusively, Makkan sūrahs.[6] A few examples manifesting that equivalence will suffice to bring this point home. Hence, we read in different contexts the following verses grouped in two sets according to such terms.

Group A:

1. *No human being (nafsun) shall be burdened with m ore than he is well to bear.* (al-Baqarah, 2:233)

2. *God does not burden any human being with more than he is well able to bear.* (al-Baqarah, 2:286)

3. *Every human being (kullu nafsin) is bound to taste death: but only on the Day of Resurrection will you be requited in full [for whatever you have done].* (Āl 'Imrān, 3:185)

4. *Because of this We ordain unto the children of Israel that if anyone slays a human being unless it be [in punishment] for murder (qatala nafsan bi-ghayri nafsin) or for spreading corruption on earth — it shall be as though he had slain all mankind.* (al-Mā'idah, 5:32)

5. *And whatever [wrong] any human being (kullu nafsin) commits rests upon himself; and no bearer of burdens shall be made to bear another's burden.* (al-An'ām, 6:164)

6. *... and no one (nafsun) knows in what land he will die.* (Luqmān, 31:34)

7. *[On the Judgement Day,] every human being (kullu nafsin) will be held in pledge for whatever [evil] he has wrought.* (al-Muddaththir, 74:38)

Group B:

1. *As it is, man [often] prays for things that are bad as if he were praying for something that is good: for man is prone to be hasty [in his judgements].* (al-Isrā', 17:11

2. *Man never tires of asking for the good [things of life]; and if evil fortune touches him, he abandons all hope, giving himself up to despair.* (Fuṣṣilat, 51:49)

3. *Is man (al-insān), then, not aware that it is We who create him out of a [mere] drop of sperm — whereupon, lo! he shows himself endowed with the power to think and to argue?* (Yā Sīn, 36:77)

4. *We have enjoined upon man (al-insān) goodness to his parents. In pain did his mother bear him, and in pain did she give him birth ...* (al-Aḥqāf, 46:15)

5. *Does man (al-insān), then, think that he is to be left to himself, to go
    about at will.* (al-Qiyāmah, 75:36)

6. *But as for man (al-insān), whenever his Sustainer tries him by His generosity
    and by letting him enjoy a life of ease, he says: 'My Sustainer has been [just-
    ly] generous towards me.* (al-Fajr, 89:15)

7. *Nay, verily man (al-insān) becomes grossly overweening whenever he believes
    himself to be self-sufficient.* (al-'Alaq, 96:6-7)

Taken randomly without any preconceived criteria except their sequence in the established (canonical) order of the text of the Qur'an,
one main feature that can be readily noticed from the above verses is
that the words *nafs* and *insān* may be interchanged without the central
message of each specific verse being seriously affected. Likewise, the
two terms converge on one essential and comprehensive meaning pertaining to the human being (*al-kā'in al-insānī*), self or person (*shakhs*) as a
whole and taken in its totality as an integral entity, male and female
alike. This comprehensive sense of *nafs* is at the centre of Muslim legal
deliberations on *hifz al-nafs* as one of the universal and necessary goals
of the Sharī'ah, which will be the subject of the following discussion. It
should be noted here that this essential and comprehensive meaning
does not in any way exclude the different shades of meaning denoted
by the specific contexts in which the terms *nafs* and *insān* occur in the
Qur'an. In fact, through such shades of meaning the Qur'an brings to
light many different (positive and negative) aspects, qualities and conditions of the human being and self, something that remains beyond our
purpose to dwell upon here.[7]

Anchoring *hifz al-nafs*: Human dignity

The high value and prime importance attached to the protection and
safeguarding of human life, or *hifz al-nafs*, flows from the fact that God
Almighty, who has created human beings, has conferred dignity upon
them (*takrīm*) in different ways and placed them on earth as His vicege-
rents (*khalīfah, khulafā'*), as mentioned in different places in the Qur'an.
This divinely conferred dignity of the humankind is, so to speak, cere-
moniously portrayed on a number of occasions in the Qur'an by God's

command to the angels to prostate to Adam, its prototype, at the very dawn of its pre-terrestrial existence. Thus, for example, we read in sūrahs al-Ḥijr (15:28-29) and al-Baqarah (2:34) respectively,[8]

1. *[28]And lo! Thy Sustainer said unto the angels: "Behold, I am about to create mortal man out of sounding clay, out of dark slime transmuted [29] and when I have formed him fully and breathed into him of My spirit, fall down before him in prostration!"*

2. *[34]And when We told the angels, "Prostrate yourselves before Adam!" they all prostrated themselves, save Iblis, who refused and gloried in his arrogance: and thus he became one of those who deny the truth.*

Regardless of the way the first human being was created, what matters for us in these and similar verses is the cosmic significance and special status God has conferred upon him and his species from the very beginning, before the descent from Eden to the earth, thus bespeaking a unique status and special mission of the new creature.[9] Indeed, this was such a momentous news that it raised the concern or at least curiosity of the angels themselves who openly sought clarification from their Lord as the Qur'an relates (al-Baqarah, 2:30):

They said: "Wilt Thou place on it such as will spread corruption thereon and shed blood—whereas it is we who extol Thy limitless glory, and praise Thee, and hallow Thy name?"

To this reservation or query by the angels with regard to the new creature came the divine answer in a practical demonstrative manner showing one of the most distinctive capacities of Adam (al-Baqarah: 2:31-33):

[31]And He imparted unto Adam the names of all things (al-asmāʾ kullahā); then He brought them within the ken of the angels and said: "Declare unto Me the names of these [things], if what you say is true." [32]They replied: "Limitless art Thou in Thy glory! No knowledge have we save that which Thou hast imparted unto us. Verily, Thou alone art all-knowing, truly wise." [33]Said He: "O Adam, convey unto them the names of these [things]." And as soon as [Adam] had conveyed unto them their names, [God] said: "Did I

> *not say unto you, 'Verily, I alone know the hidden reality of the*
> *heavens and the earth, and know all that you bring into the open and*
> *all that you would conceal'?"*

Imparting unto Adam "all the names" or "the names of all things" has been a subject of much intellectual debate and has prompted profound theological and philosophical reflections among Muslim scholars over the centuries on the nature and scope of the knowledge given to Adam which the angels did not have. Without going into the details of that debate, what seems to be the gist on which most different views converge can be summarized as follows. Starting with philology, the term *ism* (name) is a word or expression used to "identify something"[10] or to denote "a substance, an accident, or an attribute." Thus, the term *ism* conveys knowledge of the thing named (*musammā*) with the purpose of distinguishing it from other things.[11]

In philosophical or more technical language, the term *ism* is equivalent to the term "concept" (*mafhūm, muṣṭalaḥ*), whereby a meaning or an idea is distinguished from another. From this it may be legitimately inferred that the 'knowledge of all the names' imparted unto Adam denotes "man's faculty of logical definition and, thus, of conceptual thinking," in which respect by Adam is meant "the whole human race." In other words, this signifies that God has bestowed upon human beings "the faculty of conceptual thinking," thus making them superior in this regard to "all other animate beings, and even to the angels,"[12] as it appears from the scene described by the above-cited and similar Qur'anic verses. As al-Jāḥiẓ put it long ago, names circulating among people are in fact signs and indicators (*'alā-māt*) of the characteristics of things and situations (*ḥālāt*); that is, they refer to meanings, ideas and essences. It would therefore be illogical to imagine that God had imparted to Adam names without referents and words empty of meanings, for the truth is that referents and meanings are pre-existent to names and words and are for them what souls (*arwāḥ*) are for bodies (*abdān*). Were we to think that "God gave [Adam] names without meanings, it would then be like giving someone something that is lifeless, motionless, senseless and useless." This would be sheer futility and absurdiyy in view of the high status and position to which God raised this creature and made the angels prostrate themselves to him.[13]

Most probably inspired by al-Jāḥiẓ's argument, al-Iṣfahānī adduces that true knowledge does not consist of just having cognizance of certain details and particulars of things; it is rather to grasp the fundamentals (*uṣūl*) on which ramifications and offshoots (*furūʿ*) depend and to comprehend the universal meanings (*maʿānī kulliyyah*) to which particulars belong, such as knowing the essence and characteristics of man, and being cognizant of the axioms of arithmetic, the rules of geometry, and the principles of jurisprudence, theology or grammar. Knowledge of particulars and details stripped of their fundamentals is not true knowledge; it is no more than a parrot's imitation of words. Thus, according to al-Iṣfahānī, what really makes the greatness of man is not to just know and memorize names and words, but the capacity to comprehend meanings and the realities they stand for as well as "the essences of things in themselves."[14]

In the context of his psycho-sociological perspective on culture, Bennabi warned that it would be erroneous to look at the verse in question as merely a description of "a simple situation." Rather, it has a more important symbolic significance, as it depicts "the first essential function of the human mind when, in control of objects, it gives them their names."[15] As he further argues, an object remains in the shadow or darkness of non-existence in relation to human consciousness. It is only when "it gives birth to an idea" that it proves its existence and becomes present in the human mind, thus entering "the sphere of our knowledge, that is our consciousness." Once this happens, the object becomes part of the illuminated area of the mind or the realm of our consciousness, and "its presence becomes a real existence" whereby "its character is defined, and a name is ultimately given to" it.[16]

This remarkable capacity of conceptual thinking bestowed on the first prototype of mankind has been further expressed and consolidated in the Qur'an (al-Raḥmān, 55:3-4) by another capacity or quality, namely communication: "*al-Raḥmān khalaqa al-insān, ʿallamahu al-bayān.*" According to al-Iṣfahānī, the term *bayān* means circumscribing something and making it clear (*al-kashf ʿan al-shayʾ*)," thus having "a more general meaning than speech (*nuṭq*), as speech is a specific quality of man."[17] Yet, whatever other means humans happen to use for communication, speech and verbal language remain their utmost distinctive characteristic as opposed to the different kinds of the animal family. Hence, in the context of the verse in question, *bayān* refers specifically to speech and language, a signification that is clearly underscored by the verse (no. 2) immediately preceding what has been quoted above, according to which God, the Lord of Mercy (*al-Raḥmān*) "has taught the Qurʾan", being itself a divine speech of excellent quality and high eloquence.[18]

Bayān as imparted to man is not, therefore, mere vocalization of words by the tongue or drawing them by means of any kind of script; it is rather doing so in a systematic manner to express one's "internal intentions and purposes (*mā fiʾl-ḍamīr min maqāṣid wa-aghrāḍ*)." Furthermore, it means that God has put in human beings "the disposition and capacity (*istiʿdād*) to learn and to establish languages for the sake of mutual communication and knowing of one another (*taʿāruf*)," thus embodying one of the greatest divine blessings and favours (*niʿam*) bestowed on mankind, and constituting a characteristic feature setting her apart from other animal species in the world.[19] Accordingly, *bayān* "applies to both thought and speech inasmuch as it comprises the faculty of making a thing or an idea apparent to the mind and conceptually distinct from other things or ideas, as well as the power to express this cognition clearly in spoken or written language."[20] Likewise, God's imparting *bayān* unto man means that He has equipped him with the power of "articulate thought and speech", as Asad has gracefully rendered this very term.[21]

An important aspect of the conceptual connection between the two verses on God's having taught man the Qurʾan and speech, or *bayān*, must not escape our attention here, one which was a matter of reflection by a number of Muslim scholars both in the past and in modern times. As the authors of a topical work on the Qurʾan have articulated it, "Just as the human beings are distinguished by their ability to know revelation, so too are they distinguished from all other creatures by the faculty of speech through which they both articulate and comprehend." This, among other things, is an allusion "to God's giving human beings the ability to distinguish between good and evil, between what is permitted and what is forbidden, ... or between truth and falsehood, all of which is believed to be taught through revelation."[22]

The significance of speech as a distinctive feature and quality of man is in fact consequent upon a rather more important quality of this creature, that of comprehending, thinking, reasoning and feeling, these activities constituting the underlying stream and reality of linguistic expression and communication. It is through speech that humans make explicit and known their thoughts and feelings in meaningful and understandable ways orally and in written form, no matter what other means of communication they might have at their disposal. Indeed, it is through written language (*kitābah*) that the preservation and dissemination of knowledge and information have been made possible and efficient throughout the successive generations and ages of mankind. From this follows the high importance and significance in the Qur'an of such notions as pen (*qalam*), writing (*kitābah, saṭr*), book or scripture (*kitāb*), and reading (*qirā'ah*). Suffice it to mention here that the very first verses revealed to the Prophet Muḥammad in Cave Ḥirā' (al-'Alaq, 96:1-5) were not about any formal moral teaching or religious obligation, but emphatically commanding him to *read*, while at the same time underlining this command by immediately connecting it with the pen as a means of teaching. Thus we read:

> *[1]Read in the name of thy Sustainer, who has created (khalaqa)—*
> *[2]created man out of a germ-cell. [3]Read—for thy Sustainer is the Most*
> *Bountiful One [4]who has taught [man] the use of the pen— [5]taught*
> *man what he did not know!*

As Ibn al-Qayyim intimated, these verses have encompassed the levels of being or existence of all existents. Being (*wujūd*), he explains, is of four levels (*marātib*): "The first is external and objective existence (*khārijiyyah*) denoted by the expression *khalaqa;* the second is mental existence signified by the expression *'allama'l-insāna mā lam ya'lam.* The third and fourth levels consist of verbal (*lafẓiyyah*) and scriptural (*khaṭṭiy-*

yah) modes of existence: while the scriptural mode of existence is explicitly expressed by the phrase *ʿallama bi'l-qalam*, the verbal one is implied by the teaching by means of the pen, for writing (*kitābah*) is a derivative (*farʿ*) of speech (*nuṭq*), whereas speech is a derivative of conception (*taṣawwur*)." This means, as the Damascene scholar infers, "that God has made Himself known to His servants by what He has taught them in terms of script, speech and meaning." That knowledge (*ʿilm*) is the foremost way for man to know God is, in his view, "sufficient by itself as the greatest sign and proof of his nobility (*sharaf*) and excellence (*faḍl*)."[23] In fact, Ibn al-Qayyim was not the first nor the last to ascertain the significance of this verse as a testimony to human dignity and to reflect on its different aspects; he was but a link in a long chain of great minds that applied themselves to uncover the profound wisdom and far-reaching implications of this and other verses of the Qur'an.[24]

Howsoever clear and sufficient the above-discussed capacities may be as a manifestation and embodiment of human dignity and nobility (*karāmah*), uncertainty and doubt on its universality might creep into the mind, as one may entertain the idea that it is something confined to the first human being Adam, or only applicable to certain specific races or groups rather than to all humans. The answer to the possibility of such thinking indeed comes in the form of a decisive divine declaration underscoring the universality of human dignity and removing any shadow of doubt about its being universal and inclusive of all individuals and races of the species. In this respect, we read the Qur'anic decree in the voice of the majestic We (al-Isrā', 17:70):

> *Now, indeed (laqad), We have conferred (karramnā) dignity on the children of Adam, and borne them over land and sea, and provided for them sustenance out of the good things of life, and favoured them far above most of Our creation.*

This verse has been one of the Qur'anic statements mostly pondered upon and discussed by Muslim scholars of different intellectual inclinations, both in the past and, particularly, at the present. Using an unmistakably intertextual approach guided by the principle of self-referenciality according to which the Qur'an is self-explanatory,[25] eminent exegetes exerted their minds to reflect upon this verse in light of others describing physical and non-physical characteristics of human beings in themselves that make them specifically different and uniquely worthy of divinely conferred dignity in contradistinction to other creatures in the world, including the angels. Such reflections are most of the time informed by theological, philosophical and moral arguments drawing upon scientific and historical knowledge about man that has been deployed to shed light on the many Qur'anic descriptions of man's bio-physical constitution and psycho-mental make-up and characteristics as a special creature of God.[26]

Similarly, this and many other verses have been a source of great inspiration and guidance to many Muslim scholars and researchers in the modern era in their intellectual engagement with modern secular and materialistic theories and ideologies on man and society. More specifically, the verse in question indeed constitutes the bedrock of most of contemporary Islamic intellectual works on human nature, human rights, social justice and political matters.[27]

With the use of the plural form denoting and including all individuals or instances of that to which it applies grammatically and conceptually, this verse, according to Ibn Ashur, is of the category of Qur'anic statements establishing universal or generic rules pertaining to a species or genre (*aḥkām al-nawʿ*). Thus, by the children of Adam (*banī Ādam*) is meant all mankind (*jamīʿ al-nawʿ*) as such, that is, without exclusion of any of its individuals or groups.[28] Interestingly, and differently from other verses describing scenes signalling the superior status of man, such as commanding the angels to prostrate themselves before Adam or declaring him as God's vicegerent and bearer of His trust on Earth, etc.,[29] the verse under consideration announces the divine conferment of dignity on all human beings and not just on Adam in such explicit and emphatic terms as would remove any possibility of conceiving the matter otherwise. As al-Alūsī expressed it, this verse indicates that "everyone and all (*qāṭibatan*) of the human race, both the pious and sinner, are endowed with dignity and nobility and with so many beautiful things and good qualities (*maḥāsin jammah*) that defy enumeration."[30] According to al-Rāghib al-Iṣfahānī, mankind is actually the peak and purpose of the whole creation, as all other creatures in the world are intended for the service of human beings.[31]

Five kinds of favours (*minan*) are stated in the verse as having been bestowed by God on human beings, namely (1) *takrīm*, (2 & 3) making both land and sea subservient for their movement, (4) providing for them sustenance out of good things, *ṭayyibāt*, and favouring (*tafḍīl*) them above most of the creation (5).[32] Being external to human beings' selves, the three things in the middle (2, 3 & 4) clearly refer to the material bounties and natural resources by the use of which human beings satisfy their various needs in life and are mentioned as instances or manifestation of *takrīm*, and hence do not call for much elaboration (as they will be dealt with in the next chapter in connection with *ḥifẓ al-māl*). Accordingly, *takrīm* and *tafḍīl* shall be the focus of the present discussion. Two linguistic remarks are in order.

1.   The particle *laqad* at the beginning of the verse, itself a combination of two particles (*lām* and *qad*) denoting corroboration and emphasis (*tawkīd*), doubly denotes emphatic confirmation of what comes next in the verse.

2.   The double emphasis pointed out above is multiplied, so to speak, by the use of the intensified verbal form *karrama*, from which is derived the term *takrīm*. Hence, as al-Jashmī observed, while *takrīm* and *ikrām* (from the verb *akrama*) convey linguistically the same general meaning deriving from the sense of dignity and nobility (*karāmah*), the term *takrīm* rather connotes repetition and reiteration (*takrīr*) as well as multiplication and intensification (*takthīr*).[33]

Applying almost equally to the term *tafḍīl*, these linguistic considerations are of unmistakable conceptual importance. They clearly imply that divinely conferred human dignity and favour are both permanent and increasing, thus recurring in and for all individuals of the human species. Now, what are the conceptual import and practical implications of *takrīm* and *tafḍīl* in human existence?

As already mentioned, the Islamic exegetical tradition has paid considerable attention to the verse under examination with special focus on these two terms. A main trend among the scholars can be easily discerned that distinguishes between them syntactically in respect of the predicate or subject matter of each term, though both terms concern human beings. In this distinction, *takrīm* pertains to humans as such and in themselves regardless of any external considerations, whereas *tafḍīl* is relational, thus concerning them in relation to other creatures. Accordingly, *takrīm* has to do with the inherent worth and intrinsic nobility of human beings emanating from their special conformation and constitution (*taqwīm & takwīn*), their particular shape and form (*ṣūrah*), their innate dispositions and essential qualities (*istiʿdādāt & ṣifāt dhātiyyah*), all of which being, of course, the work of God. Of the physical and non-physical things Muslim scholars usually mention in this context or refer to as unlimited, five come always to the forefront as essential, namely speech (*nuṭq*), discrimination (*tamyīz*), reason and intellect (*ʿaql*), knowledge and cognition (*maʿrifah*) and the peculiar physical shape and posture (*ṣūrah*).[34]

All these constitute outward and inward characteristics and capacities that are integral to, and distinctive of, the human beings. They set them apart as a different species from the rest of creatures in kind, not only in degree. Being themselves the result of divine bestowal, they constitute the special ground of God's conferring dignity on mankind, whereby that dignity becomes inherent and innate in each and every individual as a representation and embodiment of the whole species; this will be further corroborated in a while. We must here remember one important thing of far-reaching significance. Being God-given, human dignity in the Qur'anic view and, for that matter, in the monotheistic traditions in general, is emphatically nuanced from most conceptions thereof that perceive it as a fact or reality of nature seen in essentially or purely naturalistic terms, no matter how idealized it might be. Accordingly, rather than resulting from nature as such, which is itself created, our human nature and dignity derive from "our special relationship to God that distinguishes us from the rest of creation."[35]

Coming now to the term *tafḍīl*, the following can be said. As can be clearly discerned from the syntactic structure of the verse, the last phrase on *tafḍīl* (and favoured them far above most of Our creation) comes as a conclusion to what precedes it in terms of the enumerated external bounties (2, 3 & 4) which God has provided for mankind in the wide realm of creation and enabled human beings to make use of them for their own benefit. This power of making use (*tasallut, istīlā', ghalabah*) of the things of the world by means of thinking (*ra'y*) and technique (*ḥīlah*) actually combines all aspects of mankind's favouring and elevation over most of the creation. Likewise, *tafḍīl* is consequent upon, and derivative of, *takrīm*, whence follows man's superiority and elevation in relation to other creatures within the context of the fundamental concept of *taskhīr* by virtue of which God has made the things of the world subservient to mankind.[36]

To sum up, by its explicit declaration of human beings' universal inherent dignity and relational superiority the verse we have been examining can be seen as a condensed recapitulation of all what is positively said about them in the Qur'an as well as the bounties bestowed upon them, which makes them such a unique and special species in the cosmic order of God's creation. The fact that man is described as God's *handiwork* that has been ennobled and given the essence of life by what is breathed into it of the divine spirit (*rūḥ*) is indeed a further and more resounding indication of the inherent worth and superiority of human beings. This is clearly expressed in the following Qur'anic verses (Ṣād, 38:71-75):

> [71] *[For,] Lo, thy Sustainer said unto the angels: "Behold, I am about to create a human being out of clay;* [72] *and when I have formed him fully and breathed into him of My spirit (nafakhtu fīhi min rūhī), fall you down before him in prostration!"* [73] *Thereupon the angels prostrated themselves, all of them together,* [74] *save Iblis: he gloried in his arrogance, and [thus] became one of those who deny the truth.* [75] *Said He: "O Iblis! What has kept thee from prostrating thyself before that [being] which I have created with My hands (mā mana'āka an tasjuda limā khalaqtu bi-yadayya)? Art thou too proud [to bow down before another created being], or art thou of those who think [only] of themselves as high?"*

As far as the Qur'anic account of human genesis is concerned, these verses are the earliest in the chronological sequence of revelation.[37] What may be seen as quite special about them is that they unequivocally bring into prominence the singularity and uniqueness of man as the creature whom God has created with His hands, formed fully and breathed into it of His spirit. While most of the creation, as the Qur'an tells us, come into existence by virtue of the divine majestic overwhelming will and imperative command (*kun fa-yakūn*), man's case appears to be rather different in terms of the mode of his creation (*khalq*), formation (*taswiyyah*) and animation, i.e., his endowment with the principle of life through the breathing into his body of the divine spirit. In all these essential aspects of his existence, man is attributed directly to God as being His *handiwork*. No matter how allegorical this and similar Qur'anic phrases pertaining to the creation of man might be, one of its special significations is that it epitomizes mankind's closeness to God and uniqueness and singularity in relation to other creatures.[38] This peculiarity of the process of man's coming into being has resulted in what the Qur'an has quintessentially summarized by the statement (al-Tīn, 95:4): "Verily, We [God] create man in the best conformation," thus encompassing all aspects of human existence and being outwardly as well as inwardly.[39]

The portrayal in the Qur'an of human existence, nobility, worth, vocation and destiny as willed by God, the Creator and Sustainer of all beings, goes in most cases hand in hand with an exposition of their antithesis and opposites. This is exemplified ontologically and metaphysically by Satan and his evil whisperings and promptings; internally and psychologically by human beings' own selves with their whims, vagaries, and weaknesses; and externally, in between, by fellow humans and various socio-cultural forces and circumstances, all of which remain beyond our present purpose to deal with here, but which certainly bear significantly on the issues discussed in this chapter and in the whole book.[40] However, one essential fact must not escape our attention at this juncture. As a fundamental and universal reality in the Qur'an, human dignity and superiority as manifested and embodied in human beings' characteristics and capacities has always at its helm man's "ability to discern between what is true and what is false," hence having "no excuse for not realizing God's existence and oneness." In other words, "the prospect of spiritual self-destruction" is the consequence of "a wilful disregard of the fact of God's existence and oneness, which is the core of all religious cognition and, hence, of all true prophethood."[41]

It follows from this that man's intrinsic or inherent dignity and his superiority in relation to other creatures are not merely gratuitous things or a matter of idle play, in the sense that "he is to be left to himself, to go about at will." (al-Qiyāmah, 75:36) Rather, this singularity and privileged status entail on the part of human beings the sense of gratitude and thankfulness as well as responsibility and accountability in relation to themselves, fellow humans, the rest of creation and ultimately and in the first place to God. This is because obligation, responsibility and accountability, being a corollary of, and consequent upon, freedom and choice and consistently with justice, are what makes man truly worthy of the bounties and favours bestowed on him.[42] It is undoubtedly in light of this that we can realize the significance of Muslim jurists' deliberations on the question of *taklīf* or obligation and its conditions in general and legal capacity (*alhliyyah*) in particular, the latter being the basis for both the entitlement to rights and bearing of duties,[43] all of which flow from the concept of dignity of which *'aql*, as comprehension, discernment and judgement, is the greatest manifestation.

The concept of human dignity in the Qur'an as we have attempted to elucidate its meaning in this section closely connects with, and builds on, what has already been discussed in the first chapter, and equally relates to what is dealt with in the next. Thus understood, it provides the eternal and essential ground of the sanctity and inviolability of human life whose protection and enhancement is one of the universal necessary goals of the Sharī'ah under all circumstances. It should be remembered that the sanctity of human life derives from the fact that mankind, as taught in the Qur'an (al-Ḥijr, 15:29; al-Anbiyā', 21:91; al-al-Sajdah, 32:9; Ṣād, 38:72; al-Taḥrīm, 66:12), is the recipient of a divine spirit breathed into each and every human person. In other words, we may argue that the human person to a certain extent partakes in the divine nobility and sublimity. This lays the ground for Islamic humanism at its best idealism and most realism, beyond all kinds of reductionism and vilification as well as over-glorification and idealization.[44] In fact, dignity is the bedrock and underlying principle of all rights and entitlements as well as obligations and responsibilities of both the individuals and society all through the wide range and different domains of human life and existence.[45]

The Sharīʿah Approach to *ḥifẓ al-nafs*

The phrase *ḥifẓ al-nafs* as used by Muslim scholars of Islamic jurisprudence revolves around the care for, and protection of, human life as exemplified by, and embodied in, concrete human individuals who are the real and ultimate constituents of society and the actual agents of societal development and civilization building. As is implied by Ibn Khaldūn, human social association and civilization (*ijtimāʿ, ʿumrān*) cannot exist and endure without realizing the great purpose of protecting human life, together with the other necessary universal goals for which the rules of the Sharīʿah have been enacted. Conversely, human beings cannot attain well-being and accomplishment and ensure the survival of their species except in the context of a proper socio-political order maintaining peace and security in their lives. All of this, for Ibn Khaldūn, emanates from the greatness of mankind as opposed to the rest of animal creatures.[46]

As such, human beings are inherently and innately bearers of the universal dignity their Creator has conferred upon their species. This God-given original dignity is the ground in which is rooted the notion of *ḥifẓ al-nafs* as the translation and manifestation of the most fundamental human right in the world, namely the right to life (*ḥaqq al-ḥayāt*) which constitutes the foundation of all other human rights, such as the rights to freedom, security, property, etc. In fact, such rights "are meaningful only in relation to living persons and almost worthless in relation to the deceased," hence the non-negotiability of the right to life.[47] Considering human dignity as the basis of all human rights is not in the Qur'an a matter of merely establishing a general theoretical principle or preaching an ideal. Rather, in its teachings it emphatically resuscitates in one the feeling and consciousness of one's dignity and provides specific and detailed rules to translate and actualize it in all spheres of life.[48]

Accordingly, as Ibn Ashur put it, the "preservation of human souls (*ḥifẓ al-nufūs*) means to protect human lives from being ruined either individually or collectively. This is because society or the human world (*'ālam*) comprises the individuals of the human species, and every single soul has its specific characteristics that are essential for the existence and survival of the human world."[49] In other words, Islam is equally concerned about both the individuals and society at the same time. This is because, as already stated, society comprises the individuals of the human species and every single soul or human person has specific characteristics and qualities that are essential for the existence and survival of mankind in the world, let alone the divine spirit breathed into each and every individual making him/her directly linked to the absolute being of God the Creator and Sustainer.

According to Abū Isḥāq al-Shāṭibī (d. 790H/1383AD) and other scholars before and after him, the Sharīʿah has adopted a twofold approach in order to ensure that this central and universal goal of safeguarding people's lives and protecting their selves at all levels of their being and existence be attained and sustained. This approach operates in two complementary ways, just as it does in respect of the preservation of all other essential universals or *ḍarūriyyāt*, namely *dīn* (religion/faith), *'aql* (intellect/reason), *nasl* (progeny/offspring) and *māl* (property/wealth) taken as the fundamentals and pillars (*uṣūl, arkān*) on which human society and civilization stand.[50] Likewise, their realization, safeguarding and enhancement constitute the ultimate purpose for which the Sharīʿah commands and rules have been promulgated, as they constitute the core and principles of human good on which all else depends. In other words, the twofold strategy just mentioned pertains mainly to the means and mechanisms by which these five universals are attained and maintained.[51] As will be shown in some detail in the following pages, the Sharīʿah approach to realizing *ḥifẓ al-nafs* consists of a positive and proactive aspect (*jānib al-wujūd*) on the one hand, and a 'negative', reactive or preventive aspect (*jānib al-'adam*) on the other. To put it in the language of al-Ghazālī and al-Rāzī, the said strategy consists of both *taḥṣīl* and *ibqā'*, that is, realization and preservation.[52]

1. The positive proactive aspect of ḥifẓ al-nafs

The issue here is to establish human life and strengthen its foundations by bringing it into existence in the first place through the natural process of procreation. In Islam as in most cultural and social traditions of the world since time immemorial, the normal means of such process is nothing but sanctioned and legitimate sexual relationship through marriage between man and woman, the two indispensable and inseparable facets and sides of the human race, regardless of any details of ethical or legal nature. Without such a relationship and natural path to *human procreation and production*, no new-born humans can be expected or imaginable in any normal way of being human, no matter what claims and promises latter-day prophets of cloning science and technology might make on the so-called *artificial human reproduction*, let aside what has been described as dreams and illusions and even nightmares.[53]

Put differently, and irrespective of the various forms marriage and the family might have taken in different times and climes, they stand at the root of the coming into being of human life, thus submitting to, and fulfilling, a natural universal law regulating not only human existence and survival in the world, but also that of many other species of the animal kingdom. This is part and parcel of the cosmic norm and order of the creation as willed and ordained by God, the Creator (*Khāliq*) and Originator (*Fāṭir*) of all existents. Hence, marriage and the family are "intimately connected with each other," whether or not marriage "is rooted in family, rather than family in marriage."[54] However, Islam's concern about, and care for, human life is not confined to being, that is, to the coming of human beings from non-existence (*'adam*) into existence (*wujūd*). It is equally, if not more, concerned about their becoming and destiny. Likewise, Islam cares very much about human beings' growth, development and well-being in an integrated and balanced manner throughout all stages of their life-journey from birth to death, as well as about their salvation in the Hereafter.

Indeed, as mentioned in the previous chapter, it will not be an exaggeration to say that this concern predates our birth and covers the pre-natal stages of our embryonic and foetal development in the wombs of our mothers. Taking special care of the mother during pregnancy, physically, psychologically and socially, is in actual fact and by extension caring for the little human creature dwelling and growing inside her, for anything affecting the physical health and psychological condition of the mother affects one way or another the potential human being she carries in her womb. Once born, it is the parents' immediate duty and inescapable responsibility to look after the upbringing of their offspring throughout the stages of babyhood, childhood and adolescence up to puberty and maturity age. This takes the form of careful parenting and looking after the children by providing for their basic needs of food, clothing, shelter, education, and other types of care such as education, so as to ensure their growth and development in a healthy and balanced manner, emotionally, physically and mentally. This is necessary and vital in order to prepare the person for more self-reliance in the subsequent stages of his/her life and equip him/her with the adequate means and skills to face the requirements of his/her responsibility as a member of the family and society.[55]

Should parental upbringing fail partially or totally due to natural events (such as the death of one of the parents or both) or socio-cultural circumstances (such as divorce of the spouses or their failure to assume their natural task as parents for any reason), it is incumbent upon the whole society right from next of kin and neighbours up to government agencies through different social bodies and organizations to take up this task and not leave the baby, child or adolescent to face an uncertain future and fateful destiny.

To ensure the functionality of this multifaceted and crucial purpose of the proactive and constructive aspect of the protection of human life, Islam, both in the Qur'an and the Prophetic traditions (*Sunnah*), has laid down various rules and set up different mechanisms the implications and applications of which have been elaborated and articulated by Muslim scholars in much detail both in legal and ethical terms, as can be seen in specialized *fiqh* compendia and other kinds of Islamic writings, both by classical and contemporary scholars. Historically speaking, institutions of *zakāh* and *waqf* did, and continue to, play impactful roles in Muslim societies by taking care of different categories of needy people, including orphans, and fulfilling various kinds of their needs depending on the cases and situations. It goes without saying that human life does not prosper simply through the fulfillment of material and physical needs as just outlined. There are other equally, and perhaps more, important needs that are necessary to the wholeness and balance of human life and personality. The satisfaction of such needs depends on the socio-cultural environment and political and economic system and the general atmosphere that nurture in each and every individual and group in the society the sense of security, justice, respect and dignity, and minimizes all feeling of alienation, estrangement and deprivation.[56]

However, the rich stock of ideas and experiences in the Islamic heritage and Muslim millennial legacies concerning the aspect under consideration is in much need to be contextualized and developed to suit the emerging needs of modern Muslim societies. Then, it has to be systematically operationalized in the form of educational programmes, social policies and legal regimes and procedures to satisfy the requirements of the protection and promotion of human life in such an efficient manner as would meet the challenges of the modern age posed as much by its scientific and technological advancements as by its human and ecological failures and social dislocations and breakdowns.[57]

2. The preventive 'reactive' aspect of ḥifẓ al-nafs

Just as the Sharī'ah has laid down rules and measures and taught values and norms for bringing about, enhancing and promoting human life in a positive and proactive manner, it has also made sure that once in existence human life is not object of harm and destructive action whether by external natural and/or human agents or through self-infliction such as suicide. Islam's categorical abhorrence of, and unshakable stand against aggression on human life and homicide are indeed uncompromising. Accordingly, the Qur'an has considered killing one person equivalent to killing all mankind, and conversely saving the life of one person equal to saving all of mankind. This unshakable position has been translated in the law of just retribution (*qiṣāṣ*) as stipulated in a number of Qur'anic verses to be seen shortly. Likewise, "human life, which has been declared inviolable by God, can only be destroyed for just cause."[58] The following verse lays down the general principle underpinning the prescribed law of *qiṣāṣ* in such a way that makes it a means to serving and promoting the universal value of the inviolability and sanctity of human life. Hence, it states that (al-Mā'idah, 5:32),

> *[I]f anyone slays a human being—unless it be [in punishment] for murder or for spreading corruption on earth—it shall be as though he had slain all mankind; whereas, if anyone saves a life, it shall be as though he had saved the lives of all mankind.*

Unlike modern secularized legal thinking which deems as crimes against humanity those deliberate acts which are typically part of a systematic campaign, and cause human suffering or death on a large scale,[59] the Qur'an takes a categorically different stand by seeing in the crime against one person a crime against all humanity. This emanates from Islam's view of human beings not merely in quantitative numerical terms, but more significantly in a qualitative way according to which each and every individual carries in himself/herself the essential worth and universal value of humanity inscribed in his/her inborn original nature (*fiṭrah*) by the Creator and Lord of the universe. As elaborated above, it is God Himself who has sanctioned and sublimated this essential humanity through the universal dignity (*takrīm*) which He conferred upon the children of Adam with full consideration of their complex and multidimensional nature and constitution in which materiality, spirituality, morality and rationality go hand in hand in an inextricably integrated manner shunning all bifurcation of the human person.[60]

In the spirit of this essential universal worth and dignity, the law of just retribution, legislated for intentional and deliberate killing of people, has been emphasized on different occasions by the Qur'an which places homicide among the gravest sins next to denying God's existence or associating other deities with Him. Thus we read in sūrah al-Furqān (25:68):

> *... and who never invoke any [imaginary] deity side by side with God,*
> *and do not take any human being's life—[the life] which God has*
> *willed to be sacred—otherwise than in [the pursuit of] justice, and do*
> *not commit adultery. And [know that] he who commits aught*
> *thereof shall [not only] meet with a full requital.*

Warning against the gravest sins a person is doomed by committing any of them, the Prophet (peace be upon him) is reported to have said:

> *Avoid the seven sins that doom one to Hell: Associating others with*
> *God (shirk), magic, killing a soul whom God has forbidden killing,*
> *consuming usury (ribā), consuming the property of orphans, fleeing on*
> *the day of the march (to the battlefield), and slandering chaste women.*[61]

The law of just retribution is not the only way of dealing with homicide and violation of the sanctity of people's lives in Islam, as this punishment only caters for its worldly punishment. Greater and more fateful punishment awaits those committing it in the Hereafter, as clearly stated in the Qur'an (al-Nisā', 4:93) according to which

> *whoever deliberately slays another believer, his requital shall be hell,*
> *therein to abide; and God will condemn him, and will reject him, and*
> *will prepare for him awesome suffering.*

The importance of just retribution has been further emphasized in the Qur'an in the form of a short dictum summarizing its ultimate objective as being the protection of society and humanity as a whole and not merely a revenge against the murderer. Hence, the divine compelling maxim has announced to people of sound minds that "there is life in the law of just retribution." (al-Baqarah, 2:179) This is because the very existence of such a law as an integral part of the legal system (especially the penal code), which serves the crucial purpose of maintaining peace, justice and order in society, plays a very crucial and effective role by deterring people from the very idea of contemplating taking-off someone else's life, simply because the consequence will be losing one's own life. Severe as it may appear, the capital punishment on homicide as prescribed in the Qur'an does not violate any of the universal and essential values and principles necessary for people's well-being and the proper working of human society and civilization, notably the value and imperative of justice; it is simply what justice requires. Otherwise, the door will be wide-open for anyone to kill anyone for whatever reason or pretext that might motivate, and used to justify, such an act.

Of course, Islam neither denies nor ignores the causing of people's death or infliction of lesser harms by mistake, in which respect it has also provided appropriate rules for dealing with its aftermath in a variety of ways depending on the nature of the obtaining cases and ensuing consequences. This has been described in detail in the following verse (al-Nisā': 4:92):

> *And it is not conceivable that a believer should slay another believer, unless it be by mistake. And upon him who has slain a believer by mistake there is the duty of freeing a believing soul from bondage and paying an indemnity to the victim's relations, unless they forgo it by way of charity. Now if the slain, while himself a believer, belonged to a people who are at war with you, [the penance shall be confined to] the freeing of a believing soul from bondage; whereas, if he belonged to a people to whom you are bound by a covenant, [it shall consist of] an indemnity to be paid to his relations in addition to the freeing of a believing soul from bondage. And he who does not have the wherewithal shall fast [instead] for two consecutive months. (This is) the atonement ordained by God: and God is indeed all-knowing, wise.*

Whatever the penal policy of the Sharī'ah vis-á-vis the ruining of human life deliberately or by m istake, lesser harms that might be intentionally inflicted upon people's bodies are also duly attended to by the Sharī'ah in the same spirit of justice in accordance with the gravity of harm. As it is not our aim here to undertake a detailed analysis of how Islam has dealt with those lesser harms from the juridical and legal point of view, it would suffice to point out that the matter has been firmly established in the Qur'an and the Prophetic traditions which are the foundational sources of the Sharī'ah and explicated and elaborated extensively by Muslim jurists to work out proper measures and mechanisms that would ensure the removal of the harm or at least the reduction of its effect. Reflecting on the philosophy underlying Islamic criminal justice, Ibn Ashur summarizes the over-all purpose of the Sharī'ah in all types of punishment, especially the fixed penalties (*ḥudūd*) and just retribution (*qiṣāṣ*), as consisting of "three objectives: to reform the criminal, to satisfy the victim, and to deter the imitator of criminals"[62] or potential criminal.

Islam's concern about the protection of human life from aggression and the violation of the individual's personality is not confined to the material and physical aspects, as humans are not mere biological machines to be maintained and lubricated in order to keep them operating. Rather, it is as much concerned about the non-material being of the individual for whom the emotional, moral, and spiritual elements are essential and decisive in the making of one's character and self-identity as an independent entity and responsible and efficacious agent in society. This is clearly epitomized by the categorical punishment prescribed by the Qur'an against slander and defamation which is only superseded by the punishment for homicide and adultery. Hence it is stipulated that (al-Nūr, 24:4)

> *for those who accuse chaste women [of adultery], and then are unable*
> *to produce four witnesses [in support of their accusation], flog them*
> *with eighty stripes; and ever after refuse to accept from them any tes-*
> *timony—since it is they, they that are truly depraved!*

Although the direct reference in the verse is to the accusation of 'fortified women' (*muḥṣanāt*) of pervert conduct whether by their husbands or by others, the princple it establishes actually applies to each and everyone, regardless of gender or social status. This punishment is aimed at protecting people's character and personality from being tarnished and undermined by false accusations and gratuitous allegations, for which reason a number of Muslim scholars viewed the protection of honour (*ḥifẓ al-'irḍ*) as part of the *ḍarūriyyāt* category of the Sharī'ah goals, or at least closely related to it.[63] For that matter, the Qur'an has strongly condemned and clearly forbidden all verbal and non-verbal acts aimed at belittling and deriding people and harming them psychologically and morally and undermining them socially, as clearly stated in the following verses (al-Ḥujurāt, 49:11-12):

> *O you who have attained to faith! No men shall <u>deride</u> [other] men: it*
> *may well be that those [whom they deride] are better than themselves;*

and no women [shall deride other] women: it may well be that those [whom they deride] are better than themselves. And neither shall you <u>defame</u> one another, nor <u>insult</u> one another by [opprobrious] epithets: evil is all imputation of iniquity after [one has attained to] faith; and they who [become guilty thereof and] do not repent—it is they, they who are evildoers! O you who have attained to faith! Avoid most <u>guesswork</u> [about one another]—for, behold, some of [such] guesswork is [in itself] a sin; and do not spy upon one another, and neither allow yourselves to <u>speak ill</u> of one another behind your backs. Would any of you like to eat the flesh of his dead brother? Nay, you would loathe it!

Likewise, derision, insult, defamation, ill-thinking of people and back-biting them are all stated together in the same context as things that both men and women are enjoined not to commit against one another. All these practices are of non-physical nature and are prohibited because of the psycho-moral and socio-cultural harm they cause to the individuals or groups targeted thereby.[64]

While the Qur'an considers murder as one of the gravest sins a person might commit against another person or a group of people, second only to associating other deities with God, it is no less categorical with regard to self-killing and bringing one's life to an end, whether or not assisted. As such, suicide is not only a crime against one's own self; it is also a crime against humanity. Moreover, it is a crime against the will of God Himself Who is the bestower of life and its real and ultimate owner, including the human body itself which is the vehicle thereof, wherefrom human dignity and the sanctity of life actually derive, as we have already explained. Thus, we read in the Qur'an,

1. *And spend in God's cause, and let not you own hands throw you into self-destruction.* (al-Baqarah, 2:195)

2. *you who have attained to faith! Do not devour one another's possessions wrongfully—not even by way of trade based on mutual agreement—and do not destroy one another (wa la taqtulū anfusakum): for, behold, God is indeed a dispenser of grace unto you!* (al-Nisā', 4:29)

Despite the fact that these Qur'anic statements may appear unyielding of direct evidence as to the unlawfulness and prohibition of suicide, the latter can be implied as a particular instance of its general import on forbidding self-destruction. Whatever the case may be, suicide is no doubt and ultimately an act of homicide (*qatl al-nafs*), the latter being categorically condemned and prohibited in the Qur'an with severe punishment for committing it. And yet, in order to remove any possibility of interpretive doubt in relation to the killing of oneself, the Prophet has declared in clear-cut statements that,

1. *Whoever hurls himself down from a mountain and thus kills himself will be in Hell hurling himself down therein, abiding therein and being accommodated therein for ever; whoever takes poison and thus kills himself, his poison will be in his hand; he will be tasting it in Hell, always abiding therein, and being accommodated therein forever; and whoever kills himself with a weapon, his weapon will be in his hand; he will be plunging it into his belly in Hell, abiding therein forever.*[65]

2. *He who commits suicide by throttling himself shall keep on throttling himself in the Hell-Fire (forever), and he who commits suicide by stabbing himself shall keep on stabbing himself in the Hell-Fire.*[66]

   And whoever commits suicide with piece of iron will be punished with the same piece of iron in the Hell-Fire.[67]

From these as well as from other traditions, "it appears that the sin of suicide is not less than that of murder." The suicider "will permanently reside in hell, as he killed a soul which remembered God, or which, if alive, would have remembered Him. Suicide is the result of pangs and overwhelming anxieties which are in turn so many boons for leading a man to Paradise."[68] That is, such anxieties and bangs are part of the tests and trials of life in this world which one should with patience and trust in God's succour and mercy. Thus, rather than withdrawing through the easy exit of suicide which results in absolute loss, one should turn such trials and tests into a means to salvation and eternal bliss.[69]

Finally, it is worth mentioning that though described as 'negative' or reactive, this aspect of *ḥifẓ al-nafs* is not passive in the sense of waiting until homicide or any other kinds of crime and harm against human life take place and then come for the remedial of their aftermath. As rightly argued by Ibn Ashur, despite its severity the law of just retribution is the weakest means for protecting human souls, because it consists of only a partial remedy of the loss. In his view, the most important way for protecting human life is to prevent harm and ruin before they happen, such as combating and eradicating epidemics.[70] In line with this, we can argue that it is part and parcel of Islam's preventive measures for protecting and invigorating human life to combat the cultural and social roots of all types of aggression and violation against human life through adequate education and proper socialization that would instill in people's consciousness the sense of sanctity (*ḥurmah*), and inviolability (*'iṣmah*) of the human soul and people's lives.[71]

Conclusion

Regardless of the different rules and detailed measures provided by the Sharī'ah for the protection, consolidation and promotion of human life through its twofold approach or strategy as outlined above, one very important fact must always be kept in mind. That strategy is based on Islam's fundamental view of the worth and position of human beings as God's stewards and trustees on earth, their entitlements and rights as well as their duties, obligations and responsibilities all stem from the inalienable original dignity conferred upon them by their Creator as well as from the inviolability of their being. This holds under all conditions provided they do not transgress their boundaries and infringe upon one another's life and existence physically, materially or morally, in which case the law has to interfere and settle matters within the parameters of justice and equity.

Notes

[1] Al-Farāhīdī, *Kitāʿb al-ʿAyn*, vol. 4, p. 249.

[2] Abū ʿUbayd Aḥmad b. Muḥammad al-Harawī, *al-Gharībayn fī'l-Qur'ān wa'l-Ḥadīth*, ed. Ahmad Farid al-Muzayyidi (Makkah al-Mukarramah/Riyadh: Maktabat Nizār Musṭafā al-Bāz, 1st edn., 1419/1999), vol. 5, p. 1869; Ibn Sīdeh (d. 458 AH), *al-Muḥkam wa'l-Muḥīṭ al-Aʿẓam*, vol. 8, p. 525; Ibn Manẓūr, *Lisān al-ʿArab*, vol. 6, p. 233; al-Zabīdī, *Tāj al-ʿArūs*, vol. 16, p. 559 & 561; Ismāʿīl b. Ḥammād al-Jawharī (d. slightly before 400H), *al-Ṣiḥāḥ: Tāj al-Lughah wa-Ṣiḥāḥ al-ʿArabiyyah*, ed. Ahmad Abd al-Ghafur ʿAttar (Beirut: Dār al-ʿIlm li'l-Malāyīn, 3rd edn., 1404/1984 [1376/1956]), vol. 3, p. 984; Lane, *An Arabic-English Lexicon*, vol. 8, p. 2827.

[3] See, from the lexicographical point of view, Ibn Manẓūr, *Lisān al-ʿArab*, vol. 6, pp. 233-335; al-Zabīdī, *Tāj al-ʿArūs*, vol. 16, pp. 559-564 (extensively quoting al-Suhaylī). From other perspectives (theological, philosophical and mystical, etc.), see, Abū Ḥātim al-Rāzī, *Kitāb al-Zīnah*, ed. Said al-Ghanimi (Beirut/Freiburg: Al-Kamel Verlag, 2015), pp. 364-317; Abū ʿAbd al-Raḥmān al-Sulamī, *ʿUyūb al-Nafs*, ed. Majdi Fathi al-Sayyid (Tanta: Dār al-Saḥābah, 2nd edn., 1413/1993); Ibn Sīnā, *al-Shifā': al-Ṭabīʿiyyāt, VI: al-Nafs*, ed. Georges Anawati & Saeed Zayed (Cairo: al-Hay'ah al-Miṣriyyah al-ʿĀmmah li'l-Kitāb, 1395/1975), pp. 1-237; also its English version: *Avicenna's Psychology*, trans. F. Rahman (Connecticut: Hyperion Press, Inc., 1981 [1952]); Abū ʿAlī Aḥmad b. Muḥammad b. Yaʿqūb Miskawayh, *Tahdhīb al-Akhlāq*, ed. ʿImad al-Hilali (Freiburg, Germany: Al-Kamel Verlag, 2011), pp. 237-262; Abū Ḥāmid Muḥammad b. Muḥammad b. Muḥammad al-Ghazālī, *Maʿārij al-Quds fī Maʿrifat al-Nafs*, edited and with an introduction by Ahmed Shamshuddin (Beirut: Dār al-Kutub al-ʿIlmiyyah, 1st edn., 1409/1988), pp. 39-172; Fakhr al-Dīn Muḥammad b. ʿUmar al-Rāzī, *Kitāb al-Nafs wa'l-Rūḥ wa-Sharḥ Quwāhumā*, ed. Muhammad Saghir Hassan al-Maʿsumi (Islamabad: Islamic Research Institute, 1968); also his *al-Tafsīr al-Kabīr*, vol. 26, pp. 37-54; Abū ʿAbd Allāh Muḥammad b. Abī Bakr b. Ayyūb Ibn Qayyim al-Jawziyyah, *Kitāb al-Rūḥ*, ed. Muhammad Ajmal Ayyub al-Isahi (Makkah al-Mukarramah: Sulaiman Bin Abdul Aziz Al Rajhi Charitable Foundation, 1st edn., 1433 H), pp. 613-621; Muhammad Ali Abu Rayyan, *Uṣūl al-Falsafah al-Ishrāqiyyah ʿinda Shihāb al-Dīn al-Suhrawardī* (Beirut: Dār al-Ṭalabah al-ʿArab, 1969), pp. 285-342; al-Bahiy al-Khuli, *Ādam ʿalayhi al-Salām: Falsafat Taqwīm al-Insān wa-Khilāfatih* (Cairo: Dār al-Turāth, 1985), pp. 21-24; al-Tabataba'i, *al-Mīzān fī Tafsīr al-Qur'ān*, vol. 20, pp. 189-191; Muhammad Sayyid Ahmad al-Musayyar, *al-Rūḥ fī Dirāsāt al-Mutakallimīn wa'l-Falāsifah* (Cairo: Dār al-Maʿārif, 2nd edn., 1988); Gaven Picken, *Spiritual Purification in Islam: The Life and Works of al-Muḥāsibī* (London & New York: Routledge, 2011), pp. 124-159; Naim Döner, "Mafhūm al-Rūḥ wa'l-Nafs fī Ḍaw' Āyāt al-Qur'ān al-Karīm", *BÜIFD: Bingöl University Faculty of Theology Journal*, No. 11 (2018/2), pp. 29-63.

[4] Ibn Manẓūr, *Lisān al-ʿArab*, vol. 6, p. 234; Ibn Sīdeh, *al-Muḥkam wa'l-Muḥīṭ al-Aʿẓam*, vol. 8, p. 525; al-Zabīdī, *Tāj al-ʿArūs*, vol. 16, p. 569; al-Farāhīdī, *Kitāʿb al-ʿAyn*, vol. 4, p. 249. See also, Aḥamd b. Muḥammad b. ʿAlī al-Muqrī al-

Fayyūmī, *al-Miṣbāḥ al-Munīr fī Gharīb al-Sharḥ al-Kabīr li'l-Rāfiʿī*, ed. Abdul Azim al-Shennawi (Cairo: Dār al-Maʿārif, 2nd edn., n.d.), p. 617; Ahmad Rida, *Muʿjam Matn al-Lughah: Mawsūʿah Lughawiyyah Ḥadithah* (Beirut: Dār Maktabat al-Ḥayāt, 1380/1960), vol. 5, p. 514.

[5] Mohammed Fuad Abdel-Baqi, *al-Muʿjam al-Mufahras li-Alfāẓ al-Qur'ān al-Karīm* (Cairo: Dār al-Kutub al-Miṣriyyah, 1364H), pp. 710-714.

[6] Ibid., pp. 93-94. It should also be mentioned here that the generic term *ins*, signifying the human kind as distinctive from other species (especially the *jinn*), and the plural *nās* referring to the plurality of human beings do occur in the Qur'an 18 and 224 respectively. Ibid., pp. 93 & 726-729; Laleh Bakhtiar, *Concordance of the Sublime Qur'an* (Chicago: Library of Islam & Kazi Publications, 2011), p. 511-512.

[7] See in this respect, al-Balkhī, *al-Wujūh wa'l-Naẓā'ir fi'l-Qur'ān al-Karīm*, pp. 120-121; al-Sharīf al-Murtaḍā ʿAlī b. al-Ḥusayn al-Mūsawī al-ʿAlawī, *Ghurar al-Fawā'id wa-Durar al-Qalā'id*, known as *Amālī al-Murtaḍā*, ed. Mohammed Abul Fadl Ibrahim (Beirut: al-Maktabah al-ʿAṣriyyah, 1426/2005), vol. 1, pp. 317-320; al-Ghazālī, *Maʿārij al-Quds*, p. 39; Ibn Qayyim al-Jawziyyah, *Kitāb al-Rūḥ*, pp. 622-667; ʿAbd al-Raḥmān al-Suhaylī, *al-Rawḍ al-Unuf fi Sharḥ al-Sīrah al-Nabawiyyah*, ed. Abdul Rahman al-Wakil (Cairo: Dār al-Kutub al-Ḥadīthah, 1st edn., 1378/1967), vol. 3, pp. 191-192; Muhammad Qutb, *Dirāsāt fi'l-Nafs al-Insāniyyah* (Cairo-Beirut: Dār al-Shurūq, 10th edn., 1414/1993); Ahmed Omar Hashim & Gmal Mady Abou El Azayem, *al-Nafs fi'l-Qur'ān* (Cairo: Dār al-Fayṣal, 1996); Nizar al-Ani, *al-Shakhṣiyyah al-Insāniyyah fi'l-Turāth al-Islāmī* (Amman: The International Institute of Islamic Thought, 1st edn., 1918/1998); Abdelamjid al-Najjar, *Maqāṣid al-Sharīʿah bi-Abʿād Jadīdah* (Beirut: Dār al-Gharb al-Islāmī, 1st edn., 2006), pp. 84-85.

[8] See also, Ṣād (38:71), al-Isrā' (17:61), al-Kahf (18:50), al-Aʿrāf, 7:11).

[9] Muhammad Hadi Maʿrafah, *al-Tamhīd fī ʿUlūm al-Qur'ān* (Beirut: Dār al-Taʿāruf li'l-Maṭbūāat, 1432/2011), vol. 3, p. 20.

[10] Abū Manṣūr Muḥammad b. Aḥmad al-Azharī, *Tahdhīb al-Lughah*, ed. Abdul Salam Mohamed Harun *et al.* (Cairo: Dār al-Qawmiyyah al-ʿArabiyyah li'l-Ṭibāʿah, 1384/1964), vol. 13, p. 117.

[11] Ibn Manẓūr, *Lisān al-ʿArab*, vol. 14, p. 401. According to some eminent lexigrophers and linguists, such as Abū Isḥāq al-Zajjāj and al-Jawharī, *ism* does not only imply the sense of *tasmiyyah* or designating something by giving it a specific name as a sign distinguishing it from other things; hence, being equivalent in meaning to the word *ʿalamah*. It also denotes the sense of raising, elevation and upliftment, thus being derived from the word *sumuw*, and implying that a thing given a name has been brought into prominence (*rifʿah*). See for example, Ismāʿīl b. Ḥammād al-Jawharī, *al-Ṣiḥāḥ: Tāj al-Lughah wa-Ṣiḥāḥ al-ʿArabiyyah*, ed. Ahmad Abd al-Ghafur ʿAttar (Beirut: Dār al-ʿIlm li'l-Malāyīn, 4th edn., 1990), p. 2383; al-Iṣfahānī, *Mufradāt Alfāẓ al-Qur'ān*, p. 428; al-Azharī, *Tahdhīb al-Lughah*, vol. 13, p. 117; Ibn Manẓūr, *ibid.* p. 401 & 397; al-Zabīdī, *Tāj al-ʿArūs*, vol. 38, pp. 305-306.

[12] Asad, *The Message of the Qur'an*, p. 10, note 23 & p. 514, note 83. For elaborate analysis and argumentation on what we have summarized here see for

example: al-Ṭabarī, *Jāmiʿ al-Bayān,* vol. 1, p. 484; Abū ʿAlī al-Faḍl b. al-Ḥasan al-Ṭabarsī, *Majmaʿ al-Bayān fī Tafsīr al-Qurʾān,* ed. Hashim al-Rasuli al-Mahallati & Fadlullah al-Tabataba'i (Beirut: Dar El-Marefah, 1408/1988),vol. 1-2, p. 180; Abū al-Ḥasan ʿAlī b. Ḥabīb al-Māwardī al-Baṣrī, *al-Nukat wa'l-ʿUyūn* (Beirut: Dār al-Kutub al-ʿIlmiyyah & Mu'assassat al-Kutub al-Thaqāfiyyah, n.d.), vol. 1, p. 99; Abū al-Qāsim Jār Allāh Maḥmūd b. ʿUmar al-Zamakhsharī al-Khuwārizmī, *Tafsīr al-Kashshāf,* ed. Khalil Ma'moun Sheha (Beirut: Dār al-Maʿrifah, 1430/2009), p. 71; ʿAbd al-Salām b. ʿAbd al-Raḥmān b. Muḥammad Ibn Barrajān, *Tanbīh al-Afhām ilā Tadabbur al-Kitāb al-Ḥakīm wa-Taʿarruf al-Āyāt wa'l-Nabaʾ al-ʿAẓīm,* ed. Ahmed Fareed al-Muzayyidi (Beirut: Dār al-Kutub al-ʿIlmiyyah, 1ˢᵗ edn., 1434/2013), vol. 1, pp. 184-185; al-Rāzī, *al-Tafsīr al-Kabīr,* vol. 2, p. 192; Nāṣir al-Dīn Abū al-Khayr ʿAbd Allāh b. ʿUmar b. Muḥammad al-Shīrāzī al-Shāfiʿī al-Bayḍāwī, *Anwār al-Tanzīl wa-Asrār al-Taʾwīl,* ed. Mohammed Abdur-Rahman (Beirut: Dār Iḥyāʾ al-Turāth al-ʿArabī, n. d.), vol. 1, p. 69; ʿIṣām al-Dīn Ismāʿīl b. Muḥammad al-Ḥanafī, *Ḥāshiyat al-Qūnawī ʿalā Tafsīr al-Imām al-Bayḍāwī,* with *Ḥāshiyat Ibn al-Tamjīd,* ed. Abdullah Mahmoud Mohamed Omar (Beirut: Dār al-Kutub al-ʿIlmiyyah, 1ˢᵗ edn., 1422/2001), vol. 3, pp. 128-131; Muhammad Abdu and Muhammad Rashid Rida, *Tafsīr al-Qurʾān al-Ḥakīm,* known as *Tafsīr al-Manār* (Cairo: Dār al-Manār bi-Miṣr, 3ʳᵈ edn., 1367 H), vol. 1, pp. 262-264; Ibn Ashur, *Tafsīr al-Taḥrīr wa'l-Tanwīr,* vol. 1, pp. 408-411.

[13] Abū ʿUthmān ʿAmr b. Baḥr al-Jāḥiẓ, *Rasāʾil al-Jāḥiẓ,* ed. Abdel Salam Mohamed Haroun (Cairo: Maktabat al-Khānjī, 1ˢᵗ edn., 1399/1979), vol. 1, p. 262.

[14] Al-Rāghib al-Iṣfahānī, *Tafsīr Sūratay al-Fātiḥah wa'l-Baqarah,* in Mohamed Abdel Aziz Bassiouni Ghorab, *Manhaj al-Rāghib al-Iṣfahānī fī'l-Tafsīr maʿa Taḥqīq Muddimatihi wa-Tafsīrihi li-Suratay al-Fātiḥah wa'l-Baqarah* (a doctoral dissertation submitted at Tanta University, Egypt, 1420/1999), p. 144; also his *Mufradāt Alfāẓ al-Qurʾān,* p. 428.

[15] Malik Bennabi, *The Question of Culture,* translated by Abdel Wahid Lu'lu'a and revised by Mohamed El-Tahir El-Mesawi (Kuala Lumpur: Islamic Book Trust and London: The International Institute of Islamic Thought, 1423/2003), pp. 11-12.

[16] Ibid., p. 10. Guided by a closely similar perspective, the Tunisian sociologist Mahmoud Dhaouadi worked towards developing a sociological theory on the uniqueness of human beings as singularly symbol makers and users. See his, *Toward Islamic Sociology of Cultural Symbols* (Kuala Lumpur: A.S. Noordeen, 1ˢᵗ edn., 1416/1996).

[17] Al-Iṣfahānī, *Mufradāt Alfāẓ al-Qurʾān,* p. 157. See also, Ibn Manẓūr, *Lisān al-ʿArab,* vol. 13, pp. 67-68; al-Zabīdī, *Tāj al-ʿArūs,* vol. 34, pp. 297-298; Lane, *Arabic-English Lexicon,* vol. 1, p. 288. Of great significance and relevance to the present discussion is the insightful account provided by al-Jāḥiẓ on human communication (*bayān*) and its means within a cosmo-semiotic and anthropological perspective; yet it is beyond our purpose to delve into it here. See, Abū ʿUthmān ʿAmr b. Baḥr is al-Jāḥiẓ, *al-Ḥayawān,* ed. Abdul Salam Mohammed

Haroun (Cairo: Sharikat Maktabat Muṣṭafā al-Bābī al-Ḥalabī wa-Awlādih, 2nd edn., 1389/1969), vol. 1, pp. 31-37.

[18] Abū 'Uthmān 'Amr b. Baḥr al-Jāḥiẓ, *al-Bayān wa'l-Tabyīn,* ed. Abdul Salam Mohammed Haroun (Cairo: Maktabat al-Khānjī, 6[th]edn., 1418/1998), vol. 1, p. 8.

[19] Ibn Ashur, *Tafsīr al-Taḥrīr wa'l-Tanwīr,* vol. 12/27, p. 233. See also al-Ṭabarī, *Jāmiʿ al-Bayān,* vol. 22, p. 170; Abū al-Ḥusayn al-Qāsim b. Muḥammad b. al-Mufaḍḍal al-Rāghib al-Iṣfahānī, *Tafṣīl al-Nash'atayn wa-Taḥṣīl al-Saʿādatayn,* ed. Abdelmajid al-Najjar (Beirut: Dār al-Gharb al-Islāmī, 1st edn., 1408/1988), pp. 87-89; Ibn 'Aṭiyah, *al-Muḥarrar al-Wajīz,* vol. 5, p. 223; al-Rāzī, *al-Tafsīr al-Kabīr,* vol. 2, p. 86; Abū Muḥammad al-Ḥussain b. Masʿud al-Baghawī, *Tafsīr al-Baghawī: Maʿālim al-Tanzīl,* ed. Mohammed Abdullah al-Nimr *et al.* (Riyadh: Dār Taibah, 1412 H), vol. 7, p. 441; al-Qurṭubī, *al-Jāmiʿ li-Aḥkām al-Qur'ān,* vol. 20, pp. 113-114; Abū Ḥayyān, *al-Baḥr al-Muḥīṭ,* vol. 8, p. 268; al-Bayḍāwī & al-Ḥanafī, *Anwār al-Tanzīl & Ḥāshiyat al-Qūnawī,* vol. 18, p. 345.

[20] Asad, *The Message of the Qur'an,* p. 986, note 1. See also, Abū Jaʿfar Muḥammad b. al-Ḥasan al-Ṭūsī, *al-Tibyān fī Tafsīr al-Qur'ān,* ed. Ahmed Habib Kasir al-'Amili (Beirut: Dār Iḥyā' al-Turāth al-'Arabī, n. d.), vol. 9, p. 463; Darwazeh, *al-Tafsīr al-Ḥadīth,* vol., 6, pp. 90-91; Qutb, *Fī Zilāl al-Qur'ān,* vol. 6, p. 3447; al-Tabataba'i, *al-Mīzān fī Tafsīr al-Qur'ān,* vol. 19, pp. 98-99.

[21] Asad, *The Message of the Qur'an,* p. 986.

[22] Seyyed Hossein Nasr *et al.,* *The Study Qur'an* (New York: Harper Collins Publishers, 2015), p. 1311. See also, Abū al-Faḍl Shihāb al-Dīn al-Sayyid Maḥmūd al-Alūsī al-Baghdādī, *Rūḥ al-Maʿānī fī Tafsīr al-Qur'ān al-'Aẓim wa'l-Sabʿ al-Mathānī* (Cairo: Idārat al-Ṭibāʿah al-Munīriyyh, 1353 H), vol., 27, pp. 98-99; Ahmed Mustafa al-Maraghi, *Tafsīr al-Marāghī* (Cairo: Sharikat Maktabat wa-Matbaʿat Muṣṭafā al-Bābī al-Ḥalabī wa-Awlādih, 1st edn., 1365/1946), vol. 27, p. 106; Qutb, *Fī Zilāl al-Qur'ān,* vol. 6, p. 3446; Ibn Ashur, *Tafsīr al-Taḥrīr wa'l-Tanwīr,* vol. 12/27, pp. 232-233; Muhammed Mahmoud Hijazi, *al-Tafsīr al-Wāḍiḥ* (Cairo: Mashyakhat al-Azhar, 3rd edn. 1440/2019), vol. 3, pp.578-579; Mustafa Muslim *et al. al-Tafsīr al-Mawḍūʿī li-Suwar al-Qur'ān al-Karīm* (Shajah: Sharjah University, 1st edn., 1431/2010), vol. 7, pp. 547-552.

[23] Abū 'Abd Allāh Muḥammad b. Abī Bakr b. Ayyūb Ibn Qayyim al-Jawziyyah, *Miftāḥ Dār al-Saʿādah wa-Manshūr Wilāyat al-'Ilm wa'l-Irādah,* ed. Abdul Rahman bin Hassan bin Qa'id (Makkah al-Mukarramah: Dār 'Ālam al-Fawā'id, 1st edn., 1432H), vol. 1, p. 158. It is worthy of mention here that the categorization of the modes of being (*marātib al-wujūd*) predates Ibn al-Qayyim, and is not confined to the fourfold taxanomy he seems to uphold. Other categorizations have been formulated in different terms and from different perspectives by earlier and subsequent scholars, including *mutakallimūn* and *ḥukamā',* such as al-Jāḥiẓ, al-Ghazālī and al-Jaylī.

[24] For pertinent comments on the meaning and implications of these verses from different points of view (historical, intellectual, theological and psychological), see for example, Asad, *The Message of the Qur'an,* pp. 1150-1151, notes 1 & 3; al-Zamakhsharī, *al-Kashshāf,* pp. 1212-1213; al-Qurṭubī, *al-Jāmiʿ li-Aḥkām al-Qur'ān,*

vol. 22, p. 277; Abū Ḥayyān, *al-Baḥr al-Muḥīṭ,* vol. 8, pp. 693-695; al-Maraghi, *Tafsīr al-Marāghī,* vol. 30, pp. 188-200; Darwazeh, *al-Tafsīr al-Ḥadīth,* vol.1, pp. 317-318; Qutb, *Fī Ẓilāl al-Qur'ān,* vol. 6, pp. 3935-3942; Hijazi, *al-Tafsīr al-Wāḍiḥ,* vol. 3, pp. 890-891; Ibn Ashur, *Tafsīr al-Taḥrīr wa'l-Tanwīr,* vol. 15/30, pp. 435--442.

[25] By 'self-referentiality' and 'self-explanation' reference is made to a famous methodological maxim known as *al-Qur'ān yufassiru baʿḍuhu baʿḍā* which seems to be derived from the epistemic rule stating that *al-Qur'ān yuṣaddiqu baʿḍuhu baʿḍā.* This maxim means, accoding to Ibn Taymiyyah, that what may be stated in ambiguous terms (*mujmal*) in one place of the Qur'an is explained in another palce, and so too what is expressed in a concise manner in one place is elaborated in another. Hence, the best and most reliable way is "to explicate the Qur'an by the Qur'an (*an yufassara al-Qur'ānu bi'l-Qur'ān*)." Ibn Taymiyyah, *Daqā'iq al-Tafsīr: al-Jāmʿi li-Tafsīr Ibn Taymiyyah,* compiled & edited by Mohammad al-Sayyid al-Julaynid (Damascus-Beirut: Mu'assasat ʿUlūm al-Qur'ān, 2nd edn., 1404/1984), vol. 1, p. 110. The Hanbali polymath has applied this rule throughout his numerous works, and can be considered to have paved the way to the notion of thematic study of the Qur'an. The same can also be said of the Andalusian scholar Abū Isḥāq al-Shāṭibī in his inductive method which is crucial for the construction of his Maqāṣid theory. In modern times, much emphasis has been put on the principle of 'self-referentiality' and 'self-explanation', thus making it one of the key methodological tools for the proper understanding of the Qur'anic message. This has been the case with Qur'an commentatories produced within the bounds of the established exegetical tradition and, more so, with the newly-born Qur'anic studies discipline. See in this respect, Carl Sharif El-Tobgui, *Ibn Taymiyya on Reason and Revelation: A Study of Darʿ Taʿāruḍ al-ʿAql wa-l-Naql* (Leiden-Boston: Brill, 2020), pp. 202-204; Muhammad al-Amin b. Muhammad al-Mukhtar al-Jakni al-Shinqiti, *Aḍwā' al-Bayān fī Īḍāḥ al-Qur'ān bi'l-Qur'ān* (Makkah: Dār ʿĀlam al-Fawā'id, 1st edn. 1424 H), vol. 1, pp. 8-46; Abd al-Rahman Hassan Habannakah al-Maydani, *Qawāʿid al-Tadabbur al-Amthal li-Kitāb Allah ʿAẓẓa wa-Jall* (Damascus: Dār al-Qalam, 3rd edn., 1425/2004), pp. 13-149; Ahmed Bin Mohammad al-Buraydi, "Tafsīr al-Qur'ān bi'l-Qur'ān: Dirāsah Ta'ṣīliyyah", *Majallat Maʿhad al-Imām al-Shāṭibī li'l-Dirāsāt al-Qur'āniyyah,* No. 2 (Dhul-Ḥijjah 1427 H), pp. 12-68; Stefan Wild (ed.), *Self-Referentiality in the Qur'an* (Wiesbaden: Harrassowitz Verlag, 2006); Anne-Sylvie Baoisliveau, *Le Coran par lui-même: Vocabulaire et argumentation du discours coranique autoréférentiel* (Leiden-Boston: Brill, 2014); Jonathan Hoffman, "The Ojectives of Qur'anic Self-Referentiality", *Qur'anica: International Journal of Qur'anic Research,* vol. 11, No. 1 (June 2019), pp. 1-13.

[26] In this respect see for example, al-Ṭabarī, *Jāmiʿ al-Bayān,* vol. 15, pp. 5-6; Abū Manṣūr Muḥammad b. Muḥammad b. Maḥmūd al-Māturīdī, *Ta'wīlāt Ahl al-Sunnah,* ed. Majdi Basalum (Beirut: Dār al-Kutub al-ʿIlmiyyah, 1st edn., 1426/2005), vol. 7, pp. 86-88; Abū al-Layth Naṣr b. Muḥammad b. Aḥmad b. Ibrāhīm al-Samarqandī, *Baḥr al-ʿUlūm,* ed. Ali Mohammad Muʿwwad *et al.* (Beirut: Dār al-Kutub al-ʿIlmiyyah, 1st edn., 1413/1993), vol. 2, pp. 277-278; Abū Isḥāq Aḥmad b. Muḥammad b. Ibrāhīm al-Thaʿlabī, *al-Kashf wa'l-Bayān ʿan Tafsīr al-Qur'ān,* ed. Salah Ba-Uthman *et al.* (Jeddah: Dār al-Tafsīr, 2015/1436),

vol. 16, p. 391-396; Abū al-Qāsim ʿAbd al-Karīm b. Hawāzin b. ʿAbd al-Malik al-Qushayrī al-Naysābūrī, *Laṭāʾif al-Ishārāt*, ed. Abdullatif Hassan Abdul Rahman (Beirut: Dār al-Kutub al-ʿIlmiyyah, 2nd edn., 1428/2007), vol. 2, pp. 196-198; al-Ḥākim al-Jashmī, *al-Tahdhīb fiʾl-Tafsīr*, vol. 6, pp. 4262-4264; al-Zamakhsharī, *al-Kashshāf*, p. 603; al-Rāzī, *al-Tafsīr al-Kabīr*, vol. 21, pp. 13-17; al-Qurṭubī, *al-Jāmiʿ li-Aḥkām al-Qurʾān*, vol. 13, pp. 125-129; Ibn Qayyim al-Jawziyyah, *Miftāḥ Dār al-Saʿādah*, esp. pp. 746-776; al-Alūsī al-Baghdādī, *Rūḥ al-Maʿānī*, vol. 15, pp. 117-120; al-Shinqiti, *Aḍwāʾ al-Bayān*, vol. 3, p. 726; Mohammad Taqi al-Mudarresi, *Min Hudā al-Qurʾān* (Beirut: Dār al-Qāriʾ, 2nd edn., 1429/2008), vol. 4, p. 462; Muhammad Ali Taha al-Durrah, *Tafsīr al-Qurʾān al-Karīm wa-Iʿrābuhu wa-Bayānuh* (Damascus-Beirut: Dār Ibn Kathīr, 1st edn., 1430/2009), vol. 5, p. 379.

[27] See for example, Ali Abdul Wahid Wafi, *Ḥuqūq al-Insān fiʾl-Islām* (Cairo: Dār Nahḍat Miṣr, 5th edn. 1979); Muhammad al-Ghazali, *Ḥuqūq al-Insān bayna Taʿālīm al-Islām wa-Iʿlān al-Umam al-Muttaḥidah* (Cairo: Dar Nahdat Misr, 4th edn., 2005); Muhammad Fathi Osman, *Ḥuqūq al-Insān bayna al-Sharīʿah al-Islāmiyyah waʾl-Fikr al-Qānūnī al-Gharbī* (Cairo-Beirut: Dār al-Shurūq, 1st edn., 1402/1982); Yusuf al-Qaradawi, *al-Khaṣāʾiṣ al-ʿĀmmah liʾl-Islām* (Beirut: Muʾassasat al-Risālah, 2nd edn., 1404/1983); Fahmi Huweidi, *Muwāṭinūn lā Dhimmiyyūn* (Cairo-Beirut: Dār al-Shurūq, 3rd edn., 1420/1999); Ibrahim Madkour & Adnan al-Khatib, *Ḥuqūq al-Insān fiʾl-Islām* (Damascus: Dār Ṭlās, 1st edn., 1412/1992); Edward Ghali al-Dahabi, *Muʿāmalat ghayr al-Muslimīn fiʾl-Mujatmaʿ al-Islāmī* (Cairo: Maktabat Gharīb, 1st edn., 1993); Rached al-Ghannouchi, *al-Ḥurriyyāt al-ʿĀmmah fiʾl-Dawlah al-Islāmiyyah* (Beirut: Markaz Dirāsāt al-Waḥdah al-ʿArabiyyah, 1st edn., 1993); Ahmed al-Raysuni, "Insāniyyat al-Insān qabla Ḥuqūq al-Insān", in al-Raysuni *et al.* (authors), *Ḥuqūq al-Insān Miḥwar Maqāṣid al-Sharīʿah* (Doha: Ministry of Awqaf and Islamic Affairs, 1st edn., 1423/2002), pp. 39-66; Muhammad Hashim Kamali, *The Dignity of Man: An Islamic Perspective* (Kuala Lumpur: Ilmiah Publishers, 2002); Fathi al-Durayni, *Khaṣāʾiṣ al-Tashrīʿ al-Islāmī fiʾl-Siyāsah waʾl-Ḥukm* (Beirut: Resalah Publishers, 2nd edn., 1429/2008); ʿUmar Ahmad Kasule, *Pursuit of Human Dignity and Justice* (Kuala Lumpur: A.S. Noordeen, 2008); Abdulaziz Altwaijri, *al-Karāmah al-Insāniyyah fī ḍawʾ al-Mabādiʾ al-Islāmiyyah* (Rabat: ISESCO, 2nd edn., 1436/2015); Hassan bin Musa al-Saffar, *al-Dīn waʾl-Qiyam al-Insāniyyah* (al-Qatif, SA: no publisher, 1st edn., 1441/2020), pp. 247-255; Abdulaziz Sachedina, *Islam and the Challenge of Human Rights* (Oxford • New York: Oxford University Press, 2009).

[28] Ibn Ashur, *Tafsīr al-Taḥrīr waʾl-Tanwīr*, vol. 7/15, p. 164.

[29] Darwazeh, *al-Tafsīr al-Ḥadīth*, vol. 3, p. 407-408. See especially, al-Baqarah, 2:30 & 34; al-Aʿrāf, 7:11; al-Ḥijr, 15:29; al-Isrāʾ, 17:61; al-Kahf, 18: 50 &Ṣād, 38:72.

[30] Al-Alūsī, *Rūḥ al-Maʿānī*, vol. 15, p. 117.

[31] Al-Rāghib al-Iṣfahānī, *Tafṣīl al-Nashʾatayn wa-Taḥṣīl al-Saʿādatayn*, pp. 100-102.

[32] Ibn Ashur, *Tafsīr al-Taḥrīr waʾl-Tanwīr*, vol. 7/15, p. 164.

[33] Al-Ḥākim al-Jashmī, *al-Tahdhīb fī al-Tafsīr*, vol. 6, p. 4260. See also, al-Ṭabarsī, *Majmaʿ al-Bayān*, vol. 5-6, p. 662; al-Ṭūsī, *al-Tibyān fī Tafsīr al-Qurʾān*, vol. 6, p. 503; al-Qurṭubī, *al-Jāmiʿ li-Aḥkām al-Qurʾān*, vol. 13, pp. 125-126.

[34] Al-Ṭabarsī, *Majmaʿ al-Bayān*, vol. 5-6, p. 662; al-Zamakhsharī, *al-Kashshāf*, p. 603; al-Rāzī, *al-Tafsīr al-Kabīr*, vol. 21, pp. 13016; al-Qurṭubī, *al-Jāmiʿ li-Aḥkām al-Qurʾān*, vol. 13, pp. 125-126; Abū Ḥayyān, *al-Baḥr al-Muḥīṭ*, vol. 6, p. 75; Burhān al-Dīn Abū al-Ḥasan Ibrāhīm b. ʿUmar al-Biqāʿī, *Naẓm al-Durar fī Tanāsub al-Āyāt waʾl-Suwar* (Cairo: Dār al-Kitāb al-Islāmī, n.d.), vol. 11, pp. 475-476; al-Alūsī, *Rūḥ al-Maʿānī*, vol. 15, pp. 117-118; Abū al-Ṭayyib Ṣiddīq b. Ḥassan b. ʿAlī al-Ḥussain al-Qinnūjī, *Fatḥ al-Bayān fī Maqāṣid al-Qurʾān*, ed. Abdullah bin Ibrahim al-Ansari (Sedon-Beirut: al-Maktabah al-ʿAṣriyyah, 1412/1992), vol. 7, 424; al-Qāsimī, *Maḥāsin al-Taʾwīl*, vol. 10, p. 3950; Ibn Ashur, *Tafsīr al-Taḥrīr waʾl-Tanwīr*, vol. 7/15, pp. 165-166; al-Tabatabaʾi, *al-Mīzān fī Tafsīr al-Qurʾān*, vol. 13, pp. 152-153; al-Durrah, *Tafsīr al-Qurʾān al-Karīm wa-Iʿrābuhu wa-Bayānuh*, vol. 5, p. 378.

[35] Shabir Akhtar, *The Quran and the Secular Mind: A Philosophy of Islam* (London and New York: Routledge, Taylor & Francis Group, 2008), p. 269.

[36] Ibn Ashur, *Tafsīr al-Taḥrīr waʾl-Tanwīr*, vol. 7/15, p. 166. See also, Abū al-Ḥasan ʿAlī b. Muḥammad b. Ḥabīb al-Māwardī al-Baṣrī, *al-Nukat waʾl-ʿUyūn: Tafsīr al-Māwardī*, ed. al-Sayyid Abdul Maksud bin Abdul Rahman (Beirut: Dār al-Kutb al-ʿIlmiyyah & Muʾassasat al-Kutub al-Thaqāfiyyah, n.d.), vol. 3, p. 258; al-Alūsī, *Rūḥ al-Maʿānī*, vol. 15, pp. 118-119; al-Khatib, *al-Tafsīr al-Qurʾānī liʾl-Qurʾān*, vol. 3, pp. 524-525; Hijazi, *al-Tafsīr al-Wāḍiḥ*, vol. 2, p. 376.

What we have described as Qurʾanic genesis appears in the Qurʾan six times, namely in al-Baqarah, 2:30-34; al-Aʿrāf, 7:11-27; al-Ḥijr, 15:26-44; al-Isrāʾ, 17:61-65; al-Kahf, 18:50, and Ṣād, 38:69-85. For a brief discussion of the significance and some implications of the Qurʾanic account of genesis, see Mohamed El-Tahir El-Mesawi, *Gender Issues in Islam: Recovering the Measure and Restoring the Balance*, with comments by Serene Jones and edited by Fethi B. Jomaa Ahmed (Doha: Research Center for Islamic Legislation and Ethics, 2019), pp. 26-43.

[37] Asad, *The Message of the Qurʾan*, pp. 838-839, note 52; Nasr *et al.*, *The Study Qurʾan*, p. 1114, note 71-85. See also Jalāl al-Dīn al-Suyūṭī, *al-Itqān fī ʿUlūm al-Qurʾān*, ed. Shuaib al-Anaʾut (Beirut: Resalah Publishers, 1st edn., 1429/2008), p. 35; El-Mesawi, *Gender Issues in Islam*, pp. 27-28; Darwazeh, *al-Tafsīr al-Ḥadīth*, vol. 2, p. 342.

[38] Al-Māturīdī, *Taʾwīlāt Ahl al-Sunnah*, vol. 8, p. 646; al-Alūsī, *Rūḥ al-Maʿānī*, vol. 23, p. 225; Darwazeh, *al-Tafsīr al-Ḥadīth*, vol. 2, pp. 352-356; Qutb, *Fī Ẓilāl al-Qurʾān*, vol. 5, p. 3028; Ibn Ashur, *Tafsīr al-Taḥrīr waʾl-Tanwīr*, vol. 11/23, pp. 302-303; al-Tabatabaʾi, *al-Mīzān fī Tafsīr al-Qurʾān*, vol. 17, p. 226; Hijazi, *al-Tafsīr al-Wāḍiḥ*, vol. 3, p. 251; Abd al-Rahman Hassan Habannakah al-Maydani, *Maʿārij al-Tafakkur wa-Daqaʾiq al-Tadabbur* (Damascus: Dār al-Qalam, 1st edn., 1423/2002), vol. 3, p. 691.

[39] Unlike many Qurʾan exegetes who understood the expression *asfal sāfilīn* in the verse just cited as meaning physical deterioration and degeneration, Ibn Ashur

seems to give much less significance to the physical form in which human beings are moulded as far as the meaning of the verse is concerned. In his view, "[t]here is no doubt that what is meant by the expression 'the best of moulds (*aḥsan taqwīm*)' here is the valuation of the intellect, which is the principle of right beliefs and good deeds, while the phrase 'the lowest of the low (*asfal sāfilīn*)' refers to humankind's propensity to acquire bad qualities (*radhā'il*) from false beliefs and evil deeds. Therefore, this mould has nothing to do with the human being's physical form (*ṣūrah*). This is because the human physical form does not degenerate. It is also because the exclusion (*istithnā'*) in the phrase 'excepting only such as attain to faith and do good works' precludes any possibility that the general term in the verse refers to the outward form. Moreover, righteous believers are not privileged with having beautiful physical forms to the exclusion of others." Ibn Ashur, *Treatise on Maqāṣid al-Sharī'ah*, p. 83; also his *Tafsīr al-Taḥrīr wa'l-Tanwīr*, vol. 15/30, p. 424. *Cf.* Qutb, *Fī Ẓilāl al-Qur'ān*, vol. 6, pp. 3933-3934; al-Tabataba'i, *al-Mīzān fī Tafsīr al-Qur'ān*, vol. 20, pp. 132-135; al-Maydani, *Ma'ārij al-Tafakkur wa-Daqā'iq al-Tadabbur*, vol. 2, pp. 407-408.

⁴⁰ See insightful discussions in this respect in, al-Qāḍī Abū al-Ḥasan 'Abd al-Jabbār al-Asadābādī, *al-Mughnī fī Abwāb al-Tawḥīd wa'l-'Adl*, ed. Taha Hussein, Ibrahim Madkour *et al.* (Cairo: Wazārat al-Thaqāfah wa'l-Irshād al-Qawmī, al-Idārah al-'Ammah lil-Thaqāfah, 1960-1965), vol. 11 (*al-Taklīf*), pp. 310-367; Abū Ḥāmid Muḥammad b. Muḥammad b. Muḥammad b. Aḥmad al-Ghazālī, *Iḥyā' 'Ulūm al-Dīn* (Jeddah: Dār al-Minhāj, 1ˢᵗ edn., 1432/2011), vol. 5, pp. 96-243 & *passim* (also the whole of vol. 6); Qutb, *Dirāsāt fi'l-Nafs al-Insāniyyah*; Muhammad Othman Nagati, *al-Qur'ān wa 'Ilm al-Nafs* (Cairo-Beirut: Dār al-Shurūq, 7ᵗʰ edn., 1414/1993), pp. 27-121; Samih Atef El-Zein,'*Ilm al-Nafs: Ma'rifat al-Nafs al-Insāniyyah fi'l-Qur'ān wa'l-Sunnah* (Beirut: Dār al-Kitāb al-Lubnānī / Cairo: Dār al-Kitāb al-Miṣrī, 1411/1991), vol. 1, pp. 127-205 & vol. 2, pp. 37-206; al-Maydani, *Ma'ārij al-Tafakkur wa-Daqā'iq al-Tadabbur*, vol. 2, p. 407.

⁴¹ Asad, *The Message of the Qur'an*, pp. 838-839, notes 52-58.

⁴² Al-Asadābādī, *al-Mughnī*, vol. 11, pp.134-300; M.A. Draz, *The Moral World of the Qur'an*, translated from French by Danielle Robinson & Rebecca Masterton(London-New York: I. B. Tauris, 2008), pp. 13-116; Qutb, *Fī Ẓilāl al-Qur'ān*, vol. 4, pp. 2240-2241; Darwazeh, *al-Tafsīr al-Ḥadīth*, vol. 2, pp. 355-356; Hijazi, *al-Tafsīr al-Wāḍiḥ*, vol. 3, pp. 127-128 & 793; al-Maydani, *Ma'ārij al-Tafakkur*, vol. 6, pp. 677-690; al-Maraghi, *Tafsīr al-Marāghī*, vol. 29, p. 155; al-Tabataba'i, *al-Mīzān fī Tafsīr al-Qur'ān*, vol. 20, pp. 132-135; A. Ezzati, *Islam and Natural Law* (London: Islamic College for Advanced Studies Press, ICAS, 2002), pp. 87-92; 'Umar Farrūkh, *al-Islām wa'l-Tārīkh: al-Islām fī Naẓarihi ilā Allāh wa'l-Insān wa'l-Mujtama' wa'l-Tārīkh* (Beirut: Dār al-Kitāb al-'Arabī, 1402/1983), pp. 85-110; Syed Muhammad Naquib al-Attas, *Prolegomena to the Metaphysics of Islam* (Kuala Lumpur: International Institute of Islamic Thought and Civilization, 2001), pp. 144-145; Kasule, *Pursuit of Human Dignity and Justice*, pp. 50-55;

⁴³ For discussions on the meaning, basis and conditions of *taklīf* and related moral, legal and theological issues see, al-Asadābādī, *al-Mughnī*, vol. 11, pp.367-387; Imām

al-Ḥaramayn Abū al-Maʿālī ʿAbd al-Malik b. ʿAbd Allāh b. Yūsuf al-Juwaynī, *al-Burhān fī Uṣūl al-Fiqh*, ed. Abdul Azim Mahmoud al-Deeb (al-Mansourah, Egypt: Dār al-Wafāʾ, 1412/1992), vol. 1, pp. 88-94; Abū Ḥāmid Muḥammad b. Muḥammad b. Muḥammad al-Ghazālī, *al-Mustaṣfā min ʿIlm al-Uṣūl*, ed. Mohammed Sulayman al-Ashqar (Beirut: Muʾassasat al-Risālah, 1417/1997), vol. 1, pp. 158-174; ʿAlī b. Muḥammad al-Āmidī, *al-Iḥkām fī Uṣūl al-Aḥkām*, with comments by Abdul Razzaq Afifi (Riyadh: Dār al-Ṣamīʿī, 1st edn., 1424/2003), vol.1/1, pp. 179-209; Hussein al-Nuri, *ʿAwāriḍ al-Ahliyyah maʿa'l-Muqāranah bi'l-Sharāʾiʿ al-Waḍʿiyyah* (Cairo: Maṭbaʿat Lajnat al-Bayān al-ʿArabī, 1st edn., 1954); Huda Mohammad Hassan Hilal, *Naẓariyat al-Ahliyyah: Dirāsah Muqārinah bayna al-Fiqh wa-ʿIlm al-Nafs* (Hernden, Virginia: The International Institute of Islamic Thought, 2001).

[44] Muhammad Qutb, *al-Insān bayna al-Māddiyyah wa'l-Islām* (Cairo-Beirut: Dār al-Shurūq, 10th edn., 1409/1989), pp. 69-71.

[45] al-Durayni, *Khaṣāʾiṣ al-Tashrīʿ al-Islāmī*, pp. 96-98 & 208-210.

[46] Ibn Khaldūn, *Muqaddimat Ibn Khaldūn*, pp. 43-48; *The Muqaddimah*, vol. vol. 1, pp. 79-85 & 89-93.

[47] Muhammad Hashim Kamali, *The Right to Life, Security, Privacy and Owenership in Islam* (Kuala Pumpur: International Institute of Advanced Islamic Studies Malaysia, 2013), p. xi & 1.

[48] Al-Durayni, *Khaṣāʾiṣ al-Tashrīʿ al-Islāmī*, p. 97; Kamali, *The Dignity of Man*, pp. 5-104.

[49] Ibn Ashur, *Treatise on Maqāṣid al-Sharīʿah*, p. 120.

[50] Abū Isḥāq Ibrāhīm b. Musā al-Shātibī, *al-Muwāfaqāt fī Uṣūl al-Sharīʿah*, commented upon by Abdullah Draz and Muhammad Abdullah Draz (Beirut: Dār al-Kutub al-ʿIlmiyyah, 1422/2001), vol. 1/2, pp. 7-8; Ibn Ashur, *Treatise on Maqāṣid al-Sharīʿah*, p. 120. See also, al-Ghazālī, *al-Mustaṣfā*, vol. 1, p. 417.

[51] Yusuf Hamid al-ʿAlim, *al-Maqāṣid al-ʿĀmmah li'l-al-Sharīʿah al-Islāmiyyah* (London-Washington: The International Institute of Islamic Thought, 1413/1993), pp. 133-200.

[52] Abū Ḥāmid Muḥammad b. Muḥammad b. Muḥammad al-Ghazālī, *Shifāʾ al-Ghalīl fī Bayān al-Shabah wa'l-Mukhīl wa-Masālik al-Taʿlīl*, ed. Hamad al-Kubaysi (Baghdad: Matbaʿat al-Irshād, 1390/1971), p. 159; Fakhr al-Dīn Muḥammad b. ʿUmar b. al-Ḥusayn al-Rāzī, *al-Maḥṣūl fī ʿIlm al-Uṣūl*, ed. Taha Jabir Fayyad al-Alwani (Beirut: Muʾassasat al-Risālah, 2nd edn., 1412/1992), vol. 5, p. 157.

[53] In the best of cases cloning and its sister techniques of artificial human reproduction will only deliver machine-like, senseless creatures or robots if not mere destructive monsters, thus heralding the advent and emergence of what has been called posthumanism and transhumanism. See scientific, legal, ethical, philosophical and literary discussions in this respect in:

Richard C. Lewontin, *Biology as Ideology: The Doctrine of DNA* (Ontario: House of Anan si Limited, 1995); Leon R. Kass & James Q. Wilson, *The Ethics of Human Cloning* (Washington, D.C.: The AEI Press, 1998); James M. Humber & Robert

F. Almeder, *Human Cloning* (New York: Springer Science+Business Media, LLC, 1998); Mae-Wan Ho, *Genetic Engineering Dream or Nightmare: The Brave World of Bad Science and Big Business* (Penang, Malaysia: TWN, 1998); Richard C. Lewontin, *It Ain't Necessarily So: The Dream of the Human Genome and Other Illusions* (New York: New York Review of Books, 2nd edn., 2001); National Academy of Sciences, National Academy of Engineering, Institute of Medicine & National Research Council, *Scientific and Medical Aspects of Human Reproductive Cloning* (Washington, DC: National Academy Press, 2002); Francis Fukuyama, *Our Posthuman Future: Consequences of the Biotechnology Revolution* (New York: Farrar, Straus and Giroux, 2002); Ted Peters, *Playing God? Genetic Determinism and Human Freedom* (London/New York: Routledge, 2003); Maria Aline Salgueiro Seabra Ferreira, *I Am the Other: Literary Negotiations of Human Cloning* (Wesport, Connecticut & London: Praeger, 2005); Harold W. Baillie and Timothy K. Casey (eds.), *Is Human Nature Obsolete? Genetic Engineering and the Future of the Human Condition* (Massachusetts: The MIT Press, 2005); Farida bint Sadek Zouzou, *al-Nasl: Dirāsah Maqāṣidiyyah fī Wasā'ili Ḥifẓihi fī Ḍaw' al-Taḥaddiyyāt al-Muʿāṣirah* (Riyadh: Maktabat al-Rushd, 1st edn., 1427/2006), pp. 191-231; Heiner Roetz (ed.), *Cross-Cultural Issues in Bioethics: The Example of Human Cloning* (Amsterdam-New York: Rodopi, 2006); Russ Hodge, *Genetic Engineering: Manipulating the Mechanisms of Life* (New York: Facts On File, Inc, 2009); Allen Buchanan, *Better than Human: The Promise and Perils of Enhancing Ourselves* (Oxford, UK & New York: Oxford University Press, 2011); Kerry Lynn Macintosh, *Human Cloning: Four Fallacies and their Legal Consequences* (Cambridge,, UK and New York: Cambridge University Press, 2013); Luc Ferry, *La Révolution Transhumaniste: Comment la Technomedicine et l'Uberisation du Monde Vont Boulverser nos Vies* (Paris: French and European Publications Inc., 2016). Henry T. Greely, *The End of Sex and the Future of Human Reproduction* (Cambridge, Massachusetts & London, England: The MIT Press, 2016); Henry T. Greely, *CRISPR People: The Science and Ethics of Editing Humans* (Cambridge, Massachusetts & London, England: The MIT Press, 2021).

[54] Edward Westermarck, *The History of Human Marriage* (New York and London: MacMillan and Co., 2nd edn., 1894), p. 22.

[55] See for more details, Abdullah Nasih ʿUlwan, *Tarbiyyat al-Awlād fī'l-Islām*, 2 vols. (Cairo: Dār al-Salām, 21st edn. 1412/1992); Fayiz Quntar, *al-Umūmah: Numuww al-ʿAlāqah bayna al-Ṭifl wa'l-Umm* (Kuwait: ʿĀlam al-Maʿrifah, 1992); Maha Abdullah Omar al-Abrash, *al-Umūmah wa-Makānatuhā fī'l-Islām fī Ḍaw' al-Kitāb wa'l-Sunnah* (Makkah al-Mukarramah: Umm al-Qura University, 1417/1996); Zouzou, *al-Nasl*, pp. 283-311; Ra'fat Farid Suwaylim, *Tarbiyat al-Ṭifl: Ḥuqūq al-Ṭifl fī'l-Sharīʿah al-Islāmiyyah* (Cairo: Dār al-Yusr, 1st edn., 1429/2008); Abdul Rahman Idris Abdul Rahman Fadlallah, *Ḥuqūq al-Ṭifl fī'l-Sharīʿah al-Islāmiyyah* (A doctoral dissertation submitted at the Law Fcaulty, University of Khartoum 1429/2008); Nihayah Mohammad Saeed Naseef al-Qaysi, "Ḥuqūq al-Janin fi'l-Sharīʿah al-Islāmiyyah," *Journal of The Iraqi University*, vol. 25, No. 1 (2010), pp. 217-262; Shahrazad Bousetla, "al-Ḥuqūq al-

Ma'nawiyyah wa'l-Māliyyah li'l-Ṭifl fi'l-Sharī'ah al-Islāmiyyah," *Majallat al-Ijtihād al-Qaḍā'ī,* No. 7 (2010), pp. 139-148; Raed Jamil Okasha & Monzer Arafat Zaytoun (eds.), *al-Usrah al-Muslimah fī Ẓilāl al-Taghayyurāt al-Mu'āṣirah* (Herndon: International Institute of Islamic Thought & Amman: Dār al-Fatḥ, 1ST edn., 1436/2015), pp. 181-312.

56 Al-Durayni, *Khaṣā'iṣ al-Tashrī' al-Islāmī,* pp. 210-219.

57 See for more details, al-'Alim, *al-Maqāṣid al-'Āmmah li'l-al-Sharī'ah al-Islāmiyyah,* pp. 271-297; al-Najjar, *Maqāṣid al-Sharī'ah bi-Ab'ād Jadīdah,* pp. 59-83; Ihsan Mir Ali, *al-Maqāṣid al-'Āmmah li'l-Sharī'ah al-Islāmiyyah bayna al-Aṣālah wa'l-Mu'āṣarah* (Damascus: Dār al-Thaqāfah li'l-Jamī', 1st edn., 1430/2009), vol. 2, pp. 621-650.

58 Sayyid Abul A'la Mawdūdī, *Towards Understanding the Qur'ān,* abdridged version of *Tafhīm al-Qur'ān,* translated and edited by Zafar Ishaq Ansari (Leicester: The Islamic Foundation, 1988/1408), vol. 2, p. 291.

59 This, generally speaking, seems to be the definition adopted by the United Nations following the Nuremberg trials. See in this respect, Larry May, *Crimes against Humanity: A Normative Account* (Cambridge: Cambridge University Press, 2005); Mark Lottimer and Philippe Sands, *Justice for Crimes against Humanity* (Oxford and Portland, Oregon: Hart Pubnlishing, 2003); M. Cherif Bassiouni, *Crimes Against Humanity: Historical Evolution and Contemporary Application* (Cambridge: Cambridge University Press, 2011); Norman Geras, *Crimes against Humanity: The Birth of a Concept* (Manchester and New York: Manchester University Press, 2011).

60 See for more details, al-Rāghib al-Iṣfahānī, *Tafṣīl al-Nash'atayn wa-Taḥṣīl al-Sa'ādatayn,* pp. 61-110; Abbas Mahmoud al-Aqqad, *al-Insān fi'l-Qur'ān* (Cairo: Nahḍat Miṣr, 4th edn., 2005), pp. 10-54; Murteza al-Motahhari, *Fiṭrah,* translated from the Persian by Jaafar Sadiq al-Khalili (Beirut: Mu'assasat al-Bi'thah, 1412/1992), pp. 10-80; Abdul Aziz bin Othman Altuwaijri, *al-Karāmah al-Insāniyyah fī Ḍaw' al-Mabādi' al-Islāmiyyah* (Rabat: Islamic Educational, Scientific and Cultural Organization, ISESCO, 1436/2015).

61 Abū 'Abd Allāh Muḥammad b. Ismā'īl al-Buhkārī, *Ṣaḥīḥ al-Buhkārī* (Damascus/Beirut: Dār Ibn Kathīr, 1st edn., 1423/2002), 'Kitāb al-Waṣāyā', ḥadīth 2766, p. 684; Abū al-Ḥusayn Muslim b. al-Ḥajjaj al-Qushayrī al-Naysābūrī, *Ṣaḥīḥ Muslim,* ed. Mohammed Fuad Abd al-Baqi (Cairo: Dār Iḥyā' al-Kutub al-'Arabiyyah, 1412/1991), 'Kitāb al-Īmān', ḥadīth 145, vol. 1, p. 92.

62 Ibn Ashur, *Treatise on Maqāsid al-Sharī'ah,* p. 337. The author provides a profound analysis of how these objectives are attained in the different categories of punishment depending on the cases and circumstances, but with justice and rectification being always present. (pp. 336-340. See also his discussion on judicial procedures and testimonies, pp. 317-335). For more detailed expositions on homicide and other crimes against the human self and related issues of Islamic penal doctrines and precepts of criminal justice in, Abdul Qadir Audah, *al-Tashrī' al-Jinā'ī al-Islāmī Muqāran bi'l-Qānūn al-Waḍ'ī* (Beirut: Dār al-Kitāb al-

'Arabī, n.d.), vol. 2, pp. 4-345 & vol. 1, pp. 533-635; Muhammad Abu Zahra, *al-Jarīmah wa'l-'Uqūbah fi'l-Fiqh al-Islāmī: al-'Uqūbah* (Cairo: Dār al-Fikr al-'Arabī, n.d.), pp. 298-527; Ahmad Fethi Bahansi, *al-Qiṣāṣ fi'l-Fiqh al-Islāmī* (Cairo-Beirut: Dār al-Shurūq, 5th edn., 1409/1989), pp. 12-26; also his *al-Jarā'im fi'l-Fiqh al-Islāmī: Dirāsah Fiqhiyyah Muqārinah* (Cairo/Beirut: Dār al-Shurūq, 6th edn., 1409/1988), pp. 169-243, and *al-Siyāsah al-Jinā'iyyah fi'l-Sharī'ah al-Islāmiyyah* (Cairo-Beirut: Dār al-Shurūq, 2nd edn., 1409/1988); Ahmed Omar Hashem, *al-Nafs fi'l-Qur'ān* (Cairo: Dār al-Fayṣal, 1996), pp. 57-61; Muhammad Salim El-Awa, *Fī Uṣūl al-Niẓām al-Jinā'ī al-Islāmī: Dirāsah Muqārinah* (Cairo: Nahḍat Miṣr, 2006), pp. 57-148 & 283-306; Muhammad Mohyi al-Din Awad, *al-Qānūn al-Jinā'ī: Mabādi'uhu al-Asāsiyyah wa-Naẓariyyātuhu al-'Āmmah fi'l-Sharī'ah al-Islāmiyyah* (Cairo: Cairo University Press, n.d.); Farhad Malekian, *Principles of Islamic International Criminal Law: A Comparative Search* (Leiden-Boston: Brill, 2011); Kamali, *The Right to Life, Security, Privacy and Owenership in Islam*, pp. 12-63; Luqman Zakariyah, *Legal Maxims in Islamic Criminal Law: Theory and Applications* (Leiden-Boston: Brill, 2015).

[63] Shihāb al-Dīn Ahmad b. Idrīs al-Qarāfī, *Sharḥ Tanqīḥ al-Fuṣūl fī-'Ikhtiṣār al-Maḥṣūl*, ed. Ahmad Farid al-Muzayyidi (Beirut: Dār al-Kutub al-'Ilmiyyah, 1428/2007), p. 377; Najm al-Dīn Abū al-Rabī' Sulaymān b. 'Abd al-Qawīy b. 'Abd al-Karīm b. Saʿīd al-Ṭūfī, *Sharḥ Mukhtaṣar al-Rawḍah*, ed. Abdullah bin Abdul Mohsin al-Turki (Beirut: Mu'assasat al-Risāhah, 2nd edn., 1419/1998), vol. 3, p. 209; Tāj al-Dīn 'Abd al-Wahhāb b. 'Alī al-Subkī, *Jamʿ al-Jawāmiʿ fī Uṣūl al-Fiqh*, ed. Abdelmonim Khalil Ibrahim (Beirut: Dār al-Kutub al-'Ilmiyyah, 2nd edn., 1424/2003), p. 92.

[64] See for more details, al-'Alim, *al-Maqāṣid al-'Āmmah li'l-al-Sharī'ah al-Islāmiyyah*, pp. 297-323; Mir Ali, *al-Maqāṣid al-'Āmmah li'l-Sharī'ah al-Islāmiyyah*, vol. 2, pp. 651-666.

[65] Abū 'Abd Allāh Muhammad b. Ismāʿīl al-Bukhārī, *Ṣaḥīḥ al-Bukhārī* (Damscus-Beirut: Dār Ibn Kathīr, 1st edn., 1423/2002), 'Kitāb al-Ṭibb', ḥadīth 5778, p. 1462; Abū al-Hussain Muslim b. al-Ḥajjāj al-Qushayrī al-Naysābūrī, *Ṣaḥīḥ Muslim*, ed. Mohammed Fuad Abd al-Baqi (Cairo: Dār Iḥyā' al-Kutub al-'Arabiyyah, 1st edn., 1412/1991), 'Kitāb al-Īmān', ḥadīth 175, vol. 1, pp.103-104.

[66] Al-Bukhārī, *Ṣaḥīḥ al-Bukhārī*, 'Kitāb al-Janā'iz', ḥadīth 1365, p. 329.

[67] Al-Bukhārī, *Ṣaḥīḥ al-Bukhārī*, 'Kitāb al-Janā'iz', ḥadīth 1363, p. 329; also, 'Kitāb al-Adab', ḥadīths 6047 & 6652, p. 1515 & 1647; al-Naysābūrī, *Ṣaḥīḥ Muslim*, 'Kitāb al-Īmān', ḥadīth 175, vol. 1, pp. 103-104.

[68] Margaret Pabst Battin (ed.), *The Ethics of Suicide: Historical Sources* (Oxford*New York: Oxford University Press, 2015), p. 198.

[69] For more on the question of suicide in the Islamic framework, see, al-Durayni, *Khaṣā'iṣ al-Tashrīʿ al-Islāmī*, pp. 206-209; Battin, *The Ethics of Suicide*, pp. 194-217; Mahmud Adesina Ayuba, "Euthenasia: A Muslim's Perspective," *Scriptura: Journal for Biblical, Theological and Contextual Hermeneutics*, vol. 115, no. 1 (2016), pp. 1-13; Mohamed Saeed Mohamed Saad, "Ẓāhirat al-Intiḥār wa-Aḥkāmuhā fi'l-Fiqh al-Islāmī," *Ḥawliyyat Kulliyat al-Dirāsāt al-Islāmiyyah bi-Aswān*, no. 2 (1441/2019), pp. 1985-2066.

[70] Ibn Ashur, *Treatise on Maqāṣid al-Sharīʿah*, pp. 120-121.

[71] For more details, see, al-Najjar, *Maqāṣid al-Sharīʿah bi-Abʿād Jadīdah*, pp. 84-125; also his *Qīmat al-Insān* (Rabat: Dār al-Zaytunah, 1st edn., 1417/1996).

CHAPTER THREE

Ḥifẓ al-ʿAql and *Ḥifẓ a-Māl:* Building Human Rationality and Realizing Economic Well-being

Introduction

As mentioned earlier more than once, *ḥifẓ al-ʿaql* (protection of the mind or intellect) and *ḥifẓ a-māl* (protection of wealth and property) are two of the five universal necessary goals of the Sharīʿah, thus standing with them on top of the pyramid of its system of values and purposes whose realization is aimed at by all-inclusive Islamic teachings and legislation covering the different spheres of human life. As such, *ḥifẓ al-ʿaql* is usually ranked by scholars of Islamic legal theory (*uṣūl al-fiqh*) as number three after *ḥifẓ al-dīn* and *ḥifẓ al-nafs*, while *ḥifẓ a-māl* occupies the fifth and last rank in the hierarchical order of *maqāṣid al-Sharīʿah*.

The protection of intellect pertains to fundamental internal aspects of human beings' non-physical nature and constitution, whereas the protection of wealth concerns external means and things required for serving and fulfilling a wide range of human needs in such a way as would sustain their material life and physical existence and well-being. In the following two sections of this chapter, an overall exposition of the significance and implications of these two Sharīʿah universals (*kulliyyāt al-sharīʿah*) will be made, followed in the third section by a brief concluding discussion of their relationship.

Ḥifẓ al-ʿAql: Meaning and Significance

1. The semantics of ʿaql

The noun *ʿaql* itself does not occur in the Qur'an, though it is widely used in all types of Arabic literature including pre-Islamic poetry and Prophetic traditions (Ḥadīth). However, this does not in any way imply the absence from the Qur'anic discource of the concept denoted by this specific term. Rather, the concept of *ʿaql* has been expressed some forty-nine times in the revealed text through verbal derivatives in both singular and plural forms (*yaʿqil, taʿqilūn,* and *yaʿqilūn*), thus indicating the action or activity of thinking, understanding, comprehending and reasoning, regardless of the positive or negative contexts in which such references are made.[1] On the other hand, we find in the Qur'an a number of nominal terms denoting either a physiological organ or a spiritual faculty to which are attributed many verbal forms denoting the kinds of intellectual activity mentioned above. These nouns include such terms as *ḥijr, ḥulum* (pl. *aḥlām), ṣadr* (pl. *ṣudūr), fu'ād* (pl. *af'idah), qalb* (pl. *qulūb), al-bāb,* and *nuhā*.[2] According to some Muslim scholars, such terms can be seen as synonyms of the term *ʿaql,* but with the realization that they denote different dimensions and levels of the power or faculty thus named.[3]

Of these nouns *qalb* (heart), occurring one hundred thirty-two times mostly in the plural form *qulūb*,[4] is the one to which the active verbal mode *yaʿqilūn* (derived from the root *ʿ.q.l.*), is specifically attributed as being the locus of the activity connoted by this verb. (al-Ḥajj, 22:46) In another instance, the active verbal mode *yafqahūn*[5] is also directly attributed to the plural subject *qulūb* (al-Arʿāf, 7:179) in a negative way describing those who fail to think and comprehend. Other than these two specific cases, there are a few instances where the plural noun *qulūb* is used in quite similar contexts together with the active verbal mode *yafqahūn* without there being a direct attribution of this verb to *qulūb* as a subject, though the conceptual connection between them cannot escape one's attention or be doubted. In addition to the above-mentioned verbal forms (*yaʿqilūn, yafqahūn*), the Qur'an abounds with a high score of other verbal forms deriving from different roots that denote various aspects or levels of cognition (perception, remembrance, intelligence, thinking, reflection, etc.). Here particularly it is question of expressions such as *yubṣirūn, yatadabbarūn, yatadhakkarūn, yadhdhakkarūn, yatafakkarūn, yanẓurūn,* etc., and their roots and co-derivatives.[6]

Regardless of the relative frequency of these verbal forms and whatever their (direct or indirect) grammatical and syntactic connections with *qalb* and the other noun terms, all such nouns and verbal expressions revolve around one central thing that has come to be predominantly known in Arabic as *ʿaql* to which different human languages have assigned specific terms, such as reason or mind or intellect in English, *minda* in Malay, raison in French, *grund* or *verstand* in German, *ratio* or *intellectus* in Latin, and *lógos* in Greek.

Having thus surveyed in a rather sketchy and descriptive manner the Qur'anic usage of the term *ʿaql* and other semantically related terms and verbal expressions, the question that now needs to be addressed is the following: what is exactly the meaning of this seemingly self-evident concept known as *ʿaql* and to the authority of which people usually appeal?

By consulting al-Khalīl's *Kitāb al-ʿAyn,* the oldest Arabic lexicon that has reached us, we find, together with other meanings pertaining to physical entities, actions or social events, that *ʿaql* is contrasted with ignorance (*jahl*) as being its opposite, and that the verb *ʿaqala* denotes the act of perceiving, understanding and apprehending. One of the significations pertaining to physical entities is worthy pointing out here whose significance will be realized shortly: both the noun *ʿaql* and the verb *ʿaqala* convey the sense of withhold (withholding) and bind or restrain (binding, restraining), such as when hobbling a camel by a rope in order to control its movement.[7] Subsequent philologists and lexicographers built on al-Khalīl's work and provided more linguistic and literary material confirming and supporting the different connotations of the term *ʿaql* and its derivatives in various contexts.

A quick look at the works of Ibn Manẓūr (d. 711/1311) and al-Zabīdī (d. 1205/1790) will suffice to have a clear view of the semantic development and conceptual crystallization of the meaning of *'aql* that unmistakably reflects its absorption of ethical, theological and philosophical connotations. In this respect, we read in *Lisān al-'Arab* that *'aql* is *ḥijr* and *nuhā,* thus standing in opposition to foolishness and stupidity (*ḥumq*), with both *nuhā* and *ḥijr* denoting also restrain, prevention and forbidding. Ibn Maẓūr then adds: a man described as *'āqil* is one with resolute will (or determinate course of action) and clear view (*al-jāmi'u li-amrihi wa-ra'yih*). It is also said of a person who is in control of his own self and restrains himself from following its whims and desires (*hawā*). From this an important meaning of *'aql* emerges that bears both ethical and intellectual implications. *'Aql* thus stands as man's capacity to comprehend and retain knowledge, as well as to control himself and keep away from "blameable inclinations". Hence, he is described as "a rational being.[8]

Taking stock of the heritage of Arabic lexicographical and Islamic intellectual traditions, al-Zabīdī provides perhaps the largest entry on the term *'aql* that encompasses its different linguistic connotations as recorded by linguists as well as its conceptual significations as articulated especially by Muslim theologians and philosophers based on their study of the Qur'an and Prophetic traditions as well as the intellectual traditions and philosophical works available to them.[9]

Stating first a generally agreed upon basic view that *'aql* is equivalent in meaning to knowledge (*'ilm*), al-Zabīdī then goes on listing a large number of different linguistic and lexical meanings of *'aql* and citing various statements by earlier scholars describing and defining the meaning(s) of this crucial term. Without going into a detailed discussion of al-Zabīdī's material, we shall rather focus on what is of direct bearing on our present purpose to circumscribe the conceptual signification of this term as it seems to have gradually crystallized in Muslim intellectual life seen from the perspective of al-Zabīdī himself. Hence, *'aql* is said to refer to knowledge of the qualities of things in terms of their goodness (*ḥusn*) and evilness (*qubḥ*), their perfectness (*kamāl*) and defectiveness (*nuqṣān*). It is also said of the power or faculty (*quwwah*) of discriminating between the good and the bad, of knowing the better of good things and the worse of bad things. Closely related to these meanings of *ʿaql* is its definition as an innate capacity by which the human being is prepared to acquire knowledge as well as of the knowledge arrived at thanks to the principles of that capacity.

Encompassing and grounding all the above-mentioned meanings, as al-Zabīdī seems to imply, is the view of Abū al-Maʿālī al-Juwaynī that *ʿaql* consists of certain elements of basic and necessary knowledge (*ʿulūm ḍarūriyyah*) characterizing and distinguishing a rational person (*ʿāqil*), whereby one perceives the necessity of what is necessary, the impossibility of what is impossible and the possibility of what is possible. This elementary knowledge is, so to speak, hardwired in the human mind as potentialities that come into actuality and grows gradually with the person's physical and mental growth, thus forming the foundation for all types of human inquiry and reasoning in the process of acquiring the knowledge of what one is ignorant of. As such, the great lexicographer concludes, *ʿaql* or reason has been considered the basis of obligation and responsibility (*taklīf*) once a person has reached maturity age of discernment (*bulūgh* & *tamyīz*).[10]

Before moving on to the next section, an important aspect of the Qur'anic view of reason and rationality should not escape our attention here, namely the relationship between the intellect and sense perception. Whether its locus is the brain or the heart or both or elsewhere in the human body, and no matter what kind of physiological and neurological relationship between these two organs, reason and rationality in the Qur'an are not detached or dissociated from sense perception with its different means, i.e. the physical senses, especially sight (*baṣar/ abṣār*) and hearing (*samʿ*). More specifically, the fact that the latter two senses are mentioned or referred to and paired in many Qur'anic verses, in relation to both human beings and in relation to God, clearly underscores their special importance and function.[11]

Being the immediate instruments with which the human person comes into contact with the external phenomenal world with its human and non-human existents, the different senses play a very crucial role in human cognition and acquisition of knowledge. They are the windows or channels by means of which we receive different kinds of data and information about the things and phenomena of the world in the form of sounds and words, images and shapes, tastes and smells, etc. Constituting what may be described as 'raw material', all such data and information are conveyed to the human internal faculties generally expressed by and subsumed under the concept of mind or reason or intellect (as being the generic or ultimate apprehensive/cognitive power). Then, it is the power indicated by these terms that subjects those data to different operations or processes of analysis, categorization, evaluation, judgement, conceptualization and inference.[12] This explains the Qur'an's recurrent call to people to properly use such senses as a sign of gratitude to God Who has endowed them therewith and its blame of those who fail to do so. In both respects we read:

1. *And God has brought you forth from your mothers' wombs knowing nothing—but He has endowed you with hearing, and sight, and minds (af'idah), so that you might have cause to be grateful.* (al-Naḥl, 16:78)

2. *And most certainly have We destined for hell many of the invisible beings (jinn) and men who have hearts with which they fail grasp the truth, and eyes with which they fail to see, and ears with which they fail hear.* (al-A'rāf, 7: 179)

The importance of the relationship between reason and the senses in fact cannot be expressed and stressed more beautifully than what God Himself has taught us as part of the ten commandments and general wisdom (al-Isrā', 17:36),

> *And never concern yourself with anything of which you have no knowledge: verily, [your] hearing and sight and mind—all of them—will be called to account for it [on Judgement Day].*

2. Protecting the mind and enhancing human rationality

As can be seen from the foregoing exposition and inferred from the different Qur'anic references to human understanding and reasoning briefly described above, the concept of *'aql* is multidimensional and has a clearly holistic signification that is not confined to mere theoretical understanding and discursive thinking, but combines and blends together "perceptual experience, conceptual thinking and moral judgment," thus uniting all the different aspects and means of the human cognitive experience.[13] The Qur'an, indeed, "has a high estimate of the potential of the human intellect," which is in fact "a corollary of its optimistic view of human nature."[14] However, it "does not exalt reason as autonomous and disembodied," for reason in the Islamic tradition "is intuitive and participatory." Aware of its embodiment as well as its limitations in relation to revelation and overlapping with sound intuition, reason "can be analytical and discursive, which coincides with its exegetical, legal, or analogical roles."[15]

Aided by revelation and in mutual complementarily and consolidation with it, reason in the Qur'an has to play the greatest role in human life and existence. Its role is not only to comprehend the multilayered meanings of the revelational discourse and receive its guiding messages on human conduct and relations. It has also to decipher the multiple signs in the universe pointing to the all-encompassing divine wisdom and ultimate order governing the world of creation with its diverse manifestations in both nature and history,[16] thus giving rise to different physical-natural and human-social sciences.

Likewise, reason, with its double light as theorized by al-Iṣfahānī and al-Ghazālī,[17] constitutes the solid and only ground for human responsibility and accountability in Islam whose discourse to human beings (in the Qur'an and Prophetic traditions) is not only about knowing, but about knowing and doing, cognizing and acting, at the same time. Hence, Muslim legal theorists, jurists and theologians throughout the centuries are almost one on the fact that the preservation and consolidation of the human mind or intellect, *ḥifẓ al-ʿaql*, is one of the essential goals and necessary universals (*al-kulliyyāt al-ḍarūriyyah*) of the Sharīʿah. In the event of the mind's defect or deficiency a person's conduct and liability are totally or partially affected in accordance with the degree of affliction, this will no doubt reverberate in different forms and with varying effects in accordance with the person's connections and presence in society in a chain that affects in different ways the social body and structure. This is so regardless of whether or not such reverberations be realized or recognized.[18]

It is within this perspective on the meaning, worth, function and impact of reason and rationality in human life and society that we can best appreciate Islam's unwavering position as to the prohibition of all intoxicants whatever form they might take and in whichever way they may be consumed. Yet, the Islamic teachings are not silent on hard-case circumstances of compelling necessity that might affect human beings individually or collectively, for which purpose a whole juristic theory, explicitly anchored in the Qur'an, has been developed that addresses the different aspects of necessity in terms of scope, criteria, gravity and treatment.[19]

The Qur'an has summarized the whole issue about alcoholism and its twin-sister gambling in the most concise and suggestive manner for thinking minds and live consciences. Thus, we read in sūrah al-Baqarah (2:219):

> *They will ask you about intoxicants (khamr) and games of chance (maysir). Say: "In both there is great evil as well as some benefit for man; but the evil which they cause is greater than the benefit which they bring."*

The message of this verse is further emphasized and explicated in sūrah al-Mā'idah (5:90-91) as follows:

> *[90]O You who have attained to faith! Intoxicants (khamr), and gambling, and idolatrous practices, and the divining of the future are but a loathsome evil of Satan's doing: shun it, then, so that you might attain to a happy state! [91]By means of intoxicants and games of chance Satan seeks only to sow enmity and hatred among you, and to turn you away from the remembrance of God and from prayer. Will you not, then, desist?*

As a noun derived from the verb *khamara*, meaning to conceal and obscure, *khamr* in its lexical signification "denotes every substance the use of which obscures the intellect."[20] The Qur'an takes up this original linguistic signification and uses the term in a generic manner that extends beyond the types of intoxicants known in the immediate socio-historical context of Revelation, so as to include all kinds of intoxicants. This generic meaning of the term *khamr* has been expressed in the form of general maxims by the Prophet of Islam who stated that "Every intoxicant is *khamr*, and every *khamr* is forbidden,"[21] and "Whatever intoxicates in large quantities, a small quantity thereof is forbidden."[22]

The rationale behind the prohibition of such intoxicants, be they alcoholic beverages or other substances, is their inebriating effect on the mind resulting in veiling and covering it, or simply *iskār* as always stated by Muslim scholars in their juristic deliberations. Accordingly, it is the purpose of the Sharī'ah to preserve the intactness, integrity and soundness of the human mind and protect it against anything that might corrupt it and undermine its intellectual functions of understanding, reasoning and discrimination. But, as the second of the above two verses makes it clear, the consequences of intoxicants are not confined to affecting individual minds. They have rather far-reaching effects of socio-cultural, economic, spiritual and psychological nature, taking the form of hatred, enmity and strife in society and turning people away from God. It is in this connection that we can properly realize the Prophet's description of intoxicants as the mother or root cause of disgraceful deeds and the gravest of sins, "*al-khamr umm al-fawāḥish wa akbar al-kabā'ir.*"[23] Thus, he strongly emphasizes their prohibition and sharply brings forth their loathsome character by the virtue of the fact that "the word *fawāḥish* applies to all those acts whose abominable character is self-evident."[24] Hence, as Tunisia's renowned scholar Ibn Ashur put it,

> The preservation of the intellect means the protection of people's minds from being affected by anything putting them in disorder. This is because any disorder of the intellect leads to serious corruption consisting of improper and perverted human conduct. Thus, any defect affecting the mind of an individual leads to partial corruption and evil, while any defect affecting the minds of large groups or of the entire community results in total and devastating evil.[25]

Yet, disorder and malfunctioning befalling the intellect are not solely the result of self-induced intoxicants of the kind of *khamr-*

beverages known at the time of revelation and to the early generations of Muslims or introduced subsequently through to the present age by different peoples and cultures. There are other factors, beyond mere physical intoxicating substances, which may rather be more dangerous to, and corruptive of, the mind. Such agents have been mentioned in the two Qur'anic verses (5: 90-91) quoted a while ago, namely gambling, idol-worship and divining of the future. This is further brought into focus in the same sūrah shortly after where it is stated that (al-Mā'idah, 5:103-104),

[103] It is not of God's ordaining that certain kinds of cattle, baḥīrah, sā'ibah, waṣīlah, and ḥām, should be marked out by superstition and set aside from the use of man; yet those who are bent on denying the truth attribute their own lying inventions to God. And most of them never use their reason:[104] for when they are told, "Come unto that which God has bestowed from on high, and unto the Apostle," they answer, "Enough for us is that which we found our forefathers believing in and doing." Why, even though their forefathers knew nothing, and were devoid of all guidance?

These verses revolve around two things. The first verse describes certain practices of the pre-Islamic pagan Arabs who "used to dedicate to their various deities" certain categories of animals named as *baḥīrah, sā'ibah, waṣīlah* and *ḥām,* by setting them free to pasture and prohibiting their slaughter."[26] As indicated in the same verse, such practices are simply the result of those people's failure to use their reason, thus being no more than "an illustration of the arbitrary invention of certain supposedly 'religious' obligations and prohibitions."[27] In the second verse it is question of the same people's attitude to reject the call of the Prophet and refuse to listen to the Qur'anic message by sticking to what their forefathers had been believing and practising, thus once again failing to use their mind out of blind submission to tradition.[28] In fact, the Qur'an abounds with statements describing, criticizing and condemning different forms of the corruption and subversion of reason, which all obstruct sound thinking and rational inquiry and pursuit of the truth. Citing one example will suffice to further underline this point here. Likewise, we read in sūrah al-Jāthiyah (45:23-24):

> [23]*Have you ever considered the one who takes his own desires as a deity, and whom God [thereupon] allows to go astray in the face of knowledge, sealing his hearing and heart and veiling his sight? Who, then, could guide him after God [has abandoned him]? Will you not, then, bethink yourselves?* [24]*And yet they say: "There is nothing beyond our life in this world. We die as we come to life, and nothing but time destroys us." But of this they have no knowledge whatever: they do nothing but guess.*

It is clear from this passage that the Qur'an does not limit the perversion and corruption of human reason to self-induced intoxicants of whatever kind. Rather, it confirms and "further implicates, *inter alia*, ego, social anxiety, and cultural convention in the corruption, suppression, or misuse of ʿ*aql*."[29] Thus, as al-Raysuni rightly says, the preservation of reason in the Sharīʿah "is not limited to outward measures such as prohibiting intoxicants and imposing penalties for partaking of them," for many a person has lost his/her mind "without his or her having touched a drop of liquor" or any other kind of intoxicants! "Indeed, people's minds are lost through ignorance, lethargy, idleness and blind imitation."[30]

The preservation of intellect, therefore, takes multiple forms including and transcending the legal ban on intoxicating substances and the combat against alcoholism and drug addiction, as it may be very much the case that falling prey to such corruptive factors is in fact the result, not the cause, of the mind's weakness and corruption due to other more dangerous and corruptive agents of non-physical nature. Hence, a more comprehensive approach to the preservation and protection of the intellect is required that shall take various forms of both preventive and positive constructive measures. All such measures need to converge on building and nurturing thinking, inquisitive, and critical minds driven to seeking the truth and goodness and rejecting prejudice, falsehood and evilness.[31] Such is or should be the mission and function of an education that is not confined to just stuffing the learners' minds with information and equipping them with certain practical skills, but one aimed at building their personalities in such an integrated manner so that knowledge, thinking, virtue and skill are inextricably intertwined and operate as a unified entity.

Without going into more profound and specialized philosophical and psychological discussion of *'aql* and its levels and manifestations, what has been said so far about it in this chapter serves sufficiently the purpose of the present work. In fact, a good deal of what has preceded in the first two chapters strongly connects with and complements our present discussion on the intellect, and we trust the reader's capacity to intelligently see the whole picture.

Ḥifẓ a-Māl: Meaning and Purpose

1. The Qur'anic semantics of māl and the ontology of economic wealth

Unlike the term *'aql*, the word *māl* is literally used over eighty times in many different contexts in the Qur'an in both the singular and plural modes, in long, medium and short sūrahs. In both modes, this term has a generic meaning denoting whatever one possesses, likewise constituting one's wealth or property, regardless of the specific things or substances making up such wealth, be that natural or man-made.[32] But this does not seem to be the prevailing usage of the term at the time of the Qur'anic revelation. It is interesting to note that the first Arab lexicographer al-Khalīl, did not feel the need to explain the meaning of *māl* as it is, according to him, something "known" (*ma'rūf*). However, he observes that for the Arabs *amwāl* consisted of cattle (*wa-kānat amwālu al-'Arabi an'āmahum*).[33] In quite similar vein, Ibn al-Athīr (d. 606AH/1233AD) indicates that originally *māl* referred to possessions of gold and silver, but then it came to include "all concrete things (*a'yān*) that may be acquired and possessed," following which he observes that "for the Arabs *māl* mostly referred to camels because they were the bulk of their wealth."[34]

Transcending the immediate socio-cultural and historical context of the Arabs' use of the term *māl* before and during the time of its revelation, the Qur'an has amplified its meaning and widened its scope so as to include all things that are useful, valuable and attractive to human beings, thus bringing forth the reasons for which they strive for acquiring and possessing them. In this context, it discloses the psychological relationship between human beings and *māl* as being part of their innate propensities and instinctive drives due to the fact that *amwāl* fulfill for them different kinds of needs both at the individual and collective levels that go beyond the mere biological and physical aspects of human life and existence, without in any way underestimating the importance of such aspects.

Hence, the Qur'an underlines the fact that we humans "love wealth with boundless love" (al-Fajr, 89:20) and declares that "wealth (*māl*) and children (*banūn*) are an adornment of worldly life (*zīnat al-ḥayāt al-dunyā*)," while reminding us that "good deeds, the fruit of which endures forever, are of far greater merit" in God's sight "and a far better source of hope" (al-Kahf, 18:46). It teaches us not to be so self-indulgent and lustful for, and enslaved to, money for its own sake, in an endless race to collect and accumulate it for no real and good purpose other than the mere concerns and interest of the ego and the present, thus falling under the devil's spell.[35] The psychology of money and wealth is further underscored by bringing to light its ontological roots. Referring specifically to male human beings, and by implication to women, the Qur'an announces (āl 'Imrān, 3:14) that,

> *Made beautiful for mankind (zuyyina li'l-nās) is the love of desires, for women and offspring, for hoarded treasures of gold and silver, for branded horses, cattle and plantations. These are the comforts of worldly life (matā' al-ḥayāt al-dunyā); yet with God is the best of all ends.*

This verse "describes the blessings of this world and the excessive weakness of man for them." Stating that they have been "made beautiful (*zuyyina*) for mankind", the Qur'an thus underlines the fact that love and desire for such things belong to instinctual dispositions and relate to deep impulses which are necessary for human survival. At the same time, it states clearly that such instinct-prompted desires are not an end in themselves. Instead, they are simply means for life in this world which must be harnessed to achieve human beings' higher goal and ultimate end of being closer to God and enjoying His eternal bliss.[36]

The idea of "making beautiful" the love-desire of the objects mentioned in the verse calls for further reflection necessitated by the question as to the ontological origin of such beautifying (*tazyīn*). A close syntactical and semantic analysis of the verse shows that the subject or author of the act of *tazyīn*, grammatically ascribed to the passive voice, is actually God Who has created human beings and inscribed in their inborn nature (*jibillah*) such desires. As Ibn ‘Aṭiyyah put it, God's making such things alluring to mankind is by creating and making them susceptible for utilisation and ingraining in human nature the longing for them.[37] Thus constituting the root of all human desires (*uṣūl al-shahawāt al-bashariyyah*), these fundamental desires do not change with time, space and culture. Behind this lies a profound universal wisdom serving God's purpose in the human creation.[38] In other words, the instinctive attraction to the things mentioned in the verse as being the object of human desire is an essential and integral aspect of the cosmic order governing human existence and enabling humans to fulfill their purpose provided such desire is rightfully satisfied.[39]

With this understanding of the meaning of *māl* in mind, classical Muslim jurists set out to formulate technical definitions for it. Notwithstanding the differences mirrored in their definitions as a result of the criteria used in the different juristic schools to classify wealth and property into different categories, there seems to be a universal consensus on certain essential features of *māl* that clearly reflect its psychological, economic, and social nature and function in human life. These characteristics can be summarized in three main points. First, *māl* is what human beings are inclined to by nature (*yamīlu ilayhii al-ṭab‘*) and seek to acquire and own whether individually or collectively. Second, it is something which has a real value in terms of usefulness and utility (*naf‘*) in the customary life of people as well as in terms of legality in the sight of the Sharī‘ah, or simply valuable *‘ādatan wa-shar‘an*. Lastly, *māl* consists of both movable and immovable things whose ownership is transferable from one hand to another; movables are durable, and hence can be stored for time of need and exchanged among people through different forms of transactions. *Bien entendu*, durability and saving for time of need applies equally to immovable things.

Attendant to the above-mentioned characteristics of *māl* is the idea of usufruct (*manfaʿah*) which, though contested by the Ḥanafīs on the basis of its ephemeral nature and non-susceptibility to saving (*iddikhār*), its character as commodity or merchandise is acknowledged by the majority of classical Muslim jurists, hence constituting a category of wealth and property on its own, be it in private or public ownership.[40]

It goes without saying that all types of services that fulfil material or non-material needs in human life are encompassed in this broad conception of *māl*. Similarly, money and currency in its different forms (old and new, tangible or intangible) is an integral part of *māl* so far as those forms are a matter of social convention sanctioned and regulated by the legal order and economic system under which people carry out their economic and financial activities. This seems to be the view held by most contemporary Muslim scholars across the different jusristic schools and juridical bodies.[41]

What has been said so far is not, however, all that we can learn from the Qur'an about the origin, significance and function of *māl* in human life and civilization. In fact, there is a much deeper conceptual level without which our understanding of the Islamic philosophy of wealth and property, or economic philosophy, will remain incomplete or wanting. A number of other closely related terms to *māl* should not therefore escape our attenation, though our analysis will not cover them all. Rather, we shall limit our discussion to only two of those terms, which we deem fundamental and central and hence sufficient to shed more light on the subject and put it in proper perspective. It is question of the terms *rizq* and *taskhīr*.

The term *rizq* occurs in the Qur'an 122 times half of which in the verbal mood, whereas 54 times as active participle (*ism al-fāʿil*) and the rest as substantive noun (*maṣdar*). What is of special significance for us in this statistical information is that more than fifty percent of the verbal usages of this term are attributed in different grammatical moods to God as the subject (*fāʿil*) of the act (*fiʿl*), while the seven occurrences of the active participle refer to Him as the supplier of *rizq*. Now, what does this term mean?

From the etymological point of view, the root *r.z.q* has to do with subsistence or sustenance and its means. In the Qurʾanic usage, this meaning applies to human beings and other creatures in the world as well, thus implying that subsistence and its means are both material and immaterial, physical and non-physical, tangible and intangible, seen and unseen, yet experienced and felt one way or another, directly or indirectly. That being the generic sense of the term, *rizq* in the Qurʾan is ontologically linked or attributed to God as the ultimate supplier of all means of subsistence to all kinds of creatures, each in accordance with its nature, needs and function. Hence, being *al-Razzāq* is one of God's beautiful names (*al-asmāʾ al-ḥusnà*). With its intensive or superlative mood (*mubālaghah*) applying only to God,[42] this epithet implies that He is not only the provider of the means of subsistence, but also "the Creator of what are termed *arzāq* and the Giver of their *arzāq* to His creatures."[43]

Thus, we read in the Qurʾan (Hūd, 11:6): "And there is no living creature (*dābbah*) on earth but depends for its sustenance (*rizquhà*) on God; and He knows its dwelling [on earth] and its resting-place [after death]." This is because (al-Dhāriyāt, 51:56-58) "God Himself is the Provider of all sustenance, the Lord of all might, the Eternal," Who has "created the invisible beings (*jinn*) and humankind to any end other than that they may [know and] worship" Him, without being in need for anything from them.[44] The relationship between creation and sustenance in God's power has been expressed by al-Ghazālī as follows. *Al-Razzāq*, he says, "is the one who has created the means of sustenance (*arzāq*) and those sustained (*murtazaqah*), made the former within the reach of the latter and created in them the ways of enjoying them." As he further explaines, *rizq* is of two kinds. The first kind is "outwardly (*ẓāhir*) consisting of nourishment and food which concern the outward [of humans], that is the body." The second is "inwardly and consists of knowledge and revelations (*al-maʿārif wa'l-mukāshafāt*) relating to the hearts and innermost matters (*asrār*)."[45]

Interestingly, the lexicographer Ibn Manẓūr reproduced almost verbatim al-Ghazālī's explanation; yet he clearly played down its mystical tone. Likewise, he stated that for human beings "sustenance (*arzāq*) is of two types: outward (*ẓāhirah*) relating to bodies, such as food, and inward (*bāṭinah*) pertaining to hearts and souls, such as knowledge and the sciences."[46] In other words, *rizq* in the Qur'anic context "applies to all that may be of benefit to man, whether it be concrete and tangible (like food, property, offspring, etc.) or abstract and intangible (like knowledge, piety, etc.)."[47]

God's supply of the means of sustenance is not confined to specific individuals, race or social class, but is for all human beings regardless of whether or not they believe in Him and whether obey or disobey His commands. This is made abundantly clear by the Qur'an in the following verses (al-Isrā', 17:18-20):

> [18]*Unto him who cares for [no more than the enjoyment of] this fleeting life We readily grant thereof as much as We please, [giving] to whomever it is Our will [to give]; but in the end We consign him to [the suffering of] hell; which he will have to endure disgraced and disowned!* [19]*But as for those who care for the [good of the] life to come, and strive for it as it ought to be striven for, and are [true] believers withal—they are the ones whose striving finds favour [with God]!* [20]*All [of them]—these as well as those—do We freely endow with some of thy Sustainer's gifts, since thy Sustainer's giving is never confined [to one kind of man].*

Following a description of the attitudes of the believers and un-believers towards God, this worldly life and the Hereafter in verses 18-19, verse 20 underlines the fact that those attitudes are not de-terminant factors when it comes to humans' benefiting from, and enjoying, the bounties of this world. As al-Rāzī comments, because this world is a place of labour and test (*dār al-ʿamal*) for human be-ings, it has been necessary to remove for them all kinds of excuses (*ʿudhr*) and obstacles (*ʿillah*) and provide all of them with what they need for their well-being, as God's bounty is for all and restricted to none.[48] Likewise, God's bounties in the world are bestowed on all, irrespective of their gratitude and obedience or disobedience and ingratitude to Him.[49] What has been described in detail in these and similar verses in the Qur'an has been expressed in a generic and all-encompassing manner in the following statement (al-Baqarah, 2:29):

"He it is who has created for you all that is on earth."[50]

Now, the foregoing exposition of the Qur'anic view on *rizq* reflects, and invites the mind to, the other fundamental Qur'anic concept, i.e., *taskhīr*, according to which all things of the world have been created by God who made them subservient to mankind as part of the necessary and suitable conditions for their stewardship (*khilāfah*) on earth. Thus, we read in sūrah Ibrāhīm (14:32-34):

> [32]*It is God who has created the heavens and the earth, and who sends down water from the sky and thereby brings forth [all manner] of fruits for your sustenance; and who has made ships <u>subservient</u> to you (sakhkhara lakum), so that they may sail through the sea at His behest; and has made the rivers <u>subservient</u> to you;* [33] *and has made the sun and the moon, both of them constant upon their courses, <u>subservient</u> to you; and has made the night and the day subservient to you.* [34] *And [always] does He give you something out of what you may be asking of Him; and should you try to count God's blessings, you could never compute them.*

Occurring twenty-two times in the Qur'an with God as its subject, the verb *sakhkhara* has as its object various natural phenomena on earth and in the heavens that have been mentioned in different contexts with varying degrees of detail.[51] All such phenomena have been expressed in a general and all-inclusive way in at least two places in the Qur'an. Accordingly, we read in sūrah Luqmān (31:20) that "God has made subservient to you (humans) all that is in the heavens and all that is on earth, and has lavished upon you His blessings, both outward and inward." The same message is conveyed in al-Jāthiyah (45:13) in which we are taught that "He [God] has made subservient to you, from Himself, all that is in the heavens and on earth: in this, behold, there are messages indeed for people who think." Of similar significance, though not using the same verb, is the statement in al-Baqarah (2:29) cited above stating that God "has created for you (humans) *all that is on earth*, and has applied His design to the heavens and fashioned them into seven heavens."

One essential meaning of the verb *sakhkhara* in the Qur'anic discourse has to do with God's absolute power and will by virtue of which to "Him belongs all that is in the heavens and all that is on earth", hence "He alone is self-sufficient." (al-Ḥajj, 22:64) Likewise, everything in the world is governed by a divinely designed order and runs according to specific norms and laws commensurate with its nature and function(s) in the cosmos.[52] The other meaning, which is a derivative of what has been mentioned, is that God has made the natural phenomena, thus regulated, 'subservient' to human beings, in the sense of being put at their service and hence made amenable to their intervention and action. In other words, it is part of God's cosmic design that, "alone among all living beings", man has been endowed "with a creative mind and, thus, with the ability to make conscious use of the nature that surrounds him and is within him."[53] This conscious use of natural phenomena by human beings consists first and foremost of deriving "lasting benefit from them,"[54] that is, to derive from them all that is required to meet the different human needs in this life. This understanding of the meaning of *taskhīr* in relation to human beings is corroborated by many verses in the Qur'an of which the following one will suffice to make the point. We read in sūrah al-Mulk (67:15):

> *He [God] it is who has made the earth submissive (dhalūlan) to you [humans]: go about, then, in all its regions, and partake of the suste-nance which He provides (kulū min rizqih).*

Likewise, mankind is both informed and recommended: informed that the earth has been made an easy and hospitable place for them to live in, and recommended to go around and benefit and 'eat' from the provisions made available to them in land and sea combined with un-seen bounties descending from the sky or lying underground.

It is of much significance that the Qur'anic discourse on *rizq* is not confined to such general references to what God has provided for mankind, as have been explained above. It also more specifically refers to various types of human activities and different ways through which the use of those provisions and bounties is made possible, ef-ficient and beneficial, such as cultivation and agriculture, livestock and pasturing, manufacturing and industry.[55] All this understandably goes beyond mere immediate and 'primitive' use or consumption to involve varying degrees and processes of intervention which require different levels of scientific knowledge and technological capacity in accordance with the different stages of historical development the human race has gone through.

Being thus grounded in a cosmological view of *rizq*, which is itself rooted in the fundamental concept of *taskhīr*, the notion of *māl* in the Qur'an acquires its full philosophical, spiritual and ethical dimensions both as gift and trust from God. Its characteristics as indicated above make its conception in the Islamic framework so comprehensive that it denotes and includes all types of wealth hitherto known in human history and civilization or which might be known in the future. It thus consists of the God-given natural resources and whatever human beings make out of them by way of derivation, extraction, transformation, engineering and reengineering, with money serving as the means of value-measurement and stock of value for all commercially exchangeable matters, including human labour itself. As such, all types of wealth fall under the purview of the essential notion of original permissibility (*al-ibāḥah al-aṣliyyah*). According to this principle, things in the world have been created by God for the benefit of human beings and, hence, made permissible to them, except those things which have been explicitly declared forbidden (*ḥarām* or *maḥẓūr*) by the Qur'an and the Prophet due to their harmful and/or evil nature. To this are appended such things as judged so by expert scholars through proper interpretive and analogical methods (as elaborated in the discipline of Islamic legal theory and methodology, *uṣūl al-fiqh*), based on careful study of their characteristics and effects.[56] Hence, the Qur'an exclaims (al-A'rāf, 7:32):

> *Say: "Who is there to forbid the beauty which God has brought forth for His creatures, and the good things from among the means of sustenance?" Say: "They are [lawful] in the life of this world unto all who have attained to faith—to be theirs alone on Resurrection Day".*

Commenting on this verse, Muhammad Asad has the following to say: "By declaring that all good and beautiful things of life—ie., those which are not expressly prohibited—are lawful to the believers, the Qur'an condemns, by implication, all forms of life-denying, asceticism, world-renunciation and self-mortification."[57]

Before turning to another aspect of the subject, it is worth pointing out that in most cases the word *māl* is used in the Qur'an in the plural form *amwāl*, in such possessive phrases as *amwālunā, amwālukum* and *amwāluhum* (2, 14 and 30 times respectively), whereby it is also ascribed to plural (or collective) pronouns. This is so regardless of the grammatical functions of the word *amwāl* in such phrases (i.e., as subject or object) and whether they occur in positive or negative contexts.[58] Without going into detailed discussion of this fact, we may here make the general remark that whatever money and property individuals acquire and possess, it is still an integral part of the society's overall wealth and, therefore, individuals' ownership thereof is not private in an absolute sense. Hence, it should be used in such a way as would benefit the community, let aside to be disposed of in ways detrimental to its well-being.[59]

2. *Māl and wealth in the value scheme of Islamic jurisprudence*

As explained above, *māl* consists of all kinds of natural resources God has provided for humans as well as all that results from those resources through human labour and intervention. Thus, in the Qur'anic vision, human beings cannot seriously claim any absolute and original ownership of such resources, for it is God unto whom "belong the treasures of the heavens and the earth" (al-Munāfiqūn, 63:7) who is their Real Owner.[60] Therefore people's ownership is relative and relational at the same time. It is relative in the sense that they have been delegated by their Creator and Sustainer to make use of the resources and bounties He has bestowed on them in order to fulfill their material and immaterial needs. It is relational in the sense that whatever resources and wealth individuals and groups may acquire and possess does not, and should not, stand away or above the society to which they belong, however big or small that society might be. Rather, resources and wealth owned by individuals and groups could not have been acquired without the opportunities and favourable conditions provided for them by the society itself. In fact, the totality of society contributes in many ways, direct and indirect, to the various forms of wealth and property its individuals and groups may acquire. Accordingly, such wealth and property are essentially indebted to the rest of society. Indeed, the matter goes beyond one's immediate and particular society and fellow citizens. It also includes the future generations of one's community and, indeed, all humanity in different degrees, especially at a time when human communities and societies in the world have become so much interconnected and mutually dependent through increasingly globalized financial, economic, technological and other types of systems and webs, in such a way that the fate of every society depends in varying degrees on that of others.

This vision is certainly in total opposition to the mentality and attitude of Qārūn (Korah) "who arrogantly boasted above" his fellow Israelites because of the opulent riches he had, claiming that that wealth had been given to him only by virtue of the knowledge in him: *innamā ūtihu ʿalā ʿilmin ʿindī.* (al-Qaṣaṣ, 28:76-78)[61] Such attitude and mentality are not something of a remote past that was characteristic of a certain Korah, nor are they confined to specific individuals or small groups. Instead, they express certain human propensities that can be, indeed have been, manifestly and dangerously embodied in whole societies, notably in today's world with its dominant plunderous capitalist system and ultra-greedy multinationals.

As an ethico-legal discipline, Islamic jurisprudence has been deeply embedded in the concrete realities of human life and existence. Since very early stages of its history, it has been systematically arranged in accordance with the different spheres of human activity and endeavour whereby individuals and groups seek to fulfill their different needs, material as well as immaterial. This is a prominent feature of this crucial area of Islamic scholarship and culture that cannot be missed out or ignored by any serious student of human cultural history and civilization, testifying to both its realism and normativity. In fact, this entrenchment of Islamic jurisprudence in the life-word is equally and clearly reflected in the way most canonical collections of the Prophetic traditions have been thematically classified according to the categories of issues they deal with, which all concern different and interrelated aspects and dimensions of human life and society. One may even argue that it was jurisprudence that actually set up the model to the discipline of Ḥadīth by virtue of its historical precedence.

In that context, both in its encyclopedic compendia and medium and short treatises and manuals, Islamic jurisprudence devoted a noticeably large space to economic and financial matters of different kinds and scopes dealt with in varying degrees of elaboration and systematization, thus manifestly testifying to its dynamic and realistic nature.[62] Thanks to their deliberations on the Qur'anic and Sunnaic materials pertaining to financial and economic matters and due to their tackling of various types of real-life economic activities and financial issues, Muslim jurisprudents, broadly speaking, were able to come to the essential conclusion that *ḥifẓ al-māl* is one of the five universal necessities (*al-kulliyyāt al-ḍarūriyyah al-khamsah*) constituting the higher goals of the Sharī'ah. Together, so they argued, this necessity and the other four universals (*ḥifẓ al-dīn, ḥifẓ al-nafs, al-ʿaql* and *ḥifẓ al-nasl*) constitute the foundation on which the order of the human world stands and depends for its equilibrium, well-being and continuation. To just paraphrase al-Ghazālī and al-Shāṭibī, this fivefold grand purpose of the Sharī'ah revolves around what is cardinal and essential for achieving human beings' spiritual and material well-being. If these essentials are missing or undermined wholly or partly, imbalance, corruption and strife will affect human life accordingly, in this world and in the hereafter as well.[63]

Encapsulated in the Qur'an and the Prophet's traditions by the word *māl* and other related terms as already shown, it is only natural that wealth and property be assigned in the teachings of Islam such an important place in human life and civilization simply because mankind does not consist of angelic beings or ethereal entities existing beyond matter and the physical world of nature. Humans rather consist of physically and concretely embodied beings whose subsistence in this world cannot be maintained without fulfilling a wide range of essentially material and physical needs. Indeed, lots of human beings' immaterial needs require money as, means for their fulfillment. In other words, human well-being is multidimensional in nature and embedded in the material world. Attaining it cannot, therefore, happen by merely taking care of one dimension only.

That being the case as to the crucial place and function of *māl* in human life, scholars of Islamic jurisprudence have paid considerable attention to the question of how *ḥifẓ al-māl* can be achieved in terms of both attaining (*taḥṣīl*) and retaining (*ibqāʾ*) it.[64] By this they mean the ways and means of making money and acquiring wealth as well as the ways and means of preserving them. This includes by necessity the legal and ethical criteria of lawfulness and unlawfulness of the ways money and wealth are acquired and spent, as there is no condoning in the Sharīʿah of the idea that ends justify the means (except in the very limited sense of compelling necessity, i.e., *ḍarūarh*). They did so through careful analysis of the Qurʾanic and Prophetic legal-ethical ordinances pertaining to the regulation of people's conduct in carrying out their economic and financial activities, including of course the nature and substance of the subject matter of those activities. Accordingly, *taḥṣīl* and *ibqāʾ* revolve, in al-Shāṭibī's words, around establishing the pillars of wealth and strengthening its foundations (*jānib al-wujūd*) on the one hand, and removing whatever might put it in disorder whether at the present or in the future (*jānib al-ʿadam*), on the other. This is achieved through undertaking various types of economic activities and financial transactions (*muʿāmalāt*) as well as abstaining from certain things and practices the violation of which provides grounds for punishment, such as hand amputation for theft.[65]

In other words, *taḥṣīl* consists of production and the creation of wealth, which requires and presupposes access to the resources and means necessary for the process of production, including means. This involves various types of business that include agriculture, livestock, manufacturing and services, each being carried out and enhanced by the relevant technological means. In all this labour in both its mental and physical sense plays the most crucial role whereby the human genius and abilities are applied to the different kinds of natural resources that God has provided for mankind. As for *ibqāʾ*, it concerns the protection of wealth and property, whether private or public, from being misused, squandered or usurped. On this latter aspect of *ḥifẓ al-māl* Ibn Ashur states that it "means protecting the wealth of the community from being ruined and from shifting to the hands of others without compensation. It also means protecting the different constituents* of that wealth which is valued in the Shari'ah from being destroyed for no return." It also includes "the protection of property from being transferred from one person to another within the community without the consent of its owner" or without return. This is because "the preservation of private wealth leads eventually to the preservation of the community's wealth," since "the preservation of the whole is achieved by preserving its constituent parts."[66]

Despite their emphasis on economic wealth as one of the five essential pillars of human life and society, Muslim jurists prior to the contemporary era were mostly concerned about outlining the different types of contracts governing financial and economic transactions taking place among individuals and detailing the legal stipulations and rules that would ensure their validity, transparency, equity and workability. The same can be said of specific treatises devoted totally to economic and financial subjects, which are generally known under such nomenclatures as *kharāj, amwāl, ḥisbah, kasb* or *makāsib, tijārah,* etc.[67] This may suggest the impression that those jurists lacked, or at least did not develop, a general view or theory of society's economy as a whole or as a system, which may imply the absence in their thinking of the idea of wealth distribution and economic justice in the society as a clearly spelled out and systematically articulated theory. In other words, theorizing about economics was not of noticeable clear interest for classical and 'medieval' Islamic economic jurisprudence. Admitting its validity for the sake of argument, this impression can be explained as follows. In their deliberations on economic and financial matters, Muslim jurists' approach was essentially legal as they were mainly concerned about the criteria and formal rules governing people's transactions, thus apparently taking for granted an existing economic system within which such transactions are carried out.

It is a matter of fact that we find in the writings of those jurists' insightful discussions on many economic issues, such as prices, markets and value, which have become increasingly so crucial and determinant in human economic thought only in recent centuries, es-

---

* Ibn Ashur refers here to the different types of ownership and property existing in society, i.e., private, public, etc.

pecially since the publication of Adam Smith's *The Wealth of Nations* in the last quarter of the eighteenth century and the rise and development of modern economic theories. Other issues that are central to modern economic thought, like the scarcity of resources considered as the central problem of economics,[68] may appear to lack clear and explicit presence in those works. Nevertheless, this does not and cannot mean that Muslim scholars of the past, who dealt with economic and financial issues, did not have in the back of their minds certain general theoretical notions or postulates concerning the nature and problems of the economy, just as they had with regard to the socio-political system as expressed by such concepts like *ummah* and *khilāfah* on which they produced a vast body of literature. Likewise, comprehensive comparative (synchronic and diachronic) analysis of the many chapters on different types of economic dealings across juristic schools to unearth their underlying premises is yet a serious research gap to be filled, despite the fact that some insightful historical studies in Islamic economic thought and institutions are already in existence.[69] Such comparative study needs to be complemented by a systematic effort to reconstruct and rearticulate the relevant materials and data in order to bring to light what may be considered a general Islamic theory or doctrine on economics that guided Muslim jurists in their legal treatment of economic and financial matters.[70]

3. Justice and need fulfilment: Pearls of wisdom from Ibn Khaldūn and al-Ghazālī

What we have arguably considered missing in formal juristic works with regard to economic theorizing can, in fact, be found in some other disciplines of Islamic learning and scholarship or in works that do not belong to a specific discipline but reflect a kind of 'hybrid' or interdisciplinary treatment of human social and political matters. In this respect, Ibn Khaldūn's (d. 808AH/1406AD) legacy, especially his *Muqaddimah,* usually comes to the forefront by virtue of his socio-cultural approach developed in the context of his science of human association and civilization (*'ilm al-'umrān al-basharī wa'l-ijtimā' al-insānī*). Interestingly enough, while explaining the subject matter of this science, he notices that it intersects with other sciences, such as Islamic jurisprudence. As he states, "in their deliberations on the purposes of the Sharī'ah commands (*al-maqāṣid al-sha'riyyah fi'l-aḥkām*), they [the *fuqahā'*] mention a number of purposes which all concern the preservation of civilization (*fa-innahā kullahā mabniyyatun 'al'-lmuḥāfaẓah al'l-'umrān*)."[71]

It is, we may argue, within this *maqāṣid*-informed sociological perspective that Ibn Khaldūn offered one of the most profound, comprehensive and systematic treatments of economic life before the rise of modern economics in the West. His analysis covered a wide range of economic subjects, such as production (depending mainly on agriculture and livestock), growth, commerce and trade, markets and prices, supply and demand, profit and value, labour and division of labour, taxation, professions and crafts, role of the state, welfare and poverty, etc. Ibn Khaldūn's discussion of such issues is unmistakably shaped by a clear realization of the interconnectedness of economic life with, and influence by, the prevailing socio-political order and the surrounding ecological system, both in times of peace and warfare.[72]

Of special interest to us here is a relatively large chapter which he devoted entirely to economic injustice as one (if not *the*) main factor that brings about the ruin of civilization (*al-ẓulm mu'dhin bi-kharāb al-'umrān*). The central argument of this chapter is that any offenses against people's wealth and property (*amwālihim*) destroy their incentives to earn money and own property, as they see that its ultimate destiny is that it will be robbed from them. This pushes them to stop working to make their livelihood and all business activities will slacken inasmuch as people's property is affected. Consequently, people will scatter around in all directions beyond the borders of their home country in search of sustenance, thus seeking refuge from poverty and deprivation. As a result, society will disintegrate and civilization collapse. According to Ibn Khaldūn, injustice in this context is not restricted to the confiscation of money or property from its owners without compensation or for no good reason as is generally understood; it is more general than that. Thus, taking someone's property, or using him for forced labour, or pressing against him an unjustified claim, or imposing upon him a duty not required by the Sharī'ah, all this is sheer injustice.[73]

In light of all this, Ibn Khaldūn indicates, we can realize the Law-giver's wisdom in denouncing and forbidding injustice, as it "results in the destruction and ruin of civilization," which ultimately leads to the discontinuation or eradication of the human species (*inqiṭāʿ al-nawʿ al-basharī*). This, he argues, is "the general wisdom contemplated by the *Sharʿ* in all its five necessary essential goals consisting of the preservation of *dīn* (religion), *nafs* (life), *ʿaql* (intellect), *nasl* (progeny) and *māl* (property). Since, as we have seen, "injustice calls for the eradication of the human species by causing the destruction of civilization, it contains in itself the reason for its prohibition..." For him, evidence on this in Qur'an and Sunnah is too ample to be accurately presented.[74]

Two kinds of injustice are singled out by Ibn Khaldūn as being of the greatest injustices that contribute to the ruin of civilization. The first one is the imposition on the people of unjustified tasks and using them for forced labour, thus depriving them from the value and fruit of their effort and energy which constitute the means of their sustenance and livelihood. The second injustice, which is even greater and more destructive, is appropriating people's property (*al-tasalluṭ ʿala amwāl al-nās*) by "buying their possessions for the cheapest prices and then reselling the merchandise to them at the highest possible prices through forced sales and purchases."[75] This is a clear reference to monopoly, hoarding and manipulation of the market, which Ibn Khaldun discussed quite extensively in more than one place of his work.[76] For all these evil consequences, he maintains, all unfair practices have been banned by the Sharīa'h which "has legalized cunning and bargaining (*mukāyasah*) in trading and forbidden depriving people from their property illegally."[77] In the Khaldūnian view, economic injustice as explained above runs clearly and squarely counter to God's making mankind His vicegerent (*istikhlāf*), by virtue of which He has created things in the world for the good of human beings all alike, not for the monopoly by a few of them, "as indicated in several verses of the Qur'an."[78]

A few centuries before Ibn Khaldūn, Abū Ḥāmid al-Ghazālī (d. 505AH/1111AD) was such an eminent figure whose undisputed scholarship masterly combined a wide range of disciplines. It was then only natural that economic matters be part of his intellectual preoccupations. Thus, he addressed financial and economic issues from more than one angle. As a Shāfiʿī jurist who produced a number of works dealing with all areas and topics covered by Islamic jurisprudence, al-Ghazālī dealt with financial and economic matters from a purely juridical point of view in the same way all jurists usually do.[79] As a theologian-philosopher and spiritual sage or mystic, he looked at such matters from a wider perspective that is clearly concerned with ethical, spiritual, psychological and social considerations. He did so without neglecting the specific nature of those matters or downsizing their importance in human life, a fact which he himself emphasizes strongly in his taxonomy of the universal necessities constituting the core of *maqāṣid al-sharīʿah* and revolving around the promotion of people's welfare. People's well-being, he indicates, lies in "safeguarding their faith, their life, their intellect, their posterity and their wealth. Whatever ensures the safeguarding of these five fundamentals (*uṣūl*) is *maṣlaḥah* [to be attained], and whatever undermines them is *mafsadah* the prevention of which is *maṣlaḥah*." As he further explains, it is for this purpose that certain deterrents (*zawājir*) have been set up in the Sharīʿah, such as the punishments on robbery and theft, for the protection of people's property and wealth on which they depend by necessity for their sustenance (*maʿāsh*).[80]

Firmly rooted in such a holistic vision of human well-being, al-Ghazālī devoted a considerable space of his well-known encyclopaedic *Iḥyāʾ ʿUlūm al-Dīn,* generally perceived as a work on *taṣawwuf* or mysticism, to matters economic and financial. In three main chapters of this work's quarter on customary matters (*rubuʿ ʿal-ʿadāt*),[81] he presents what can be described as a psycho-spiritual and social ethics of economic life and activity, without however neglecting the purely juridical parameters governing economic activities and financial transactions through different contractual formulas, thus integrating in one stream their inward and outward dimensions. At the opening of Book 3 on the ethics of earning and livelihood, al-Ghazālī lays down a general proposition according to which, in the religious perspective of Islam, human struggle and endeavour in this world is not confined to the purpose of the Hereafter (*al-maʿād*) at the expense of one's livelihood (*maʿāsh*). On the contrary, "earning a livelihood is a means and aid to the Hereafter."[82]

In light of this, he classifies people with regard to economic pursuit in three categories as follows. 1. Those indulging completely in mundane affairs and totally ignoring the Hereafter; they will be ultimately doomed (*mina'l-hālikīn*). 2. Those seeking the Hereafter at the expense of mundane life. 3. Lastly, there is the category of people of, or closest to, the middle course or balance and moderation (*iʿtidāl*). While keeping their Hereafter as the ultimate goal, they engage in worldly affairs as a means to it, thus caring to earn a livelihood. For al-Ghazālī, people deviating from the middle course will not attain the pleasure of the straight path, nor will those making worldly pursuits a means to the pleasures of the Hereafter succeed in so doing if they do not abide by the norms and rules of the Sharīʿah.[83] As he further elaborates, profound inquiry proves that people following the path of balance and moderation are actually the best category, for they give this world and the next their due and are reliable guides to the success and pleasures of both worlds, including the prophets whom God has sent to establish what is good for the people in this life and in the next (*iqāmat maṣāliḥ al-ʿibād fi'l-maʿāsh wa'l-maʿād*).[84] This middle way of balance and moderation emphasised by al-Ghazālī is what the Qur'an has taught in many verses such as,

1. *And neither allow thy hand to remain shackled to thy neck, nor stretch it forth to the utmost limit [of thy capacity], lest thou find thyself blamed [by thy dependents], or even destitute.* (al-Isrā', 17:29)

2. *... and who [i.e. ʿibād al-Raḥmān], whenever they spend on others, [51] are neither wasteful nor niggardly but [remember that] there is always a just mean between those [two extremes].* (al-Furqān, 25:67)

3. *Seek, instead, by means of what God has granted thee the abode of the Hereafter, and neglect not thy portion of the world, and be thou kind even as God hath been kind to thee, and seek not corruption in the earth.* (al-Qaṣaṣ, 28: 77)

Within such ethico-spiritual framework as outlined above al-

Ghazālī articulated his economic views both in a holistic and realistic manner clearly taking account of society as a whole, notwithstanding the mystic and ascetic spirit overshadowing many of his works, especially the *Iḥyā'* and *Mīzān*. In this connection he shows that earning a livelihood is one of the excellent endeavours praised and encouraged by the Islamic teachings, in which respect he cites as evidence a number of Qur'anic verses and Prophetic statements. In this connection, we read in the Qur'an verses such as the following:

1. *(...) and We made the day for your livelihood.* (al-Naba', 78:11)[85]

2. *Indeed, [O men,] We established you on earth, and provided you thereon with means of livelihood, [yet] how seldom are you grateful!* (al-A'rāf, 7:10)

3. *(...) then when the prayer has ended, disperse in the land and seek out God's bounty.* (al-Jumu'ah, 62:10)

As for the Prophet (peace be upon him), we read with al-Ghazali such statements as,

1. *There are sins which are not expiated except by the anxieties of earning a livelihood.*

2. *The truthful tradesman will be resurrected on Resurrection Day with those of great faith and martyrs.*

3. *He who seeks worldly bounties in a lawful way, thus refraining from begging, putting in effort for family members and being kind to his neighbour, will meet God with a face as bright as a full moon.*

4. *God loves a person who labours for saving himself from depending on others, and He hates a person who pursues knowledge to take it as a means to livelihood.*[86]

Whatever the import of these verses and traditions, they are only a part of what al-Ghazālī has produced as evidence of Islam's positive view on earning money and possessing property, themselves making only a small portion of the Qur'anic and Prophetic material concerning human economic life and activity in various respects, which is beyond our purpose to dwell upon here.[87]

However, al-Ghazālī notes, this positive view and attitude concerning the pursuit of mundane life through economic and financial activities has been objected by some people on the basis of other Qur'anic verses and Prophetic traditions that seem to clash with the above-mentioned ones. To this effect, they cite the verse stating that: "Your worldly goods and your children are but a trial and a temptation, whereas with God there is a tremendous reward." (al-Taghābun, 64:15) As for the Prophet, he is reported to have said that "it has not been revealed to him to accumulate wealth and be among traders, but rather *to extol his Sustainer's limitless glory and praise Him, and be of those who prostrate themselves before Him in adoration, and worship his Sustainer till death comes to him.*"[88] Accordingly, certain scholars and mystic teachers counselled that people seeking the Hereafter and resigning themselves to God must confine themselves in respect of material life to bare necessity and subsistence level (*ḍarūrah* and *sadd al-ramaq*). The reason for this is that we often live under circumstances where the lawful and unlawful in people's dealings are intermixed in such a way that it is very difficult to discriminate between them or even to determine which of them is preponderant. Therefore, so they believe, in order to be on the safe side and safeguard one's destiny in the next world, true piety requires one to keep away from all that is doubtful and uncertain, let alone that which is evidently and clearly unlawful.[89]

Al-Ghazālī's answer to such view and position operates on two planes. First, the so-called or alleged conflict of the Qur'anic and Prophetic statements on earning and the pursuit of wealth is due to a misunderstanding of such texts and narrations and inattention to their contexts, however different they might appear. This misunderstanding flows from the failure to realize their reconciliation by looking into the different wise considerations underlying them within the respective contexts. Second, the negative judgement and condemnation of earning and property is due to a misconception of the place and purpose of wealth and property (*rutbat al-māl*) both in human life and within the scheme of the purposes (*maqāṣid*) of Islamic teachings as well as unawareness of the nature and dynamics of the real life-world including the arena of economic life and activities.[90]

As far as the issue of textual conflict is concerned, al-Ghazālī explains that it is no question in this context of saying that trade and commerce (*tijārah*) are the best of all professions in all respects and under all circumstances; the matter is rather relative and relational, depending on the purpose and objective of undertaking a business. Such purposes are mainly two: either to seek self-sufficiency (*kifāyah*), or to seek accumulation of wealth (*tharwah*) and getting more than self-sufficiency. If a trade or business is pursued for the sake of getting more than self-sufficiency and accumulating money and wealth without using it for good causes and spending it in charity, it is blameworthy. The reason behind this is that such kind of pursuit makes one obsessed with, and engulfed in, the vanities and material pleasures of this world, whose love is the main cause of all sins. The situation becomes even worse if the undertaker of a business commits betrayal (*khā'in*) and fraud in his dealings, thus falling in injustice (*ẓulm*) and impiety (*fisq*).[91] If, on the contrary, one seeks through the engagement in trade to attain sufficiency and sustenance for himself and his dependents, thus shunning the idleness of joblessness (*baṭālah*) and self-abasement by destitution and begging (*su'āl*), then this is even better than engaging in physical worship (*al-ʿibādāt al-badaniyyah*).[92] That is why the law of Islam condemns begging and reliance on others, and encourages striving through a trade or business to seek earning and make a living.[93]

As for the place and purpose of *māl* in human life and in the scheme of *maqāṣid*, they can be properly realized, in al-Ghazālī's point of view, in the context of his classification and categorization of the kinds of bounties and blessings (*khayrāt, niʿam*) and the types of pleasure and happiness (*saʿādāt*). In this respect, he uses a number of criteria and adopts more than one perspective whose details do not concern us much here.[94] Our purpose is rather to look at the position al-Ghazālī assigns to money and wealth within his scheme of blessings and happiness. In the sixth and last classification which he considers as an all-encompassing (*qismah ḥāwiyyah*) one combining all kinds of bounties and blessings, both *khayrāt* and *saʿādāt* are divided into four categories of which three are intrinsic to man's being, whereas the fourth is extrinsic or external to that being. The intrinsic bounties and blessings are other-worldly (*ukhrawiyyah*), phsycho-spiritual (*nafsiyyah*), and physical (*badaniyyah*). The extrinsic kind of bounties is inextricably linked to, and closely surrounding (*muḥīfah*), man's being. It consists mainly of four things: property (*māl*), family (*ahl*), dignity and honour (*jāh*) and nobility of clan (*karam al-ʿashīrah*). While the first category of bounty and happiness is sought for its own sake as it pertains to the ultimate goal of being closer to God and attaining His pleasure, the other three are complementary to each other and serve as means to that ultimate goal.[95]

Of special interest here is the place and function of *māl* not only with regard to the third category of physical (*badaniyyah*) bounties and blessings, but to all the other categories of al-Ghazālī's scheme presented above. As he clearly puts it, the psycho-spiritual virtues and merits (i.e., knowledge and illumination, good conduct, continence and self-restraint, and justice) drawing us nearer to God can only be achieved through realizing the merits and virtues of our physical being, namely of health (*ṣiḥḥah*), strength (*quwwah*), beauty (*jamāl*) and long life (*ṭūl al-ʿumur*). These, in turn, depend on the extrinsic category of bounties and blessings surrounding our being, in which *māl* is a crucial factor for the sustenance and growth of the human body. Thus, despite its extrinsic nature in relation to our being in the world, and though ranked last in the third category of *khayrāt* and *saʿādāt*, *māl* in al-Ghazālī's thinking plays a pivotal role in human well-being and destiny. All such dimensions, he further teaches, need to be taken care of in a sustained and balanced manner that can only be achieved through God's guidance, aid and protection. This balance and equilibrium, he argues, is implied by the divine decree (al-Raḥmān, 55:7-9):

> [7]*And the skies He raised high, and has devised [for all things] a measure,*[8]*so that you [too, O men,] might never transgress the measure [of what is right):* [9]*weigh, therefore, [your deed] with equity, and cut not the measure short!*[96]

It is within this framework, especially in view of the place and function of *māl,* that al-Ghazālī tackles a wide range of *ḥalāl* and *ḥarām* issues and rebuts the position of those who counselled confining oneself to the level of mere necessity and subsistence (*ḍarūrah* and *ramaq*) due to uncertainty arising from the intermixedness of the lawful and unlawful in the world. Not denying that such teaching may be relevant and applicable to certain categories of people who are only a minority in society, al-Ghazālī unambiguously states that this does not hold for the general public and all members of the society. His argument runs as follows:

> If people were to limit themselves to partake of only as much as would save off hunger (*sadd al-ramaq*), they would soon weaken and disease would kill them off. Then all deeds would become invalid, all industry would come to a halt, and the whole world (*dunyā*) would be ruined. Certainly, the ruin of world would mean the ruin of religion because the world is the seedbed (*mazra'ah*) of the Afterlife.[97]

Moreover, and here al-Ghazālī is his realist at best, we cannot expect or even imagine the world to be totally free from the unlawful unless all people stop sinning and doing wrong, "and that is impossible." Likewise, since "it is not stipulated that all people stop doing wrong in the world in order for anything to be lawful, is not to be stipulated in a city either, unless the city is entirely cut off. Therefore, such abstinence is no more than the prudence of the overly suspicious (*muwaswisīn*), as it was never recorded from the Messenger of God (may God bless him and grant him peace) or any of his Companions. Nor, for that matter, is it imaginable among any people anywhere, or at any time."[98]

Accordingly, al-Ghazālī does not hesitate on the necessity of earning and seeking wealth provided people undertake such endeavour as part of the collective duties (*furūḍ al-kifāyāt*). This is because if crafts (*ṣinā'āt*) and trade (*tijārāt*) were to be abandoned, the sources of living would fall in idleness, and people would be ruined. Indeed, the survival, welfare and well-being of all of them depends on their co-operation so that each group of them engages in a different kind of work and business. Were all of them to take part in one and the same craft or profession, all other professions and crafts would perish, and people's lives would be under the threat of destruction. In this regard, al-Ghazālī clearly subscribes to the idea of the division of labour and complementarity of the different types of professions and industries in realizing the various interests of individuals and overall welfare and well-being of society and public common good. For him, this accords with people's different purposes, interests, dispositions and potentials in relation to the various industries and professions. Of the different professions and businesses, he further indicates that some are essential, while others are not and hence can be dispensed with due to their being means to seeking mere luxuries and adornment in this life. This means that people should rather engage in professions and businesses that of essential importance to the whole society.[99]

Underlying all this, for al-Ghazālī, is a general principle and established fact that "there can be no doubt that the best of this world and the next are what the law (*shar'*) intended," and that "sending people back to living on as much as is essential, or enough to care for their needs, or to eating only what they can gather or hunt, *would lead to the ruination of the world to start with, and by means of it to the ruination of religion.*" This, in his view, is something self-evident for which "there is no reason to seek a proof."[100]

In order that such pursuit be both beneficial and praiseworthy, those engaged in it have to observe certain considerations or conditions in the earning and use of money and property, which al-Ghazālī calls *waẓā'if al-māl*. These considerations mainly concern the sources of money and means of getting it, its spending, the amount to be earned and the intention in using it.[101] First and foremost, being the last in the category of extrinisinc bounties, *māl* in whatever form, notably *dirhims* and *dīnars*, can only be a means to serving man's legitimate ends, never to be served or sought after for its own sake (*khādimān wa-lā khādima lahumā*). It has to be used to fulfil people's needs of food, clothing, shelter, marriage, etc. for the sake of sustaining and maintaining the human body. Caring for the body stems from the fact that it is the vehicle (*markabah*) of the human soul and embodiment of the self (*nafs*) which is the agent of psycho-spiritual, moral and intellectual accomplishment and virtues.[102]

All other considerations flow and follow from this essential view on the worth and function of money and wealth depriving them of any absoluteness or sublimity in relation to human beings as both individuals and community. Pivotal amongst those considerations is fairness and transparency in respect of which al-Ghazālī devoted a good deal of discussion on different forms of injustice in economic activities and financial transactions. These injustices include those causing public harm and general damage to the society, such as monopoly and hoarding (especially in foodstuff and similar essential goods), and stretch over to all kinds of mischievous practices affecting individuals and specific groups in different ways, such as cheating and fraud in weight, quality, price, etc. in all crafts and business activities.[103]

In his discourse on earning and economic behaviour al-Ghazālī exhibits a sharp awareness of the double-edged nature of money and wealth. Like many things in the world, they are prone to use, abuse and misuse.[104] They can be object of proper use for good ends to secure one's own welfare and contribute to that of others, seeking thereby God's pleasure. Their potential misuse and abuse can be such that they are not limited to only pursuing frivolous luxuries and hence forgetting the Hereafter,[105] but also as means to exploiting, abasing and dominating others. Because of this Abū Ḥāmid considers wealth and property as the "greatest temptation" or test facing humans in the world.[106] This is the reason why he keeps reminding us of the wisdom (*ḥikmah*) and objective (*maqṣūd*) for which *māl* has been created, namely "to fulfill the people's needs," in which respect it should be handled and disposed of with justice (*ʿadl*) by spending it on that for which it is created not on that for which it is not created, for the sake of fulfilling real and genuine needs not in pursuit of mere wants and insatiable consumerism. In other words, money "should be saved where it should, and be spent where it should," in moderation (*wasaṭ*) and away from the blameworthy extremes of extravagance and niggardliness, as taught by the Qur'an (al-Isrā' (17:29; al-Furqān (25:67).[107]

With all that taken into account, al-Ghazālī sets out to provide a roadmap for whomever would engage in trade and commerce and, for that matter, in any kind of profession or business. For this he has devoted the last three chapters of *kitāb al-kasb* and keeps returning to it in other parts of the *Iḥyāʾ*.[108] In this context, he indefatigably emphasizes time and again the paramount place of justice, fairness and transparency in all economic activities and financial dealings as essential aspects of the general and universal rule (*ḍābiṭ kullī*) of reciprocity by virtue of which one "should not desire for one's brethren except what one desires for oneself" (*an lā yuḥibba li-akhīhi illā mā yuḥibbu li-nafsih*).[109] Thus guided, one should carry out business not only with the spirit of seeking one's own livelihood and securing the welfare of one's dependents, but also, more importantly, with the spirit of fulfilling one of the collective duties (*furūḍ al-kifāyāt*) for the sake of the people's general welfare.[110] Caring for people's good and public interest (*maṣāliḥ al-ʿibād*) is, in al-Ghazālī's view, among the greatest forms of worship (*min aʿẓam al-ʿibādāt*), as described by the Messenger of God (may peace and blessing be upon him): "The whole creation is the family of God, and the most beloved to God among human beings are those who are most beneficial to His creation."[111]

However, al-Ghazālī's socio-economic thinking does not stop at emphasizing justice and fairness and appealing to them as essential requirements in human economic activities and financial transactions. He also is not merely contented with laying much stress on their functional nature as means to serving the public interest and general welfare of society. Deeply rooted, as stated earlier, in a clearly spelled out spiritual and ethical vision, al-Ghazālī's economics[112] seems to rather consider justice and fairness as the normal requirement that should govern people's dealings and relations, a borderline below which there is nothing but injustice, wrongdoing and lack of social responsibility. It is an economics stipulating and requiring a higher level of morality in economic behaviour and financial practice which people need to strive for, namely benevolence. This is because, as he reminds us, God has commanded us "to observe both justice (*ʿadl*) and benevolence (*iḥsān*), for justice is only a means to salvation and functions just as capital functions in commerce, [while] benevolence is a means to success (*fawz*) and happiness (*saʿādah*), and serves like profit in commerce." Therefore, intelligent and wise people cannot content themselves with only maintaing their capital by "merely observing justice and avoiding injustice." Hence, observing justice and avoiding injustice are mandatory (*wājib*), whereas benevolence is not and, hence, it arises from goodwill (*tafaḍḍul*).[113]

Obviously, the profit meant by our great sage does not consist only of the rewards one will get in the Hereafter in lieu of the money and wealth one forgoes for the sake of fellow humans here and now, though this is what matters most. It may take the form of worldly reward by being blessed with more success in business and good reputation and high regard among people for one's generosity and benevolence. In this connection, al-Ghazālī mentions six things through which business people can attain benevolence. They consist mainly of selling, buying and pricing, loans and debts, assisting the poor and needy as well as the ways *iḥsān* can be realized in all that, depending on the categories and situations of the people one would be engaged with.[114] It is in this light that we can appreciate his strong criticism "of 'excessive' profit-making" and manipulation and artificiality of prices through malpractices, such as hoarding, especially in foodstuffs and other necessities,[115] which in our time take different forms of financial speculations and manipulations in financial and stock markets.

The foregoing exposition of al-Ghazālī's views on economics might give the impression that his focus is on the micro level of economic life and financial activities of individuals at the expense of a general conception of the economy as a public arena where the state should play an important role. This impression is true, but only in a limited and specific sense in so far as voluntary individual behaviour of business people and individual economic agents is crucial in shaping and determining the nature and orientation of economic life and financial activities. It is in fact for this reason that al-Ghazālī puts greater emphasis on personal conduct and self-discipline, not only in the world of economics and finance, but in all walks of life. However, this does not mean that he is oblivious to the macro level of economic life or dismissive of the public role of the state.[116] In fact, he shows sharp awareness that certain areas and issues in the society's economic life cannot be attended to by individual economic actors. Taking care of them should rather be part and parcel of the public duties of the state to which he assigns "the fulfillment of the *Sharīʿah*-mandated social obligations *(furūḍ kifāyah)*" in addition to its role in maintaining peace, security and order, were the society's affairs to run properly.[117]

In this context, issues pertaining to the public treasury are symmetrical in al-Ghazālī's economic thinking; hence, he paid considerable attention to both public revenues and public expenditures. Various areas of public expenditures are identified by him not simply as a matter of public interest so as to have certain immediate general needs of the people fulfilled by the state, such as providing food and shelter for the poor and needy. Quite explicitly and most importantly too, he emphasizes the importance of laying down the proper infrastructure (such as bridges, canals, roads, etc.) necessary for facilitating and promoting economic growth and social development and realizing the benefit and good of society as a whole.[118] In this connection, al-Ghazālī exhibits great concern about the need for economy and efficiency in the use of public funds which should be expended wisely and justly in a prioritized manner according to the hierarchy of the society's needs in order to serve the public interest and general well-being.[119]

Just as al-Ghazālī insists on justice in the individuals' dealings and businesses in the market, so too he emphasizes that for justice to prevail, it is the duty of the state to remove poverty and distress in the society by directing public funds and expenditures to this very purpose. Clearly bringing to the fore the concept of distributive justice, he states that,

> When the ruler's *(sultan's)* subjects fall into penury or suffer distress, it is his duty to come to their aid, especially in times of drought or when they are incapable of earning their livelihood (due to high prices). It is then the duty of the ruler to provide the subjects with food and extend financial assistance from the public treasury, and take good care to stop his officials from oppressing the subjects; for in that case, the people would become impoverished and quit the territory, the royal revenues would be shattered, profit would accrue to hoarders,

and the ruler would (incur) curses and bad name. It was for this reason that the kings of old times practiced the utmost frugality in such situations, and were accordingly able to grant aid from their treasuries to the subjects.[120]

Al-Ghazālī's psycho-spiritual philosophy of economics and his emphasis on ethical considerations in economic life and behaviour are reminiscent of ideas of economics of altruism, gift economy, moral economy, and even spiritual economy.[121] All such terms and similar nomenclatures have been gaining prominence over the last decades in writings by different authors who are critical of the increasingly devastating economic injustices and gravely widening financial gaps, internally at the level of individual societies and countries and externally at the global level of the whole world between nations and countries. Such injustices and gaps are actually tearing apart humanity between tiny financial oligarchies (not exceeding at best 10% of the population) controlling and monopolizing over 80% of the total wealth on the one side, and increasingly impoverished and destitute majorities millions of whom live far below the so-called poverty line, on the other. The economic philosophy as advocated by al-Ghazālī and like-minded thinkers, especially in today's world, is not only concerned with efficiency, growth, profit-making, economic development and the making and increase of wealth for their own sake. It is equally, indeed more, concerned about justice, equity, distribution, and transparency for the sake, benefit and welfare of all and everyone. Such a philosophy is a call to liberate the destiny of nations and countries from the destructive grips of surveillance capitalism with its 'elect' few and self-styled oligarchs and tycoons of financial power and economic wealth. These oligarchs and tycoons are the ones who plunder both the natural resources of the globe, as well as the capital and labour of whole nations and countries in the world through their octopus-like cross-border corporations and local handmaiden satellites, thus exponentially multiplying the rates of inequality and destitution coupled with uncertainty and insecurity in today's populations of the globe and jeopardizing the lives of future generations.[122]

4. Infāq: Towards a humane economy

Our (seemingly digressive) excursus with Ibn Khaldūn and al-Ghazālī[123] in fact leads us back to where we started our investigation on *māl*, namely the semantic and conceptual analysis of this and other related terms depicting the nature and kinds of property and wealth as a divine gift and trust constituting a great manifestation of the innumerable bounties God has bestowed upon mankind. What we have learnt from these two great minds actually directs our attention to another very important aspect of the Islamic view on *māl* and economic life. The crucial Qur'anic term translating this aspect in full is *infāq* (spending), as being the other side of the coin in relation to money and wealth as a major subject of human pursuit.

Of the more than seventy instances where the concept of *infāq* is expressed in different Qur'anic contexts, sixty-eight occur in verbal forms with various conjugation moods mostly ascribed to plural pronouns. The other four cases occur in nominative forms, namely *nafaqah* (al-Baqarah, 2:270; al-Tawbah, 9:121), *nafaqāt* (al-Tawbah, 9:54), *infāq* (al-Isrā', 17:100) and *munfiqīn* (Āl 'Imrān, 3:17). From the chronological viewpoint, most of the said instances belong to Madīnan revelations of which sūrah al-Baqarah has the lion's share (20), succeeded by al-Tawbah (10), Āl 'Imrān (6), al-Anfāl and al-Ḥadīd (5), al-Mumtaḥanah (4), al-Nisā' (3), etc.[124] This phenomenon can be explained in general terms by the fact that it was in the Madīnan era that the Muslim community emerged as an independent society with its own central authority and specific institutions, thus facing multiple individual and public needs and demands that require economic and financial resources to meet them.

The Qur'anic discourse on *infāq*, as exemplified in the general statistical data referred to above, can be said to be characterized by two main features. On the one hand, it is exhortative, praising and rejoicing. It calls upon people and exhorts them to spend of their money and wealth in good causes as a means to gaining divine pleasure, such as spending on the poor, the needy, the orphans, etc. Those doing so are highly praised and given good tiding of the high status and better rewards which God will bestow on them both in this world and in the

Hereafter. Citing two examples will suffice to make this point:

1. *Those who spend their possessions for the sake of God and do not thereafter mar their spending by stressing their own benevolence and hurting [the feelings of the needy] shall have their reward with their Sustainer, and no fear need they have, and neither shall they grieve.* (al-Baqarah, 2:262)

2. *[29]Those who follow God's revelation, and are constant in prayer, and spend on others, secretly and openly, out of what We have provided for them as sustenance—it is they who may look forward to a trade that will never fail, [30]sinceHe will grant their just rewards, and give them yet more out of His bounty.* (Fāṭir, 35:29-30)

On the other hand, the same discourse is blameful and warnful. It blames those who hoard their money and riches and do not spend them on good causes or expend them for bad purposes to obstruct truth and promote falsehood and other forms of corruption, oppression and evilness, such as bribery. In both cases, such people are warned against the bad end and miserable destiny awaiting them both in this life and the next. Again two examples will suffice to illustrate this point. Hence, we read in the Qur'an:

1. *But for those who lay up treasures of gold and silver and do not spend them for the sake of God—give them the tiding of grievous suffering [in the life to come]: on the Day when that [hoarded wealth] shall be heated in the fire of hell and their foreheads and their sides and their backs branded therewith, [those sinners shall be told:] "These are the treasures which you have laid up for yourselves! Taste, then, [the evil of] your hoarded treasures!"* (al-Tawbah, 9:34)

2. *Behold, those who are bent on denying the truth are spending their riches in order to turn others away from the path of God; and they will go on spending them until they become [a source] of regret for them; and then they will be overcome.* (al-Anfāl, 8:36)

However, the presence of the concept of *infāq* in the Qur'an is not restricted to this term and its co-derivatives, nor is the Qur'anic discourse on it limited to the exhortative and blameful features mentioned above. Rather, there is a set of other terms and expressions in the

Qur'an giving *infāq* a juridically more specific, assertive and binding nature consolidating and concretizing the spiritual and ethical character of it which we have already just pointed out. This set consists mainly of four terms, namely *ītā'*, *ṣadaqah*, *ḥaqq* and *zakāh*. Being derived from the root *a.t.y.*, the noun *ītā'* itself is used only twice in the Qur'an (al-Anbiyā', 21:73; al-Nūr, 24:37) in connection with *zakāh*. However, its meaning denoting the act of spending (or giving out) is expressed through its co-derivative verbal singular and plural forms (*ātā, ātaw, ātū, ātaytum, yu'tūn, tu'tū,* etc.) at least fourty times in both Makkan and Madīnan verses. In most of these cases, it is associated with *zakāh* and *māl,* both of them being the object of the act of spending.[125] Occurring thirteen times in singular (5) and plural (8) forms, the term *ṣadaqah* carries both the sense of general and voluntary charity and that of a specific financial duty, thus being synonymous with the term *zakāh* in its technical meaning, as will be seen below.[126]

The notion of financial duty just mentioned takes us readily to the term *ḥaqq*. Though occurring only five times in relation to the subject of our inquiry, this term has a crucial significance in the following discussion of the concept of *infāq*. Chronologically speaking, all five instances belong to Makkan sūrahs, namely al-An'ām (6:141), al-Isrā' (17:26), al-Rūm (30:38), al-Dhāriyāt (51:19) and al-Ma'ārij (70:24-25). Irrespective of their chronological sequence in the order of revelation as well as their grammatical structure however, the central message of these verses is that there is in people's wealth and property a certain portion that should be given to some specific groups in society. This portion is clearly described as *ḥaqq* to be delivered to those groups; hence it is a duty upon those who are well-off and in possession of wealth. Let us cite the verses in question so that we can get the general picture of that *ḥaqq* and its implications. Thus we read,

1. [15]*[But,] behold, the God-conscious will find themselves amid gardens and springs,* [16]*enjoying all that their Sustainer will have granted them [because], verily, they were doers of good in the past:* [17]*they would lie asleep during but a small part of the night,* [18]*and would pray for forgiveness from their innermost hearts;* [19]*and [would assign] in all that they possessed a due share unto such as might ask [for help] and such*

as might suffer privation: *wa-fī amwālihim ḥaqqun li'l-sā'ili wa'l-maḥrūm*. (al-Dhāriyāt, 51:15-19)

2. [22]*Not so, however, those who consciously turn towards God in prayer,*[23] *[and] who incessantly persevere in their prayer,* [24]*and in whose possessions there is a due share, acknowledged [by them],* [25]*for such as ask [for help] and such as are deprived [of what is good in life]: wa'l-ladhīna fī amwālihim ḥaqqun ma'lūmun li'l-sā'ili wa'l-maḥrūm*. (al-Ma'ārij, 70-22-25)

3. [38]*Hence, give his due to the near of kin, as well as to the needy and the wayfarer; this is best for all who seek God's countenance: for it is they, they that shall attain to a happy state!* [39]*And [remember:] whatever you may give out in usury so that it might increase through [other] people's possessions will bring [you] no increase in the sight of God—whereas all that you give out in charity, seeking God's countenance, (will be blessed by Him:] for it is they, they (who thus seek His countenance] that shall have their recompense multiplied!* (al-Rūm, 30:38-39)

4. *It is He [God] Who has brought into being gardens—[both] the cultivated ones and those growing wild—and the date-palm, and fields bearing multiform produce, and the olive tree, and the pomegranate: [all] resembling one another and yet so different! Eat of their fruit when it comes to fruition, and give [unto the poor] their due on harvest day. And do not waste [God's bounties]: verily, He does not love the wasteful.* (al-An'ām, 6:141)

5. [26]*And give his due to the near of kin as well as to the needy and the wayfarer, but do not squander [thy sustenance] senselessly.* [27]*Behold, the squanderers are, indeed, of the ilk of the satans—in as much as Satan has indeed proved most ungrateful to his Sustainer.* (al-Isrā', 17:26-27).

From the examination of these Qur'anic passages, the following general remarks can be made. The first two passages prasingly describe some of the major spiritual and moral characteristics of people of faith who are God-conscious. Thus, they highlight some of the behavioural qualities of such people, including the way they behave in relation to their economic wealth and possessions (*amwālihim*) in which respect they realize and are mindful that their wealth involves a portion that should not be kept with them, but should rather be given to some others as being their due or right (*ḥaqq*). On the other hand, the other three passages (3, 4 & 5) contain a straightforward command to give whatever is due (*ḥaqq*) in one's wealth and property to specified categories of people (i.e., the next of kin, the needy and the wayfarer) in order to meet their basic needs in life. In all these verses, though they belong to the Makkan stage of revelation, we see a clear and positive response in the Qur'an towards the problem of poverty that is reflected in its ethical and juridical language.[127]

As Ibn Ashur pertinently states in his comment on al-Isrā' (17:26), three aspects of great social significance are brought into focus by the mentioning of such categories as deserving the enjoined right. Caring financially about the next of kin (*dhu'l-qurbā*) is close and similar in purpose to the commandment of being benevolent (*iḥsān*) to one's parents made earlier in the same sūrah (17:23).[128] It nurtures kinship unity and the sense of belonging among its members, and strengths their bonds, thus bringing about great benefit that translates in the form of cohesion and security among the group. As for giving to the needy (*miskīn*), it serves the purpose of social solidarity in society at large, so that none of its members should live in distress and misery, not forgetting the fact that the needy in most cases is someone crippled by the inability to work or stricken by poverty to attain sufficiency. Lastly, providing financial care to the wayfarer (*ibn al-sabīl*) concerns the purpose of consolidating and perfecting the society's social order, because the one who passes by, having no relatives or acquaintances with whom to seek accommodation, might be in great need of shelter, food and protection against the danger and harm of adverse agents, such as thieves and bad weather.[129] All these considerations revolve around instilling and promoting the values of mercy, compassion and generosity that will engender an atmosphere of peace and security in society.

Likewise, we are in the presence of a general principle which the Qur'an clearly establishes in both ethical and juridical terms as a compelling rule that should, together with other rules enunciated throughout the Qur'anic discourse, govern people's conduct with respect to economic wealth and property. This rule prescribes on the owners of such wealth and property to forgo a part thereof for the sake of specific categories of fellow human beings. In this connection, the following fact should not escape our attention. Immediately after the command to give that due to those entitled to it, the Qur'an (al-Rūm, 30:39) makes a contrast between lending in usury (*ribā*) and giving out in charity (*zakāh*), as being in total opposition to one another, in spirit and intention as well as in consequence and end, ethically, spiritually and materially, in this life as well as in the next. It thus lays the ground for a different type of economic behaviour that shall shun all usurious and exploitative financial dealings.[130]

The last observation brings us directly to the term *zakāh* which occupies a central place in the Qur'anic semiotic and conceptual field of *infāq*. While the set of verses we have been reflecting upon explicitly enunciate the notion of *ḥaqq* as a financial duty on those who are well-off towards those in need, the amount or rate of that right remains unspecified and its implementation may depend on one's personal judgement if not mere convenience, especially when human God-consciousness and spirituality weaken. Settling this and other issues is what the purpose of the legislation of *zakāh* is all about.

Let us first start with the statistical information relating to the occurrence of this term in the Qur'an. In this very nominal form, the term *zakāh* occurs thirty-two times; in thirty of these occurrences it is used in the technical meaning denoting a specific financial obligation, while in the other two (al-Kahf, 18:81; Maryam, 19:15) it is used in a general linguistic meaning pertaining to purity and cleanliness. Its use in the technical sense is divided between the Makkan and Madīnan revelations to the ratio of one third to two thirds, whereby it is used twenty times in nine sūrahs revealed in Madīnah and ten times in nine sūrahs revealed in Makkah.[131]

Looking more closely at the instances of the technical usage of the term under discussion reveals the following facts. In twenty-five of them *zakāh* is associated and paired with *ṣalāh* or prayer as part and parcel of what the conduct and practice of sincere believers is or should be like. In this respect, some of the verses are descriptive (seventeen times), while the others are prescriptive (eight times).[132] Furthermore, *zakāh* is in one instance mentioned with prayer in a sequence of verses describing qualities and behaviour of the believers (al-Mu'minūn, 23:1-4), whereas in another case it is associated with piety and God-consciousness, *taqwā* (al-A'rāf, 7:56).

In all these twenty-seven cases, the Qur'anic usage of *zakāh* takes place in positive contexts expressing praise and appreciation. Moreover, the term *zakāh* is used twice (al-Nisā': 4:77; Fuṣṣilat, 41:7) in negative contexts with reference to unbelievers and detractors of faith who fail to perform what is due to their Creator (prayer) and to give out what is due to their fellow humans (*zakāh*), and go on perpetrating mischief. Finally, the last instance in our statistical data on the usage of *zakāh* in the Qur'an is its juxtaposition with *ribā*, as we have already shown. Thus being conclusively established by a multitude of Qur'anic verses[133] as the twin-sister of prayer and one of the essential pillars of the Islamic order of life, the imperativeness of *zakāh* can be said to have been summed up and firmly grounded by the following verse (al-Bayyinah, 98:5):

> *And they have not been enjoined commanded naught else but to worship God, keeping sincere religious faith in Him and turning away from all that is false (ḥunafā'), to perform regular prayer (ṣalāh), and to spend in charity (zakāh). That is the ever-true upright religion (dīn al-qayyimah).*[134]

To further give this obligation its juristic practicality and full socio-economic bearing beyond all generality and ambivalence, the Qur'an explicitly lays down a list of the categories of people (*aṣnāf* or *maṣārib*) eligible to it. Hence we read (al-Tawbah, 9:60):

> *The alms are meant only (innama's-ṣadaqāt) for the poor (al-fuqarā') and the needy (masākīn), and those who are in charge thereof (al-'āmilūn 'alayhā), and those whose hearts are to be won over (al-mu'allafah qulūbuhum), and for the freeing of human beings from bondage (riqāb), and [for] those who are overburdened with debts (ghārimīn), and [for every*

struggle] in God's cause (sabīl Allāh), and [for] the wayfarer (ibn al-sabīl): [this is] a duty enjoined by God, and God is all-knowing, wise.

It is an established fact in the Islamic tradition right from Prophet Muḥammad (peace be upon him) that this verse gave the legislation on *zakāh* its definitive character as the foremost *ḥaqq* due on wealth and property of everyone by identifying its target groups (*maṣārif al-zakāh*).[135] It thus concluded in more specific terms a general Qur'anic discourse on *zakāh* by cirumscribing "all the purposes for which the *zakāh* funds may be expended"[136] without, however, limiting the scope of *infāq* and charity to *zakāh* and to the categories of people eligible to it.[137]

The centrality of *zakāh* as concept and institution and its practical implications for the Islamic socio-economic system in general and for the personal life of a wide range of social groups in particular have thus been deeply ingrained in the Islamic ethos as a spiritual and material matter deserving utmost attention. Owing to that, and guided by the Prophet's practice and teaching, Muslim scholars throughout the centuries laboured to delimit its subject matter on different accounts in light of the prevailing economic and social conditions of the day. That is, to identify the kinds and requirements of *zakatable* wealth and the amount or rate due in each kind once it has satisfied the required conditions, to delineate the juristic rules and procedures regulating the collection and distribution of the *zakāh* funds including their methods of computation, and to determine the criteria by which to identify those who practically and genuinely deserve it. Nothing can perhaps attest to the place of *zakāh* in Muslim consciousness and life better than the the following. Large chapters covering its various aspects have been devoted to it in almost all of the authoritative collections of Prophetic traditions and literally in every juristic compendium and treatise across the different guilds of Islamic jurisprudence. This bears strong witness to its necessity and practicality at the same time. In modern times, an increasing volume of scholarly works has been produced by both jurists and economic specialists on the socio-economic aspects and implications of *zakāh* in the context of the modern world.[138]

At any rate, what concerns us here most is the social and economic philosophy underlying the legislation of *zakāh* in the wider framework of the Islamic view on economics and society. As a personal duty in every individual's wealth exceeding or just reaching the *niṣāb*, i.e. minimum level (in kind or value) and satisfying a number of other conditions,[139] *zakāh*, when institutionally functioning efficiently and systematically, "ensures a constant readjustment of the distribution" of the society's wealth, thus constituting "on the economic plane the best guarantee that any human community could possibly hope for against the disintegrating forces of class hatred."[140] By its rootedness in the individual's conscience pairing his/her obligatory daily prayers, *zakāh* is being grounded on the very foundation of the socio-economic and ethical order of society and provides an inbuilt mechanism that precedes and survives states and governments. Likewise, it makes the community responsible for, and capable of, remedying its economic and social ills internally by caring for the welfare of its members by its own means. In the words of de Zayas, "the Institution of *Zakāt* lays special stress on rehabilitation: on promptly restoring the impoverished individual to a condition of self-sufficiency, thereby enabling him to once more take his place as a productive member of the social group, actively contributing to its prosperity."[141]

In fact, very profound psychological considerations can be realized that underlie the legislation of *zakāh* and which actually take us back to what we have already said about the instinctive bond between human nature and *māl,* that is, *zīnah* and *tazyīn,* which constitutes the ontological basis of wealth and property. Thanks to this strong bond, human beings are instinctively driven to the pursuit of money and wealth not just to satisfy their actual needs, but also to accumulate thereof as much as possible to the extent that such a pursuit may become an end in itself. This may, and often does, give rise not only to money worship, but most seriously to arrogance, oppression, subjugation and exploitation of others, if not outright enslavement. Such attitudes arise from of a feeling of power, self-sufficiency and aboveness, hence driving one into an endless quest and insatiable desire for power and dominance in which money and economic wealth turn into destructive tools if left uncontrolled from within the human person and not simply from without. Failing such self-control enhanced and consolidated by proper and efficient legal and institutional frameworks, society can only slip into the abyss of absurd economics and finance and unstopping impoverishment and deprivation of the quasi-totality of the people, thus plunging the whole planet into successive economic crises and financial crushes.[142]

Therefore, it is part of Islam's strategy to free the human self from the grips of money and purify the mind and heart from its luring and destructive temptations, or at least diminish their hold on them. This emancipation takes place through instilling and nurturing in people's consciousness that money is not and should not be an end in itself, but a means to fulfill one's genuine and real needs as well as the needs of deprived fellow human beings out of consideration of, and care for, human brotherhood and in quest of the pleasure of God who is the real bestower and ultimate owner of whatever riches one might possess, for which reason one must be grateful to Him by spending for His sake. In other words, Islam aims at making man the master not the slave of money and wealth, so that he can dispense with it at will and whenever required, for the sake of good purposes and greater causes transcending the self and ego, thus aspiring and striving to rise up to noble ideals and lofty values.[143]

Through the legislation of *zakāh* and other forms of *infāq*, Islam "induces the social group to think and feel as a whole" and to realize "that the prosperity of the group is the best safeguard for the prosperity of the individual, and that the poverty of the individual inevitably jeopardizes the prosperity of the group."[144] To state it otherwise, the interest and well-being of the individual are intertwined with, and dependent upon, those of the community. This means that whatever wealth and property one might have must necessarily function for the community's good and benefit on top of which comes the alleviation, if not eradication, of poverty. This necessity stems from the reality, already mentioned, of one's indebtedness to the society for being able to make money and get rich.[145] By constituting the backbone of the society's social order and solidarity and providing a constant mechanism for wealth and income distribution, *zakāh* accomplishes social functions and fills economic disparities and financial gaps in which the state and its public institutions and treasury are most of the time defective, either because of the paucity of means and resources or simply due to mis-management and corruption, regardless of the nature of the political system that is in place. In this way, *zakāh* plays a pivotal role in building and consolidating a truly sustainable civil society that will not be totally dependent on the state for its survival and the minimum welfare of its members.

The Islamic view on *māl, rizq* and *infāq* as it emerges from the preceding exposition may be seen as one that favours spending over wealth accumulation, let alone wealth hoarding and monopolization.[146] The foremost reason behind this is to ensure that wealth in society, be it private or public, circulates rather than stagnates or freezes, and is inclusive rather than exclusive. This can take place through a process that would translate and realize the Qur'anic dictum (al-Ḥashr, 59:7): *kay lā yakūna dūlatan bayna al-aghniyā'i minkum,* that is, it should not be going around and around among, and in the hands of, those who are already rich. This bias (one may say) towards spending concerns no doubt the fulfilment of consumer needs that enables people to live a decent and dignified life. It also simultaneously pertains to the funding of different types of activities and productive projects aimed at keeping the society's economy resilient and growing and capable of facing not only the demands of the present, but also those of the future. Finally, it should be kept in mind that this philosophy of spending does not operate in isolation from other values and principles enunciated in the Qur'an. Foremost of them is the rule of moderation and balance whose observation is mentioned as one of the behavioural qualities of true servants of God (*'ibād al-Raḥmān*). To this effect we read in sūrah al-Furqān (25:67):

> *They are those who are neither wasteful nor niggardly when they spend, but keep to a just balance.*[147]

This rule governs both private and public spending, whereby one's look and concern are not merely focused on, and confined to, the present and the immediate interests of the personal and collective self, but are equally directed to one's own future (as individual and society) and to the generations of the future. Put differently, the obligations of the society and its members embrace both the present and the future, and this is an essential dimension of human solidarity and caring for the common good.[148]

Conclusion

Reason and rationality are the major distinctive characteristic of human beings setting them apart from all other creatures in the world of nature, including the most 'advanced' and 'smart' animal kinds that we might encounter on earth, thus reflecting and manifesting the singularity of human consciousness at its best. This is a fact that stands beyond any shadow of doubt, no matter what similarities and closeness between humans and their animal neighbours might be imagined or even discovered.[149] As our semantic inquiry on *'aql* has shown, human reason and intellection in the Qur'anic view is multi-faceted and multi-layered, being ethically and spiritually anchored and physically and historically embedded, in which respect language and speech stand out as the most efficient and enduring tool expressing that consciousness. This does not mean, however, that such grounding and embeddedness take place automatically and in a mechanical way or even intuitively all through, despite the fact that intuition undeniably plays a great part in human life and existence including in the processes of human comprehension, cognition and knowledge; indeed, intuition is at the origin of all our life affairs, as established by different intellectual and philosophical traditions.[150]

As such and, interestingly, to the astonishment of the angels, mankind has been raised by the Almighty Creator and Lord of the universe to such a preeminent status and noble mission as the divinely appointed trustee and vicegerent on earth. By virtue of this ennobling appointment and as a manifestation thereof, diverse and bountiful resources in land, sea and the skies have been made subservient to human beings as means for their sustenance and survival, to the exclusion of none, as they all belong to the one and same human family. Making use of such resources to extract different types of benefit to satisfy the wide range of human physical and non-physical needs comes, generally speaking, under the purview of such encompassing Qur'anic concepts as *rizq* and *māl*.

From this spring all kinds of economic thinking and socio-political doctrines about wealth and property in human society and civilization. The Qur'an, as we have seen, has its own outlook on the place, significance and purpose of economic pursuit in human life and existence as essentially revolving around the realization and promotion of human common good and the well-being of both the individuals and society all through the different races and denominations of the larger body of humanity, including the present and future generations.

It is here, and by virtue of that grounding and embeddedness, that mankind is faced with one of the greatest tests on how human reason and rationality can guide individuals and communities on the proper use of economic and financial resources for the benefit of all and everyone within the parameters and values of justice, equity, solidarity and benevolence.

Notes

[1] See in this respect, Abdel-Baqi, *al-Muʿjam al-Mufahras*, pp. 468-469; Bakhtiar, *Concordance of the Sublime*, p. 338. See also, Balil Abd al-Karim, *Qur'anic Terminology: A Linguistic and Semantic Analysis*, translated from the Arabic by Nancy Roberts (London-Washington: The International Institute of Islamic Thought, 1438/2017), pp. 81-82.

[2] Abdel-Baqi, *al-Muʿjam al-Mufahras*, pp.194, 216-217, 304-305, 510, 550-551, 644, 722; Bakhtiar, *Concordance of the Sublime Quran*, pp. 138, 154, 288, 368, 400-401 & 461-461.

[3] See in this regard Abū ʿAbd Allāh Muḥammad b. ʿAlī al-Ḥakīm al-Tirmidhī, *Bayān al-Farq bayna al-Ṣadr wa'l-Qalb wa'l-Fu'ad wa'l-Lubb*, ed. Ahmad Abdel Hamid al-Sayeh (Cairo: Markaz al-Kitāb li'l-Nashr, 1997), pp. 18-73; Mohammed Ali El Jouzou, *Mafhūm al-ʿAql wa'l-Qalb fi'l-Qur'ān wa'l-Sunnah* (Beirut: Dār al-ʿIlm li'l-Malāyīn, 1980), pp. 101-129; Syed Muhammad Naquib al-Attas, *The Concept of Education in Islam: A Framework for an Islamic Philosophy of Education* (Kual Lumpur: Ta'dib International, 2018), pp. 13-14; Abd al-Karim, *Qur'anic Terminology*, pp. 85-87.

[4] Abdel-Baqi, *al-Muʿjam al-Mufahras*, pp. 550-551; Bakhtiar, *Concordance of the Sublime Quran*, pp. 400-401; Hanna E. Kassis, *A Concordance of the Qur'an*, with foreword by Fazlur Rahman (California-London: University of California Press, 1983), pp. 903-905; Abd al-Karim, *Qur'anic Terminology*, pp. 83-84.

[5] See Qur'an: al-Anʿām, 6:25; al-Tawbah, 9:87 & 127; al-Isrā', 17:47; al-Kahf, 18:57; and al-Munāfiqūn, 63:3.

[6] In statistical terms and significantly enough, these verbal expressions occur more than eighty times in contexts denoting reflection, pondering, investigation, understanding, comprehension. See Abdel-Baqi, *al-Muʿjam al-Mufahras*, pp. 121, 252, 272-274, 525, 705-706; Bakhtiar, *Concordance of the Sublime Quran*, pp. 400-401; Abd al-Karim, *Qur'anic Terminology*, p. 83-84.

[7] Al-Farāhīdī, *Kitāʿb al-ʿAyn*, vol. 3, p. 203.

[8] Ibn Manẓūr, *Lisān al-ʿArab* (, vol. 11, p. 458; also vol. 4, p. 170 & vol. 15, p. 346; Lane, *An Arabic-English Lexicon*, vol. 5, p. 2115).

[9] It is worth mentioning that al-Zabīdī's encyclopedic lexicon is in actual fact an elaboration and extension of al-Fayrūzābādī's (1329-1414) famous *al-Qāmūs al-Muḥīṭ* which was mainly a combination and summary of the Andalusian Ibn Sīdeh's (398/1007-458/1066) *al-Muḥkam* and al-Ṣaghānī's (577/1181-650/1252) *al-ʿUbāb al-Zākhir*, as he himself clearly mentions. Majd al-Dīn Muḥammad b. Yaʿqūb al-Fayrūzābādī, *al-Qāmūs al-Muḥīṭ*, ed. Anas Mohamed al-Shami and Zakaria Jabir Ahmad (Cairo: Dār al-Ḥadīth, 1429/2008), pp. 25-26.

[10] Al-Zabīdī, *Tāj al-ʿArūs*, vol. 30, pp. 18-20; also, Lane, *An Arabic-English Lexicon*, vol. 5, pp. 2113-2114.

The summary provided by al-Zabīdī of the technical meaning of *ʿaql* as epistemologically conceptualized by al-Juwaynī is, generally speaking, quite adequate and accurately represents the views of most Muslim scholars, especially theologians (*mutakallimūn*) and legal theorists (*uṣūliyyūn*). According to those scholars, including al-Juwaynī who has been specifically referred to by the great lexicographer, the terms *wujūb al-wājibāt, istiḥālat al-mustaḥīlāt* and *jawāz al-jā'izāt* constitute fundamental epistemological principles on which the whole edifice of human knowledge stands. They are considered as part of the elementary innate knowledge (*ma'rifah awwaliyyah fiṭriyyah*) with which God has endowed human beings. Granting that 2 plus 2 equals 4 is necessary and cannot be otherwise, while saying that a person x can physically be in two different places at the same time is impossible and does not allow for any degree of probability to be otherwise. On the contrary, saying that it will be raining this afternoon in the Gombak area because of clouds accumulating in the sky is neither necessary nor impossible, as it may or may not rain. So, it belongs to the category of what is possible. This necessary elementary knowledge is thus immediate and intuitive, and is both physical or sensual and non-physical or non-sensual.

On al-Juwaynī's epistemological scheme see, Imām al-Ḥaramayn Abū al-Ma'ālī 'Abd al-Malik b. 'Abd Allāh b. Yūsuf al-Juwaynī, *al-Burhān fī Uṣūl al-Fiqh*, ed. Abdul Azim Mahmoud al-Deeb (al-Mansourah, Egypt: Dār al-Wafā', 1412/1992), vol.1, 95-132; *al-Irshād ilā Qawāṭi' al-Adillah fī Uṣūl al-I'tiqād*, ed. Mohammad Yousof Moussa *et al.* (Cairo: Maktabat al-Khānjī, 1369/1950), pp. 3-16; Sohaira Z. M. Siddiqui, *Law and Politics under the Abbasids: An Intellectual Portrait of al-Juwaynī* (Cambridge, UK: New York: Cambridge University Press, 1st edn., 2019), pp. 109-132; Ibn al-Amīr (d. 736H), *al-Kāmil fī Uṣūl al-Dīn fī Ikhtiṣār al-Shāmil fī Uṣūl al-Dīn*, ed. Gamal Abdel Nasir Abdel Monim (Cairo: Dār al-Salām, 1st edn., 1431/2010), vol. 1, pp. 173-187.

For other scholars' views on *'aql* or intellect see for example, al-Ḥārith b. Asad al-Muḥāsibī, *al-'Aql wa-Fahm al-Qur'ān*, ed. Hossain al-Quwatli (Beirut: Dār al-Fikr, 1st edn., 1391/1971); Gavin Picken, *Spiritual Purification in Islam: The Life and works of al-Muḥāsibī* (London and New York: Routlegde, 2011), pp. 98-201; Abū Bakr Muḥammad b. al-Ṭayyib b. al-Bāqillānī, *Kitāb al-Tamhīd*, ed. Revd. Richard Joseph McCarthy (Beirut: Librarie Orientale, 1957), pp. 6-14; al-Qāḍī Abū al-Ḥasan 'Abd al-Jabbār al-Asadābādī, *al-Mughnī fī Abwāb al-Tawḥīd wa'l-'Adl*, ed. Taha Hussein, Ibrahim Madkour *et al.* (Cairo: Wizārat al-Thaqāfah wa'l-Irshād al-Qawmī, al-Idārah al-'Ammah lil-Thaqāfah, 1960-1965), vol. 12 (*al-Naẓar wa'l-Ma'ārif*); Abū al-Qāsim al-Ḥusayn b. Muḥammad b. al-Mufaḍḍal al-Rāghib al-Iṣfahānī, *Kitāb al-Dharī'ah ilā Makārim al-Sharī'ah*, ed. Aldou Elyazid al-Ajami (Cairo: Dār al-Salām, 1st edn., 1428/2007), pp. 133-135 and 168-169. Abū Ḥāmid al-Ghazālī, *Mishkāt al-Anwār*, ed. Abu Al 'Ala 'Afifi (Cairo: al-Dār al-Qawmiyyah li'-Ṭibā'ah wa'l-Nashr, 1383/1964), pp. 48-49; Fakhr al-Dīn Muḥammad b. 'Umar al-Rāzī, *Nihāyat al-'Uqūl fī Dirāyat al-Uṣūl*, ed. Saeed A. Foudeh (Beirut: Dār al-Dhakā'ir, 1st edn. 1436/2015), vol. 1, pp. 116-121; Sayf al-Dīn al-Amidī, *Abkār al-Afkār fī Uṣūl al-Dīn*, ed. Mohammad Ali al-Mahdi (Cairo: Dār al-Kutub wal-Wathā'iq al-Qawmiyyah, 2nd edn., 1424/2004), vol. 1, pp. 72-94. A succinct yet comprehensive account of the different views on *'aql* in the various Islamic intellectual traditions can be found in, Muḥammad b. 'Alī al-Tahānawī, *Mawsūʿat Kashshāf Iṣṭilāḥāt al-Funūn wa'l-ʿUlūm,* ed. Rafiq al-Ajam *et al.* (Beirut: Maktabat Lubnān Nāshirūn, 1ˢᵗ edn. 1996), pp. 1194-1201.

[11] Abdel Baqi, *al-Muʿjam al-Mufahras,* p. 121-123 and 358-360; Bakhtiar, *Concordance of the Sublime Quran,* pp. 84-85, 256-257.

[12] For a comprehensive discussion of what we have briefly touched upon here, see Abd al-Karim, *Qur'anic Terminology,* pp. 164-171.

[13] Ibrahim Kalin, *Reason and Rationality in the Qur'an* (Amman: The Royal Aal Al-Bayt Institute for Islamic Thought, 2012), p. 33.

[14] Shabir Akhtar, *The Quran and the Secular Mind: A Philosophy of Islam* (London and New York: Routledge, Taylor & Francis Group, 2008), pp. 69 & 267-294. In chapter 8 stretching over this range of pages, Akhtar offers one of the most profound discussions on human nature, its dimensions, and characteristics in the Qur'an.

[15] Ibid., p. 58.

[16] Ibid., pp. 217-237. See also, Ramon Harvey, *Transcendent God, Rational World: A Māturīdī Theology* (Edinburgh: Edinburgh University Press, 2021), pp. 59-102.

[17] Abū al-Ḥussain al-Qāsim b. Muḥammad b. al-Mufaḍḍal al-Rāghib al-Iṣfahānī, *Tafṣīl al-Nash'atayn wa-Taḥṣīl al-Saʿādatayn,* ed. Abdelmajid al-Najjar (Beirut: Dār al-Gharb al-Islāmī, 1ˢᵗ edn., 1408/1988), pp. 140-143; also his *Kitāb al-Dharīʿah,* pp. 153-165. Abū Ḥāmid Muḥammad b. Muḥammad b. Muḥammad al-Ghazālī, *Maʿārij al-Quds fī Maʿrifat al-Nafs,* edited and with an introduction by Ahmed Shamshuddin (Beirut: Dār al-Kutub al-ʿIlmiyyah, 1ˢᵗ edn., 1409/1988), pp. 72-74. The idea of the double light has been rearticulated by Draz in his discussion on the foundation and orgin of moral knowledge and moral obligation. To the question: "On which foundation rests the Qur'anic law of duty, from which sources does it take its authority?", he offers the following answer: "the distinction between good and evil, before being a divine law, is an inner revelation, inscribed the human soul", wherby "virtue takes its influence from its own nature and its intrinsic value," and "therefore Reason and Revelation are but two lights revealing the same object, a dual translation of the one single original reality, rooted at the heart of things." M. A. Draz, *The Moral World of the Qur'an,* translated from the French by Danielle Robinsob and Rebecca Masterton (London-New York: I.B. Tauris, 2008), p. 8.

[18] On the destructive effects and consequences of alcoholism see for example, Benjamin Kissin & Henri Begleiter (eds.), *Social Aspects of Alcoholism* (New York: Springer Science+Business Media, 1976); George E. Vaillant, *The Natural History of Alcoholism Revisited* (Cambridge, Massachsetts & London, England: Harvard University Press, 1995 [1983]); Marc Galanter (ed.), *The Consequences of Alcoholism: Medical, Neuropsychiatric, Economic, Cross-Cultural* (New York-Boston-Dordrecht-London-Moscow: Kluwer Academic Publishers, 1998).

[19] See in this regard, Ḍiyā' al-Dīn Abū al-Maʿālī ʿAbd al-Malik b. ʿAbd Allāh b. Yūsuf al-Naysābūrī, Imām al-Ḥaramyn Juwaynī, *al-Ghiyyāthī: Ghiyyāth al-Umam fī'l-Tiyāth al-Ẓulam,* ed. Abbul Azim Mahmoud Aldeeb (Jeddah: Dār al-Minhāj,

3rd edn., 1433/2011), pp. 529-552; Wahbah al-Zuhayli, *Naẓariyyat al-Ḍarūrah al-Sharʿiyyah* (Beirut: Muʾassasat al-Risālah, 4th edn., 1405/1985); John Makdisi, "Hard Cases and Human Judgment in Islamic and Common Law", *Indiana International & Comparative Law Review*, vol. 2, issue 1 (1991), pp. 191-220; Yacoub Al Bahussain, *al-Mufaṣṣal fiʾl-Qawāʿid al-Fiqhiyyah* (Riyadh: Dār al-Tadmuriyyah, 2nd edn., 1432/2011), pp. 238-272.

[20] Asad, *The Message of the Qurʾan*, 2011), p. 194, note 105.

[21] Abū al-Ḥusayn Muslim b. al-Ḥajjāj al-Qushayrī al-Naysābūrī, *Ṣaḥīḥ Muslm*, ed. Muhammad Fuad Abdel-Baqi (Cairo: Dār Iḥyāʾ al-Kutub al-ʿArabiyyah, 1421/1991), "Kitāb al-Ashribah", No. 2003:73-75, vol. 3, pp. 1587-1588.

[22] Abū ʿĪsā Muḥammad b. Īsā al-Tirmidhī, *al-Jāmiʿ al-Kabīr*, ed. Bashshar Awwad Marouf (Beirut: Dār al-Gharb al-Islāmī, 1996), "Abwāb al-Ashribah", No. 1865, vol. 3, p. 442.

[23] In line with this description and characterization of intoxicants, we read in the same narration that "he who consumes them will rape his mother and paternal and maternal aunts." ʿAlī b. ʿUmar al-Dāraquṭnī, *Sunan al-Dāraquṭnī* ed. Adel A. Abdel Mawgoud *et al.* (Beirut: Dār al-Maʿrifah, 1422/2001), "Kitāb al-Ashribah", No. 4531, vol. 3, p. 495. For a comprehensive and detailed analysis of the psychological, socio-cultural and economic effects and consequences of alcoholism and its treatment from an Islamic perspective, see Malik Badri, *Ḥikmat al-Islām fī Taḥrīm al-Khamr: Dirāsah Nafsiyyah Ijtimāʿiyyah* (Herndon, Virginia: The International Institute of Islamic Thought, 1416/1996); *cf.* Yusuf Hamid al-ʿAlim, *al-Maqāṣid al-ʿĀmmah liʾl-Sharīʿah al-Islāmiyyah* (London-Washington: The International Institute of Islamic Thought, IIIT, 1413/1993), pp. 376-392. See also references cited earlier on alcoholism.

[24] Sayyid Abul Aʾla Mawdudi, *Towards Understanding the Qurʾān*, abridged version of *Tafhīm al-Qurʾān*, translated and edited by Zafar Ishaq Ansari (Leicester: The Islamic Foundation, 1988/1408), vol. 2, p. 291.

[25] Muhammad al-Tahir Ibn Ashur, *Treatise on Maqāṣid al-Sharīʿah*, trans. Mohamed El-Tahir El-Mesawi (London/Washington: The International Institute of Islamic Thought, 1427/2006), p. 121

[26] Asad, *The Message of the Qurʾan*, p. 199, note 124.

[27] Ibid.

[28] This very attitude is condemningly mentioned in a number of other Qurʾanic verses, such as al-Baqarah (2:170): "And when it is said to them, 'Follow what God has revealed,' they say, 'Nay, we shall follow [only] what we found our forefathers following.' Why, even if their forefathers did not use their reason at all, and were devoid of all guidance?"

[29] Sherman A. Jackson, "Apprehending and Concretizing *Maqāṣid al-Sharīʿah* in the Modern World", in Mohamed El-Tahir El-Mesawi (ed.), *Maqāṣid al-Sharīʿah: Explorations and Implications* (Petaling Jaya, Malaysia: Islamic Book Trust, 2018), p. 113.

[30] Ahmad al-Raysuni, *Imām al-Shāṭibī's Theory of the Higher Objectives and Intents of Islamic Law,* translated from the Arabic by Nancy Roberts (London–Washington: The International Institute of Islamic Thought, 1426AH/2005CE), p. 265.

[31] Ibid., pp. 114-119.

[32] Ibn Manẓūr, *Lisān al-ʿArab,* vol. 11, pp. 635-636; al-Zabīdī, *Tāj al-ʿArūs,* vol. 30, pp. 427-428; Lane, *An Arabic-English Lexicon,* vol. 9, p. 3026.

[33] Al-Farāhīdī, *Kitāʿb al-ʿAyn,* vol. 4, p. 173. From the grammatical viewpoint, this statement can alternatively be read as: '*wa-kānat amwāla al-ʿArabi anʿāmuhum.*'

[34] Majd al-Dīn Abū al-Saʿādāt al-Mubārak b. Muḥammad al-Jazarī Ibn al-Athīr, *al-Nihāyah fī Gharīb al-Ḥadīth wa'l-Athar,* ed. Tahir Ahmed al-Zawi and Mahmoud Mohamed al-Tanahi (Cairo: al-Maktabah al-Islāmiyyah, 1383/1963), vol. 4, p. 373.

[35] For more elaboration of the ideas outlined here see, Abū Muḥammad ʿAbd al-Ḥaqq b. Ghālib Ibn ʿAṭiyah al-Andalusī, *al-Muḥarrar al-Wajīz fī Tafsīr al-Kitāb al-ʿAzīz,* ed. Abdul Salam Abdul Shafi Mohammad (Beirut: Dār al-Kutub al-ʿIlmiyyah, 2nd edn., 1422/2001), vol. 1, p. 408 & vol. 3, p. 420; Fakhr al-Dīn Muḥammad b. Ḍiyāʾ al-Dīn ʿUmar al-Rāzī, *Tafsīr al-Rāzī,* known as *al-Tafsīr al-Kabīr,* vol. 7, pp. 210-204 & vol. 21, pp. 131-133; Muhammad al-Tahir Ibn Ashur, *Tafsīr al-Taḥrīr wa'l-Tanwīr* (Tunis: al-Dār al-Tūnusiyyah li'l-Nashr, 1984), vol. 3/3, pp. 178-180; al-Tabataba'i, *al-Mīzān fī Tafsīr al-Qur'ān,* vol. 13, p. 315 & vol. 20, pp. 319-321.

[36] Ali Ozek *et al.* (trans.), *The Majestic Qur'an: An English Rendering of its Meanings* (Chicago: The Nawawi Foundation / London: The Ibn Khaldun Foundation, 4th edn., 2000), p. 51, note 131.

[37] Ibn ʿAṭiyah, *al-Muḥarrar al-Wajīz,* vol. 1, p. 408.

[38] As elaborated by Ibn Ashur, this universal wisdom manifests itself as follows. The inclination of man and woman toward one another is rooted in their divinely given nature (*ṭabʿ*) for the purpose of the survival of the human species (*baqāʾ al-nawʿ*) through a sexually motivated pursuit of procreation (*dāʿī ṭalab al-tanāsul*). This has been so in order for the survival of the species not to be subject to self-constraining (*takalluf*) that might be followed by boredom and disgust. Similarly, the parents' love of their children, emanating from an internal deep feeling that they are part and parcel of them, drives them naturally to take care of their offspring, thus serving the purpose of the species' survival against the natural extinction decreed upon its individuals by death. Furthermore, the survival of mankind is attained through offspring in another way by protecting the weak thereof. Since the human being is prone to weakness after strength, parents will be protected by their children when they are weak due to old age. Likewise, just as parents take care of their weak offspring, so too children take care of their weak parents. Finally, gold and silver and the other things mentioned with them refer to money and different kinds of wealth to which human beings are instinctively attracted and by means of which they fulfill their needs. Ibn Ashur, *Tafsīr al-Taḥrīr wa'l-Tanwīr,* vol. 3/3, pp. 178-182.

[39] Al-Tabataba'i, *al-Mīzān fī Tafsīr al-Qur'ān*, vol. 3, pp. 110-114.

[40] For more details see, ʿAlī Ḥaydar, *Durar al-Ḥukkām Sharḥ Majallat al-Aḥkām*, translated from Ottoman Turkish by Fahmī al-Ḥusaynī (Riyadh: Dār ʿĀlam al-Kutub, 1423/2003), vol. 1, pp. 115-116; Muhammad Abu Zahrah, *al-Milkiyyah wa'l-ʿAqd fī'l-Sharīʿah al-Islāmiyyah* (Cairo: Dār al-Fikr al-ʿArabī, 1996), pp. 47-77; Ali al-Khafif, *Buḥūth wa-Maqālāt fī'l-Tashrīʿ al-Islāmī* (Cairo: Dār al-Fikr al-ʿArabī, 1431/2010), pp. 179-224; Nazih Hammad, *Qaḍāyā Fiqhiyyah Muʿāṣirah fī'l-Māl wa'l-Iqtiṣād* (Damascus: Dār al-Qalam, 2001), pp. 29-62; Rifat al-Sayyid al-Awadi (ed.), *Mawsūʿat al-Iqtiṣād al-Islāmī* (Cairo: Dār al-Salīm & Herndon, Virginia: The International Institute of Islamic Thought, IIIT, 1430/2009), vol. 1, pp. 139-149; Taysir Mohamed Barmou, *Naẓariyat al-Manfaʿah fī'l-Fiqh al-Islāmī* (Beirut: Dār al-Nawādir, 2008).

[41] One of the most extensive discussions on money and currency as a medium of measurement, exchange and store value is provided by al-Ghazālī in different works of his. See especially, Abū Ḥāmid Muḥammad b. Muḥammad b. Muḥammad b. Aḥmad al-Ghazālī, *Iḥyā' ʿUlūm al-Dīn* (Jeddah: Dār al-Minhāj, 1st edn., 1432/2011), vol. 7, pp. 305-512. For recent treatments of this issue, see for example, Shawqi Ismail Shehata & Abu Bakr al-Siddiq Metwally, *Iqtiṣādiyyāt al-Nuqūd fī Iṭār al-Fikr al-Islāmī* (Cairo: Maktabat Wabah, 1983); Muhammad Umer Chapra, *Towards a Just Monetary System* (Leicester, UK: The Islamic Foundation, 1985/1405); Iraj Toutounchian, *Islamic Money and Banking: Integrating Money in Capital Theory* (Sinapore: John Wiley & Sons [Asia] Pte. Ltd., 2009), esp. pp. 1-161; Rafiq Yunus al-Masri, *al-Nuqūd fī'l-Iqtiṣād al-Islāmī* (Damascus: Dār al-Maktabī, 1314/2013); Baqir al-Hassani *et al.* (authors), *Dirāsāt Islāmiyyah fī'l-Iqtiṣād wa'l-Naqd* (Beirut: Center of Civilization for the development of Islami thought, 1st edn., 2011), pp. 169-311; Rayyan Tawfiq Khalil, *Naẓariyyat al-Nuqūd fī'l-Fiqh al-Islāmī al-Muqāran* (Amman: Dār al-Fatḥ, 1st edn., 1435/2014).

[42] Muḥyiddin Aṭiyah, *al-Kashshāf al-Iqtiṣādī li-Āyāt al-Qur'ān al-Karīm* (Hernden, Virginia: The International Institute of Islamic Thought, 1st edn., 1412/1991), pp. 266-280.

[43] Al-Rāghib al-Iṣfahānī *Mufradāt Alfāẓ al-Qur'ān*, ed. Safwan Adnan Dawoodi (Damascus: Dār al-Qalam, 1430/2009), p. 352.; Lane, *Arabic-English Lexicon*, vol. 3, p. 1077.

[44] For more elaboration on the concept and meaning of worship in these verses, see Asad, *The Message of the Qur'an*, p. 965, note 38.

[45] Abū Ḥāmid al-Ghazālī, *al-Maqsad al-Asnā fī Sharḥ Asmā' Allāh al-Ḥusnā*, ed. Bassam Abdul Wahab al-Jabi (Beirut: Dār Ibn Ḥazm, 1324/2003), pp. 84-85. *Cf.* Murtaza Mutahhari, *al-Fikr al-Islāmī wa-ʿUlūm al-Qur'ān* (Beirut: Dār al-Irshād, 1st edn., 1430/2009), pp. 239-247.

[46] Ibn Manẓūr, *Lisān al-ʿArab*, vol. 10, p. 115.

[47] Asad, *The Message of the Qur'an*, p. 4, note 4. For further and profound discussions on the meaning and dimensions and implications of the concept of *rizq*, see: al-Qāḍī Abū al-Ḥasan ʿAbd al-Jabbār al-Asadābādī, *al-Mughnī fī Abwāb al-*

Tawḥīd wa'l-ʿAdl, ed. Taha Hussein, Ibrahim Madkour *et al.* (Cairo: Wizārat al-Thaqāfah wa'l-Irshād al-Qawmī, al-Idārah al-ʿAmmah lil-Thaqāfah, 1960-1965), vol. 11 (*al-Taklīf*), pp. 27-60 & 81-84; Ibn Ashur, *Tafsīr al-Taḥrīr wa'l-Tanwīr,* vol. 1, p. 234-237; al-Tabataba'i, *al-Mīzān fī Tafsīr al-Qur'ān,* vol. 3, pp. 158-163 & vol. 18, pp. 380-381.

[48] Al-Rāzī, *al-Tafsīr al-Kabīr,* vol. 20, p. 182.

[49] Al-Tabataba'i, *al-Mīzān fī Tafsīr al-Qur'ān,* vol. 13, pp. 66-67.

[50] For an imformative and more comprehensive survey and reasonable semantic analysis of the term *rizq* in the Qur'an and Prophetic traditions and the different articulations of this concept by different Islamic schools of thought, see, Fatih Muhammad Sulayman, *al-Taṭawwur al-Dilālī li--Muṣṭaḥāt al-ʿAqīdah* (Beirut: Dār al-Kutub al-ʿIlmiyyah, 1st edn., 1440/2019), pp. 223-241.

[51] See Abdel Baqi, *al-Muʿjam al-Mufahras,* pp. 347-348; Bakhtiar, *Concordance of the Sublime Qur'an,* p. 1074. Derived from the same root *s-kh-r* the passive participle *musakhkhar* occurs four times in the Qur'an, of which three are in the feminine plural form, all referring to different natural phenomena.

[52] Ibn Ashur, *Tafsīr al-Taḥrīr wa'l-Tanwīr,* vol. 5/8, pp. 168-169.

[53] Asad, *The Message of the Qur'an,* p. 916, note 11.

[54] Ibid., p. 452, note 46.

[55] See for example for the following verses, al-Baqarah, 2: 205; Āl ʿImrān, 3:117; al-Anʿām, 6:136, 141; al-Aʿrāf, 7:96; Hūd, 11:38; Yūsuf, 12:47; al-Naḥl, 16:11, 14, 67; al-Isrā', 17:18-20, 91; al-Kahf, 18:32-43; al-Anbiyā', 21:78, 80; al-Mu'minūn, 23:18-21, 27; al-Shuʿarā', 26:128-129, 149; Saba', 34:10-11; Yā Sīn, 36:71-73; al-Dukhān, 44:26; al-Fatḥ, 48:29; Qāf, 50:9; al-Raḥmān, 55:10-12; al-Wāqiʿah, 56:63-64; al-Hadid, 57:25; al-Qalam, 68:22.

[56] For elaborate discussions on the theory of original permissibility see, Abū Isḥāq Ibrāhīm b. Mūsā al-Shāṭibī, *al-Muwāfaqāt fī Uṣūl al-Sharīʿah,* ed. Abdullah Draz (Beirut: Dār al-Kutub al-ʿIlmiyyah, 1422/2001), vol. 1/1, pp. 76-105, also its English translation as, *The Reconciliation of the Fundamentals of Islamic Law,* trans. Imran Ahsan Khan Nyazee (London: Garnet Publishers, 2014), vol. 1, pp. 77-10; Muhammad Salam Madkour, *Naẓariyyat al-Ibāḥah ʿinda al-Uṣūliyyīn wa'l-Fuqahā'* (Cairo: Dār al-Nahḍah al-ʿArabiyyah, 2nd edn., 1984); Muhammad Sidqi bin Ahmad bin Mohammad al-Burnu, *al-Wajīz fī Qawāʿid al-Fiqh al-Kulliyyah* (Beirut: Mu'assasat al-Risalah, 4th edn., 1416/1996), pp. 191-200; Ahmad b. Abdullah Aldhuwayhi, *Qāʿidat al-Aṣl fī'l-Ashyā' al-Ibāḥah* (Riyadh: Al-Imam Muhammad Ibn Saud Islamic University, 1428/2007).

[57] Abdel Baqi, *al-Muʿjam al-Mufahras,* p. 683. It should be noted that it is used 3 times in indefinite form (*amwālan*) and 11 times with the definite article (*al-amwāl*).

[58] Asad, *The Message of the Qur'an,* p. 248, note 24.

[59] Ibn Ashur, *Tafsīr al-Taḥrīr wa'l-Tanwīr,* vol. 3/4, pp. 234-236; al-Tabataba'i, *al-Mīzān fī Tafsīr al-Qur'ān,* vol. 4, pp. 175-180.

[60] See also, al-Anʿām, 6:50; Hūd, 11: 31; al-Ḥijr, 15: 21; al-Isrāʾ, 17:100.

[61] Abhorrence of, and warning against, arrogance because of one's power, wealth, race, etc. is one of the Qurʾan's recurrent themes, considered as one of destructive factors of human life and society. In fact, it has been addressed in the earliest revelation in Makkah with its essential cause clearly brought to light as being the feeling of independence and self-sufficiency. Thus, we read in sūrah al-ʿAlaq (96:6-8): "Nay, verily, man becomes grossly overweening whenever he belives himself to be self-sufficient: fr, belhold, unto thy Sustainer all must return." Of similar significance is the story of the man with the two gardens (ṣaḥib al-jannatayn) related in sūrah al-Kahf (18:32-43) whose wealth drove him to arrogance and self-destruction.

[62] See for example, *al-Muwaṭṭaʾ*, *Kitāb al-Aṣl*, *al-Mudawwanah*, *al-Umm*, *al-Nawādir waʾl-Ziyādāt*, *Aḥkām al-Qurʾān* & *Sharḥ Mukhtaṣar al-Taḥḥāwī*, *al-Muḥallā*, *al-Ḥāwī al-Kabīr*, *al-Mabsūṭ fī Fiqh al-Imāmiyyah*, *Nihāyat al-Maṭlab*, *al-Mabsūṭ*, *al-Wasīṭ fiʾl-Madhhab*, *al-Byān waʾl-Taḥṣīl*, *Aḥkām al-Qurʾān*, *al-Mughnī*, *al-Muktaṣar al-Fiqhī*, *al-Baḥr al-Zakhkhār*, and *al-Fiqh al-Islāmī wa-Adillatuh* (respectively by Mālik ibn Anas, Muḥammad b. al-Ḥassan al-Shaybānī, Suḥnūn, al-Shāfiʿī, Abū Bakr al-Jaṣṣāṣ, Ibn Abī Zayd al-Qayrawānī, Ibn Ḥazm, al-Māwardī, Abū Jaʿfar al-Ṭūsī, Abū al-Maʿālī al-Juwaynī, Shams al-Aʾimmah al-Sarakhsī, Abū Ḥāmid al-Ghazālī, Ibn Rushd, Abū Bakr Ibn ʿArabī, Ibn Qudāmah al-Maqdisī, Ibn ʿArafah, Aḥmad b. Yaḥyā b. al-Murtaḍā, Wahba al-Zuhayli).

[63] Abū Ḥāmid Muḥammad b. Muḥammad b. Muḥammad al-Ghazālī, *Shifāʾ al-Ghalīl fī Bayān al-Shabah waʾl-Mukhīl wa-Masālik al-Taʿlīl*, ed. Hamad al-Kubaysi (Baghdad: Maṭbaʿat al-Irshād, 1390/1971), p. 162; also his *al-Mustaṣfā min ʿIlm al-Uṣūl*, ed. Mohammed Sulayman al-Ashqar (Beirut: Muʾassasat al-Risālah, 1417/1997), vol. 1, p. 417; al-Shātibī, *al-Muwāfaqāt*, vol. 1/2, p. 7. On the socio-historical and cultural significance of the universal necessities, see Ibn Ashur, *Treatise on Maqāṣid al-Sharīʿah*, pp. 118-123.

[64] Al-Ghazālī, *Shifāʾ al-Ghalīl*, p. 159; Fakhr al-Dīn Muḥammad b. ʿUmar b. al-Ḥusayn al-Rāzī, *al-Maḥṣūl fī ʿIlm al-Uṣūl*, ed. Taha Jabir Fayyad al-Alwani (Beirut: Muʾassasat al-Risālah, 2nd edn., 1412/1992), vol. 5, p. 157.

[65] Al-Shātibī, *al-Muwāfaqāt*, vol. 1/2, pp. 7-8; also *The Reconciliation of the Fundamentals of Islamic Law*, trans. Imran Ahsan Khan Nyazee (London: Garnet Publishers, 2014), vol. 2, pp. 9-10. For an elaborate exposition of these two aspects or twofold approach to *ḥifẓ al-māl*, see Yusuf Hamid al-ʿAlim, *al-Maqāṣid al-ʿĀmmah liʾl-Sharīʿah al-Islāmiyyah* (London-Washington: The International Institute of Islamic Thought, IIIT, 1413/1993), pp. 467-568, Ibn Ashur, *Treatise on Maqāṣid al-Sharīʿah*, pp. 118-123.

[66] Ibn Ashur, *Treatise on Maqāṣid al-Sharīʿah*, pp. 121.

[67] Though very much fewer in number compared to comprehensive juristic compemdia and manuals (such as mentioned in a previous note), this category of literature is of high intellectual and historical value as it mostly addresses practical issues of day-to-day of the general public in the different kinds of life,

financial and economic dealings or having to do with policy matters where the main addressees are state officials. Of this category mention can be made of treatises such as *Kitāb al-Kharāj* by Abū Yūsuf (d. 182 AH/798 AD), *al-Iktisāb* by Muḥammad b. al-Ḥassan al-Shaybānī, *Kitāb al-Amwāl* by Abū ʿUbayd (d. 224AH/837CE), *Kitāb al-Tabaṣṣur bi'l-Tijārah* by al-Jahiz (d. 250H), *Aḥkām al-Sūq* by Yaḥyā b. ʿUmar al-Kinānī (d. 289H), and *Bughyat al-Irbah fī Maʿrifat Aḥkām al-Ḥisbah* by Ibn al-Daybaʿ (d. 944H).

[68] In a kind of characterization of modern western economic thought, some critics have dubbed scarcity as an invention of modernity. By this is meant the fact that the "materials that were employed in the construction of this phenomenon had been at hand since the Greeks, but the moderns refashioned the materials into something new." Nicholas Xenos, *Scarcity and Modernity* (London and New York: Routledge, 1989), p. 7 (See his elaboration of this thesis in the first chapter from which the above citation has been taken).

[69] An illuminating, though concise, work has been produced the Syrian economist Rafiq Yusus al-Masri to trace out the premises underlying Muslim jurists' economic thinking and deliberations on the different types of economic activities and financial transactions. See his, *Ishāmāt al-Fuqahā' fi'l-Furūḍ al-Asāsiyyah li-ʿIlm al-Iqtiṣād* (Damascus: Dār al-Maktabī, 1ˢᵗ edn., 1421/2001).

[70] See in this respect, Muhsen Khalil, *Fi'l-Fikr al-Iqtiṣādī al-ʿArabī al-Islāmī: Dirāsah li-Maqūlatay al-ʿAmal wa'l-Milkiyyah* (Baghdad: Manshūrāt Wazārat al-Thaqafāh wa'l-Iʿlām, 1982); Abdul Azim Islahi, *Economic Concepts of Ibn Taimiyyah* (Leicester: The Islamic Foundation, 1996/1417 [1988/1408], also his *History of Islamic Economic Thought: Contributions of Scholars to Economic Thought and Analysis* (Cheltenham, UK: Northampton, MA, USA: Edward Elgar, 2014 [2005]); *Muslim Economic Thinking and Institutions in the 10ᵗʰ AH/16ᵗʰ CE Century* (Jeddah: Islamic Economic Research Centre, King Abdulaziz University, 1430AH/2009CE); S.M. Ghazanfar (ed.), *Medieval Islamic Economic Thought: Filling the 'Great Gap" in European Economics* (London and New York: Routledge, 2003); Fuad Adullah al-Omar, *Muqaddimah fī Tārīkh al-Iqtiṣād al-Islāmī wa-Taṭawwurih* (Jeddah: IDB Islamic Research and Training Institute, 1424/2003); Ahmed El-Ashker & Rodney Wilson, *Islamic Economics. A Short History* (Leiden-Boston: Brill, 2006), esp. pp. 155-283; Benedikt Koehler, *Early Islam and the Birth of Capitalism* (Lanham-Boulder-New York-London: Lexington Books, 2014).

[71] Ibn Khaldūn, *Muqaddimat Ibn Khaldūn*, p. 43. In addition to the jurists, Ibn Khaldūn mentions the *ḥukamā'*, the *uṣūliyyūn* (legal theorists), etc. It should be remembered here that the author of *The Muqaddimah* himself was no stranger to Islamic jurisprudence both in theory and practice, as teacher as well as judge. See his autobiography, ʿAbd al-Raḥmān b. Muḥammad al-Ḥaḍramī al-Ishbīlī, *Riḥlat Ibn Khaldūn*, ed. Moḥammad b. Tāwīt al-Ṭanjī (Beirut: Dār al-Kutub al-ʿIlmiyyah, 1425/2004), pp. 36-64 & 225-246.

[72] Ibn Khaldūn, *Muqaddimat Ibn Khaldūn*, esp. pp. 255-265 & 333-399.

[73] *Muqaddimat Ibn Khaldūn*, pp. 262-263.

[74] *Muqaddimat Ibn Khaldūn*, p. 263; *The Muqaddimah*, vol. 2, p. 107.

[75] *Muqaddimat Ibn Khaldūn,* p. 264.

[76] *Muqaddimat Ibn Khaldūn,* pp. 264-265 & 368-369.

[77] *Muqaddimat Ibn Khaldūn,* p. 265.

[78] *Muqaddimat Ibn Khaldūn,* p. 353. For much more elaborate analysis of Ibn Khaldun's economic thought, see the following: Mohammad Ali Nash'at, *Rā'id al-Iqtiṣād Ibn Khaldūn* (Cairo: Maṭba'at Dār al-Kutub al-Miṣriyyah, 1944); Joseph J. Spengler, "Economic Thought of Islam: Ibn Khaldun", *Comparative Studies in Society and History,* vol. 6, No. 3 (April, 1964), pp. 268-306; Abdalla M. Batta, *Ibn Khaldun's Principles of Political Economy: Rudiments of New Science* (Ph.D. thesis submitted at The American University, 1988); Syed Shorbagi Abdel Maula, *al-Fikr al-Iqtiṣādī 'inda Ibn Khaldūn: al-As'ār wa'l-Nuqūd* (Dammam: Al-Imam Muhammad Ibn Saud Islamic University, 1409/1989); Shawqi Ahmad Dunya, *'Ulamā' al-Muslimīn wa-'Ilm al-Iqtiṣād: Ibn Khaldūn Mu'assis 'Ilm al-Iqtiṣād* (Riyadh: Dār Mu'ādh, 1414/1993); Elseyed Mohammad Ashur, *Ruwwād al-Iqtiṣād al-'Arab* (Cairo: Dār al-Amal, 1ˢᵗ edn., 1419/1998), pp. 119-162; S. C. Karatas, *Economic Theory of Ibn Khaldun and Rise and Fall of Nations* (Manchester, UK: Foundation for Science Technology and Civilisation, 2006); Zubair Hasan, "Labour as a Source of Value and Capital Formation: Ibn Khaldun, Ricardo, and Marx: A Comparison", *Journal of King Abdulaziz University: Islamic Economics,* vol. 20, No. 2, pp. 39-50 (2007 AD/1428 AH); M. Umer Chapra, "Ibn Khaldun's theory of development: Does it help explain the low performance of the present-day Muslim world?", *The Journal of Socio-Economics,* 37 (2008), pp. 836-863; Christos P. Baloglou, "The Tradition of Economic Thought in the Mediterranean World from the Ancient Classical Times through the Hellenistic Times until the Byzantine Times and Arab-Islamic World," in Jurgen Georg Backhaus (ed.), *Handbook of the History of Economic Thought: Insights on the Founders of Modern Economics* (New York-Dordrecht-Heidelberg-London: Springer, 2012), pp. 69-72; Harry Landreth and David C. Colander, *History of Economic Thought* (Boston-Toronto: Houghton Mifflin Company, 4ᵗʰ edn., n.d.), p. 35; Abdul Azim Islahi, "Ibn Khaldun's Theory of Taxation and Its Relevance", *Turkish Journal of Islamic Economics,* vol. 2, No. 2 (August 2015), pp. 1-19.

[79] In this context, al-Ghazālī authored books such *al-Wasīṭ, al-Wajīz, Ma'ākhidh al-Khilāf, Taḥsīn al-Ma'ākhidh, al-Khulāṣah,* and *al-Ta'līqah.*

[80] Al-Ghazālī, *al-Mustasfā,* vol. 1, p. 417 & *Shifā' al-Ghalīl,* p. 160.

[81] Al-Ghazālī, *Iḥyā',* vol. 3, pp. 235-339 (*kitāb al-kasb wa'l-ma'āsh*) & 341-595 (*kitāb al-ḥalāl wa'l-ḥarām*). It should be pointed out that al-Ghazālī's treatment of such matters is not confined to these chapters, as we find him touching on them in various ways and from different perspectives in other places of the book, such as in *kitāb dhamm al-dunya* etc. in the quarter of *muhlikāt* (vol. 6, pp. 114-253) and *kitāb al-shukr* in the quarter of *munjiyyāt* (vol. 7, pp. 302-355).

[82] Al-Ghazālī, *Iḥyā',* vol. 3, p. 238. What has just been described as a psycho-spiritual and social ethics of economic life is also explained in some detail in a

small-sized book by al-Ghazālī. See, Abū Ḥāmid Muḥammad b. Muḥammad b. Muḥammad b. Aḥmad al-Ghazālī, *Mīzān al-ʿAmal* (Jeddah: Dār al-Minhāj, 2nd edn., 1441/2020), pp. 264-281.

83 Al-Ghazālī, *Iḥyāʾ*, vol. 3, p. 238.

84 Al-Ghazālī, *Mīzān*, p. 275. It should be mentioned here that al-Ghazālī's favouring in *Mīzān* of the third category of people in respect of their attitude to mundane life and economic pursuit runs, at least apparently, counter to what is stated in the *Iḥyāʾ* where he considers people falling under the second category as the truly successful. See note 93 for an explanation of this remark.

85 This is one of a group of verses in the same sūrah which, in one sequence (6-16), enumerate God's worldly bounties to humans, which read as follows: *"⁶Did We not make the earth smooth, ⁷and make the mountains to keep it stable? ⁸Did We not create you in pairs, ⁹give you sleep for rest, ¹⁰the night as a cover, ¹¹and the day for your livelihood? ¹²Did We not build seven strong [heavens] above you, ¹³and make a blazing lamp? ¹⁴Did We not send water pouring down from the clouds ¹⁵to bring forth with it grain, plants, ¹⁶and luxuriant gardens?"*

86 These Prophetic statements are available in the Ḥadīth collections of al-Ṭabarānī (*al-Awsaṭ*), Abū Nuʿaym (*Ḥilyah*), al-Tirmidhī (*Sunan*), Ibn Mājah (*Sunan*), Ibn Abī Shaybah (*al-Muṣannaf*), al-Bayhaqī (*Shuʿab al-Īmān*), and others.

87 Al-Ghazālī, *Iḥyāʾ*, vol. 3, pp. 239-246; vol. 7, pp. 343-344.

88 Ibid., *Iḥyāʾ*, vol. 3, p. 246. The italicized lines are a parapharese of the last two verses of sūrah al-Ḥijr (15:98-99). On the tradition cited by al-Ghazālī and its chain of narrators see, Ibn Abī al-Shaykh Abū Muḥammad ʿAbd Allāh b. Muḥammad b. Jaʿfar b. Ḥayyān al-Aṣbahānī, ed. Saleh bin Mohamed al-Wunayyan (d.369H), *Akhlāq al-Nabiy s.A.w.s. wa-Ādābuh*, ed. Salih Mohamed al-Wunayyan (Riyadh: Dār al-Muslim, 1st edn., 1418/1998), No. 853, vol. 4, pp. 184-186.

89 Al-Ghazālī, *Iḥyāʾ*, vol. 3, pp. 390-412.

90 Ibid., vol. 3, pp. 390-412; *Mīzān*, p. 178 & 264.

91 Al-Ghazālī, *Iḥyāʾ*, vol. 3, p. 247.

92 Ibid., vol. 3, p. 247. What al-Ghazālī means by physical worship does not include obligatory acts of worship, such as the five daily prayers, fasting during the month of Ramaḍān, performing the pilgrimage once in a lifetime, etc. It only concerns what is beyond such compulsory duties, this consisting of supererogatory acts of worship, such as virgil prayers, fasting on certain specific days of the week or the moth.

93 Al-Ghazālī, *Iḥyāʾ*, vol. 3, p. 246.

94 For details of al-Ghazālī's different classifications of the kinds of blessings and happiness and their underlying criteria see, *Iḥyāʾ*, vol. 7, pp. 329-340.

95 Ibid., *Iḥyāʾ*, vol. 7, p. 342; *Mīzān*, pp.178-179. It is worth mentioning here that in his *Mīzān*, clearly intended to educate the general public, al-Ghazālī

totally omitted discussing the other five classifications of the kinds of *khayrāt* and *saʿādāt* which he elaborated in the *Iḥyāʾ* and which may be of special interest to certain esoteric people, mainly the Sufis who were supposedly the main target audience in the latter work.

[96] Al-Ghazālī, *Iḥyāʾ*, vol. 7, pp. 340-342; *Mīzān*, pp.178-179. It is worth noting that al-Ghazālī provides an interesting and insightful analysis showing the sociological and historical significance of the four things (i.e., property, family, dignity and honour and nobility of clan) which constitute the category of the extrinsic bounties and blessings in response to those whould look down upon them as mere worldly vanities. His elaboration on such matters is indeed worthy of serious study. See *Iḥyāʾ*, vol. 7, pp. 343-355; *Mīzān*, pp.179-185.

[97] Al-Ghazālī, *Iḥyāʾ*, vol. 3, p. 413. English translation by Yusuf T. Delorenzo as, *al-Ghazālī on the Lawful and Unlawful: Kitāb al-Ḥalāl waʾl-Ḥarām* (Cambridge: Islamic Texts Society, 2020 [2014]), p. 72.

[98] Al-Ghazālī, *Iḥyāʾ*, vol. 3, p. 398; Delorenzo, *al-Ghazālī on the Lawful and Unlawful*, p. 56.

[99] Al-Ghazālī, *Iḥyāʾ*, vol. 3, pp. 323-324 & 417; vol. 6, pp. 93-103. Al-Ghazālī's profound analysis of human beings' need for the different crafts and industries and their interconnectedness and mutual dependence in the context of the division of labour, is worth noting here. He shows that just as there arise various forms of cooperation and cooridination among the people involved in those crafts aand industries, there also emerge disputes and conflicts as well as issues and needs that cannot be attended to and resolved by individuals or private groups in the community. This is the reason why what he describes as "political matters" (i.e., the state and its different institutions) are necessary (*umūrun siyāsiyyah lā-budda minhā*) for the purpose of resolving disputes, realizing justice and maintaining peace and order internally as well as defending the society against threats and aggression externally. All this, al-Ghazālī stipulates, requires the existence of a legal system (*qānūn*) that regulates people's conduct and sets the bounds for them. *Iḥyāʾ*, vol. 6, pp. 95-98; vol. 7, pp. 395-397.

[100] Al-Ghazālī, *Iḥyāʾ*, vol. 3, p. 418; Delorenzo, *al-Ghazālī on the Lawful and Unlawful*, p. 78. (italics added)

[101] Al-Ghazālī, *Iḥyāʾ*, vol. 6, pp. 220-222; *Mīzān*, pp. 264-281.

[102] Al-Ghazālī, *Iḥyāʾ*, vol. 7, p. 342; *Mīzān*, p. 265.

[103] Al-Ghazālī, *Iḥyāʾ*, vol. 3, pp. 284-307; *Mīzān*, p. 265.

[104] Al-Ghazālī, *Iḥyāʾ*, vol. 7, p. 355.

[105] Shaikh Mohammad Ghazanfar and Abdul Azim Islahi, *Economic Thought of al-Ghazali* (Jeddah: Scientific Publishing Center, King Abdulaziz University, 1st edn., 2011/1432), p. 20.

[106] He says, "the temptations and afflictions of this world are so many and of various types obtaining in all aspects of life. Yet, money and wealth (*amwāl*) constitute the greatest temptation and the most destructive affliction, and none

can dispense with them. Once they exist, hardly can anyone be safe from them, and once they are lost, one is given to destitution which might lead to ingratitude; and once they are available, they lead to transgression and great loss. In short, just as they have merits, so to they have demerits." *Iḥyā'*, vol. 6, pp. 113-114, also p. 214 & 279.

[107] Al-Ghazālī, *Iḥyā'*, vol. 6, p. 208; also pp. 338-339; *Mīzān*, pp. 274-275.

[108] Al-Ghazālī, *Iḥyā'*, vol. 6, pp. 284-339.

[109] Ibid., *Iḥyā'*, vol. 3, p. 292; also pp. 299, 303-304.

[110] Ibid., *Iḥyā'*, vol. 3, p. 323. See also, Ghazanfar and Islahi, *Economic Thought of al-Ghazali*, pp. 31-35.

[111] Al-Ghazālī, *Mīzān*, p. 276. Although the soundness and authenticity of this tradition has been disputed by Ḥadith scholars, resulting in the conclusion that it is very weak, if not outright fabricated, its purport and message are corroborated and consolidated by a number of ḥadīths the soundness and authenticity of which is a matter of agreement. On both the said debate and its narrator (Yūsuf b. 'Aṭiyah al-Ṣaffār) and the alternative traditions, see, Muhammad Nasir al-Din al-Alabani, *Silsilat al-Aḥādīth al-Ḍa'īfah wa'l-Mawḍū'ah* (Riyadh: Maktabat al-Ma'ārif, 1412/1992), vol. 4, 372-373 (ḥadīth 1900) & vol. 8, pp. 85-86 (ḥadīth 3590); also his *Silsilat al-Aḥādīth al-Ṣaḥīḥah* (Riyadh: Maktabat al-Ma'ārif, 1ST edn., 1416/1996), vol. 2, pp. 574-576 (ḥadīth 906); Fadil bin Khalaf al-Humadah al-Raqqi (ed.), *Mawsū'at Ibn Abī al-Dunyā* (Riyadh: Dār Atlas al-Khaḍrā', 1st edn., 1433/2012), vol. 1, pp. 276-285 (ḥadīths 893-929).

[112] The term "economics of al-Ghazālī" is a happy coinage by Ghazanfar and Islahi in their pioneering work on the economic thought of this great scholar. See, *Economic Thought of al-Ghazali*, pp. 23-44.

[113] Al-Ghazālī, *Iḥyā'*, vol. 6, p. 308; *Mīzān*, p. 278. In this connection al-Ghazālī quotes a number of Qur'anic verses, such as (al-Naḥl, 16:90): "God commands justice (*'adl*), doing good (*iḥsān*), and generosity towards relatives and He forbids what is shameful, blameworthy, and oppressive. He teaches you, so that you may take heed."

[114] Al-Ghazālī, *Iḥyā'* vol. 3, pp. 308-321; see also Adi Setia (trans.), *The Book of the Proprieties of Earning and Living: Kitāb Ādāb al-Kasb wa-al-Ma'āsh* (Kuala Lumpur: IBFIM, 2013), pp. 85-98.

[115] Ghazanfar and Islahi, *Economic Thought of al-Ghazali*, pp. 26-29.

[116] This is a major theme which al-Ghazālī dealt with extensively in different places of his *magnum opus* work. See for example, *Iḥyā'*, vol. 4, pp. 709-3784; vol. 4, pp. 174-715; vol. 6, pp. 114-723; vol. 7, 205-464; & vol. 8, pp. 10-190.

[117] Ghazanfar and Islahi, *Economic Thought of al-Ghazali*, pp. 45-49.

[118] Al-Ghazālī, *Iḥyā'*, vol. 3, p. 467. See also his counsels and anectodes concerning what the ruler must do and abstain from doing in order to serve the people and promote their well-being in the spirit of both justice and compas-

sion in, *al-Tibr al-Masbūk fī Naṣīḥat al-Mulūk,* ed. Ahmed Shamsuddin (Beirut: Dār al-Kutub al-ʿIlmiyyah, 1st edn., 1409/1988), pp. 43-82.

[119] Al-Ghazālī, *Iḥyāʾ*, vol. 3, pp. 513-540. For a detailed exposition of al-Ghazālī's views on the role of the state in managing and using financial resources to serve the purposes we have just mentioned, see Ghazanfar and Islahi, *Economic Thought of al-Ghazālī,* pp. 45-62.

[120] Al-Ghazālī, *al-Tibr al-Masbūk fī Naṣīḥat al-Mulūk,* p. 80. We relied, with slight modification, in the translation of this quote on F. R. C. Bagley (trans.), *Ghazālīs Book of Counsel for Kings, Naṣīḥat al-Mulūk* (London: Oxford University Press, 1964), pp. 101-102.

[121] See for example, Kenneth Boulding (ed.), *The Economics of Human Betterment* (London & Basingstoke: The Macmillan Press Ltd., 1984); Robert Scott, *Kenneth Boulding: A Voice Crying in the Wilderness* (New York: Palgrave Macmillan, 2015); M. R. Griffiths and J. R. Lucas, *Ethical Economics* (Hampshire & London, UK: Macmillan Press Ltd., 1996); M. Teresa Lunati, *Ethical Issues in Economics: From Altruism to Cooperation to Equity* (London: Macmillan Press Ltd., 1997); Thomas Donaldson & Thomas W. Dunfee, *Ties That Bind* (Boston, Massachusetts: Harvard Business School Press, 1999); Robin Hahnel, *Of the People, By the People: The Case for a Participatory Economy* (Philadelphia: Soapbox, 2012); L.-A. Gérard-Varet *et al.* (eds.), *The Economics of Reciprocity, Giving and Altruism* (London: Macmillan Press, 2000); Rebecca M. Blank and William McGurn, *Is the Market Moral: A Dialogue on Religion, Economics and* Justice (Washington, D.C., Brookings Institution Press, 2004); Vincent Jeffries (ed.), *The Palgrave Handbook of Altruism, Morality and Social Solidarity* (New York: Palgrave Macmillan, 2014); M. R. Griffiths & J. R. Lucas, *Value Economics: The Ethical Implications of Value for New Economic Thinking* (London: Palgrave Macmillan, 2016); Jean Tirole, *Economics for the Common Good,* translated from the French by Steven Rendall (Princeton and Oxford: Princeton University Press, 2017); Wilfred Dolfsma and Ioana Negru, *The Ethical Formation of Economists* (London and New York: Routledge, 2019).

[122] See in this connection, Richard B. Freeman (ed.), *Inequality Around the World* (New York: Palgrave Macmillan, 2002); Erik S. Reinhert, *How Rich Countries Got Rich and Why Poor Countries Stay Poor* (London: Constable, 2007); Anthony B. Atkinson, *Inequality: What Can Be Done about It?* (Cambridge, Massachusetts & London, England: Harvard University Press, 2015); Thomas Piketty, *Why Save the Bankers?: And Other Essays on our Economic and Political Crisis,* translated from the French by Seth Ackerman (New York: Houghton Mifflin Harcourt, 2016); also by the same author: *L'Economie des Inégalités* (Paris: Editions la Découverte, 2004 [1997]); *Capital in the Twenty-First Century,* translated from the French by Arthur Goldhammer (Cambridge, Massachusetts & London, England: The Belknap Press of Harvard University Press, 2014); *Capital and Ideology,* translated from the French by Arthur Goldhammer (Cambridge, Massachusetts & London, England: The Belknap Press of Harvard University Press, 2020) Anthony B. Atkinson & Thomas Piketty (eds.), *Top Incomes: A Global Perspective*

(Oxford, UK & New York: University Press, 2010); Ann Harrison, *Globalization and Poverty* (Chicago & London: The University of Chicago Press, 2007); John Weeks, *Capital, Exploitation and Economic Crisis* (London and New York: Routledge, 2010); Joseph E. Stiglitz, *The Price of Inequality: How Today's Divided Society Engangers our Future* (New York- London: W. W. Norton & Company, 2012); José A. Scheinkman *et al.*, *Speculation, Trading, and Bubbles* (New York: Columbia University Press, 2014); Ernesto Screpanti, *Global Capitalism and The Great Crisis* (New York: Monthly Review Press, 2014); *Gabriel* Zucman,*The Hidden Wealth of Nations: The Scourge of Tax Havens,* translated from the French by Teresa Laven der Fagan (Chicago & London: The University of Chicago Press, 2015); Sebastiano Fadda and Pasquale Tridico (eds.), *Inequality and Uneven Development in the Post-Crisis World* (London and New York: Routledge, 2018); Shoshana Zuboff, *The Age of Surveillance Capitalism: The Fight for A Human Future at the New Frontier vof Power* (London: Profile Books, 2019); Chuck Collins, *How Billionaires Pay Millions to Hide Trillions*(Camridge, UK Medford, USA: Polity Press, 2021).

[123] It has not been the purpose of this 'digression' to provide an historical account of Islamic economic thought, nor should it be understood to express any judgemental view on the contributions of other Muslim scholars who stand out as prominently as al-Ghazālī and Ibn Khaldūn. Suffice it to remember that between them stands such a polymath as Ibn Taymiyyah (d. 728H) whose economic and socio-political thought deserves more systematic study than what it has so far received. It is not out of place to mention that the so-called "Great Gap" in the history of human economic thought as seen through a Western canon is a gap only according to the myopic attitude and exclusive conceptions of those who so described it, such as Joseph Schumpeter (*History of Economic Analysis,* 1954. Otherwise, the alleged dark ages were not actually dark all over the planet, especially in Muslim lands where civilization flourished in all fields of thought and knowledge including the economic arena. See for details, Abbas Mirakhor, "Muslim Contributions to Economics," in Baqir Al-Ḥasani and Abbas Mirakhor (eds.), *Essays on Iqtiṣād: The Islamic Approach to Economic Problems* (Silver Spring, MD: NUR Corp., 1410/1989), pp. 81-113; Shawqi Ahmad Dunya, *'Ulama' al-Muslimīn wa-'Ilm al-Iqtiṣād: Ibn Khaldūn Mu'assis 'Ilm al-Iqtiṣād* (Dār Mu'ādh, 1414/1993); Misbah Oreibi (ed.), *Contribution of Islamic Thought to Modern Economics* (Hernden, Virginia: The International Institute of Islamic Thought, 1st edn., 1418/1998); Abdul Azim Islahi, *Economic Concepts of Ibn Taimīyah* (Leicester: The Islamic Foundation, 1996 [1988]); also his, *History of Islamic Economic Thought: Contributions of Muslim Scholars to Economic Thought and Analysis* (Cheltenham, UK: Northampton, MA, USA: Edward Edgar, 2014); S. M. Ghazanfar (ed.), *Medieval Economic Thought: Filling the "Great Gap" in European economics* (London and New York: RoutledgeCurzon, 2003); Ahmed A.E. El-Shaker and Rodney Wilson, *Islamic Economics: A Short History* (Leiden-Boston: Brill 2006).

[124] Abdel Baqi, *al-Mu'jam al-Mufahras,* pp. 715-716; Kassis, *A Concordance of the Qur'an,* pp. 822-823; Bakhtiar, *Concordance of the Sublime Qur'an,* p. 513; pp. 291-299.

[125] Abdel Baqi, *al-Mu'jam al-Mufahras,* pp. 8-10.

[126] Abdel Baqi, *al-Mu'jam al-Mufahras,* p. 406; Kassis, *A Concordance of the Qur'an,* pp. 822-823; Bakhtiar, *Concordance of the Sublime Qur'an,* p. 513; Aṭiyah, *al-Kashshāf al-Iqtiṣādī li-Āyāt al-Qur'ān al-Karīm,* pp. 107-118. It should be pointed out, however, that the sense of charity and voluntary spending is not expressed in the Qur'an only in the nominal form mentioned here. It is also expressed through certain modes of the active participle or *nomen agentis,* notably *muṣṣaddiq* and *mutaṣaddiq* each of which occurs twice in plural masculine and feminal form in the context of a description of good human qualities.

[127] Yusuf al-Qaradawi, *Fiqh al-Zakāh: A Comprehensive Study of Zakah Regulations and Philosophy in the Light of the Qur'an and Sunnah,* translated by Mozer Kahf and revised & edited by Iqbal Siddiqui (Kuala Lumpur: Islamic Book Trust, 2011), pp. 10-18.

[128] Ibn Ashur, *Tafsīr al-Taḥrīr wa'l-Tanwīr,* vol. 11/26, pp. 347-351 & vol. 14/29, pp. 171-175.

[129] Ibn Ashur, *Tafsīr al-Taḥrīr wa'l-Tanwīr,* vol. 7/15, pp. 77-78. In order to realize the importance and implications of what Ibn Ashur has said about the wayfarer, one need only think of the countless homeless people and the waves of refugees, old and young, male and female, who constitute a highly visible reality of the general social scene in most cities and many countries of the world and the millions of displaced people and refugees testifying to ever-increasing levels of destitution and privation galringly inhumane condition.

[130] Al-Ṭabarī, *Jāmi' al-Bayān,* vol. 18, pp. 503-507; al-Māturīdī, *Ta'wīlāt Ahl al-Sunnah,* vol. 8, pp. 280-282; al-Rāzī, *al-Tafsīr al-Kabīr,* vol. 25, pp. 127-128; Qutb, *Fī Ẓilāl al-Qur'ān,* vol. 5, pp. 2771-2772; Ibn Ashur, *Tafsīr al-Taḥrīr wa'l-Tanwīr,* vol. 10/21, pp. 105-106; Darwazeh, *al-Tafsīr al-Ḥadīth,* vol. 5, pp. 453-454; al-Tabataba'i, *al-Mīzān fī Tafsīr al-Qur'ān,* vol. 16, pp. 190-191; Abd al-Rahman Hassan Habannakah al-Maydani, *Ma'ārij al-Tafakkur wa-Daqā'iq al-Tadabbur* (Damascus: Dār al-Qalam, 1st edn., 1423/2002), vol. 15, pp. 262-264.

What we have described as a general principle prescribing a certain right in people's wealth and property brings to the mind the view or theory maintained by many Muslim scholars both in the past and in the present, especially within the framework of Islamic jurisprudence. This view claims that the Makkan revelations of the Qur'an were not concerned with legislation (*tashrī'*) on social, economic and political matters. Their thrust was to instill and consolidate faith and morality in the hearts and minds of the early Muslims in Makkah through different modes of discourse, including the narration of the stories of previous messengers and their communities. Likewise, so the argument goes, only after the migration to Madīnah did the Qur'an turn to matters of legislation and juridical proclamation. This view gave rise to the notion of the so-called 'juridical verses' (*āyāt al-aḥkām*) which do not count more than five hundred, as estimated by Abū Ḥāmid al-Ghazālī, Fakhr al-Dīn al-Rāzī, and others. It prevailed despite the fact that some scholars, like 'Izz al-Dīn b. 'Abd al-Salām, Shihāb al-Dīn al-Qarāfi and Najm al-Dīn al-Ṭūfī, expressed their reservation about it and intimated that juristic rules are not confined to prescriptive and proscriptive verses of the Qur'an, but can also be obtained from all types of verses through systematic interpretation and inference. It was Abū Isḥāq al-Shāṭibī, however, who made the most comprehensive and bold epistemological and methodological effort to demolish the said theory and demonstrate how legislation for human social affairs is an esstential feature of the Makkan revelations that provide the foundations and universal principles of the juridical and legal provisions proclaimed in the Madīnan ones. See al-Shāṭibī, *al-Muwāfaqāt*, vol. 2/3, pp. 3-318. See also, Wael B. Hallaq, "The Primacy of the Qur'an in al-Sahtibi's Legal Theory," in Wael B. Hallaq and Donald P. Little (eds.), *Islamic Studies Presented to Charles J. Adamas* (Leiden-New York-Kobenhavn-Koln: E.J. Brill, 1st edn., 1991), pp. 69-90; pp. 24-29; Mohamed El-Tahir El-Mesawi, "From al-Shāṭibī's legal hermeneutics to thematic exegesis of the Qur'an," *Intellectual Discourse*, vol. 20, No. 2 (2012), pp. 194-207.

[131]Abdel Baqi, *al-Mu'jam al-Mufahras*, pp. 331-332; Bakhtiar, *Concordance of the Sublime Qur'an*, p. 235. The Makkan verses are al-A'rāf, 7:156; al-Kahf, 19:31, 55; Maryam, 19:31, 55; al-Anbiyā', 21:73; al-Mu'minūn, 23:4; al-Naml, 27:3; al-Rūm, 30:39; Luqmān, 31:4; Fuṣṣilat, 41:7; and al-Muzzammil, 73:20. The Madīnan verses are al-Baqarah, 2:43, 83, 110, 177, 277; al-Nisā', 4:77, 162; al-Mā'idah, 5:12, 55; al-Tawbah, 9:5, 11, 18, 71; al-Ḥajj, 22:41, 78; al-Nūr, 24:37, 56; al-Aḥzāb, 33:33; al-Mijādilah, 58:13; and al-Bayyinah, 98:5.

[132] These two groups of verses consist of the following. 1. The descriptive: al-Baqarah, 2: 177, 277; al-Nisā', 4:162; al-Mā'idah, 5:55; al-Tawbah, 9:18, 71; al-Kahf, 19:31, 55; al-Ḥajj, 22:41; Maryam, 19:31, 55; al-Mu'minūn, 23:4; al-Nūr, 24:37; al-Naml, 27:3 and Luqmān, 31:4. 2. The prescriptive: al-Baqarah, 2:43, 83, 110; al-Mā'idah, 5:12; al-Tawbah, 9:5, 11; al-Anbiyā', 21:73; al-Ḥajj, 22:78; al-Nūr, 24:56; al-Aḥzāb, 33:33; al-Mijādilah, 58:13; al-Muzzammil, 73:20 and al-Bayyinah, 98:5.

[133] We have limited our statistical survey of the Qur'anic pronouncments on *zakāh* to the verses which explicitly and verbally use the term itself. Otherwise, much more can be adduced where the concept is implied and implicitly referred to in different ways and contexts. Think for example of the following verses at the very opening of sūrah al-Baqarah (2:1-3):

> *¹Alif. Lām. Mīm. ²This is the Scripture [the Qur'an] about which there is no doubt, a guidance for all the God-conscious ³who believe in the unseen (al-ghayb), are constant in prayer, and spend on others out of what We provide for them as sustenance.*

For this reason, some scholars went so far as to "claim that *zakāh* is associated with prayers in eighty-two places in the Qur'an," but, as al-Qaradawi rightly observed, "this is an exaggeration." al-Qaradawi, *Fiqh al-Zakāh*, p. xlvii.

[134] *Cf.* al-Rūm, 30:30.

[135] Abū Sa'd al-Muḥsin b. Muḥammad b. Karāmah al-Bayhaqī, al-Ḥākim al-Jashmī, *al-Tahdhīb fī al-Tafsīr*, ed. Abdul Rahman b. Sulayman al-Salimi (Cairo: Dār al-Kitāb al-Miṣrī & Beirut: Dār al-Kitāb al-Lubnānī, 1440/2019), vol. 4, p. 3161; Ibn 'Aṭiyah al-Andalusī, *al-Muḥarrar al-Wajīz fī Tafsīr al-Kitāb al-'Azīz*, vol. 3, p. 47; Abū 'Alī al-Faḍl b. al-Ḥasan al-Ṭabarsī, *Majma' al-Bayān fī Tafsīr al-*

Qur'ān, ed. Hashim al-Rasuli al-Mahallati & Fadlullah al-Tabatabae (Beirut: Dar El-Marefah, 1408/1988), vol. 5-6, p. 64; Abū Bakr Muḥammad b. 'Abd Allāh Ibn al-'Arabī, *Aḥkām al-Qur'ān,* ed. Mohammad Abdul Qadir 'Ata' (Beirut: Dār al-Kutub al-'Ilmiyyah, 2ⁿᵈ edn., 1424/2003), pp. 519-520; al-Qurṭubī, *al-Jām'i li-Aḥkām al-Qur'ān*, vol. 10, pp. 245-246; al-Rāzī, *al-Tafsīr al-Kabīr,* vol. 14, p. 102; Abū Ḥayyān, *al-Baḥr al-Muḥīṭ*, vol. 5, p. 71; Muhammad Abdu and Muhammad Rashid Rida, *Tafsīr al-Qur'ān al-Ḥakīm,* known *Tafsīr al-Manār* (Cairo: Maṭba'at al-Manār, 1ˢᵗ edn., 1338H), vol. 10, p. 569; Darwazeh, *al-Tafsīr al-Ḥadīth,* vol. 9, pp. 461-462; Ni'mat Abdel Latif Mashhour, *al-Zakāh: al-Usus al-Shar'iyyah wa'l-Dawr al-Inmā'ī al-Tawzī'ī* (Herndon, Virginia: The International Institute of Islamic Thought / Beirut: al-Mu'assasah al-Jāmi'iyyah li'l-Dirāsāt wa'l-Nashr wa'l-Tawzī', 1ˢᵗ edn., 1413/1993), pp. 29-33.

[136] Asad, *The Message of the Qur'an,* p. 324, note 85. See also, al-Rāzī, *al-Tafsīr al-Kabīr,* vol. 14, p. 107; Abū Ḥayyān, *al-Baḥr al-Muḥīṭ,* vol. 5, p. 71; Darwazeh, *al-Tafsīr al-Ḥadīth,* vol. 9, p. 461; Ibn Ashur, *Tafsīr al-Taḥrīr wa'l-Tanwīr,* vol. 6/10, p. 235.

[137] Darwazeh, *al-Tafsīr al-Ḥadīth,* vol. 9, p. 462; al-Qaradawi, *Fiqh al-Zakāh,* pp. 639-351.

[138] See for instance, Farishta G. de Zayas, *The Law and Institution of Zakāt* (Kualal Lumpur: The Other Press, 2003 [1960]); Mashhour, *al-Zakāh: al-Usus al-Shar'iyyah wa'l-Dawr al-Inmā'ī al-Tawzī'ī*; Abdullah b. Mansour al-Ghufayli, *Nawāzil al-Zakāh: Dirāsāt Fiqhiyyah Ta'ṣīliyyah li-Mustajiddāt al-Zakāh* (Riyadh: Bank al-Bilad & Dār al-Maymān, 1ˢᵗ edn., 1429/2008); Ali Muhyi al-Din al-Qaradaghi, *Buḥūth fī Qaḍāyā al-Zakāt al-Mu'āṣirah* (Beirut: Dār al-Bashaer al-Islāmiyyah, 1ˢᵗ edn., 1430/2009); Mohammad Naim Yasin, *Qaḍāyā Zakwiyyah Mu'āṣirah* (Amman: Dār al-Nfaes, 1ˢᵗ edn., 1437/2016); Konstantinos Retsikas, *A Synthesis of Time: Zakat, Islamic Micro-Finance and the Question of the Future in 21ˢᵗ Century Indonesia* (Switzerland: Springer Nature, 2020).

[139] de Zayas, *The Law and Institution of Zakāt,* pp. 3-48; al-Qaradawi, *Fiqh al-Zakāh,* pp. 73-355.

[140] de Zayas, *The Law and Institution of Zakāt,* p. xxiii. See also al-Rāzī, *al-Tafsīr al-Kabīr,* vol. 14, p. 105.

[141] de Zayas, *The Law and Institution of Zakāt,* pp. xxiii. For more on the socio-economic implications of *zakah* see, Rauf. A. Azhar, *Economics of an Islamic Economy* (Leiden-Boston: Brill, 2010), pp. 229-234,

[142] See in this respect, Herb Goldberg and Robert T. Lewis, *Money Madness: The Psychology of Saving, Spending, Loving and Hating Money* (New York: William Morrow and Company, Inc., 1978); Ann Harrison (ed.), *Globalization and Poverty* (Chicago and London: The University of Chicago Press, 2007); George Cooper, *The Origin of Financial Crises* (New York: Vintage Books, 2008); Nimi Wariboko, *God and Money: A Theology of Money in a Globalizing World* (Plymounth, UK: Lexington Books, 2008); Sebastian Mallaby, *More Money than God: Hedge Funds and the Making of a New Elite* (New York: The Penguin Press, 2010); James Rickards, *Currency Wars: The Making of the Next Global Crisis* (New York: Portfolio/Penguin, 2012); Laurence Cockcroft,

Global Corruption: Money, Power and Ethics in the Modern World (Lnodon-New York: I. B. Tauris, 2012); Jürgen von Hagen and Michael Welker (eds.), *Money as God?: The Monetization of the Market and its Impact on Religion, Politics, Law, and Ethics* (Cambrideg, UK: Cambridge University Press, 2014); Serge Latouche, *Décoloniser l'Imaginaire: La Pensée Créative contre l'Economie de l'Absurde* (Paris: Parangon, 2003); Bernard Stiegler, *Automatic Society,* vol. 1. *The Future of Work,* translated from the French by Daniel Ross (Cambridge, UK: Polity Press, 2016.

[143] Al-Rāzī, *al-Tafsīr al-Kabīr,* vol. 14, pp. 103-107; Sayyid Qutb, *al-ʿAdālah al-Ijtimāʿiyyah fi'l-Islām* (Beirut-Cairo: Dār al-Shurūq, 1415/1995 [1954]), pp. 38-44; Muhammad Baqir al-Sadr, *Iqtiṣādunā* (Beirut: Dār al-Taʿāruf li'l-Maṭbūʿāt, 20th edn., 1408/1987), pp. 633-636; *al-Madrasah al-Isāmiyyah* (Cairo: Dār al-Kitāb al-Maṣri/ Beirut: Dār al-Kitāb al-Lubnānī, 2011); Rauf A. Azhar, *Economics of an Islamic Economy* (Leiden. Bodton: Brill, 2010); Ayman Reda, *Prophecy, Piety and Profits* (New York: Palgrave Macmillan, 2018); Hussain Mohi-ud-Din Qadri, *Business Ethics in Islam* (Londan and New York: Routledge, 2020).

[144] de Zayas, *The Law and Institution of Zakāt,* pp. 3-48; al-Qaradawi, *Fiqh al-Zakāh,* pp. 73-355. *Cf.,* Qutb, *al-ʿAdālah al-Ijtimāʿiyyah fi'l-Islām,* pp. 57-62.

[145] Yusuf al-Qaradawi, *Mushkilat al-Faqr wa-Kayfa ʿAlajahā al-Islām* (Beirut: Mu'ssasat al-Risālah, 1406/1985); Eltigani Abdelgadir Hamid, *Mushkilat al-Faqr: Muqaddimāt hi Usul al-Iqtisad al-Siyāsī fi'l-Islām* (Khartoum: Institute for Research and Social Studies, 1994), pp. 19-40; also his *al-Naṣ al-Qur'ānī wa-Uṣul al-Ijtimāʿ al-Siyāsī,* pp. 114-151.

[146] See for a more detailed discussion, Qutb, *al-ʿAdālah al-Ijtimāʿiyyah fi'l-Islām,* pp. 63-74 & 108-125.

[147] Of similar import is God's command in sūrah al-Isrā' (17:29-30):

> [29]*And neither allow your hand to remain shackled to your neck, nor stretch it forth to the utmost limit, lest you end up blamed [by your dependants], or even destitute.*[30]*Your Lord gives abundantly to whoever He will, and sparingly to whoever He will: He knows and observes His servants thoroughly.*

[148] See in this regard, al-Bahiy al-Khouli, *al-Tharwah fi Zill al-Islām* (Kuwait: Dār al-Qalam, 4th edn., 1401/1981); Muhammad Baqir al-Sadr, *Iqtiṣādunā* (Beirut: Dār al-Taʿāruf li'l-Maṭbūʿāt, 20th edn., 1408/1978); M. Umer Chapra, *Islam and the Economic Challenge* (Leicester, UK: The Islamic Foundation/Hernden, Viriginia: The International Institute of Islamic Thought, 1992/1412H); also by the same author: *The Islamic Vision of Development in the Light of Maqāṣid al-Sharīʿah* (London-Washington: The International Institute of Islamic Thought, 1429AH/2008CE); *The Future of Economics: An Islamic Perspective* Leicester, UK: The Islamic Foundation, 2000/1420H); Abbas Mirakhor and Hossein Askari, *Islam and the Path to Human and Economic Development* (New York: Palgrave Macmillan, 2010); Hossein Askari, Zamir Iqbal and Abbas Mirakhor, *Introduction to Islamic Economics* (Singapore: Wiley, 2015); Abbas Mirakhor and Hossien Askari, *Ideal Islamic Economy* (New York: Palgrave

Macmillan, 2017); Jomo K.S. (ed.), *Islamic Economic Alternatives* (Houndmills & London: Macmillan Academic and Professional Ltd., 1992); James Simon Watkins, *Islamic Finance and Global Capitalism: An Alternative to Market Economy* (Gewerbestrasse, Switzerland: Palgrave Macmillan, 2020); Abbas Mirakhor *et. al.* (eds.), *Handbook of Ethics of Islamic Economics and Finance* (Berlin-Boston: De Gruyter, 2020).

[149] See in this respect, Mortimer J. Adler, *The Difference of Man and the Difference it Makes* (New York: Fordham University Press, 2005 [1967]); Mary Midgley, *Beast and Man: The Roots of Human Nature* (London and New York: Routledge, 2002 [1979]); Roy F. Naumeister, *The Cultural Animal: Human Nature, Meaning and Social Life* (Oxford: New York: Oxford University Press, 2005); Raymond Tallis, *Aping Mankind: Neuromania, Darwinitis and the Misrepresentatin of Humanity* (Durham, UK & Bristol, USA: Acumen Publishing Limited, 2011).

[150] See in this regard, Mehdi Ha'iri Yazdi, *The Principles of Epistemology in Islamic Philosophy: Knowledge by Presence* (New York: State University of New York Press, 1992); Ibrahim Kalin, *Knowledge in Later Islamic Philosophy: Mulla Sadra on Existence, Intellect, and Intuition* (Oxford – New York: Oxford University Press, 2010); Gila Sher and Richard Tieszen (eds.), *Between Logic and Intuition: Essays in Honor of Charles Parsons* (Cambridge: Cambridge University Press, 2000); David G. Myers, *Intuition: Its Powers and Perils* (New Haven & London: Yale University Press, 2002 Robert Audi, *The Good in the Right: A Theory of Intuition and Intrinsic Value* (Princeton and Oxford: Princeton University Press, 2004); Mark Quirk, *Intuition and Metacognition: Keys to Developing Expertise* (New York: Springer Publishing Company, Inc., 2006); Frederick Grinnell, *Everyday Practice of Science: Where Intuition and Passion Meet Objectivity and Logic* (Oxford: Oxford University Press, 2009); Emily Carson and Renate Huber (eds.), *Intuition and the Axiomatic Method* (Dordrecht: Springer, 2006).

Epilogue

Being centered around goodness and human common good, the idea of *maqāṣid al-Sharīʿah* transcends both in depth and breadth the prevailing conceptions of utility and well-being in socio-economic thought and ethical theories, including their articulations by Muslim legal theorists and moral thinkers. In most cases, such conceptions fall short, in different ways, of embracing the totality of the human condition in its multidimensional and complex nature, thus falling in various kinds of narrow-mindedness and reductionism. As a matter of fact, the formulations of *maqāṣid* by classical and post-classical Muslim scholars clearly point to that multidimensionality and complexity by emphasizing the necessity of the five universals (*al-kulliyyāt al-khamsah*) as constituting the foundation and pillars (*arkān*) of human socio-historical existence from which all human needs and benefits branch out. However, very few in our time have realized and picked up this aspect in a systematic and analytical way in order to explore its intellectual and methodological implications for the study of man and society, despite the trendy character of the writings of *maqāṣid* alluded to in the Introduction.

This is mainly due to the fact that, in addition to being generally entrapped, so to speak, in the juridical and legalistic paradigm mentioned above, some sort of pragmatic tendency seems to have dominated much of the literature produced in the name of *maqāṣid al-Sharīʿah*, which mainly expresses itself through a discourse on the notion of *maṣlaḥah*. To a great extent, it is a narrow-minded utility-centered trend for which *maṣlaḥah*, one would dare to say, serves as a justificatory means and at best an interpretative tool rather than a comprehensive conception of the total human good and well-being encompassing all apsects of human life and existence. Worst still, with the rise, spread and boom of Islamic banking and finance industry struggling to prove its suitability and efficiency in the context of the dominant capitalistic economic system and its prevailing colossal financial institutions, one can speak of the spectre of intellectual distortion whereby the concept of *maṣlaḥah* may be used to sanction and legalize financial practices that may otherwise be dubious, economically, socially and ethically.

As the semantic-conceptual inquiry carried out in this book has enabled us to show, the idea of *maqāṣid al-Sharīʿah* has much deeper underpinnings in the Qur'an that go far beyond the juridical and legal and even moral considerations expounded by different scholars in the past as well as in modern times. It is true that some of its formulations by such scholars succeded to capture its general signifi-cance as being a reflection of the Islamic worldview and condensed embodiment of the universal and enduring values enshrined in the Qur'an. However, its deeper theoretical and methodological implica-tions cannot be said to have gained equal prominence. Our rereading of its central terms (*dīn, nasl, nafs, ʿaql* and *māl*) within their wider Qur'anic semantic field and semiotic context has taken us, we may humbly claim, to hitherto not well explored intellectual horizon.

Anchoring these central notions are ontological, axiological and epistemological considerations that constitute what may be described as the meta-juridical and philosophical structure underlying *maqāṣid al-Sharīʿah*. The latter stand in respect of this deeper structure as the upper structure manifesting and translating those considerations in the different spheres of human life and existence through the spiri-tual values, moral norms and legal rules constituting the Islamic code of human conduct individually and collectively. That grounding structure is expressed succinctly and in an encompassing manner by the fundamental concepts of *mīthāq, fiṭrah, khilāfah, amānah* and *task-hīr,* which all converge and are unified thanks to a divinely designed nexus to give rise to a universal sense of humanity and human dignity and good that supersedes all bounds of time, space and race and calls people to ascend beyond narrow-mindedness, selfishness and ego-centrism under whatever guise and in whatever form they may present themselves historically and culturally.

Thus semantically and conceptually understood and philosophically grounded, *maqāṣid al-Sharīʿah* provide a normative, comprehensive and dynamic framework that puts the study of human affairs and social phenomena on a staight and sure path of wholeness and integralism, whereby such affairs and phenomena can be seen and dealt with in their multidimensionality, interconnectdenss, and complementarity. Accordingly, all spiritual, ethical, social, economic, political, intellectual, scientific and technological matters will not appear, as is often the case in secular and matrerialistic thinking, as contradictory and conflicting aspects of human life and existence that require caring for some of them at the expense of the others or sacrificing some for the sake of others. Instead, most if not all such matters can find their significance and relational value and their proper place and function as integral parts of a total truth that embodies human reality and condition at the level of the person, the community, the society and the world at large, with our ennobled universal humanity in its wholeness, holism and integrality making up the essential and common thread of all socio-cultural, economic and political configurations and institutions, endowing them with life, purpose and functionality. Thus, *maqāṣid al-Sharīʿah* furnish a holistic view of the human condition and an integrated approach to its problems, wherefrom a comprehensive vision of human needs and interests necessarily flows.

Such integralist framework has been for long lacking in the human-and-social science disciplines impoverished and shallowed by various types of reductionist and fragmentating epistemologies and methodologies shaped mainly by a predominantly secular-materialistic world-view. This has been the case for so many decades despite profound criticisms and serious questioning of the premises of the dominant paradigm by increasing numbers of expert scholars and philosophers and strong warnings against its grave consequences for the present and future of mankind. It is not therefore surprising that, realizing the gravity of the dangers facing the human race as a result of such reductionism and fragmentation, many would now and then talk not only about the dehumanization of the human race, but also about its extinction one way or another, thus heralding what has been described as post-humanity and post-human future. Announcing the death of God with the illusion of deifying man was actually putting mankind on a precipice toward self-destruction through alienation, rarefaction, dislocation, disorientation and loss of meaning. This is a situation into which secular humanism and gross materialism animated with a sense of absurdity have plunged modern civilization and the world population in varying degrees and in different forms. Realizing this situation is no novel news in the world of academia and scientific research, nor in the world of politics and policy making. Rather, it is already a big theme preoccupying many great minds of different intellectual persuasions and scientific backgrounds as well as various institutional bodies of different jurisdictions in the world, a matter that is beyond our purpose to discuss here.

Looking at *maqāṣid al-Sharī'ah* as a normative framework for approaching the question of human good and well-being and as an alternative paradigm for the study of the problems of man and society (rather than a mere utility-centered juristic theory) does not in any way preclude or ignore or underestimate the dynamic nature and empirical and historical aspects of such matters. On the contrary, being deeply rooted in the Qur'an as shown in the different chapters of the book, this framework and paradigm are rather characterized by an astounding concern for socio-historical facts and empirical realities of nature and society, and can in no way be imprisioned in any kind of a closed idealism that is blind to the empirical world of man and his environment or oblivious to the different problems besetting it. This characteristic stems from the very nature of the Qur'anic discourse itself.

The Qur'an, in fact, clearly calls upon human beings to use their minds and reflect not only on its verses and grasp its wisdom and guidance, but also, and more emphatically perhaps, to ponder on the different facts and phenomena of nature, society and history, all of which being manifestations and signs (*āyāt*) of divine wisdom in the creation as well as sources of knowledge and lessons (*'ibar*) of great importance and impact in human life and existence. Likewise, the Qur'anic discourse is not merely prescriptive, in the sense that it is only concerned with teaching values, enunciating commandments and instituting rules to govern human behaviour and regulate people's relationships and dealings. It also abounds with descriptive statements about multitudes of facts, phenomena and processes relating to man, nature and the universe, in such wise that they outnumber its prescriptive statements, be they ethical or legal. The purpose of such descriptive statements is not simply to bring specific empirical information to the human consciousness about what is being described (which is the object of natural-physical and human-social sciences) and to direct it to its pragmatic usefulness and cultural significance. Those descriptions are rather meant to awaken the intellect both to the significance of those phenomena in themselves and to their importance in relation to human existence.

The Qur'an thus invites the human mind to study such phenomena and facts in order to know their characteristics and causal connections, discover the laws governing them, fathom their reality and underlying wisdom, and realize their moral and spiritual significance and implications, inasmuch as this is within human capacity. In like manner, the Qur'an establishes an essential bond between the two books of creation and revelation whose messages are intended for the education and benefit of mankind, God's trustee and vicegerent on earth. This is clearly epitomized by the fact that in many different contexts we find the Qur'anic discourse engaged in a multidirectional movement embracing various matters of moral, legal, spiritual, physical and historical nature, thus bringing into light their ultimate and fundamental interconnectedness in different ways and for specific and various purposes.

Seen from this vantange point, the normative framework and paradigmatic alternative furnished by *maqāṣid al-Sharīʿah* as expounded in the present work is call to all those concerned with opening new avenues and exploring new grounds in dealing with human affairs in a seriously flawed civilization and profoundly troubled world.

Select Bibliography

ʿAbd Al-ʿĀṭī, Ḥammūdah, *The Family Structure in Islam* (Petaling Jaya, Malaysia: The Other Press, 2008).

Abd-Allah, Umar al-Faruq, *al-Īmān Fiṭrah: Dirāsah li'l-Īmān al-Fiṭrī fi'l-Qur'ān wa'l-Sunnah wa-Kathīr mina'l-Milal wa'l-Niḥal* (Abu Dhabi: Dār al-Faqīh, 1ˢᵗ edn., 1435/2014).

Abdel-Maula, Syed Shorbagi, *al-Fikr al-Iqtiṣādī ʿinda Ibn Khaldūn: al-Asʿār wa'l-Nuqūd* (Dammam: Al-Imam Muhammad Ibn Saud Islamic University, 1409/1989).

Abderrahmane, Taha, *al-Mafāhīm al-Akhlāqiyyah bayna al-I'timaāiyyah wa'l-ʿAlmāniyyah,* 2 vols. (Rabat: Dār al-Amān, 1ˢᵗ edn., 2021).

_________, *Bu's al-Dahrāniyyah: al-Naqd al-I'timānī li-Faṣl al-Akhlāq ʿan al-Dīn* (Beirut: Arab Network for Research and Publications, 2014).

_________, *Shurūd mā-baʿd al-Dahrāniyyah: al-Naqd al-I'timānī li'l-Khurūj min'l-Akhlāq* (Beirut: al-Mu'assasah al-ʿArabiyyah li'l-Fikr wa'l-Ibdāʿ, 2016).

_________, *Su'āl al-Akhlāq: Musāhamah fi'l-Naqd al-Akhlāqī li'l-Ḥadāthah* (Casablanca/Beirut: al-Markaz al-Thaqāfī al-Arabī, 2000).

Abul Fadl, Zainab Abdul Salam, *al-ʿArḍ al-Qur'ānī li-Qaḍāyā al-Nikāḥ wa'l-Furqah* (Cairo: Dār al-Ḥadīth, 1427/2006).

Adler, Mortimer J., *The Difference of Man and the Difference it Makes* (New York: Fordham University Press, 2005).

Aṣfahānī, Abū al-Ḥusayn al-Qāsim b. Muḥammad b. al-Mufaḍḍal al-Rāghib al-, *Tafṣīl al-Nash'atayn wa-Taḥṣīl al-Saʿādatayn,* ed. Abdelmajid al-Najjar (Beirut: Dār al-Gharb al-Islāmī, 1ˢᵗ edn., 1407/1988).

Ali, Ihsan Mir, *al-Maqāṣid al-ʿĀmmah li'l-Sharīʿah al-Islāmiyyah bayna al-Aṣālah wa'l-Muʿāṣarah* (Damascus: Dār al-Thaqāfah li'l-Jamīʿ, 1st edn., 1430/2009).

Allen, Ann Taylor, *Feminism and Motherhood in Western Europe, 1890-1970* (New York: Palgrave MacMillan, 2005).

Al-Qadi, Wadad Kadi, "The Primordial Covenant and Human History in the Qur'an," in *Proceedings of the American Philosophical Society,* vol. 147, No. 4 (December 2003).

Alwani, Zainab Taha al-, *al-Usrah fī Maqāṣid al-Sharīʿah* (Herndon: International Institute of Isllamic Though, 1ST edn., 1434/2013).

Andersen, Jensine (ed.), *Religion in the Mind: Cognitive Perspectives o n Religious Belief, Ritual, and Experience* (Cambridge, UK: Cambridge University Press, 2001).

Askari, Hossein, Iqbal, Zamir and Mirakhor, Abbas, *Introduction to Islamic Economics* (Singapore: Wiley, 2015).

Attas, Syed Muhammad Naquib al-, *The Concept of Education in Islam: A Framework for Islamic Philosophy of Education* (Kuala Lumpur: Ta'dib International, 2018).

__________, *Islam and Secularism* (Kuala Lumpur: International Institute and Civilization, 1993).

Awadi, Rifat al-Sayyid al- (ed.), *Mawsūʿat al-Iqtiṣād al-Islāmī* (Cairo: Dār al-Salīm & Herndon, Virginia: The International Institute of Islamic Thought, IIIT, 1430/2009).

ʿAwān, Maḥmūd, "The Faith community and World Order in the perspective of Islam," in Ismāʿīl Rājī al Fārūqī (ed.), *Triologue of Abrahamic Faiths* (Herndon, Virginia: International Institute of Islamic Thought, 1411/1991).

Awa, Muhammad Salim el-, *Fī Uṣūl al-Niẓām al-Jināʾī al-Islāmī: Dirāsah Muqārinah* (Cairo: Nahḍat Miṣr, 2006).

Azhar, Rauf A., *Economics of an Islamic Economy* (Leiden. Bodton: Brill, 2010).

Azhar, Rauf A., *Economics of Islamic Economy* (Leiden-Boston: Brill, 2010).

Badri, Malik, *Ḥikmat al-Islām fī Taḥrīm al-Khamr: Dirāsah Nafsiyyah Ijtimāʿiyyah* (Herndon, Virginia: The International Institute of Islamic Thought, 1416/1996).

Bahansi, Ahmad Fethi, al-Jarāʾim fi'l-Fiqh al-Islāmī: Dirāsah Fiqhiyyah Muqārinah (Cairo/Beirut: Dār al-Shurūq, 6th edn., 1409/1988).

Balkhī, Muqātil b. Sulaymān al-, *al-Wujūh wa'l-Naẓā'ir fi'l-Qur'ān al-Karīm*, ed. Ahmad Farid al-Muzayyidi (Beirut: Dār al-Kutub al-'Ilmiyyah, 1st edn., 1429/2008).

Bar, Muhammad Ali al-, *Khalq al-Insān bayna al-Ṭibb wa'l-Qur'ān* (Jeddah: al-Dār al-Su'ūdiyyah, 4th edn. 1403/1983).

Barmou, Taysir Mohamed, *Naẓariyat al-Manfa'ah fi'l-Fiqh al-Islāmī* (Beirut: Dār al-Nawādir, 2008).

Batta, Abdalla M., *Ibn Khaldun's Principles of Political Economy: Rudiments of New Science* (Ph.D. thesis submitted at The American University, 1988).

Bennabi, Malik, *The Qur'anic Phenomenon: An Essay of a Theory on the Qur'an*, translated by Mohamed El-Tahir El-Mesawi (Kuala Lumpur: Islamic Book Trust, 2004).

Berger, Peter L., (ed.), *The Desecularization of the World: Resurgent Religion and World Politics* (Washington, DC: Ethics and Public Policy Center, 1999).

_______, *A Rumor of Angels: Modern Society and the Rediscovery of the Supernatural* (New York: Anchor Books, 1970).

_______, *The Social Reality of Religion* (Middlesex, England: Penguin Books, 1973).

Boyer, Pascal, *The Naturalness of Religious Ideas: A Cognitive Theory of Religion* (California: University of California Press, 1994).

Braggett, David & Jerry L. Walls, *God and Cosmos: Moral Truth and Human Meaning* (Oxford, UK & New York: Oxford University Press, 2016).

Brennane, Teresa (ed.), *Between Feminism and Psychoanalysis* (New York and London: Routledge, 1st edn., 1989).

Buttler, Judith, *Gender Trouble: Feminism and the Subversion of Identity* (New York an d London: Routledge, 1st edn., 1990).

Cassirer, Ernst, *An Essay on Man* (New Haven and London: Yale University Press, 1992 [1944]).

Calogero, Rachel M. *et al.* (eds.), *Self-Objectification in Women: Causes, Consequences, and Counteractions* (Washington, DC: American Psychological Association, 2011).

Chapra, M. Umer, *The Islamic Vision of Development in the Light of Maqasid al-Shariah* (London-Washington: The International Institute of Islamic Thought, 1429AH/2008CE).

_______, *The Future of Economics: An Islamic Perspective* Leicester, UK: The Islamic Foundation, 2000CE/1420AH).

__________, *Islam and the Economic Challenge* (Leicester, UK: The Islamic Foundation/Hernden, Viriginia: The International Institute of Islamic Thought, 1992CE/1412AH).

Cooper, David, *The Death of the Family* (Middleessex, England: Pelican Books, 1972).

Draz, M.A., *Introduction to the Qur'an,* translated by Ayeshah Abdel-Haleem (London/New York: I.B. Tauris, 2000).

__________, *al-Dīn: Buḥūth Mumahhidah li-Dirāsat Tārīkh al-Adyān* (Cairo: Hindawi Foundation for Education and Culture, 2016 [1952]).

Dzervarli, M. Sait, "Divine Wisdom, Human Agency and fiṭra in Ibn Taymiyya's Thought," in Birgit Krawietz and Georges Tamer (eds.), Islamic Theology, Philosophy and Law: Debating Ibn Taymiyya and Ibn Qayyim al-Jawziyyah (Berlin/Boson: De Gruyter, 2013).

Eaton, Gai, *Remembering God: Rfelections on Islam* (Cambridge: Islamic Texts Society, 2000).

Eggen, Nora S., "The *Mīthāq*: A Study in Trust Relationships in the Qur'an," in Håkan Rydving (ed.), *Micro-Level Analyses of the Qur'ān* (Uppsala: Uppsala Universitet, 2014).

El-Ashker, Ahmed & Rodney Wilson, *Islamic Economics: A Short History* (Leiden-Boston: Brill, 2006).

Eliade, Mircea, *The Quest: History and Meaning in Religion* (Chicago & London: The History of Chicago University Press, 1969).

__________, *The Scared and the Profane: The Nature of Religion,* translated from the French by Williard R. Trask (New York: Harcourt, Brace & World, Inc., 1959).

El-Mesawi, Mohamed El-Tahir, "*Maqāṣid al-Sharī'ah*: Meaning, Scope and Ramifications", *Al-Shajarah* (ISTAC Journal of Islamic Thought and Civilization), vol. 25, No. 2, 2020.

__________, (ed.), *Maqāṣid al-Sharī'ah: Explorations and Implications* (Petaling Jaya, Malaysia: Islamic Book Trust, 2018).

__________, "Human nature and the universality of the Sharī'ah: Fiṭrah and Maqāṣid al-Sharī'ah in the works of Shāh Walā Allāh and Ibn 'Āshūr," *Al-Shajarah*, vol. 14, No. 2 (2009).

Ezzati, A., *Islam and Natural Law* (London: Islamic College for Advanced Studies PRESS, 2002).

Farrin, Raymond, "Sūrat al-Nisā' and the Centrality of Justice," *Al-Bayān – Journal of Qur'ānic and Ḥadīth Studies,* No. 14 (1015).

Fārūqī, Ismāʿīl Rājī al-, "The nation-state and social order in the perspective of Islam," in al Fārūqī (ed.), *Trialogue of Abrahamic Faiths* (Herndon, Virginia: International Institute of Islamic Thought, 3rd edn., 1991).

__________, *Al Tawḥīd: Its Implications for Though and Life* (Hernden, Virginia: The International Institute of Islamic Thought, 1412/1992).

Ghazanfar, S.M. (ed.), *Medieval Islamic Economic Thought: Filling the 'Great Gap" in Europen Economics* (London and New York: Routledge, 2003).

Ghazanfar, Shaikh Mohammad and Abdul Azim Islahi, *Economic Thought of al-Ghazali* (Jeddah: Scientific Publishing Center, King Abdulaziz University, 1st edn., 2011/1432).

Ghazālī, Abū Ḥāmid al-, *Iḥyāʾ ʿUlūm al-Dīn* (Jeddah: Dār al-Minhāj, 1st edn., 1432/2011).

__________, *Mīzān al-ʿAmal* (Jeddah: Dār al-Minhāj, 2nd edn., 1441/2020).

Gould, Stephen Jay, *Rocks of Ages: Science and Religion in the Fullest of Life* (New York: The Ballantine Publishing Group, 1999).

Grassie, William, *The New Sciences of Religion: Exploring Spirituality from the Outside In and Bottom Up* (New York: Palgrave MacMillan, 2010).

Guenther, Sebastian, "The Ten Commandments and the Qur'an," *Journal of Qur'anic Studies,* vol. 9, No. 2, 2007.

Hallaq, Wael B., *Reforming Modernity: Ethics and the New Human in the Philosophy of Abdurrahman Taha* (New York: Columbia University, 2019).

Hamid, Eltigani Abdelgadir, *al-Naṣṣ al-Qurʾānī wa-Uṣūl al-Ijtimāʿ al-Siyāsī: Madākhil Taʾsīsiyyah* (Doha: Muntadā al-ʿAlāqāt al-ʿArabiyyah al-Dawliyyh, 2020).

Hammad, Nazih, *Qaḍāyā Fiqhiyyah Muʿāṣirah fī'l-Māl wa'l-Iqtiṣād* (Damascus: Dār al-Qalam, 2001).

Hanafi, Sari, *ʿUlūm al-Sharʿ wa'l-ʿUlūm al-Ijtimāʿiyyah: Naḥwa Tajāwuz al-Qaṭīʿah* (Beirut: Markaz Nuhḥū, 1st edn., 2021).

Hare, John E., *God's Command* (Oxford, UK & New York: Oxford University Press, 2015).

Harvey, Ramon, *The Qur'an and the Just Society* (Edinburgh: Edinburgh University Press, 2019).

Hashas, Mohamed & Mutaz al-Khatib (eds.), *Islamic Ethics and the Trusteeship Paradigm* (Leiden-Boston: Brill, 2020).

Hashim, Mazin Muwaffaq, *Maqāṣid al-Sharīʿah al-Islāmiyyah: Madkhal ʿUmrāni* (Hernden, Virginia: The International Institute of Islamic Thought, 1st edn., 1435/2014).

Hassan, Hassan Abdullah, *al-Jāmiʿah al-Ḥaḍāriyyah: Mafhūmuhā wa-Waẓāʾifuhā wa-Mutaṭallabātuhā* (Herndon-Amman: International Institute of Isllamic Though, IIIT, 1ST edn., 1442/2021).

Ḥassani, Baqir al- *et al.* (authors), *Dirāsāt Islāmiyyah fiʾl-Iqtiṣād waʾl-Naqd* (Beirut: Center of Civilization for the development of Islamic Thought, 1st edn., 2011).

Huda, Jamilah Alam al-, *al-Naẓariyyah al-Islāmiyyah fiʾl-Tarbiyyah waʾl-Taʿlīm*, 2 vols., translated from Persian by Abbas Safi (Beirut: Center of Civilization for the Development of Islamic Thought, 1st edn., 2011).

Hughes, Aaron W. (ed.), *Theory and Method in the Study of Religion: Twenty Five Years On* (Leiden-Boston: Brill, 2013).

Ibn Ashur, Muhammad al-Tahir, *Treatise on Maqāṣid al-Sharīʿah*, translated from the Arabic and annotated by Mohamed El-Tahir El-Mesawi (London-Washington: The International Institute of Islamic Thought, 1427/2006).

__________, *Uṣūl al-Niẓām al-Ijtimāʿī fiʾl-Islām*, ed. Mohamed El-Tahir El-Mesawi (Amman: Dar al-Nafaes, 1st edn., 1421/2001).

Ibn Khaldūn, ʿAbd al-Raḥmān b. Muḥammad, *Muqaddimat Ibn Khaldūn*, ed. Darwish al-Juwaydi (Sidon-Beirut: al-Maktabah al-ʿAṣriyyah, 2nd edn., 1416/1996).

Ibn Sīnā, *Avicenna's Psychology*, trans. F. Rahman (Connecticut: Hyperion Press, Inc., 1981 [1952]).

Idnopulos, Thomas A. & Brian G. Wilson (eds.), *What is Religion? Origins, Definitions, and Explanations* (Leiden-Boston-Koln: Brill, 1998).

Islahi, Abdul Azim, *Economic Concepts of Ibn Taimiyyah* (Leicester: The Islamic Foundation, 1996/1417 [1988/1408).

__________, *History of Islamic Economic Thought: Contributions of Scholars to Economic Thought and Analysis* (Cheltenham, UK - Northampton, MA, USA: Edward Elgar, 2014 [2005]).

__________, *Muslim Economic Thinking and Institutions in the 10th AH/16th CE Century* (Jeddah: Islamic Economic Research Centre, King Abdulaziz University, 1430 AH/2009 CE).

Iṣfahānī, Abū al-Qāsim al-Ḥusayn b. Muḥammad b. al-Mufaḍḍal al-Rāghib al-, *Kitāb al-Dharīʿah ilā Makārim al-Sharīʿah*, ed. Aldou Elyazid al-Ajami (Cairo: Dār al-Salām, 1st edn., 1428/2007).

Izutsu, Toshihiko, *Ethico-Religious Terms in the Qurʾan* (Montreal & Kingston-London-Ithaca: McGill-Queen's University Press, 2002 [1959]).

James, William, *Varieties of Religious Experiences: A Study in Human Nature*, centenary edition with a foreword by Micky James & new introduction by Eugene Taylor and Jeremy Carrette (London & New York: Routledge, 2002).

Jawziyyah, Abū ʿAbd Allāh Muḥammad b. Abī Bakr b. Ayyūb Ibn Qayyim al-, *Kitāb al-Rūḥ*, ed. Muhammad Ajmal Ayyub al-Isahi (Makkah al-Mukarramah: Sulaiman Bin Abdul Aziz Al Rajhi Charitable Foundation, 1ˢᵗ edn., 1433 H).

Johnson, Adam Lloyd *et al.* (eds.), *A Debate on God and Morality* (New York and London: Routledge, 1ˢᵗ edn. 2021).

Jomo K.S. (ed.), *Islamic Economic Alternatives* (Houndmills & London: Macmillan Academic and Professional Ltd., 1992).

Juwaynī, Ḍiyāʾ al-Dīn Abū al-Maʿālī ʿAbd al-Malik b. ʿAbd Allāh b. Yūsuf, Imām al-Ḥaramyn al-, *al-Ghiyyāthī: Ghiyyāth al-Umam fiʾl-Tiyāth al-Ẓulam*, ed. Abbul Azim Mahmoud Aldeeb (Jeddah: Dār al-Mimhāj, 3ʳᵈ edn., 1433/2011).

Kalin, Ibrahim, *Reason and Rationality in the Qurʾan* (Amman: The Royal Aal Al-Bayt Institute for Islamic Thought, 2012).

Kattani, Mohamed al-, *Manẓūmat al-Qiyam al-Marjiʿiyyah fiʾl-Islām* (Rabat: Markaz al-Dirāsāt waʾl-Abḥāth fiʾl-Qiyam, Rabita Mohamadia des Oulémas, 2ⁿᵈ edn., 1433/2011).

Khalil, Muhsen, *Fiʾl-Fikr al-Iqtiṣādī al-ʿArabī al-Islāmī: Dirāsah li-Maqūlatay al-ʿAmal waʾl-Milkiyyah* (Baghdad: Manshūrāt Wazārat al-Thaqafāh waʾl-Iʿlām, 1982).

Kissin, Benjamin & Henri Begleiter (eds.), *Social Aspects of Alcoholism* (New York: Springer Science+ Business Media, 1976).

Kurdustani, Muthanna Amin al-, *Ḥarakāt Taḥrīr al-Marʾah miʾl-Musāwāt ilaʾl-Jandar* (Cairo: Dār al-Qalam, 1ˢᵗ edn., 1425/2004).

Langermann, Y. Tzvi (ed.), *Monotheism and Ethics: Historical and Contemporary Intersections among Judaism, Christianity and Islam* (Leiden-Boston: Brill, 2012).

Layne, Linda L., *Motherhood Lost: A Feminist Account of Pregnancy Loss in America* (New York and London: Routledge, 2003).

Lumbard, Joseph E. B., "Covenant and Covenants in the Qurʾan," *Journal of Qurʾanic Studies,* vol. 17, No. 2, 2015.

Madkour, Muhammad Salam, *Naẓariyyat al-Ibāḥah ʿinda al-Uṣūliyyīn waʾl-Fuqahāʾ* (Cairo: Dār al-Nahḍah al-ʿArabiyyah, 2ⁿᵈ edn., 1984).

Malekian, Farhad, *Principles of Islamic International Criminal Law: A Comparative Search* (Leiden-Boston: Brill, 2011).

Malkawi, Fathi Hasan, *al-Fikr al-Tarbawī al-Islāmī al-Muʿāṣir* (Herndon-Amman: International Institute of Isllamic Thought, IIIT, 1ST edn., 1442/2021).

Masson, Denise, *L'Eau, le Feu, la Lumière d'après la Bible, le Coran et les traditions monothéistes* (Paris: Desclée de Bouwer, 1985).

Mawdūdī, Sayyid Abul Aʿlā al-, *Worhsip in Islam: An Indepth Study bof ʿIbādah, Salāh and Ṣawm*, translated and edited by Ahmad Imam Shafaq Hshemi (Lesicestershire: The Islamic Foundation, 2014 CE/1435 AH).

__________, *al-Dīn al-Qayyim* (Beirut: Mu'assasat al-Risālah, 1404/1984).

__________, *Towards Understanding the Qur'ān*, abdridged version of *Tafhīm al-Qur'ān*, translated and edited by Zafar Ishaq Ansari (Leicester: The Islamic Foundation, 1988/1408).

__________, *al-Muṣṭalaḥāt al-Arbaʿah fi'l-Qur'ān*, translated from Urdu by Muhammad Kazim Sabbaq (Kuwait: Dār al-Qalam, 5th edn., 1391/1971).

Mirakhor, Abbas et.al. (eds.), *Handbook of Ethics of Islamic Economics and Finance* (Berlin-Boston: De Gruyter, 2020).

Mirakhor, Abbas & Askari, Hossien, *Ideal Islamic Economy* (New York: Palgrave Macmillan, 2017).

Mirakhor, Abbas & Askari, Hossein, *Islam and the Path to Human and Economic Development* (New York: Palgrave Macmillan, 2010).

Miskawayh, Abū ʿAlī Aḥmad b. Muḥammad b. Yaʿqūb, *Tahdhīb al-Akhlāq*, ed. ʿImad al-Hilali (Freiburg, Germany: Al-Kamel Verlag, 2011).

Mohamed, Yasien, *Human Nature in Islam* (Kuala Lumpur: A.S. Noordeen, 1419/1998).

Mohammed, Kamelia Helmy, *al-Mawāthīq al-Dawliyyah wa-Atharuhā fī Hadm al-Usrah: Bidāyatan min Ta'sīs Muaẓẓamāt al-Umam al-Muttaḥidah fī 1945 ḥattā Awā'il 2019* (Self-publishing, 1st edn., 1441/2020).

Morsi, Kamal Ibrahim, *al-ʿAlāqah al-Zawjiyyah wa'l-Ṣiḥḥan al-Nafsiyyah fi'l-Islām wa-ʿIlm al-Nafs* (Kuwait: Dār al-Qalam, 2nd edn., 1415/1995).

__________, *al-Tarbiyyah al-Islāmiyyah: Uṣūluhā wa-Taṭawwurahā fi'l-Bilād al-ʿArabiyyah* (Cairo: Dār al-Maʿārif, 1987).

Motahhari, Murteza al-, *Fiṭrah*, translated from the Persian by Jaafar Sadiq al-Khalili (Beirut: Mu'assasat al-Biʿthah, 1412/1992).

Najjar, Abdelamjid al-, *Fī Fiqh al-Tadayyun Fahman wa-Tanzīlan* (Doha: Ministry of Endowments [Awqaf] and Islamic Affairs, Ummah Book Series, 1989).

__________, *Maqāṣid al-Sharīʿah bi-Abʿād Jadīdah* (Beirut: Dār al-Gharb al-Islāmī, 1st edn., 2006).

__________, *Qīmat al-Insān* (Rabat: Dār al-Zaytunah, 1ˢᵗ edn., 1417/1996).

'Alim, Yusuf Hamid al-, *al-Maqāṣid al-ʿĀmmah li'l- al-Sharīʿah al-Islāmiyyah* (London-Washington: The International Institute of Islamic Thought, IIIT, 1413/1993).

Nash'at, Mohammad Ali, *Rā'id al-Iqtiṣād Ibn Khaldūn* (Cairo: Maṭbaʿat Dār al-Kutub al-Miṣriyyah, 1944).

Nashshar, Ali Sami al-, *Nash'at al-Dīn: al-Naẓariyyāt al-Taṭawwuriyyah wa'l-Mi'allihah* (Cairo: Dār al-Salām, 1430/2016).

Nasr, Seyyed Hossein, *The Heart of Islam: Enduring Values for Humanity* (London & New York: HarperCollins, 2002).

__________, *et al.*, *The Study Qur'an* (New York: Harper Collins Publishers, 2015).

Nielsen, Kai, *God and the Grounding of Morality* (Ottawa-Paris: University of Ottawa Press, 1991).

'Ulwan, Abdullah Nasih, *Tarbiyyat al-Awlād fi'l-Islām,* 2 vols. (Cairo: Dār al-Salām, 21ˢᵗ edn. 1412/1992).

O'Connor, Andrew J., "Qur'anic Covenants Reconsidered: mīthāq and 'ahd in Polemical Context," *Islam and Christian-Muslim Relations,* vol. 30, No. 1 (2019).

Omar, Fuad Adullah al-, *Muqaddimah fī Tārīkh al-Iqtiṣād al-Islāmī wa-Taṭawwurih* (Jeddah: IDB Islamic Research and Training Institute, 1424/2003).

Othman, Nabih Abdul Rahman, *Muʿjizat Khalq al-Insān bayna al-Ṭibb wa'l-Qur'ān* (Makkah al-Mukarraman: Muslim World League, n.d.).

Ozek, Ali *et al.* (trans.), *The Majestic Qur'an: An English Rendering of its Meanings* (Chicago: The Nawawi Foundation / London: The Ibn Khaldun Foundation, 4ᵗʰ edn., 2000).

Pals, Daniel L., *Nine Theories of Religion* (New York: Oxford University Press, 2015).

Pickering, W.S.F., *Durkheim's Sociology of Religion: Themes and Theories* (Cambridge, UK: James Clarke Co. Ltd, 1984).

Qadri, Hussain Mohi-ud-Din, *Business Ethics in Islam* (Londan and New York: Routledge, 2020).

Qaradawi, Ysusf al-, *Fiqh al-Usrah wa-Qaḍāyā al-Mar'ah* (Turkey: al-Dār al-Shāmiyyah, 1ˢᵗ edn., 1438/2017).

__________, *al-ʿIbādah fi'l-Islām* (Cairo: Maktabat Wahbah, 24ᵗʰ edn., 1416/1995).

Qarni, Ali bin Abdaulah bin Ali al-, *al-Fiṭrah: Ḥaqīqatuhā wa-Madhāhib al-Nās fīhā* (Riaydh: Dār al-Muslim, 1424H).

Qutb, Muhammad, *Dirāsāt fī'l-Nafs al-Insāniyyah* (Cairo/Beirut: Dār al-Shurūq, 10th edn., 1414/1993).

__________, *Manhaj al-Tarbiyyah al-Islāmiyyah* (Cairo/Beirut: Dār al-Shurūq, 14th edn., 1414/1993).

Raḍiyy, al-Sayyid al-Sharīf al-, *Ḥaqā'iq al-Ta'wīl fī Mutashābih al-Tanzīl,* ed. Muhammad al-Rida Al Kashif al-Ghita (Beirut: Dār al-Adwā', 1406/1986).

Raysuni, Ahmad al-, *Imām al-Shāṭibī's Theory of the Higher Objectives and Intents of Islamic Law,* translated from the Arabic by Nancy Roberts (London–Washington: The International Institute of Islamic Thought, 1426AH/2005CE), p. 265.

__________, (ed.), *Iʿmāl al-Maqāṣid bayna al-Tahayyub wa'l-Tasayyub* (London: Al-Furqan Islamic Heritage Foundation, 1st edn., 1435/2014).

__________, *Qawāʿd al-Maqāṣid* (London: Al-Furqan Islamic Heritage Foundation, 1st edn., 1441/2020).

Rāzī, Abū Ḥātim al-, *Kitāb al-Zīnah,* ed. Said al-Ghanimi (Beirut/Freiburg: Al-Kamel Verlag, 2015).

Reda, Ayman, *Prophecy, Piety and Profits* (New York: Palgrave Macmillan, 2018).

Richman, Robert J., *God, Free Will, and Morality* (Dordrecht, Holland: D. Reidel Publishing Company, 1983).

Rodker, Narges, *Fiminizme (al-Ḥarakah al-Niswiyyah): Mafhūmuhā, Uṣūluhā al-Naẓariyyah wa-Tayyārātuhā al-Ijtimāʿiyyah,* translated from the Persian b y Hiba Dhafir (Beirut: al-Markaz al-Islāmī li'l-Dirāsāt al-Istrātījiyyah, 1440/2019).

Sadr, Muhammad Baqir al-, *Iqtiṣādunā* (Beirut: Dār al-Taʿāruf li'l-Maṭbūʿāt, 20th edn., 1408/1978).

Schloss, Jefferey & Michael Murray (eds.), *The Believing Pramate: Scientific, Philosophical, and Theological Reflections on the Origin of Religion* (Oxford-New York: Oxford University Press, 2009).

Shaltut, Mahmud, *al-Waṣāyā al-ʿAshr* (Cairo: Dār al-Shurūq, 5th edn., 1404/1984).

Shami, Rashad Abdullah al-, *al-Waṣāyā al-ʿAshr fī'l-Yahūdiyyah: Dirāsah Muqārinah fī'l-Masīḥiyyah wa'l-Islām* (Dār al-Zahrā' li'l-Nashr, 1414/1993).

Shāṭibī, Abū Isḥāq Ibrāhīm b. Mūsā al-, *The Reconciliation of the Fundamentals of Islamic Law,* trans. Imran Ahsan Khan Nyazee (London: Garnet Publishers, 2014), vol. 2.

Shāṭibī, Abū Isḥāq Ibrāhīm b. Mūsā al-, *al-Muwāfaqāt fī Uṣūl al-Sharī'ah*, ed. Abdullah Draz (Beirut: Dār al-Kutub al-'Ilmiyyah, 1422/2001).

__________, *The Reconciliation of the Fundamentals of Islamic Law*, trans. Imran Ahsan Khan Nyazee (London: Garnet Publishers, 2014), vol. 1.

Smith, Huston, *Why Religion Matters* (New York: HarperSanFransico, 2001).

Smith, Wilfred Cantwell, *The Meaning and End of Religion* (Minneapolis: Fortress Press, 1991 [1962]).

Sorokin, Ptirim, *The Crisis of Our Age* (Oxford, England: Oneworld Publications, 1992 [1941]).

Spalek, Basia & Alia Imtoual (eds.), *Religion, Spirituality and the Social Sciences: Challenging Marginalisation* (Bristol: The Policy Press, Un iversity of Bristol, 2008).

Spengler, Joseph J., "Economic Thought of Islam: Ibn Khaldun", *Comparative Studies in Society and History*, vol. 6, No. 3 (April, 1964), pp. 268-306.

Tabataba'i, Mohammad Hossein al-, *al-Mīzān fī Tafsīr al-Qur'ān* (Beirut: Mu'assasat al-A'lamī li'l-Maṭbū'āt, 1417/1997).

__________, *al-Jawāhir al-Nūrāniyyah fī'l-'Ulūm wa'l-Ma'ārif al-Insāniyyah* (Beirut: Dār al-Maḥajjah al-Bayḍā', 1426/2005).

Thrower, James, *Religion: The Classical Theories* (Edinburgh: Edinburgh University Press, Year: 1999).

Tirmidhī, al-Ḥakīm al-, *Taḥṣīl Naẓā'ir al-Qur'ān*, ed. Hosni Nasri Zaydan (Cairo: Maṭba'at al-Sa'ādah, 1st edn., 1389/1969).

Toutounchian, Iraj, *Islamic Money and Banking: Integrating Money in Capital Theory* (Sinapore: John Wiley & Sons [Asia] Pte. Ltd., 2009).

Trigg, Roger, *Religion in Public Life: Must Faith Be Privatized?* (Oxford, UK and New York: Ixford University Press, 2007), also his *Beyond Matter: Why Science Needs Metaphysics* (West Conshohocken, Pennsylvania: Templeton Press, 2015).

Turabi, Hasan al-, *Qaḍāyā al-Tajdīd: Naḥwa Manhaj Uṣūlī* (Beirut: Dār al-Hādī, 1421/2000);

__________, *al-Īmān: Atharuhu fī Ḥayāt al-Insān* (Jeddah: Manshūrāt al-'Aṣr al-Ḥadīth, 1404/1984 [1394/1974]).

'Ulwan, Abdullah Nasih, *Tarbiyyat al-Awlād fī'l-Islām*, 2 vols. (Cairo: Dār al-Salām, 21st edn. 1412/1992).

Umrani, Mohamed al-Kaddi al-, *Fiqh al-Usrah al-Muslimah fī'l-Mahājar* (Beirut: Dār al-Kutub al-'Ilmiyyah, 1st edn., 1422/2001).

Vaillant, George Eman, *The Natural History of Alcoholism Revisited* (Cambridge, Massachsetts & London, England: Harvard University Press, 1995).

Vasalou, Sophia, *Ibn Taymiyya's Theological Ethics* (New York: Oxforn University Press, 2016).

Walī Allāh, Shāh, *Ḥujjat Allāh al-Bālighah*, ed. Mohamed Sharif Sakr (Beirut: Dār Iḥyā' al-Turāth, 1413/1992).

Walī Allāh, Shāh, *The Conclusive Argument from God*, trans. Marcia K. Hermansen (Leiden-New York-Koln: EJ. Brill, 1996).

Watkins, James Simon, *Islamic Finance and Global Capitalism: An Alternative to Market Economy* (Gewerbestrasse, Switzerland: Palgrave Macmillan, 2020).

Weiss, Bernard, "Covenant and Law in Islam," in Edwin B. Firmage *et al.* (eds.), *Religion and Law: Biblical-Judaic and Islamic Perspectives* (Winona Lake: Eisenbrauns, 1990).

Zayas, Farishta G. de, *The Law and Institution of Zakāt* (Kualal Lumpur: The Other Press, 2003 [1960]).

Xenos, Nicholas, *Scarcity and Modernity* (London and New York: Routledge, 1989).

Zakariyah, Luqman, *Legal Maxims in Islamic Criminal Law: Theory and Applications* (Leiden | Boston: Brill, 2015).

Zaytoun, Raed Jamil Okasha & Monzer Arafat (eds.), *al-Usrah al-Muslimah fī Ẓill al-Taghayyurāt al-Muʿāṣirah* (Herndon: International Institute of Islamic Thought & Amman: Dār al-Fatḥ, 1ST edn., 1436/2015).

Zellentin, Holger M. (ed.), *The Qur'an's Reformation of Judaism and Christianity: Return to the Origins* (London and New York: Routledge, 2019).

Zouzou, Farida Sadiq, *al-Nasl: Dirāsah Maqāṣidiyyah fī Wasā'il Ḥifẓihi fī Ḍaw' al-Taḥaddiyyāt al-Muʿāṣirah* (Riyadh: Maktabat al-Rushd, 1427/2006).

Notes on the Authors

Dawood Abdel Malik al-Hidabi is a professor of education at the International Islamic University Malaysia, IIUM. In addition to over 140 published papers, he co-authored several textbooks. He held many academic administrative positions both in his home country Yemen and in Malaysia, and is member of advisory boards of a number of journals in the Arab world and elsewhere. He was the founding president of the University of Science and Technology, Sanaa (1994-2007). Since he joined IIUM in April 2016 he has served in many administrative capacities in its management structure. He is also the chairman of the Islamic Agency for Quality Assurance and Accreditation of the Federation of Universities of the Islamic world (FUIW). His latest administrative appointment entrusted him with the directorship of the International Institute for Muslim Unity, IIMU, one of the active institutes under the auspices of IIUM.

Mohamed El-Tahir El-Mesawi is a professor in Islamic legal theory and Islamic contemporary thought at the International Islamic University Malaysia, IIUM. With an academic background in economics and sociology and keen interest in philosophy, he has been for years engaged in interdisciplinary research with main focus on *maqāṣid al-Sharīʿah*, human nature and values, and social theory. He has to his credit more than 30 journal articles and 14 published books in Arabic, English and French, in addition to a score of conference papers in Malaysia and abroad. He is member of many journal editorial and advisory boards. Aside of his teaching duties, he is currently the editor of the *International Jour-*

nal of Muslim World Studies published by the International Institute for Muslim Unity.

Waleed Fekry Faris is a professor in Mechanical Engineering and Aerospace Department at the International Islamic University Malaysia, with a record of more than 120 articles published in internationally indexed scientific Journals, no less than 110 Conference papers and six books on engineering. In addition to his discipline, he is an active researcher and practitioner of strategic planning, quality management, integration of knowledge, leadership and spirituality, in which respect he has published at least 6 books in both English and Arabic. At present, he is deputy dean for postgraduate studies and research at the International Institute of Islamic Thought and Civilization, ISTAC-IIUM.

Index

A

'Abd Allāh b. 'Abbās, 17
Abderrahmane, Taha, xx-xxi
Abū Isḥāq
    al-Shāṭibī, 93, 108, 187
    al-Zajjāj, 76, 105
Abū 'Ubayd, 76
accountability, 35, 91, 123
accumulation of wealth, 149
activity of thinking, 118
Adam, 25, 44, 72, 76, 80, 85-86, 97,
    142
    children of, 86
    knowledge of all the names, 81
adultery, 4, 47, 98, 100
aḥādīth al-aḥkām, xv
aḥsantaqwīm, 46
alcoholism, 124, 127, 174
Alūsī, al-, 86
altruism, 157
alienation, 96, 194
amānah, 23, 31, 192
Āmidī, Sayf al-Dīn al-, xv
'Āmirī, Abū al-Ḥasan al-, xvvi (n. 17)

animal
    genus, 45
    kingdom, 94
animals, 20, 38, 40, 42, 126
animate beings, 81
'aql, viii, xix, 88, 91, 93, 117-122, 127-
    128, 139, 144, 169, 171(n. 10),
    192
ḥifẓ al-'aql, xii, 1, 117, 123
Arabic, 119
    discourse, 118
    discourses, 75
    language, 2, 5, 11
    lexicographical tradition, 2
    lexicography, 2, 6, 120
    lexicon, 119
    sources, vii
    Arabic-Islamic semiotic field, xx
Arabs, 8, 128
    pre-Islamic pagan, 126
arrogance, 37, 80-89, 166, 178
Asad, Muhammad, 24, 28, 55 (n.11),
    59 (n.42), 83, 136
asfalsāfilīn, 46, 110
Attas, Syed Muhammad Naquib al-,
    viii, 3, 6-7, 9, 11-13

āyāt, xv, 17, 42, 195
  al-aḥkām, 186
  muḥkamāt, 17

B

balance, viii, xix, 146, 150, 168
Balkhī, Muqātil al-, vii, 4-5
bayān, 82-83
behaviour
  abnormal sexual, 45
  economic, 153-154, 163
  homosexual, 46
behavioural qualities, 161, 168
being(s), 12-3, 17, 21, 84, 87, 88, 121, 136, 150, 160, 191
  and values, ix
  articulation of, viii
  concept of being, viii
  createdness of all, 9
  levels of being or existence, 84
  modes of, 107
  physical, 150
  human, 9, 50, 83-85, 88, 90-91, 94, 129-130, 132, 135, 137, 153, 167, 175 (n. 38)
    distinct species, 38
    essential unity of origin, 50
    essential qualities, 88
    intrinsic nobility of, 88
    physical and mental growth, 35, 48, 121
    physical constitution and structure, 46
    physical deterioration, 46, 110
    relational superiority, 89
    special status, 38, 80
    survival of their species, 92
  sublime, 9

benefit, 2, 29, 89, 124, 133, 135-137, 156-157, 162, 167, 169-170, 195
  kinds of, 2
benevolence, 154-155, 159, 170
Bennabi, Malik, 28, 33, 82
Bergson (Henri), 28, 66 (n. 83)
best conformation, 46, 90
Bible, 60
biological
  constitution, 41
  laws, 46
  survival, 46
  bonds, 43, 162
Bouchikhi, Chahid El-, xvv(n. 13)
bounties, 43, 89, 91, 133, 135, 137, 147, 152, 158
  and blessings, 149, 182
  external, 89
  extrinsic bounties and blessings, 150
  intrinsic, 150
  material, 87
  physical (*badaniyyah*), 150
bounty, 133, 147, 161
bunuwwah, 42
business, 140, 143, 149, 151, 153-156
  activities, 143, 153

C

capacity, 121, 146
  innate, 121
  legal, 91
  of communication, 82
  of conceptual thinking, 82
  to comprehend, 82
  to distinguish, 29
  technological, 136
capacities, 22, 80, 85, 88, 90

capitalism
  surveillance, 157
  capitalist system, 138
Cassirer, Ernst, 64
categorization, 107, 122, 149
Cave Ḥirā', 84
children, 16-17, 25, 39, 42-44, 47-48,
  78, 85-86, 95, 97, 129, 148, 175
Christianity, 26, 30
  post-Christiansociety, 62 (n.65)
civilization, 2, 28, 43, 51, 75, 92, 136,
  138, 143-144, 194, 196
  ruin of, 143-144
cloning science and technology, 94
cognition, 24-25, 28-29, 83, 88, 91,
  119, 122, 169
commandments, 4, 6, 18-19, 23, 25,
  50-51, 58, 80, 84, 90, 162-163,
  195
  divine, 28
  Ten Commandments, 19, 60
    (n.48 and 50), 122
  al-waṣāyāal-ʿashr, 18, 58 (n.45)
commerce, 143, 149, 153-154
commercialization of sex, 49
commodity, 131
community, xix, 8, 13, 16, 34, 36,
  125, 137-138, 141, 166-167, 182
  (n. 99), 193
  faith, 36
  human, 166
  IIUM, xi
  individual and, xix, 10, 16
  individuals and, 153
  Muslim, 13, 31, 134, 158
compassion and generosity, 162
concrete human individuals, 92
concrete realities, 138
conduct, xviii, 2, 7-8, 17-18, 23, 33,

35, 100, 123, 125, 140, 150, 155,
  163-164, 192
  and action, 18
conformation and constitution, 88
consciousness, 11, 13, 82, 92, 124,
  169
  God-, 163-164
  human, 18, 33, 82, 169, 195
    existence and, 76
  Muslim, 165
  realm of consciousness, 82
  singularity of human, 160
consumerism, 30, 153
consumption, 135
contracts, 44, 141
conviction, 12, 35
corruption, 28, 37, 39, 78, 80, 97,
  125-127, 139, 146, 159, 168
cosmic
  significance, 52, 80
  wisdom, 42
cosmological view, 136
cosmopolis, 12
covenant, 26-27, 29, 99
  allegorical interpretation, 63
  between God and humanity, 27
  continuous, 29
  theme, 65
  primordial (*awwal*), 26-27, 29
  recurring, 28
  universal (*ʿāmmi*), 27
  unmediated and universal, 27
Covid-19 pandemic, xiii
crafts, 143, 151, 153
creation, 9, 23, 26, 29, 40, 43, 51-52,
  85-88, 90-91, 94, 123, 132, 140,
  154, 195
  and sustenance, 132
  book of, 195

human, 30, 130
  of wealth, 140
  realm of, 89
crimes against humanity, 101
criminality, 49
criteria
  of good and evil, 16
  of lawfulness and unlawfulness,
    140
critical minds, 127
cultural convention, 127
culture, 82, 130
  human, 51
  Islamic life and, xx
  Islamic scholarship and, 138
  Muslim life and, 68 (n.99)
  sensate, 49

D

ḍarūiyyāt, viii-ix, xii, 1, 24, 45, 75, 93,
    100
  category, 100
Day of Judgement, 4
debt, 13
  existential, 13
nature of, 13
debts, 12, 155, 164
defamation, 100, 101
degeneration, 46, 110
dehumanization, 194
dependents, 146, 149, 154
deprivation, 96, 143, 167
desire(s), 129-130, 154, 166
  false, 32
fundamental human, 130
destitute majorities, 157
destitution, 149, 157
devotional and ritual worship, 32

dhāt, 14, 77
dhurriyyah, 39
dignity, 35, 79, 86-88, 96, 150
  God-given original dignity, 92
  human, 85, 88, 101, 193
  universality of, 85
  human dignity and superiority, 90
  human beings' universal inherent
    dignity, 89
  of the humankind, 79
  of mankind, 88
  original, 103
  personal, 47
  universal, 92, 97
  worth and, 97
dīn, viii, xix, 2-16, 21-22, 29, 31, 34,
    49, 93, 192
  al-fiṭrah, 30
  all-encompassing concept, 15
  all-inclusive concept, 8
  basic meanings, 3, 8, 21
  firm conviction, 9
  ḥifẓ al-dīn, xii, 1, 22-23, 34, 51, 75,
    117, 139
  judicial power, 3
  kingdom, 12
  preservation of, 144
  primary significations, 3, 8, 11-13,
    21
  plurality and diversity of significa-
    tions, 14
  unified essential meanings, 12
  uṣūl al-dīn, 20
discourse(s), xvii, xx, 123, 153, 159
  ethical, viii
  intellectual, 18
  Islamic juristic, xviii
  juristic, xvii
  legal, xv

modes of, 186 (n. 130)
new, xxi
on *maqāṣid al-Sharīʿah*, ix
on the Sharīʿah objectives, xvi
Qur'anic, viii, xviii, 3, 40, 118,
   135, 158-159, 163, 165
revelational, 123
written and oral, 21
discrimination, 88, 125
discursive thinking, 123
disillusionment, 49
disposition(s), 12, 26, 83, 88
   innate, 25
   original, 26
   positive, 46
dispositions, 88
   instinctual, 129
divine
   call, 9
   guidance, 19, 27
   messages, 18, 26
   wisdom, 42, 123, 195
Draz, Muhammad A., 7
drug addiction, 127
Durkheim (Emile), 62 (n.65)
duties, 35, 91
   collective, 151, 154
   compulsory, 181 (n. 92)
   practical, 35
   public, 156
   rights and, 91, 103

E

earning, 145, 147-153, 156
   earning and livelihood, 145
Eaton (Gai), 41
economic
   activities, 140, 145, 153-154

and financial activities, 131, 140,
   148
and financial issues, 142
and financial resources, 158, 170
growth,156
injustice, 143-144, 157
issues, 141, 145
justice, 141
life, 143, 145, 148, 155, 157-158
life and activity, 145
philosophy, 131, 157, 166
pursuit, 146, 181
system, 96, 131, 141, 192
wealth and possessions, 162
economics, 141-142, 154-158, 166-
   168
   and society, 166
   of altruism, 157
   psycho-spiritual philosophy of,
      157
   role of the state, 155
economy,
   gift, 157
   moral, 157
   spiritual, 157
education, 34-35, 42, 47-48, 95, 103,
   127, 195
   continuous process, 35
   vocation, 48
   formal, 35
efficiency, 35, 156-157, 192
egotism, 49
ego-centrism, 195
El-Awa, 5
emancipation, 167
embellishments, 2
embryonic development, 38, 41
Enlightenment
   European, 30

rationalism, 2
enslavement, 166
epidemic, 103
epistemicrule, 108
equity, 43, 103, 141, 150, 157, 170
essences of things, 82
estrangement, 96
eternal
   essence, 19
   truths, 18
ethical
   discourse, viii
   naturalism, xviii
ethico-
   legal system, 1
   spiritual framework, 146
evil, 18, 23, 28-29, 78, 84, 90, 101,
   124-125, 136, 144, 159
   evilness, 120, 127, 159
   nature, 136
excellence, 36, 38, 85
existence, xv, 9, 11-14, 18, 22, 24-25,
   28, 30, 33, 35, 40, 47, 51, 75, 80,
   82, 85, 90-91, 93-94, 96, 98, 103,
   117, 142, 191
   and survival of mankind, 93
   external and objective, 84
   God's, 91
   human, 13, 14, 28, 31, 42, 46, 75,
   76, 87, 90, 94, 130, 195
      and consciousness, 76
      and survival, 94
      life and, 18, 41, 92
      social, 33
      socio-historical, 191
   mental existence, 84
   metaphysical realm of, 12
   modes of, 85
   non-existence, 82, 94
   physical and metaphysical realms
      of, 9
   potential existence, 39
   pre-embryonic and pre-natal
      pre-natal stage of, 40
   pre-terrestrial, 80
   realms of, 9
   seen and unseen realms of, xxi
   supernatural realm of, 30
exploitation, 166
exploitative financial dealings, 163
extracts, 41
extravagance, 153

F

fairness, 17, 153-154
faith, xvii, 2-6, 16-17, 19, 22, 26, 34,
   36, 50-51, 93, 100-101, 124, 136,
   145, 147, 161, 164
   common fundamentals of, 20
falsehood, 16, 18, 29, 127, 159
family, 2, 15, 39, 42-45, 47-51, 72, 83,
   94-95, 147, 150, 154, 169
   ascendants, 43
   basic institution, 43, 51
   bonds, 49
   collapse of the, 49
   conceptual vilification and, 43
   descendants, 37, 43
   equity and harmony, 43
   feelings and ties, 42
   ideological destruction, 49
   institution, 49
   life, 15, 39, 48
   rights and obligations, 43
   system, 43
   ties of kinship, 50
   values and ties, 49

faqr, 14

Fasi, Allal al-, xxiii

fatherhood, 42, 48

favours, 83, 87, 91, 168

Fārūqī, (Ismāʿīl) al-, viii, 51

fiṭrah, xviii, 25-26, 28, 30-31, 46, 51, 97, 192

   dīn al-fiṭrah, 30

   fiṭrat Allāh, 30

   fundamentals of, 29

   uṣūl fiṭriyyah, 29

   Qur'anic concept of, 28

filiation, 42

financial

   and economic dealings, 179

   and economic matters, 139, 145

   duty, 160, 163

   oligarchies, 157

   speculations, 155

   transactions, 140, 145, 153-154

fisq, 4, 149

forefathers, xviii, 126, 174 (n. 28)

freedom, 91-92

fragmentation, 194

fundamentals (*uṣūl*), 20, 29, 34, 82, 93, 145

   common, 20

furūḍ kifāyah, 151, 154, 156

Furgaç, Ahmet İzzet, 7

G

gambling, 124, 126

Garden, 44

genderism, 73

general public, 151, 181

general well-being, 156

generosity, 79, 155

Ghazālī, (Abū Ḥāmid) al-, vii, xv, 14,

93, 107, 123, 132, 139, 142, 144-147, 149-158, 182, 185-186

   economics, 154

   Iḥyāʾ ʿUlūm al-Dīn, 145, 147, 154

   Mīzān, 147, 181

gift, 136, 157-158

   economy, 57

globalism, xix

goals

   Sharīʿah, 34, 39, 45, 75, 79, 139

      necessary essential goals, 144

      ultimate, xix

      universal essential, 51

   Millenium Development Goals (MDGs), xi

   Seventeen Sustainable Development Goals (SDGs), xi

God,

   absolute power, 134

   absolute knowledge, 38

   al-Ḥayy al-Qayyūm, xxv

   all-inclusive creative power, 38

   all-inclusive Ego, 32

   beautiful names, 132

   Creator, 1-2, 9, 13-14, 22, 25, 27, 50, 90, 92-94, 97, 103, 132, 137, 164, 169

   cosmic command, 27

   cosmic design, 135

   creation, 25, 38, 45, 89

   creation of human beings, 25

   creative power, 40, 42

   creative will, 22, 27

   existence, 25, 90, 97

   existence and oneness, 25, 90

   given natural resources, 136

   God's bond, 28

   God's command, 80

   God-conscious, 160-161

God's divinity, 9
God's final message, 34
God's *handiwork*, 89-90
God's messengers, 17
God's prescriptions, 24
God'swill, 11, 22, 28, 44
human beings' indebtedness to,
    22
immutable pattern of, 43
imparting *bayān*, 83
judgement and reward, 10
Law giver, xvi, 23, 27
legislative command, 27
Legislator, 23, 27
Lord, 4, 13, 16-17, 22, 24-25, 27,
    40, 80, 83, 97, 132, 169
Master of the universe, 38
obedience and submission to, 2-3,
    6, 8, 133
Oneness of, 4, 6, 17, 20, 34
Originator, 94
plan and purpose in the creation,
    40
power, 132
Provider, 13, 22, 24, 50, 132
purpose, 130
Rabb, 22
Razzāq, 22, 132
relation with humans, 27
relationship between man and, 13
Sustainer, 1, 2, 9, 22-23, 25, 50-
    51, 79-80, 84, 89-90, 93, 137,
    148, 159-161
will and plan, 44
will of, 9, 35, 101
wonders in the creation, 44
good
    common, xiv, 169
    community's, 167

human common, xx, 19, 91, 170,
    191
    and well-being, 170
human total, 192
principles of human, 93
sense of, 29
public common, 152
goodness, 29, 35-36, 39, 78, 120, 127,
    191
science of, xxi
Gould, Stephen, 73 (n.133), 74
    (n.138)
gratitude, xxii, 22, 47, 91, 122, 133
growth, 47, 94-95, 143, 150, 157
Gwynne (Rosalind W.), 28

H

ḥājiyyāt, viii, 2, 20, 45
ḥalāl, 150
Hamid, Eltigani Abdelgadir, ix, xxii,
    xxv (n.13)
ḥarām, 136, 150
Ḥanafīs, 163
ḥaqq, 29, 92, 160, 162-163, 165
harm, 1, 9, 29-30, 43, 47, 75, 96, 99,
    101, 103, 136, 162
harmony, 9, 43
ḥarth, 37, 39
hearing, 37-38, 121-122, 127
hedonism, 30, 49
Helali, Abderrahman, 25
Hereafter, xvi, 1, 10, 94, 98, 133,
    145-146,148, 153, 155, 159
hermeneutics and methodology, 7
ḥifẓ
    al-'irḍ, 100
    al-nufūs, 93
ḥijr, 118, 120

higher end, 33

ḥisāb, 3-4, 6

homicide, xv, 20, 75, 96-98, 100, 102-
103

    capital punishment, 98

homo religiosus, 24

homosexuality, 45, 46

hudā, 4-5, 19

ḥukm, 4, 6

human

    activity, 138

    agency, 33, 96

    and social science disciplines, 36

    artificial reproduction, 94, 112
      (n.53)

    body, 6, 41, 76-77, 101, 121, 150,
      152

    community, 166

    brotherhood, 167

    communal life, 42

    condition, xxi, 14, 28, 191, 193

    condition and reality, xxi

    development, 36

    difference, 45

    economic activities, 154

    economic life, 147

    embryo, 38

    good human being, xxi

    inquiry, 121

    internal faculties, 122

    knowledge, 172

    offspring, 39

    primordial nature, 26, 28

    reality, 44, 193

    procreation and reproduction, 41,
      45

    reproduction, 42

    responsibility, 52, 123

    social affairs, xxi, 187

social association, 92

social edifice, 18

social life, 12, 47

social relationships, 43

solidarity, 169

soul, 33, 103, 152

spirituality and morality, 22

survival, 129

ties, 43

understanding, 122

world, 93, 139

humanism

    Islamic, ix, 52, 91

    secular, 2, 194

humanity, xviii, 27, 29, 34, 49, 52,
138, 157, 170, 193-194

    crimes against, 97

    essential, 97

    universal sense of, 193

humankind, 43, 45, 132

humans, 9, 17, 24, 50, 83, 90-91, 100,
129, 155, 164

I

ʿibādah, 9, 24, 31

Ibnal-Athīr,128

Ibn al-Qayyim, 84, 107

Ibn Ashur (Muhammad al-Tahir),
viii, xv, xxiii, 19-20, 29, 46, 59
(n.47), 61 (n.57), 73, 80, 86, 90,
97, 112, 127, 128, 149, 162, 173

    Maqāṣid al-Sharīʿah al-Islāmiyyah,
      xxiii

Ibn ʿAṭiyyah, 130

Ibn Barrajān, 27

Ibn Khaldūn, 32-33, 92, 142-144,
158, 185

    science of human association, 142

theory of social cohesion, 32
The Muqaddimah, 32, 142
Ibn Manẓūr, 76, 120, 132
Lisān al-ʿArab, 120
Ibn Sīdeh, 76
Ibn Taymiyyah, 27, 108, 185
ibqāʾ, 93, 140
iddikhār, 131
idealism, xix, 91, 194
identity, 43, 47, 100
Iṣfahānī, al-Rāghib al-, vii, 5-6, 20, 82, 86, 123
iḥsān, 154-155, 162
ijtihād, xiv, xvi
maqāṣidī, xiv, xvi
ill-thinking, 101
ʿilm, xxi, 85, 120 ,142
al-ṣalāḥ, xxii
immutable core, 11
inborn drives, 46
indebtedness, 3, 6, 7, 12, 14, 22, 25, 167
existential, 25
individual(s), 28, 39, 88, 93, 97, 100, 155, 167
and collective levels of human life, 15
and community, xix, 10
and group, 96
and society, 51
as physical being, 13
as spirit, 13
conscience,166
economic agents, 155
impoverished, 166
interests, 32
minds, 125
Muslim, 34
ownership, 137

personality, 100
inductive method, xv, 108
industries, 152
inequality, 157
infāq, 158-160, 165, 167-168
Qurʾanic discourse on, 158
semiotic and conceptual field, 163
injustice, 143-144,149,153-154
economic, 143
insān, 38, 77-79, 82
instinctive
attraction, 130
cognition of God, 26
natural inclination, 44
sense, 48
integrated total reality, 15
intellect, xii, xxi, 88, 93, 111, 117, 119, 121-124, 128, 144-145, 195
human, 123
preservation of, 125, 127
intellectual
historicism, xviii
traditions, xviii, 2, 120
and behavioural degeneration, 46
intellectualism, xix
intelligence, xxii, 119
interconnectedness, viii, ix, xx, 22, 45, 50, 143, 182, 195
interdisciplinary research, xxii
interest(s), 129, 152, 156
and well-being, 32
general, xiv
human, 193
individual, xvi
public, 154, 167
particular, xiv
International Islamic University Malaysia (IIUM), xi
intervention, 135-137

i'tidāl, 146

intoxicants, 124-125, 127, 174
   prohibition of, 124-125

Iqbal, (Muhammad), 32

iskār, 125

Islam, viii, xix, 7, 9, 11, 13, 15, 22, 26,
   28, 30-32, 34, 41, 43-44, 47, 75,
   93-95, 98-99, 123, 125, 145, 149,
   167
   communal nature of, 16
   positive view on earning, 147
   strategy, 167
   teachings of, xiv, xvii-xix, 6,1 5,
      24, 29, 36, 45, 76, 139
   worship in, 24

Islamic
   criminal justice, 99
   economic jurisprudence, 141
   ethos, 165
   intellectual traditions, 120
   jurisprudence, xx, 1-2, 92, 137-
      139, 143, 145, 165, 186
   legal theory, 117, 136
   scholarship, ix, xix, 138
   socio-economic system, 165
   teachings, 16, 117, 124, 147-148
   thought, viii, xiv, 7
   tradition, 123, 165
   view on *māl*, 158, 168
   way of life, xx

ism, 81, 91, 131

Israelites, 138

istikhlāf, 144

Izutsu, Toshihiko, 25

'Izzal-Dīn b. 'Abd al-Salām, 186

J

Jabbār, 'Abd al-, 29

Jaffer, 27

James, William, 53

Jaylī, al-, 107

Jāḥiẓ, al-, 81-82, 107

jibillah, 130

Jomier, Jacques, 31

Judaism, 26, 30

judgement, 6, 8, 12, 37 ,91, 122, 148,
   163

juridical parameters, 145

juridicalverses, 186

juridical-legalistic paradigm, xiv juristic rules, 165, 186

jurists, xii, xv, 1, 5-76, 123, 141, 145,
   165

just retribution, xv, 96-98, 100, 103

justice, 9, 12-13, 17, 35-36, 91, 96,
   98-99, 103, 150, 153-154, 156-
   157, 170
   economic justice, 86

Juwaynī, Abū al-Ma'ālī al-, xv, 121,
   171
   epistemological scheme, 172
     (n.10)

K

Kafawī, al-, 14

Keyserling, Hermann von, 33

Khalīl b. Aḥamad, al-, 77, 119

khamr, 124-125
   khamr-beverages, 126

Khan, Wahiduddin, 7

khilāfah, 23, 134, 142, 192

kinds of creatures, 23, 38, 132

kinship
   ties, 20
   unity,162

knowledge, xvii-xviii, 9, 26, 34-36, 38,

80-82, 85, 120-122, 127, 132-133,
138, 169, 195
    acquisition of, 36, 122
    and cognition, 88
    and illumination, 150
    dissemination of, 84
    elementary, 121
    function of, 27
    human, 172 (n. 10)
    Islamic, xx
    of God, 20
    of particulars, 82
    of right and wrong, 18
    necessary, 35, 121
    elementary knowledge, 121
    real, 82
    scientific, 136
        and historical, 86
        scientific sources and methods
            of, 76
    true, 21,
kulliyyāt al-ḍarūriyyah, al-, xi, xv, xix, 1,
75, 123, 139

L

labour, 44, 133, 136-137, 140, 143-
144, 157
    division of, 143, 152
    human, 137
    forced, 144
lawful, 23, 136-148, 151
legal
    discourse, xv
    norms, 23, 48
    rules, 45, 192
    theorists, xv, xvii, 172
    theory, xx
legislation, xv, 20, 45, 117, 163, 165-

167, 186-187
    of *zakāh*, 163, 166-167
lexicographers, 77, 119
life, ix, xii, xvi, xxi, 9, 10, 14, 22-23,
33, 35, 37, 45, 85, 87, 98, 101,
127, 135-136, 144, 146, 150, 152,
159, 161-163
    animal, 41
        vegetative and animal life, 41
    human, 2, 8, 11, 18, 31, 41, 48,
        50-51, 76, 79, 91-92, 94-95,
        100, 103, 129-130, 139, 145,
        169, 193
        and existence, 2, 15, 22, 24,
            41, 49, 51, 75, 92, 123, 129,
            138, 169-170, 192-193, 195
        and society, 48, 141, 178 di-
            mensions of, 18, 138
        protection of, 24, 95, 100
        wholeness and balance, 96
        and civilization, 131, 139
    communal, 42
    cultural and social, xviii
    inviolability of, 97
    protection of, 92
    realities of, 138
    sanctity of, 91, 97
    social, 12, 47
    dignified, 168
    dimensions of, 138
    dynamics of the real, 148
    essence of, 89
    economic life, 139, 143, 155
    family, 48
    Islamic, xx
    Islamic order of, 165
    laws of biological, 46
    Life of the Eternal and Absolute, xxi
    manifestations of, xxi

material, 117

mundane, 146, 148, 181

Muslim intellectual, 120

organic, 41

personal, 75, 165

principle of, 90

real world of ,15

social, 49

tests and trials of, 102

way of, 8, 16

wordly, 133

linguistic analysis, viii

literalist traditionalism, xix

livelihood, 39, 143-144, 146-147, 154, 156

localism, xix

loftyvalues,167

M

mafsadah, 1, 145

maṣaḥah, 1

maṣāliḥ, xvi, 146, 154

maṣlaḥah, xvii, 145, 192

making beautiful, 130

Magianism, 25

māl, viii, xix, 93, 117, 128-131, 136-137, 144, 148-149, 152-153, 158, 160, 166, 170, 192

function of, 131, 139, 150

ḥifẓ al-māl, xii, 1, 87, 117, 139-140

waẓā'if al-māl, 152

amwāl, 128-129, 137, 141, 144

male-female pair, 41-42, 44

man, xxi, 12-13, 28-29, 32, 37-39, 41-42, 46, 51, 77-80, 82-86, 89-91, 94, 102, 120, 124, 126, 128-129, 133, 135, 167, 191,194-195

bio-physical constitution, 86

coming to life, 50

creation from water, 40

existential experience, 12

faculty, 81

inherent dignity, 91

innate disposition, 25

moral obligation, 28

natural disposition, 30

singularity and uniqueness, 90

special creature of God, 86

manfaʿah, 131

mankind, ix, xix, 8, 14-15, 17-19, 23-26, 32-34, 41-43, 47, 49, 52, 78, 82-84, 86, 89, 91-92, 96-97, 129-130, 134-135, 139-140, 144, 158, 169-170, 194-195

closeness to God, 90

essential unity, 32

maʿrifah, 24, 88

maqāṣid, vii-ix, xi-xviii, xx-xxi, 18, 22, 83, 117, 143, 145, 148-149, 191-195

structure and categories of, xvi

theory of, viii, xi, xiv, 2

maqāṣid al-Sharīʿah, vii, ix, xi-xii, xiv-xvi, xviii, xx-xxi, 18, 22, 117, 191-195

five categories, ix

theory of, xi, 2

methodological and epistemological tenets, xiii

normative framework, 195

markets, 143, 155

marriage, 2, 40, 42-51, 94, 152

and the family, 45, 51-52, 94

devaluation of, 49

first historical covenant, 51

institution of, 44

relationship, 51

same-sex, 46
sanctity and inviolability of, 49
special status, 45
social and psychological equilibrium, 47
Masri, Rafiq Yusus, al-, 179
Masson, Denise, 71 (n.113)
L'Eau, le Feu, la Lumiè re d'aprè s la Bible, le Coran et les traditions monothé istes, 71 (n. 113)
material sustenance, 23
Mawdūdī, Abul Aʿla, viii, 6, 8-9, 11, 63 (n.67)
Message(s), xxiv, 3-5, 17, 44, 124, 134, 160
central, 79
divine, xvi, 26
essentials of the religious God's final, 34
guiding, 123
of prophets, 20
of the Qur'an, 18-19, 26
Qur'anic, 126
one common, 20
religious, 17
universal message, 18
mind, 82, 121, 123, 125, 195
mīthāq, 25, 27-28, 31, 51, 192
al-nubuwwah, 27
al-rubūbiyyah, 27
mischief, 164
mischievous practices, 153
miskīn, 162
moderation, 146, 153, 168
and balance, 168
modern
age, 96
economic thought, 142
economics, 143

Muslim societies, 96
Western economic thought, 179
modernist and post-modernist fashions, xix
modernity, 7, 179
European, 7
money, 129, 131, 136-137, 139, 140, 143, 147, 149, 152-153, 155, 158-159, 166-167
double-edged nature of, 153
monopolization, 168
worship, 166
monotheistic religious traditions, 30
moral
and legal code, 23
economy, 157
judgment, 123
Muḥammad (Prophet), 17-18, 20
community, 20
guidance, xv
legal-ethical ordinances, 140
Messenger of God, 151, 154
mission, 18
prophethood, 68
Prophet's Companions, 58 (n.45)
prophetic example, 11
practice and teaching, 165
statements, 147
Sunnah, 1
traditions, xv, xviii, 11, 95, 99, 118, 138, 148, 165
muṣāharah, 43
multinationals, 138
Muslim
academic institutions, xviii
community, 31, 34, 158
ethos, 45
intellectual history, 4

jurisprudents, ix, 139

jurists, 44, 91, 99, 141-142

classical, 130-131

legal theorists, xii, 1, 75, 123, 191

mind, viii

Qur'an exegetes, 20, 25

scholars, xiv, xix, 7, 14, 22, 24, 29, 39-40, 59, 81, 83, 85-86, 88, 92, 95, 100, 118, 125, 131, 142, 165, 171, 186, 191

scholarship, 7, 39

societies, 95

theologians, 120

ummah, 34

world, xxi

mutual dependence, 182

Muwāfaqāt, al-, xvi

mysticteachers, 148

N

nafs, viii, xix, 41, 77, 79, 102, 144, 152, 192

ḥifẓ al-nafs, xii, 1, 75-76, 79, 92-94, 96, 103, 117, 139

semantics of the term, 76

totality and essence of a thing, 77

Najjar, (Abdelmajid) al-, xvii, xxvi (n.16), 56 (n. 21)

nasab, 40-41, 43, 47

ḥifẓ al-nasab, 40, 45, 47

Nashshar, Ali Sami al-, 7

nasl, viii, xix, 1, 37, 39-40, 45, 49, 93, 144, 192

ḥifẓ al-nasl, xii, 1, 37, 39-40, 45, 47, 51, 139

Nasr, Seyyed H., 26

natural

cosmic laws, 42

disposition, 25-26

God-ordained natural process, 41

human feelings, 44

innate inclination, 3, 47

instincts, 46, 47

theology, 31

universal law, 94

world, 23, 74

naturalistic theories, 30

nature, 88, 97, 99, 101, 117, 123, 125, 127, 130

and the creation, 40

conscious use of, 135

fact of, 48

human, 10, 21, 23-25, 28, 29 (n.83), 30, 34, 50, 86, 88, 123, 130, 166

beings', 28

God-given, 25

innate, 29

normative, 46

primordial, 28

inborn, 130

of Adam's knowledge, 81

norms of, 46

original, 26

phenomena of, 195

social, 42

world of, 23, 38

necessity and subsistence, 148, 151

need(s), 2, 14, 24, 96, 167, 175 (n. 38)

actual, 166

basic, 95, 162

consumer, 168

different kinds of, 129

emerging, 96

essential, 44

general, 20, 156

hierarchy of society's, 156

human, 117, 135, 191 ,193
   natural, 33
   individual and public, 158
   material and physical, 96, 131, 139
      and immaterial, 137-138
   people's, 152-153
   physic al and non-physical, 169
   real, 167
   sexual, 44
   society's, 156
   various, 87
needy, 158-159, 161-162, 164
   needy people, 96
   the poor and the, 155-156
next of kin, 50, 95, 162
niggardliness, 153
norms, 11, 22, 32,
   and criteria, 16,
   and rules of the Sharī'ah, 146
   ethical, 45
   legal, 23, 48
   moral norms and commands of
      religion, 62 (n. 65)
   religious teachings and, 11
   revealed ruled and, xviii,
   of religion, 10
   social, 42
   specific, 135
   universal norms of nature, 46
   values and, 11, 22, 35, 96
nuhā, 118, 120
nuṭq, 83, 85, 88

O

objective(s), 33, 100, 114 (n. 62), 153
   ethical, 45
   of the Sharī'ah, xi
   Islam as objective faith, 13

necessary, 22,
   Sharī'ah, xvi, 2,
   ultimate, 98
obligations, 9, 12, 29, 31, 35, 43, 52,
   84, 91-92, 103, 121, 126, 163, 164,
   169
   and duties, 35
   and responsibilities, 92, 103
   social, 156
ontology and axiology, xx
offspring, xxi, 25, 38-40, 47, 50-51,
   93, 95, 129, 133, 175
   legitimacy, 8, 42
   protection of, 37, 51
oligarchs, 157
ontological rootedness, 28
oppression, 159, 166
original
   constitution, 38
   context, xvii
   human nature, 51
   human reality, 41
   interpretation, xix
   nature, 26, 29, 97
order,
   cosmic, 31, 89, 130
   of the universe, 31
   social, 162, 167
orphans, 17, 19, 50, 96, 98, 158
ownership, 130, 137, 141
   individuals', 137
   original, 137
   private, 131
   public, 131

P

pact, 27
   existential primordial, 25

paganism, 30, 66 (n. 83)
parenthood, 48
    father, 39,
        fatherhood, 42, 48
        ubuwwah, 42
    mother, 39, 78, 95, 125
        motherhood, 42, 48
    parental upbringing, 95
    parenting, 48, 95
particularism, xix
Pasha, Ahmed Izzet, 7
penalties, xv, 47, 99, 127
people
    character and personality, 100
    consciousness, 103, 167
    good, 154
    lives, 93, 98, 103, 151
    minds, 48, 125, 127
    wealth and property, 143, 160
perception, 11, 119, 121
person, 8, 10, 46, 77, 79, 95-98, 101,
    120-121, 123-124, 127, 141, 147
    abilities, 36
    human, 47, 75, 91, 93, 97, 121,
        167
    physical and mental growth, 35,
    rational (*ʿāqil*), 121
persons, 38, 92
personality, 36, 45, 48, 96, 100
phenomena, 30, 193, 195
    of the world, 122
    natural, 134-135
        and social, 42
    of nature, 195
    social, 134-135, 193
phenomenon, 14-15, 32, 40, 137, 158,
    185 (n.68)
    cosmic, 28, 40
    linguistic, 3

marriage, 42-43
    of *aḍdād*, 53 (n. 2)
    of religion, 15,
    syntactical, 141
    Qur'anic, 14
philosophy of spending, 168
posthumanism, 112
poverty, 14, 17, 143, 156, 157, 162,
    167
    ontological and existential mean-
        ing of, 14
prayer, 2, 20, 32, 124, 147, 159, 161,
    163-164
    cognitive value of, 32
preservation of honour, 24
prices, 141, 143-144, 156
    manipulation and artificiality of,
        155
principe du sens, 33
procreation, 38, 41-42, 45, 175 (n. 38)
    human, 39, 41, 94
        and begetting, 41, 46
        and education, 42
        and production, 39, 41, 45, 94
        motivated pursuit of, 175
        process of, 40, 94
    procreational function, 48
production, xxii, 140, 143
    process of, 140
professions, 143, 149, 151
profit
    profit and value, 143
    profit-making, 155, 157
progeny, xii, 1, 93, 144
    and offspring, 93
    protection of human offspring
        and, 37
    tilth and, 37, 39
    preservation of, 1

property, xii, 92-93, 133, 137, 144, 145, 147, 150,
   earning and, 148
   economic weath and, 163
   kinds of, 158
   money and, 152
   orphan's, 17, 19, 98
   people's wealth and, 143
   protection of, 141
prophet, 15-18, 20-21, 23, 26, 31, 34, 84, 98, 102, 125-126, 136, 147-148, 165
   Abraham, 5, 19, 23
   Jesus, 19, 23
   Lot, 46
   Moses, 19, 23
   Moses' tablets, 60
   Noah, 19, 20, 23
protection
   of honour, 100
   of human life, 24, 75, 79, 95-96
   of intellect, 117
   of offspring, 37, 51
   of people's minds, 125
   of society and humanity, 98
   of wealth and property, 140
psyche, 48
public
   expenditures, 156
   harm, 153
   interest, 154, 156
   revenues, 156
   spending, 168
punishment, xv, 4, 8, 47, 78, 97, 98-100, 102, 140
   ḥadd, 24
   homicide, xv
   theft, xv
purity and certainty of lineage, 47

purpose of economic pursuit, 170

Q

qalb, 118, 119
Qaradawi, al-, 187 (n.133)
Qarāfī, Shihāb al-Dīnal-, 186
Qārūn (Korah), 138
qualities, 18, 36, 79, 86, 93, 120, 164
qulūb, 118
Qur'an,
   and Prophetic traditions, 120, 123
   authority of the, 25
   commentaries, 108
   exegetes, 110
   Makkan revelations, 186
   message of the, 18, 19, 26
   self-referentiality, 108
   semantic world of the, 5
Qur'anic
   account of human genesis, 44, 89
   and Prophetic material, 147
   and Prophetic statements, 148
   and Prophetic teachings, 21
   concept, 3, 134
   concepts, 170
   contexts, 3-4, 77, 158
   core values, ix
   juridical verses, 24
   message, 126
   perspective, 15, 32
   phenomenon, 14
   profound underpinnings, xx
   references, 122
   revelation, xv, xvi, 8, 128
   semantic and conceptual world, 31
   semantic fields, viii
   studies, ix

terminology, viii

terms, vii, 25, 41, 71

text, xx

usage, 2, 10, 16, 21, 119, 132, 164

verses, xv, xviii, 10, 16, 19, 39, 81, 89, 97, 121, 126, 147-148, 164

version of the Ten Command-ments, 60

view, 88, 121, 134, 169

vision, 137

vocabulary, 4, 5, 8

worldview, 27

Qurṭubī, al-, 20

R

race(s), 32, 50, 85, 133, 178 (n. 61)

human, 81, 86, 94, 136, 194

unity of the, 50

radical feminism, 73 (n.132)

rational intellectualism, xviii

rationality, ix, 21, 97, 121-122

Raysuni, (Ahmed) al-, 127

Rāzī, Fakhr al-Dīn al-, xv, 93, 133, 186

realism, xix, 91, 138

reality, vii, xix, 5, 9, 25, 27, 39, 76, 81-82, 84, 88, 90, 167, 194-195

realm of human purposes, 74

reason, 29, 119, 124, 127, 169, 170

and intellect, 88

and rationality, 124, 169, 170

faculty of, 28

human, 127

perversion and corruption of, 127

power of, 29,

preservation of, 127, 169

Qur'anic view of, 121

reasoning, xvii, 8, 28, 84, 118, 121-

122, 125

reductionism, 11, 91, 191, 194

methodological, xxi

reflection, 3, 7, 83, 119, 130, 192

rūḥ, 76, 89

religio naturalis, 30

religion, vii, xii, xvi, xxi, 1, 4, 6-7, 9-13, 15-16, 19-24, 26, 28-34, 51, 62, 93, 144, 151-152, 164

acquired, 10

ʿādah, 3

cosmic phenomenon, 28

function of, 64

God-less new, 30

ideal religion,10

integrative function of, 31-33, 62 (n.65)

millah, 3

judgement and requital, 6, 8

judicial power, 3

natural, 30, 31

of human nature, 30

phenomenon of, 15

positive, 30-31

preservation of, 1, 22, 34

of Islam, 11, 13, 19

Qur'anic concept of, 8

scope of, 14, 24

source of moral values, 23

study of religion, 6-7, 53

sublime values and ideal norms of, 10

ultimate existential questions, 51

total submission, 9, 20

unified essential meanings, 12

unity and wholeness of, 11

Western conceptions of, 9

religiosity, 10, 11, 25

religious
    ethics, 62 (n.65)
    naturalism, 30
    significance, 9
remembrance, 26, 119, 124
resources, 137, 140, 168-169
    bountiful, 169
    natural, 87, 137, 140, 157
responsibility, 35, 91, 95, 121, 154
revealed books, 19
revealed religions, 20
revelation, viii, 9, 21, 125
ribā, 98, 163-164
right(s), 17-18, 25, 34, 44, 92, 95, 150, 162-163
    and entitlements, 5, 35, 92
    obligations and human, 86, 92
rizq, 131-136, 168, 170
    concept of, 176
    arzāq, 133

S

sabīl, 6, 162, 165
ṣadaqah, 160
ṣalāh, 163, 164
salvation, 21-22, 94, 102, 154
saving, 31, 96, 131, 147
scarcity, 142, 179 (n. 68)
scarcity of resources, 142
Schumpeter, Joseph, 185 (n.123)
    History of Economic Analysis, 185
    Great Gap,185
secular age, 62
security, 47, 92, 96, 156, 162
self, ix, 26, 75, 77, 79, 101, 120, 152
    collective, xix
    human, ix, 26, 167
        protection of, 75

-abasement, 149
-control, 167
-destruction, 91, 101-102, 194
-discipline, 155
-identity, 100
integral entity, 77
-killing,101
-mortification, 136
-sufficiency, 149, 166, 178
semantic
    and conceptual analysis, vii, 8, 11, 15, 158
    approach, ix, xiii
    -conceptual analysis, xix
    -conceptual method, 25
seminal fluid, 39, 41
sensate culture, 49
sense of belonging, 162
sense perception, 121
servants of God, 168
Shah Wali Allah, 29
Sharīʿah, ix, xi, xiii, xv, xvi, xvii, xviii, xx, 1, 6, 20-21, 31, 43, 45-48, 51, 76, 91-93, 96, 99-100, 103, 117, 123, 125, 127, 130, 139-141, 143, 145-146, 156,193
    cardinal goals of the, xix
    epistemic foundation, xvi foundational textual sources, vii, 7
    goals, ix, xiii, 34, 39, 45, 75, 79, 100, 139
        highest, xii
        objectives, xi, xvi, 2
        universals, xvi, 117
Shāṭibī, Abū Ishāq al-, vii, xv-xvi, xix, 93, 108, 139-140, 187
shirʿah, 21
Shmasuddin, Muhammad Mahdi, 24
significance of speech, 84

siḥr, 40-43
sincerity, 6, 35
slander, 47, 100
Smith, Adam, 142
    The Wealth of Nations, 142
social
    development, 92, 156
    dynamics, 49
    fabric, 39, 47
    norms, 42
    regulation, 62
    solidarity, 162
societies, 12, 16, 34, 49, 138, 157
    human, 29, 170
    organized, 12
society, xiv, xxi, 2, 9, 23, 31, 35, 48, 86, 92, 95-96, 100, 124, 125, 137-138, 141, 143, 147, 151-154, 156, 158, 160, 162, 166-168, 191, 193-195
    civil, 168
    human, 29, 33, 43, 50-51, 75, 93, 98, 170
        and civilization, 33, 50, 93, 98
    overall wealth of, 137
    totality of society, 137
    solidarity, 167, 170
    social cohesion and, 32
soul (s), 17, 36, 76-77, 98-99, 102
    inviolability (*'iṣmah*) human, 103
    preservation of human, 93
sovereignty and supreme authority, 8
special extracts, 41
species, 30, 51, 80, 85-86, 88, 94, 144, 175 (n.38)
    animal, 41, 83
    unique and special, 89
    human, 25, 42, 45, 52, 87, 93, 144
    continuation of, 49

preservation and continuation of, 44
survival, 44, 92
speech, 50, 76, 83-85, 88, 169
    and language, 83
spirit, 11, 13, 36, 76, 154, 163
    divine, 37-38, 80, 89-91, 93
    human, 28
    mystic and ascetic, 147
    of justice, 99
    of *Tawḥīd,* 11
spiritual
    faculty, 118
    piety, 44
spirituality, 97, 163
    human, 23
spouses, 39, 43, 95
stewards, 103
stewardship,134
subjugation,166
submission, 6, 8, 20, 35, 50, 126
submissiveness, 3
subsistence, 132, 139
    means of, 132
sufficiency, 149, 162
    self-, 149, 166
suicide, 49, 96, 101, 102
superior status of man, 86
supply and demand, 143
sustenance, 22, 42, 51, 85, 87, 132-136, 143-145, 149-150, 159, 161, 169
system
    of belief, 7
    socio-political, 142
    of laws, 8
systematic semantic analysis, 25

T

tafḍīl, 87, 88

taḥṣīl, 93, 140

taḥsīnī, xvii

taḥsīniyyāt, viii, 2

taklīf, 52, 91, 121

takrīm, 79, 87-89, 97

taqwā, 164

taskhīr, 89, 131, 134-136, 192

Tawḥīd, 4, 6, 20

taxonomy, xii, 75, 145

tazyīn, 130, 166

Ṭūfī, Najm al-Dīn al-, 186

thankfulness, xxii, 22, 91

thematic inference, xx

theologians, 76, 123, 172

thinking, 5, 7, 8, 36, 81, 82, 84, 85,
    89, 97, 119, 123, 124, 126, 127,
    141, 150, 154, 156, 170, 193
    minds, 124

Tirmidhī, al-Ḥakīm al-, vii, 5, 6

trade, 101, 143, 149, 151 ,153, 159

transhumanism, 112

trustee, 23, 103, 169, 195

truth, 4-5, 9-10, 13, 16-17, 27-29, 33,
    49, 51, 80-81, 84, 89, 122, 126-
    127, 159, 193
    and falsehood, 16, 84

truthfulness, 20

Turabi (Hassan), al-, viii, 7, 9-11, 56
    (n.21)

tycoons of financial power, 157

U

ugliness, 29

uṣūl al-fiqh, xiv, xv, xvi, xx, 117, 136

ultimate goal, xix,1 46, 150

umūmah, 42

ummah,142

United Nations, 114

unity
    of belief, 50
    of the human race, 50
    of the whole, 11

universal
    and necessary objectives, 22
    essential goals, 51
    human beings, 36
    necessary goals, 91, 117
    necessities, ix,1-2, 34, 145
    norms of nature, 46
    religious and ethical truths, 21
    value of humanity, 97
    necessities, ix, 1-2, 34, 139, 145
    wisdom, 130, 175

universalism, xix

universals, xv, xxi, 20, 93, 191
    essential, 93
    necessary, xi, xii, xv, xix, xxi, 1,
        20, 123

unlawfulness and prohibition, 102

upbringing, 47, 95

usefulness, 130, 195

usufruct, 131

usurious, 163

usury, 98, 161, 163

utility, 130, 191, 192, 194

V

value(s), xviii, 10, 18, 23, 44, 49, 142,
    162
    system of, xiv, 35, 167-168, 117
    and being, xx
    and norms, 35
    core, 18
    family, 49

fundamental, 18
hierarchy of, ix
moral, xviii, 23, 42, 48
   essential, 21
   universal, xviii
   universal and essential, 98
noble, 44
Qur'anic core, ix
vicegerent, 23, 86, 144,169,195
virtue, 35-36, 127, 150, 152
virtues, 30, 150, 152
   merits and, 150
   psycho-spiritual, 150

W

Wajdi, Mohammed Farid, 7
waqf, 95
water, 40, 134
wayfarer, 161-162, 165, 186
wealth, xii- xiii, xxi, 93, 117, 128-131,
   136-141, 145, 148-149, 151, 153,
   155, 157-160, 162-163, 165-168,
   170, 175
   accumulation, 168
   and income distribution, 168
   and property, 117, 130 ,131, 137,
      139-140, 148, 153, 162-163,
      165, 167, 170
   distribution, 141
   hoarding, 168
   ontological basis of wealth and
   property, 128, 166
   philosophy of wealth, 131
   pursuit of,148
well-being, ix, xvi,1-2, 21-22, 24, 36,
   47, 92, 94, 98, 117, 133, 137, 139,
   145, 150-151, 157 167, 170, 191-
   192,194

common good and, 170
holistic vision, 145
physical existence and, 117
spiritual and material,139
wisdom, xvi, 18, 23, 27, 35, 36, 39,
   45, 49, 51, 85, 122, 142, 144, 153,
   194, 195
woman, 39, 41, 42, 51, 94
   self-objectification of women, 49
world, vii-viii, xiv, xviii-xix, 1-2, 9, 16,
   19, 22-24, 27, 29-30, 32, 35, 37-
   38, 41, 46, 83, 86, 89, 92-94, 102,
   122-123, 127, 129, 132-136, 138-
   139, 144-146, 148-153, 155, 157-
   158, 165, 169, 193-194, 196
   world renunciation, 136
   secularized and globalized, 7
   vision of, 9
worldview, ix
   Islamic, xiv, xx, 36, 192
   materialistic, 193
worship, 126
   devotional and ritual, 32
worth and position, 103
wrong, 18, 25, 78, 151
wujūd, 84, 93, 94, 140

Z

Zabīdī, al-, 6, 76, 120-121, 171
zakāh, 160, 163-166, 168
   aspects and implications of, 165
   funds,165
   maṣārif, 164
   zakatable wealth, 165
Zayas, de, 166
Zein, Ibrahim M., ix, xxii
zīnah,166

9 789867 052697